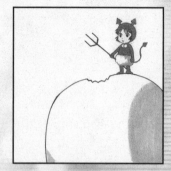

Toshiaki Iwashiro

I went to the dentist for the first time in years...
It wasn't pretty.

What a bummer.

Toshiaki Iwashiro was born December 11, 1977, in Tokyo and
has the blood type of A. His debut manga was the popular
Mieru Hito, which ran from 2005 to 2007 in Japan in
Weekly Shonen Jump, where *Psyren* was also serialized.

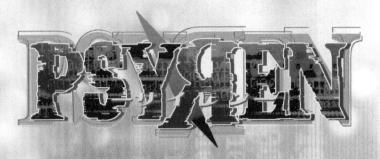

PSYREN VOL. 12
SHONEN JUMP Manga Edition

STORY AND ART BY TOSHIAKI IWASHIRO

Translation/Camellia Nieh
Lettering/Annaliese Christman
Design/Matt Hinrichs
Editor/Joel Enos

PSYREN © 2007 by Toshiaki Iwashiro
All rights reserved.
First published in Japan in 2007 by SHUEISHA Inc., Tokyo.
English translation rights arranged by SHUEISHA Inc.

The rights of the author(s) of the work(s) in this publication to be so
identified have been asserted in accordance with the Copyright, Designs
and Patents Act 1988. A CIP catalogue record for this book is available
from the British Library.

Printed in the U.S.A.

Published by VIZ Media, LLC
P.O. Box 77010
San Francisco, CA 94107

10 9 8 7 6 5 4 3 2 1
First printing, September 2013

www.viz.com

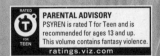

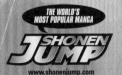

THE WORLD'S
MOST POPULAR MANGA

www.shonenjump.com

SHONEN JUMP MANGA EDITION

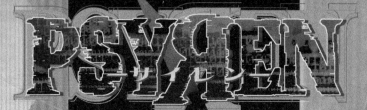

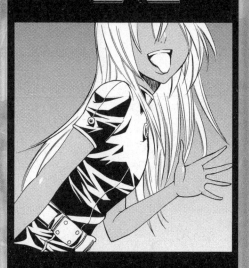

12

BLOOD AND DETERMINATION

Story and Art by
Toshiaki Iwashiro

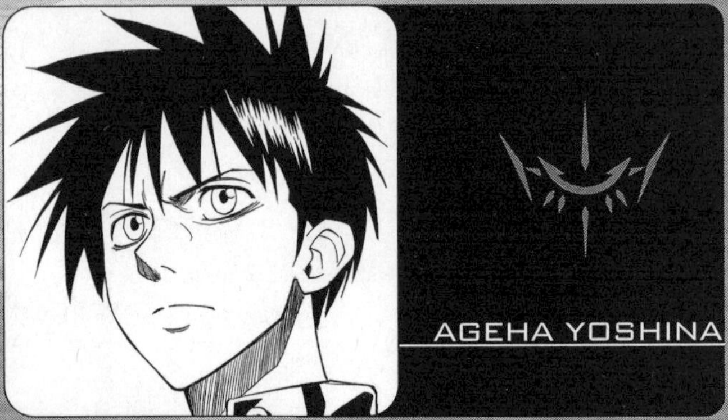
AGEHA YOSHINA

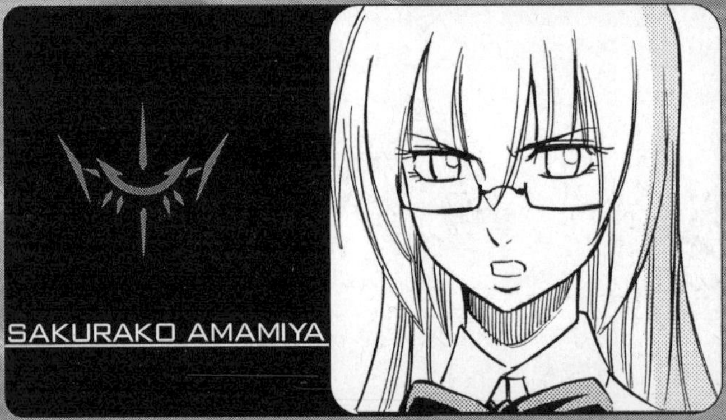
SAKURAKO AMAMIYA

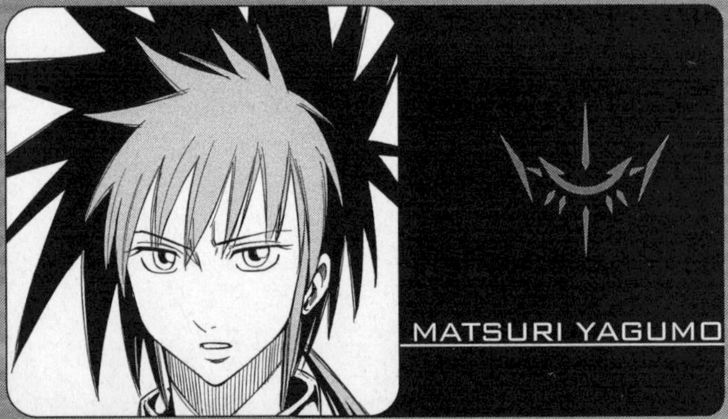
MATSURI YAGUMO

Characters

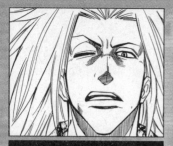

GRANA

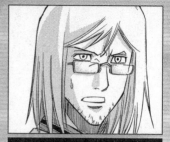

KOHEI IBA

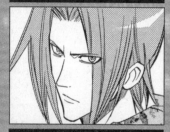

MIROKU AMAGI

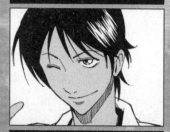

AOI YUSAKA

Story

WHILE SEARCHING FOR HIS MISSING FRIEND, SAKURAKO AMAMIYA, HIGH-SCHOOLER AGEHA YOSHINA HAPPENS UPON A RED PHONE CARD EMBLAZONED WITH THE WORD PSYREN AND SOON FINDS HIMSELF CAUGHT UP IN A LIFE-OR-DEATH GAME IN THE BIZARRE PSYREN WORLD.

AGEHA'S FRIEND KAGETORA AND HIS TEAM HEAD TO THE SPRING BREEZE ACADEMY TO LOOK FOR INFORMATION ABOUT MIROKU AMAGI, THE MAN WHO IS DESTINED TO BRING ABOUT THE END OF THE WORLD. THERE THEY ARE CONFRONTED BY JUNAS, FUTURE STAR COMMANDER OF THE SHADOWY GROUP KNOWN AS W.I.S.E! AS KAGETORA CLASHES WITH JUNAS, MIROKU TAKES ON GRANAR, AN INCREDIBLY POWERFUL PSIONIST WHOM MIROKU HOPES TO RECRUIT FOR HIS NEW WORLD ORDER. MEANWHILE, AGEHA AND SAKURAKO VISIT AGEHA'S FATHER'S LAB TO LEARN THE SECRETS OF THE OUROBOROS ASTEROID AND FIND KOHEI IBA, THE ONLY SURVIVING RESEARCHER FROM THE DOOMED GRIGORI RESEARCH PROJECT.

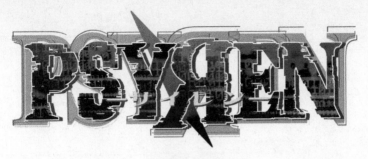

VOL. 12
BLOOD AND DETERMINATION
CONTENTS

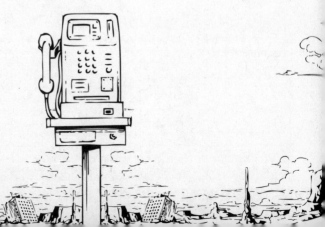

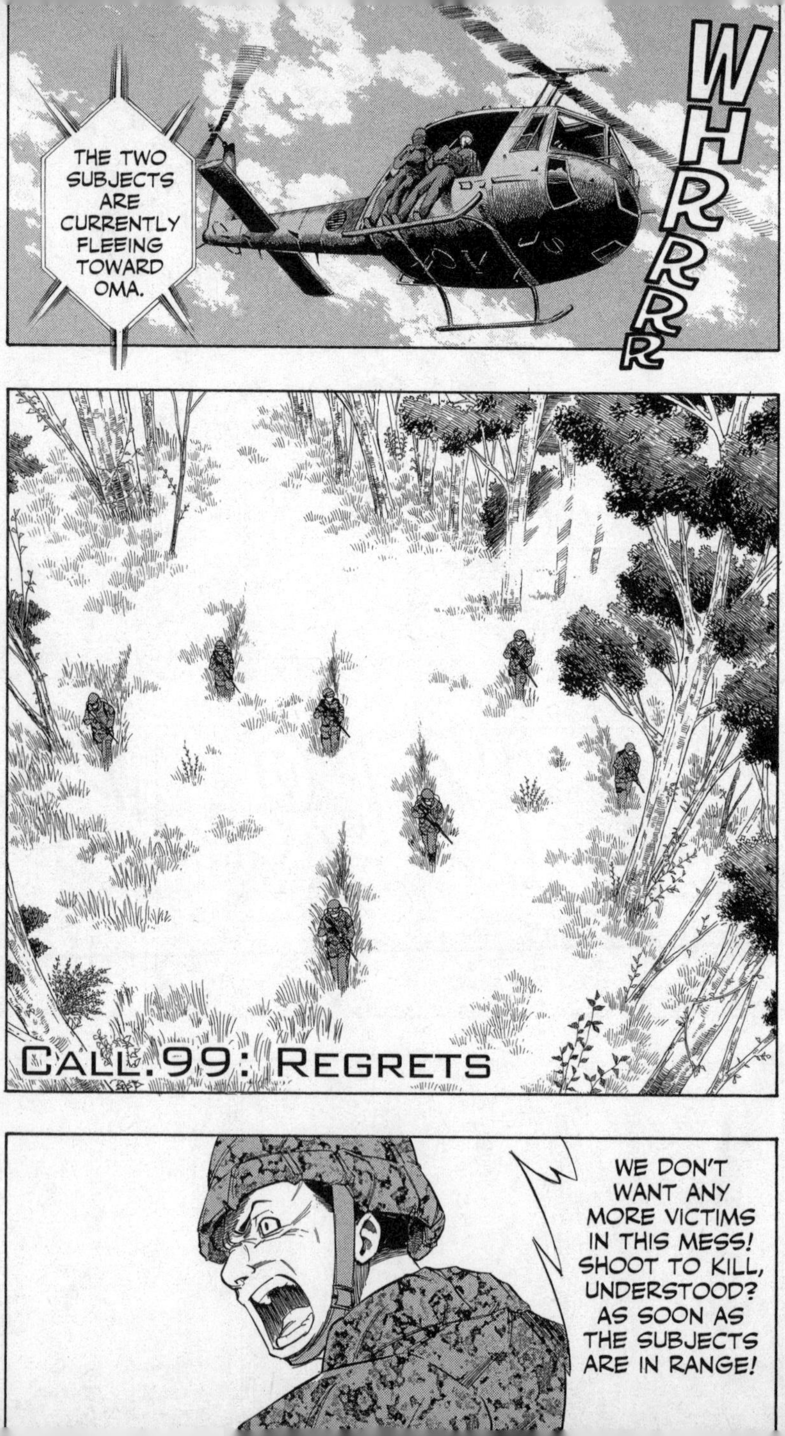
WHRRRRR
THE TWO SUBJECTS ARE CURRENTLY FLEEING TOWARD OMA.
CALL.99: REGRETS
WE DON'T WANT ANY MORE VICTIMS IN THIS MESS! SHOOT TO KILL, UNDERSTOOD? AS SOON AS THE SUBJECTS ARE IN RANGE!

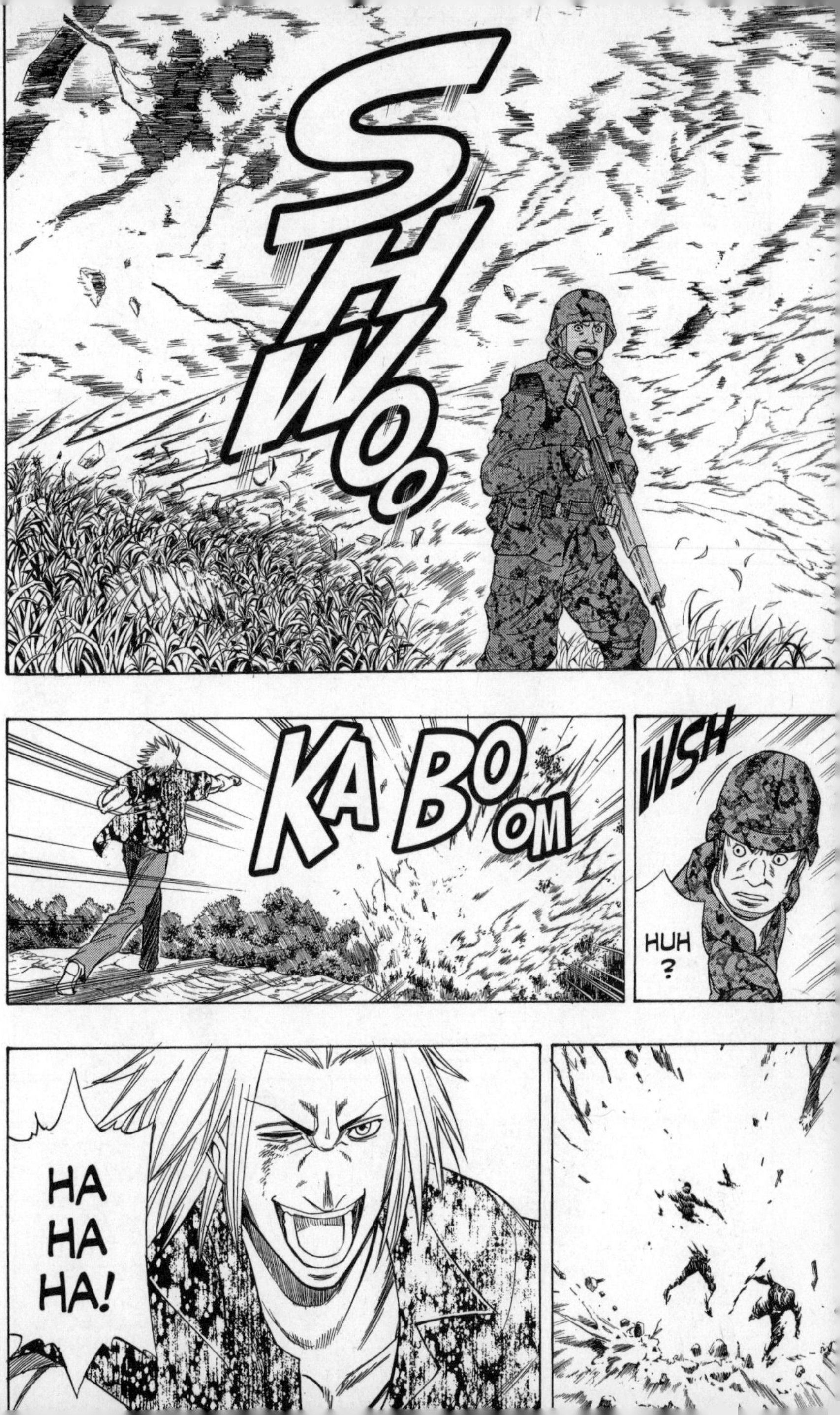
SHWOO
WSH
HUH?
KABOOM
HA HA HA!

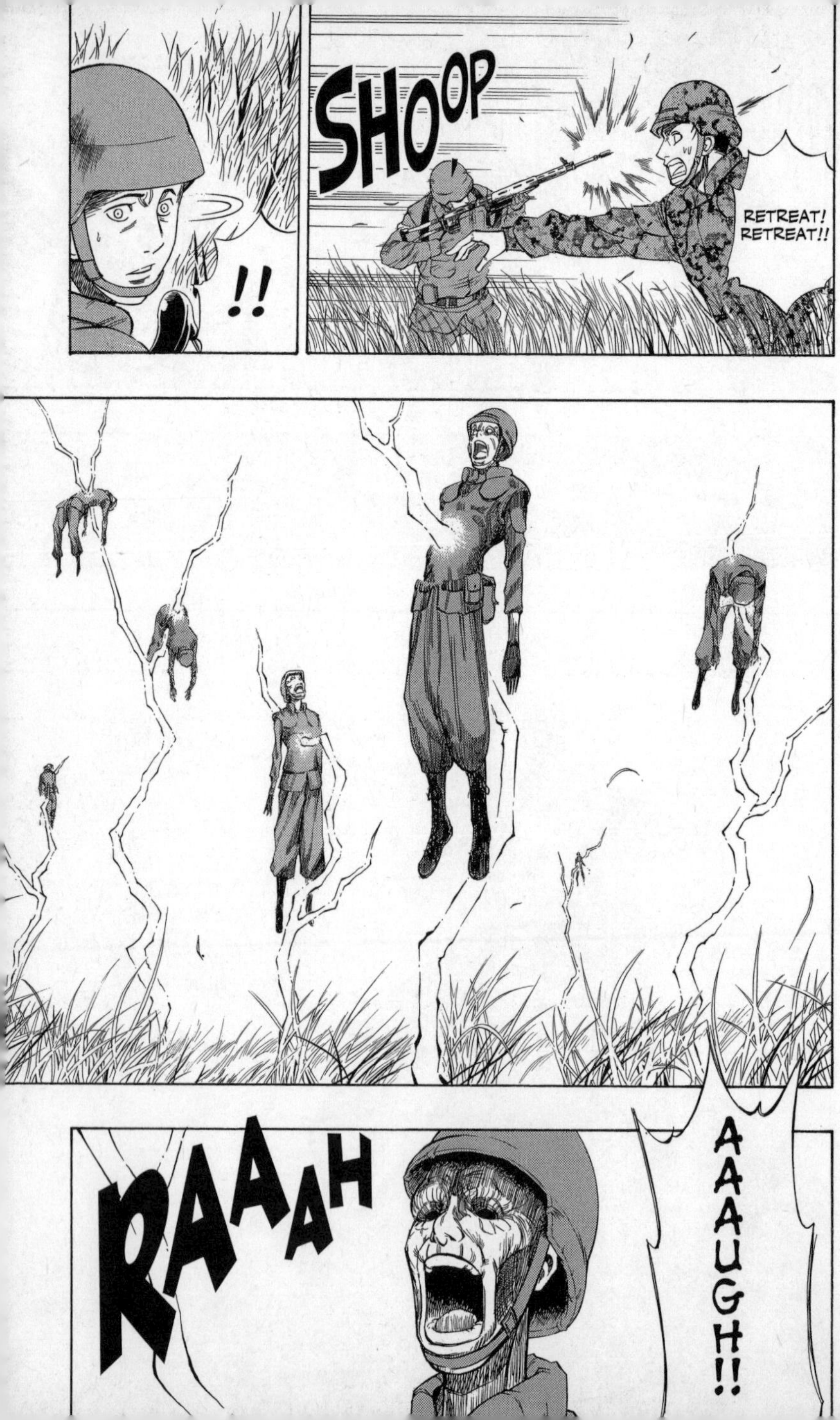
RETREAT!
RETREAT!!
SHOOP
!!
AAAUGH!!
RAAAH

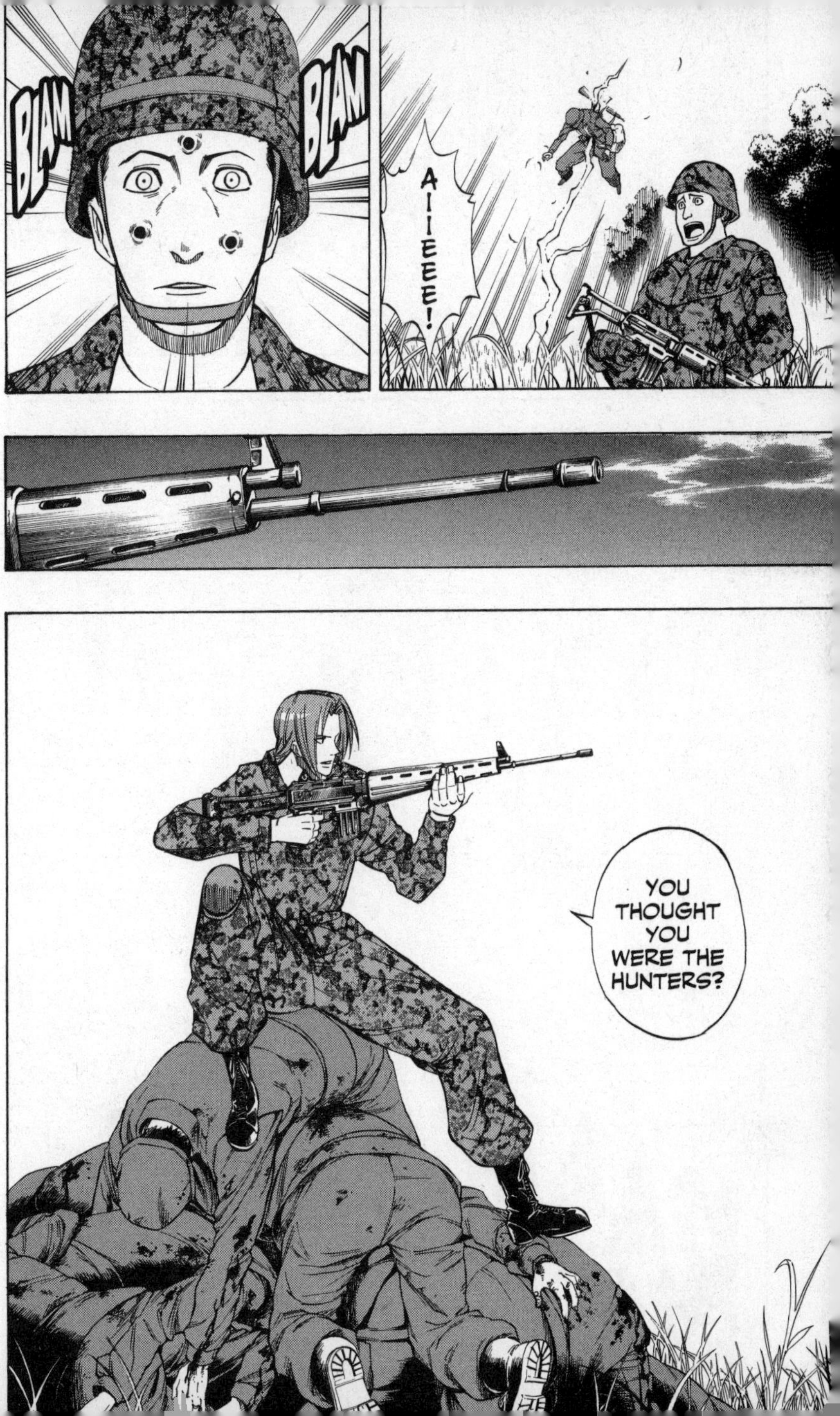
AIIEEE!
BLAM
BLAM
YOU THOUGHT YOU WERE THE HUNTERS?

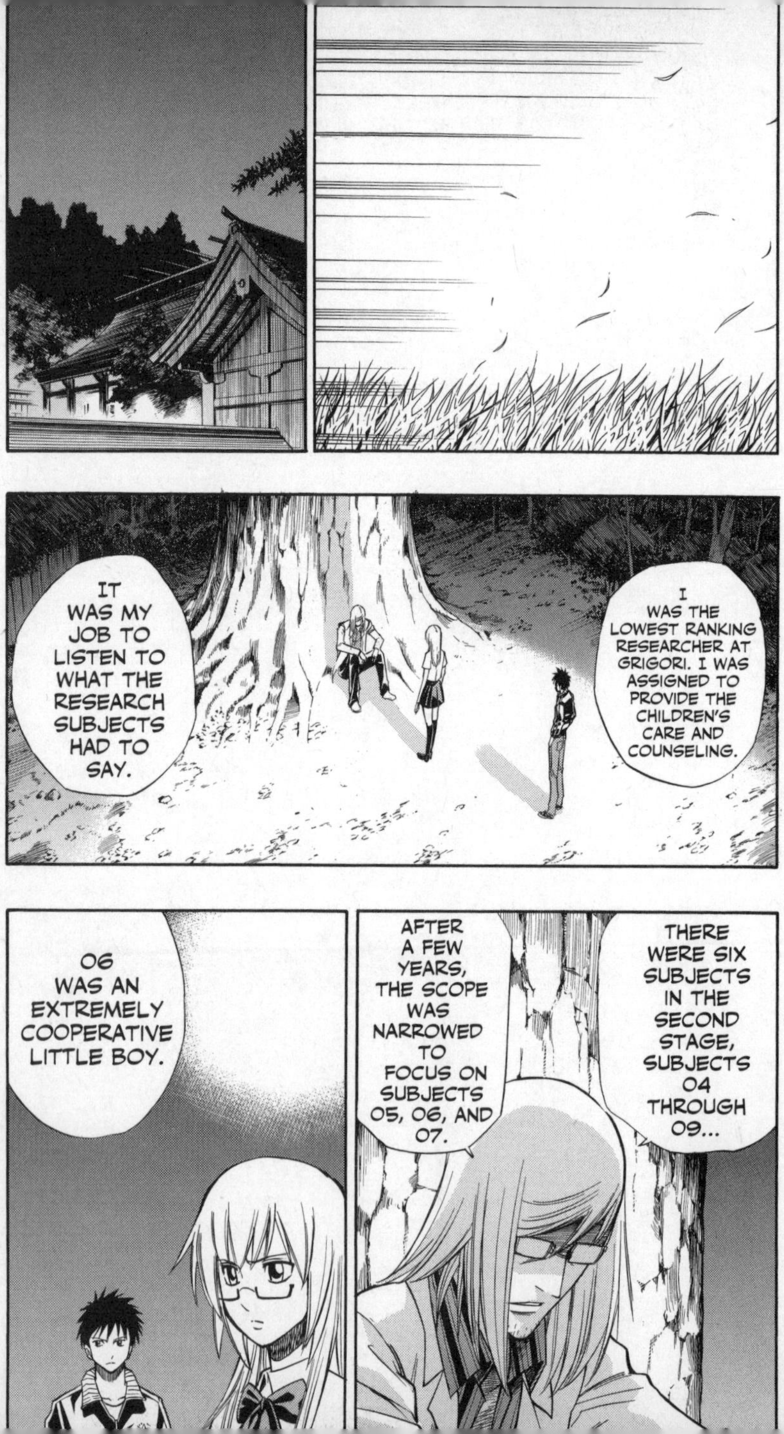
I WAS THE LOWEST RANKING RESEARCHER AT GRIGORI. I WAS ASSIGNED TO PROVIDE THE CHILDREN'S CARE AND COUNSELING.
IT WAS MY JOB TO LISTEN TO WHAT THE RESEARCH SUBJECTS HAD TO SAY.
THERE WERE SIX SUBJECTS IN THE SECOND STAGE, SUBJECTS 04 THROUGH 09...
AFTER A FEW YEARS, THE SCOPE WAS NARROWED TO FOCUS ON SUBJECTS 05, 06, AND 07.
06 WAS AN EXTREMELY COOPERATIVE LITTLE BOY.

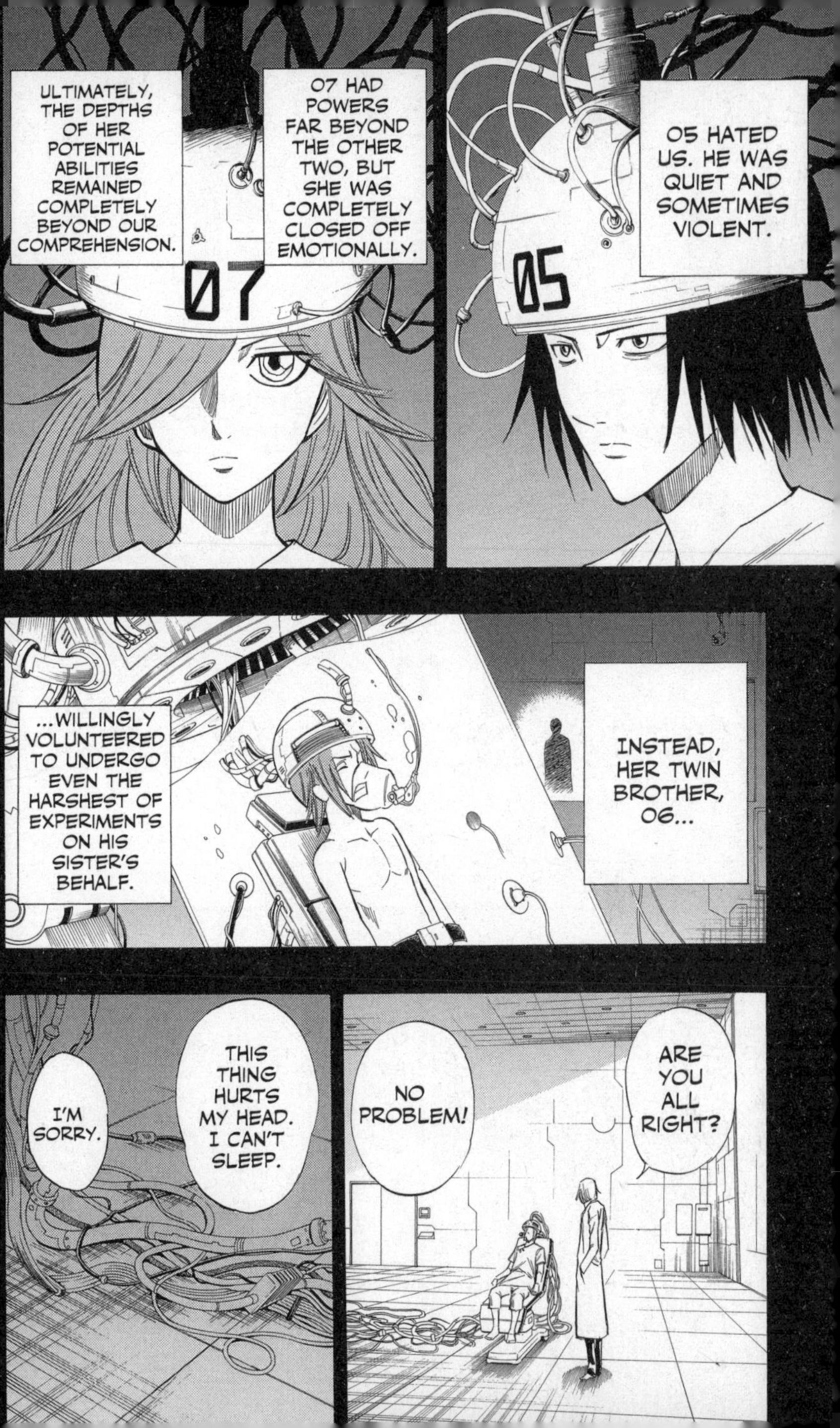
05 HATED US. HE WAS QUIET AND SOMETIMES VIOLENT.
07 HAD POWERS FAR BEYOND THE OTHER TWO, BUT SHE WAS COMPLETELY CLOSED OFF EMOTIONALLY.
ULTIMATELY, THE DEPTHS OF HER POTENTIAL ABILITIES REMAINED COMPLETELY BEYOND OUR COMPREHENSION.
INSTEAD, HER TWIN BROTHER, 06...
...WILLINGLY VOLUNTEERED TO UNDERGO EVEN THE HARSHEST OF EXPERIMENTS ON HIS SISTER'S BEHALF.
ARE YOU ALL RIGHT?
NO PROBLEM!
THIS THING HURTS MY HEAD. I CAN'T SLEEP.
I'M SORRY.

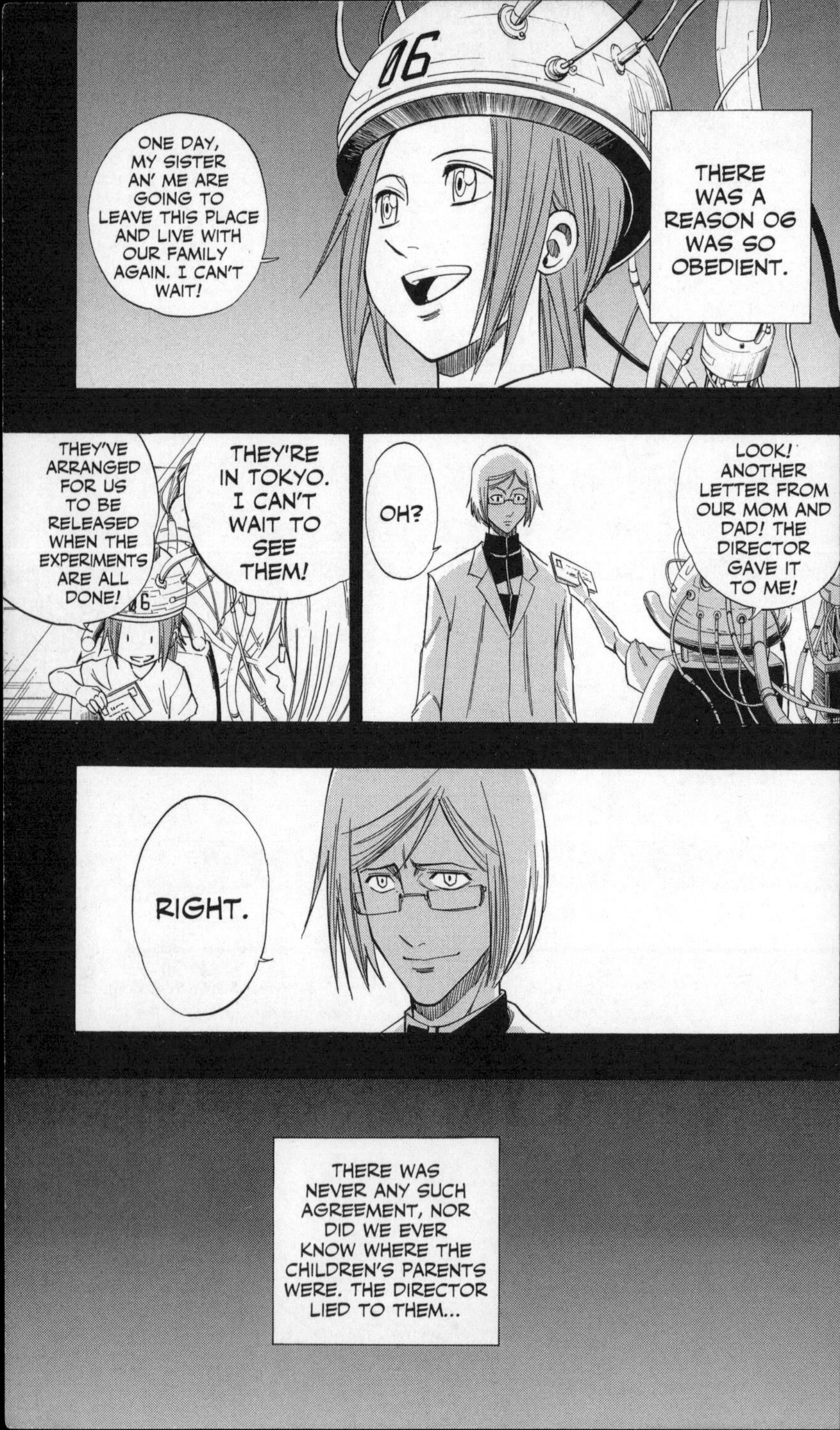
THERE WAS A REASON 06 WAS SO OBEDIENT.
ONE DAY, MY SISTER AN' ME ARE GOING TO LEAVE THIS PLACE AND LIVE WITH OUR FAMILY AGAIN. I CAN'T WAIT!
06
LOOK! ANOTHER LETTER FROM OUR MOM AND DAD! THE DIRECTOR GAVE IT TO ME!
OH?
THEY'RE IN TOKYO. I CAN'T WAIT TO SEE THEM!
THEY'VE ARRANGED FOR US TO BE RELEASED WHEN THE EXPERIMENTS ARE ALL DONE!
RIGHT.
THERE WAS NEVER ANY SUCH AGREEMENT, NOR DID WE EVER KNOW WHERE THE CHILDREN'S PARENTS WERE. THE DIRECTOR LIED TO THEM...

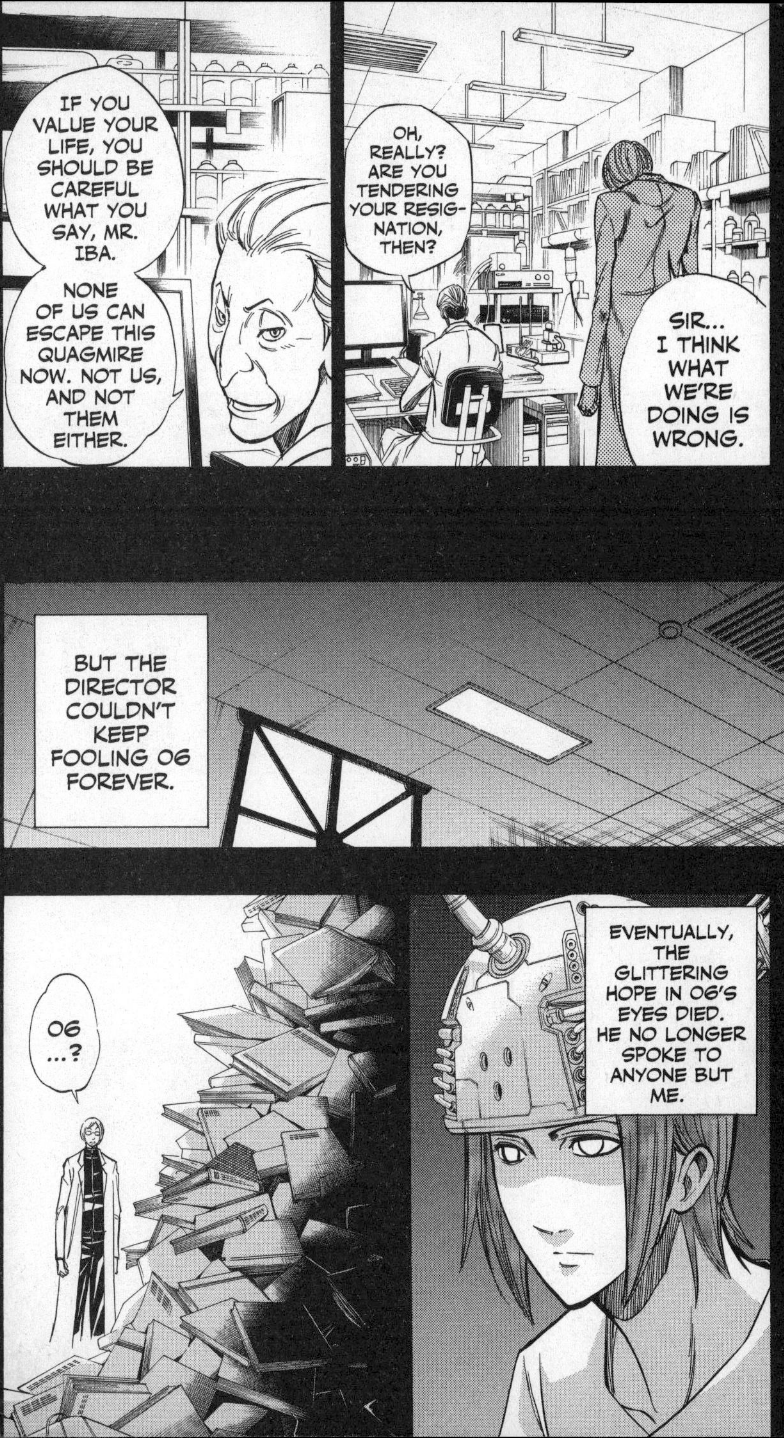
SIR... I THINK WHAT WE'RE DOING IS WRONG.
OH, REALLY? ARE YOU TENDERING YOUR RESIGNATION, THEN?
IF YOU VALUE YOUR LIFE, YOU SHOULD BE CAREFUL WHAT YOU SAY, MR. IBA.
NONE OF US CAN ESCAPE THIS QUAGMIRE NOW. NOT US, AND NOT THEM EITHER.
BUT THE DIRECTOR COULDN'T KEEP FOOLING 06 FOREVER.
EVENTUALLY, THE GLITTERING HOPE IN 06'S EYES DIED. HE NO LONGER SPOKE TO ANYONE BUT ME.
06 ...?

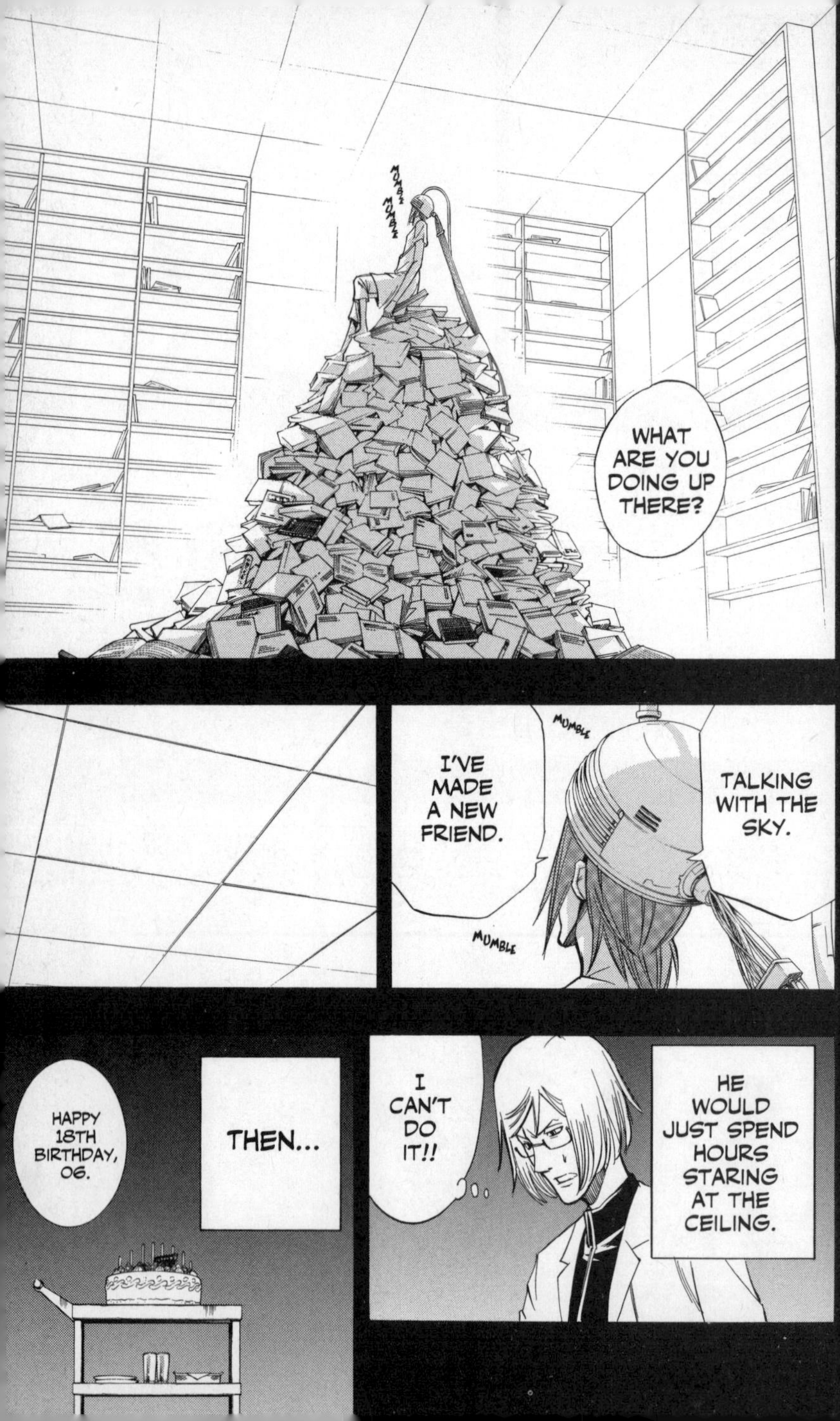
MUMBLE
MUMBLE
WHAT ARE YOU DOING UP THERE?
TALKING WITH THE SKY.
MUMBLE
I'VE MADE A NEW FRIEND.
MUMBLE
HE WOULD JUST SPEND HOURS STARING AT THE CEILING.
I CAN'T DO IT!!
THEN...
HAPPY 18TH BIRTHDAY, 06.

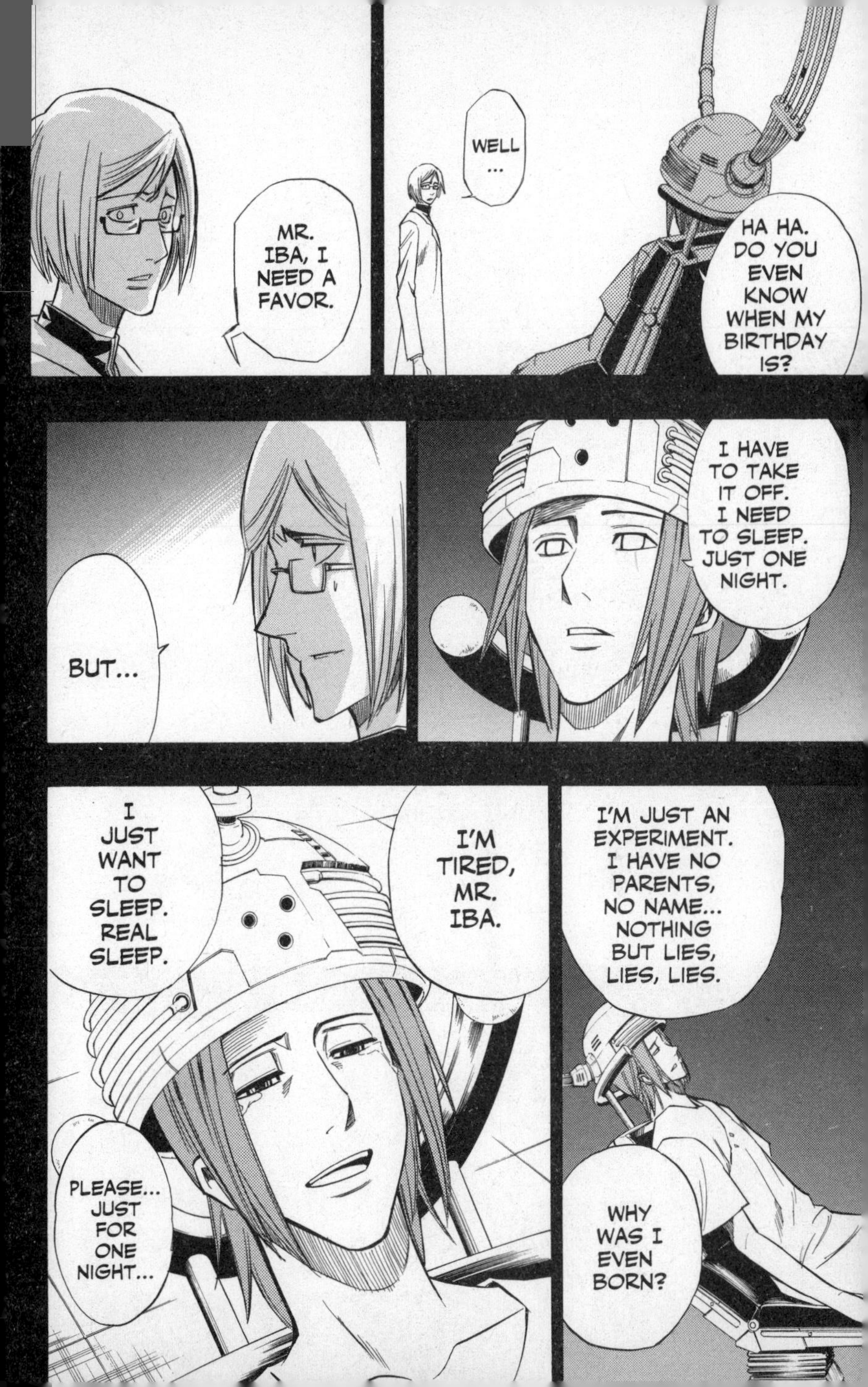
HA HA. DO YOU EVEN KNOW WHEN MY BIRTHDAY IS?
WELL...
MR. IBA, I NEED A FAVOR.
I HAVE TO TAKE IT OFF. I NEED TO SLEEP. JUST ONE NIGHT.
BUT...
I'M JUST AN EXPERIMENT. I HAVE NO PARENTS, NO NAME... NOTHING BUT LIES, LIES, LIES.
WHY WAS I EVEN BORN?
I'M TIRED, MR. IBA.
I JUST WANT TO SLEEP. REAL SLEEP.
PLEASE... JUST FOR ONE NIGHT...

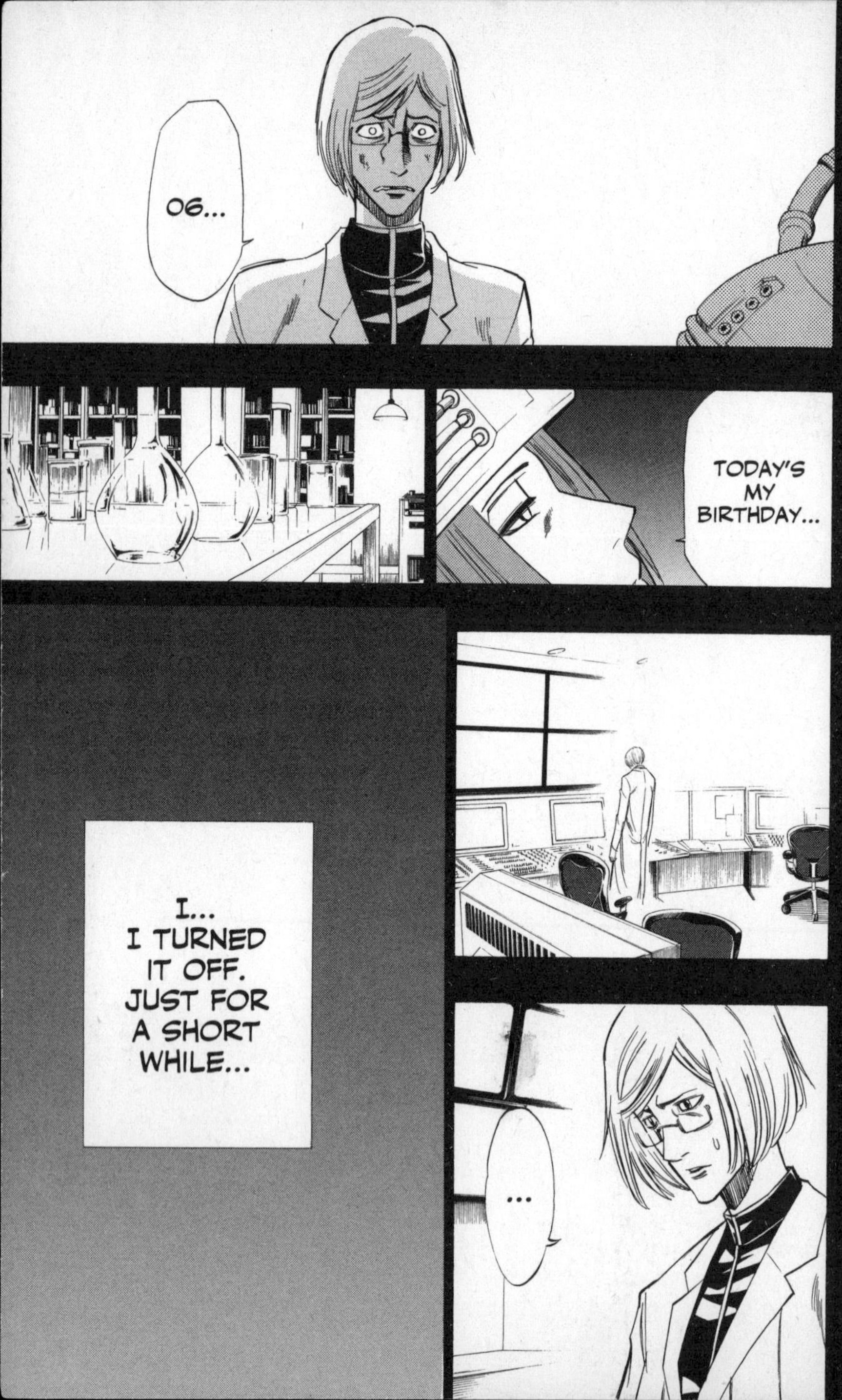
06...
TODAY'S MY BIRTHDAY...
...
I... I TURNED IT OFF. JUST FOR A SHORT WHILE...

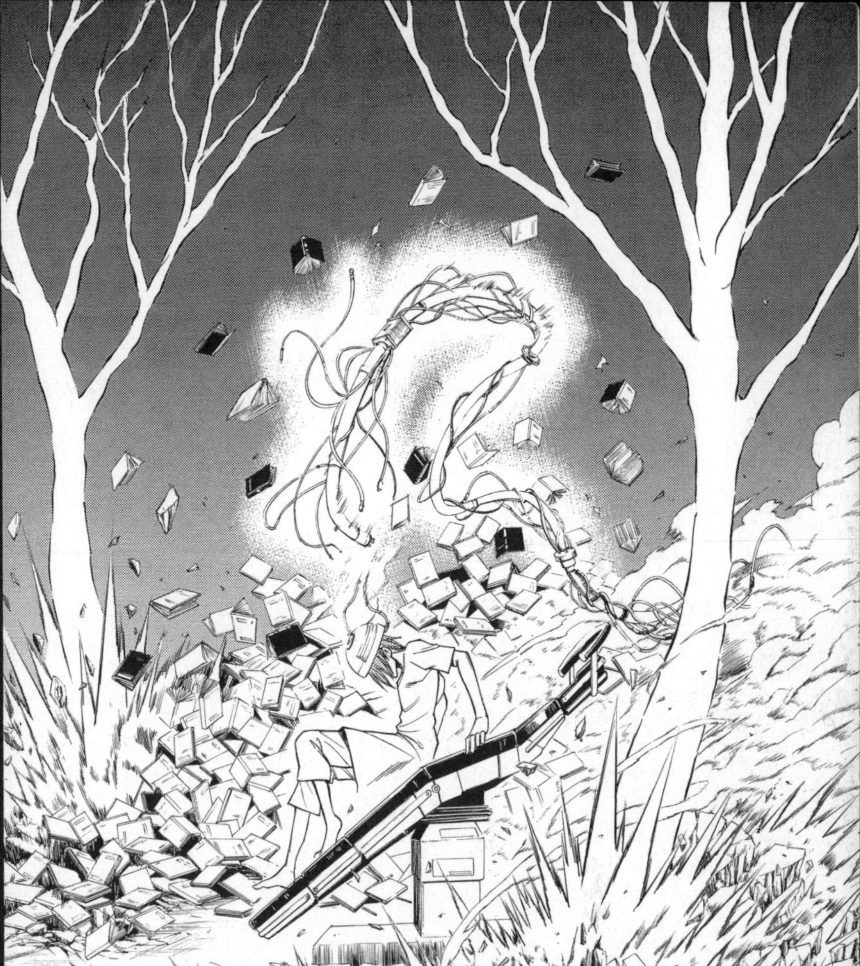

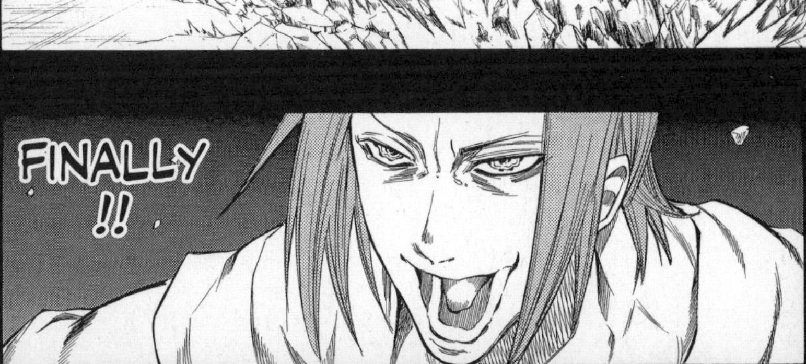
FINALLY
!!

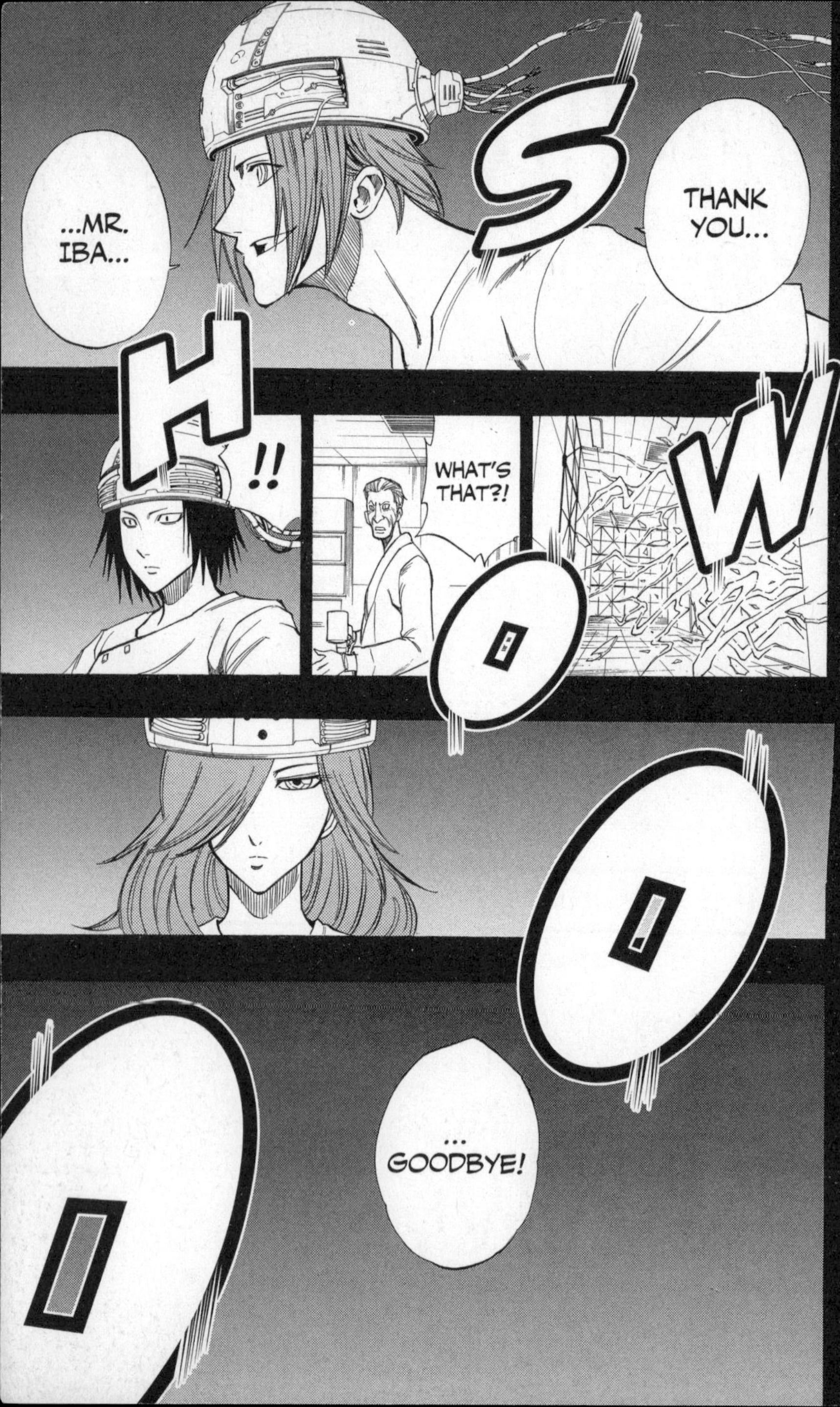
THANK YOU...
...MR. IBA...
SHWOOO
WHAT'S THAT?!
!!
... GOODBYE!

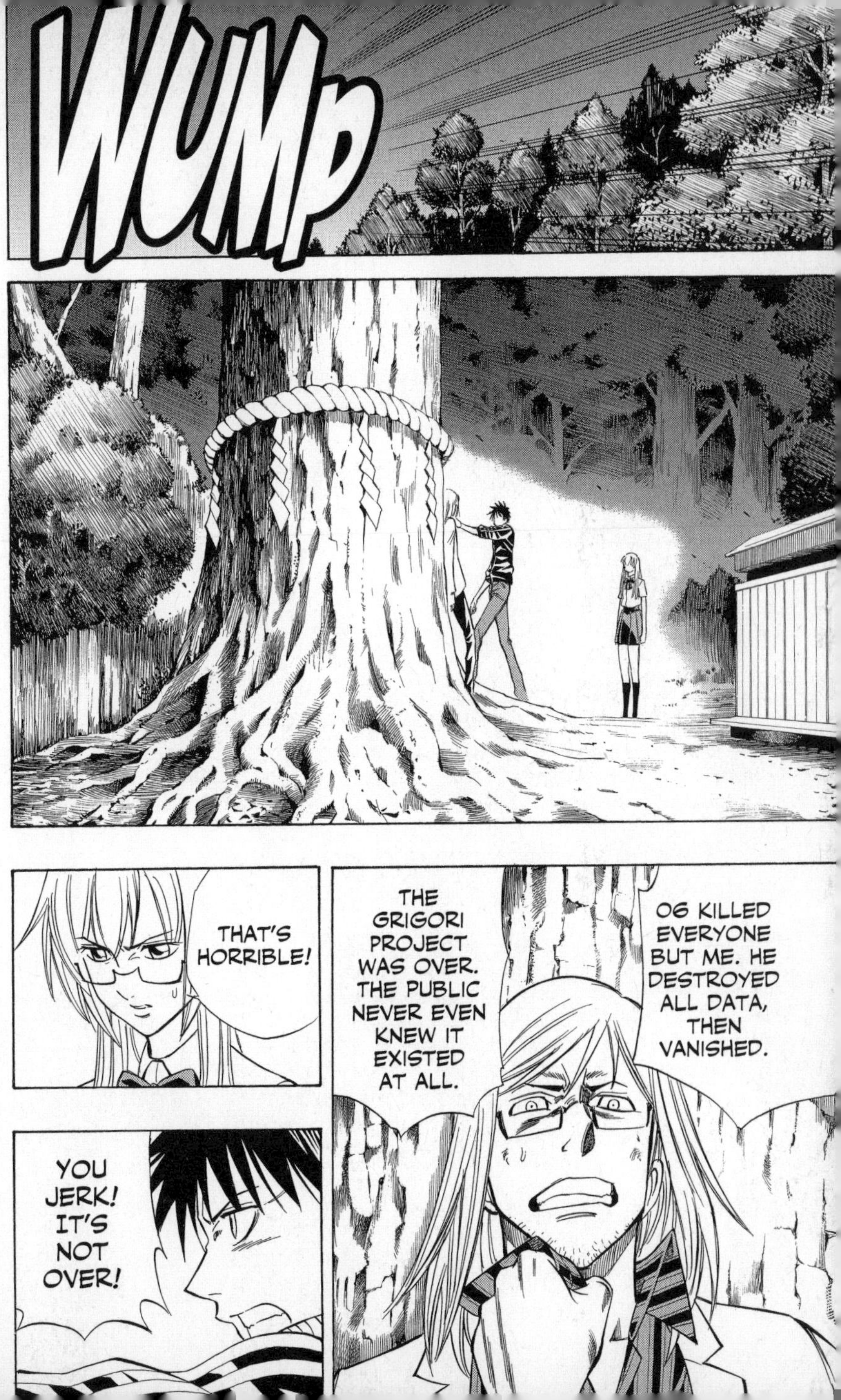
WUMP
06 KILLED EVERYONE BUT ME. HE DESTROYED ALL DATA, THEN VANISHED.
THE GRIGORI PROJECT WAS OVER. THE PUBLIC NEVER EVEN KNEW IT EXISTED AT ALL.
THAT'S HORRIBLE!
YOU JERK! IT'S NOT OVER!

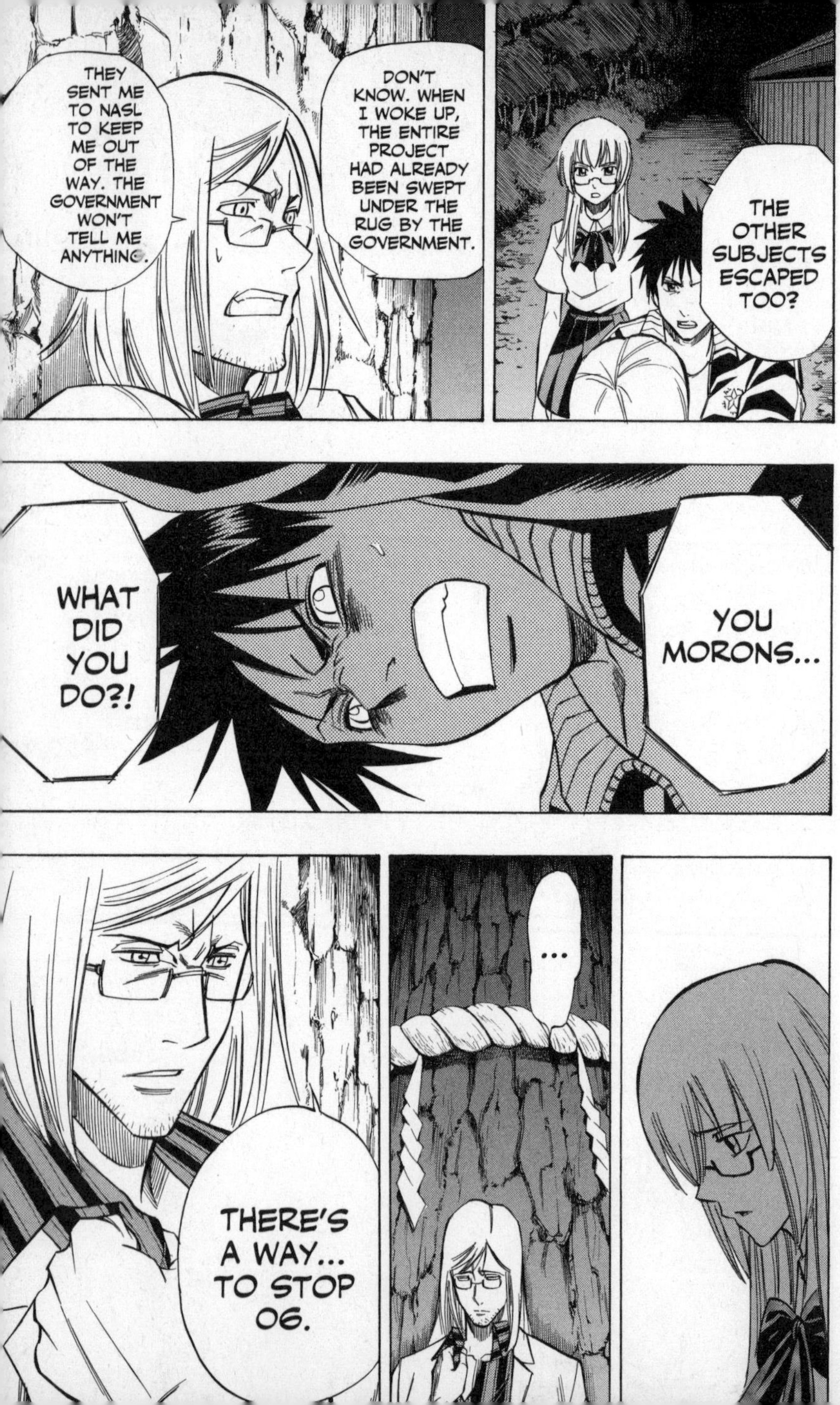
THE OTHER SUBJECTS ESCAPED TOO?
DON'T KNOW. WHEN I WOKE UP, THE ENTIRE PROJECT HAD ALREADY BEEN SWEPT UNDER THE RUG BY THE GOVERNMENT.
THEY SENT ME TO NASL TO KEEP ME OUT OF THE WAY. THE GOVERNMENT WON'T TELL ME ANYTHING.
YOU MORONS...
WHAT DID YOU DO?!
...
THERE'S A WAY... TO STOP 06.

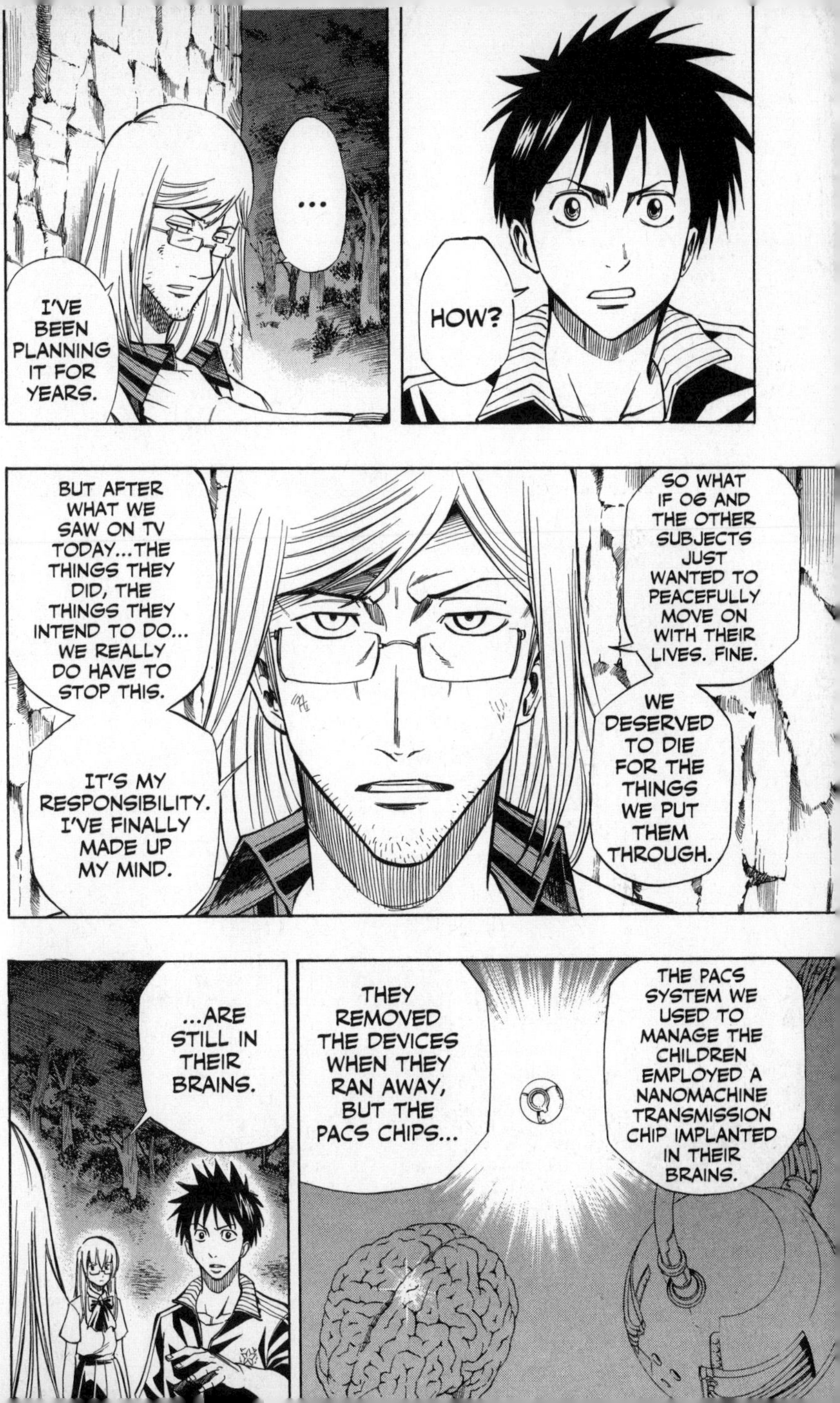
HOW?
...
I'VE BEEN PLANNING IT FOR YEARS.
SO WHAT IF 06 AND THE OTHER SUBJECTS JUST WANTED TO PEACEFULLY MOVE ON WITH THEIR LIVES. FINE.
WE DESERVED TO DIE FOR THE THINGS WE PUT THEM THROUGH.
BUT AFTER WHAT WE SAW ON TV TODAY...THE THINGS THEY DID, THE THINGS THEY INTEND TO DO... WE REALLY DO HAVE TO STOP THIS.
IT'S MY RESPONSIBILITY. I'VE FINALLY MADE UP MY MIND.
THE PACS SYSTEM WE USED TO MANAGE THE CHILDREN EMPLOYED A NANOMACHINE TRANSMISSION CHIP IMPLANTED IN THEIR BRAINS.
THEY REMOVED THE DEVICES WHEN THEY RAN AWAY, BUT THE PACS CHIPS...
...ARE STILL IN THEIR BRAINS.

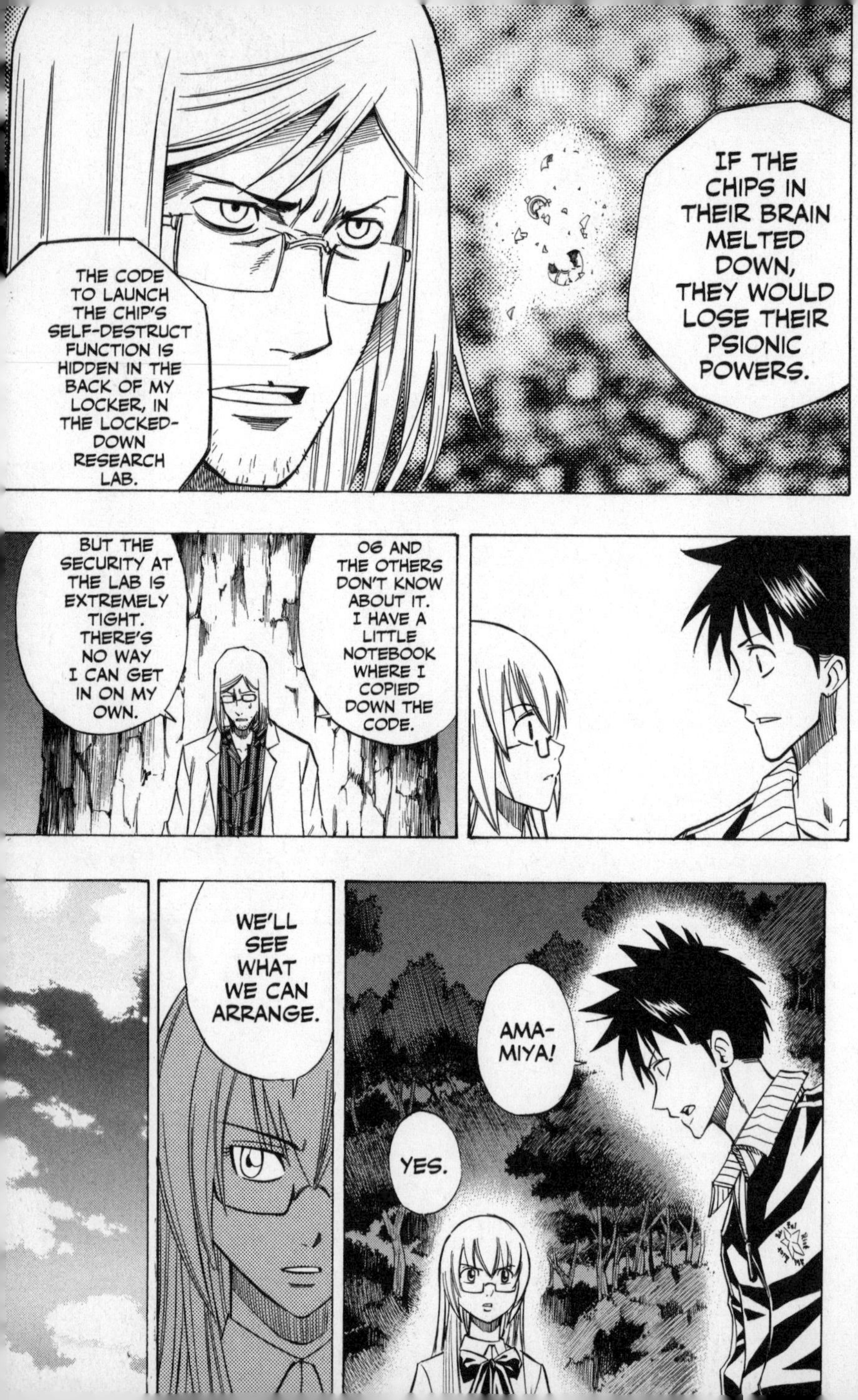
IF THE CHIPS IN THEIR BRAIN MELTED DOWN, THEY WOULD LOSE THEIR PSIONIC POWERS.
THE CODE TO LAUNCH THE CHIP'S SELF-DESTRUCT FUNCTION IS HIDDEN IN THE BACK OF MY LOCKER, IN THE LOCKED-DOWN RESEARCH LAB.
06 AND THE OTHERS DON'T KNOW ABOUT IT. I HAVE A LITTLE NOTEBOOK WHERE I COPIED DOWN THE CODE.
BUT THE SECURITY AT THE LAB IS EXTREMELY TIGHT. THERE'S NO WAY I CAN GET IN ON MY OWN.
AMA-MIYA!
YES.
WE'LL SEE WHAT WE CAN ARRANGE.

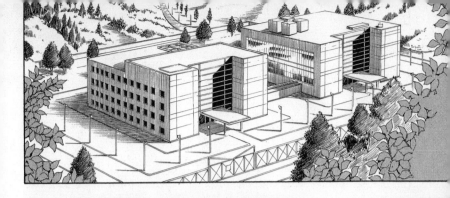

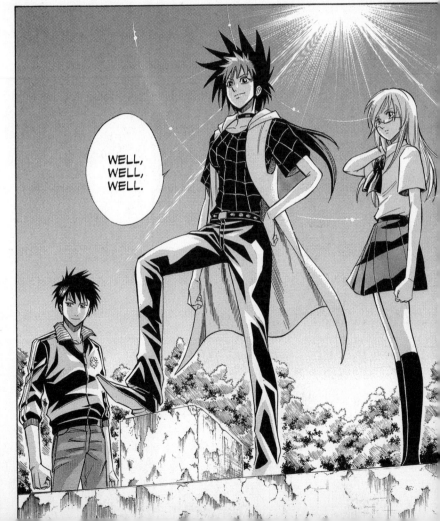

WELL,
WELL,
WELL.

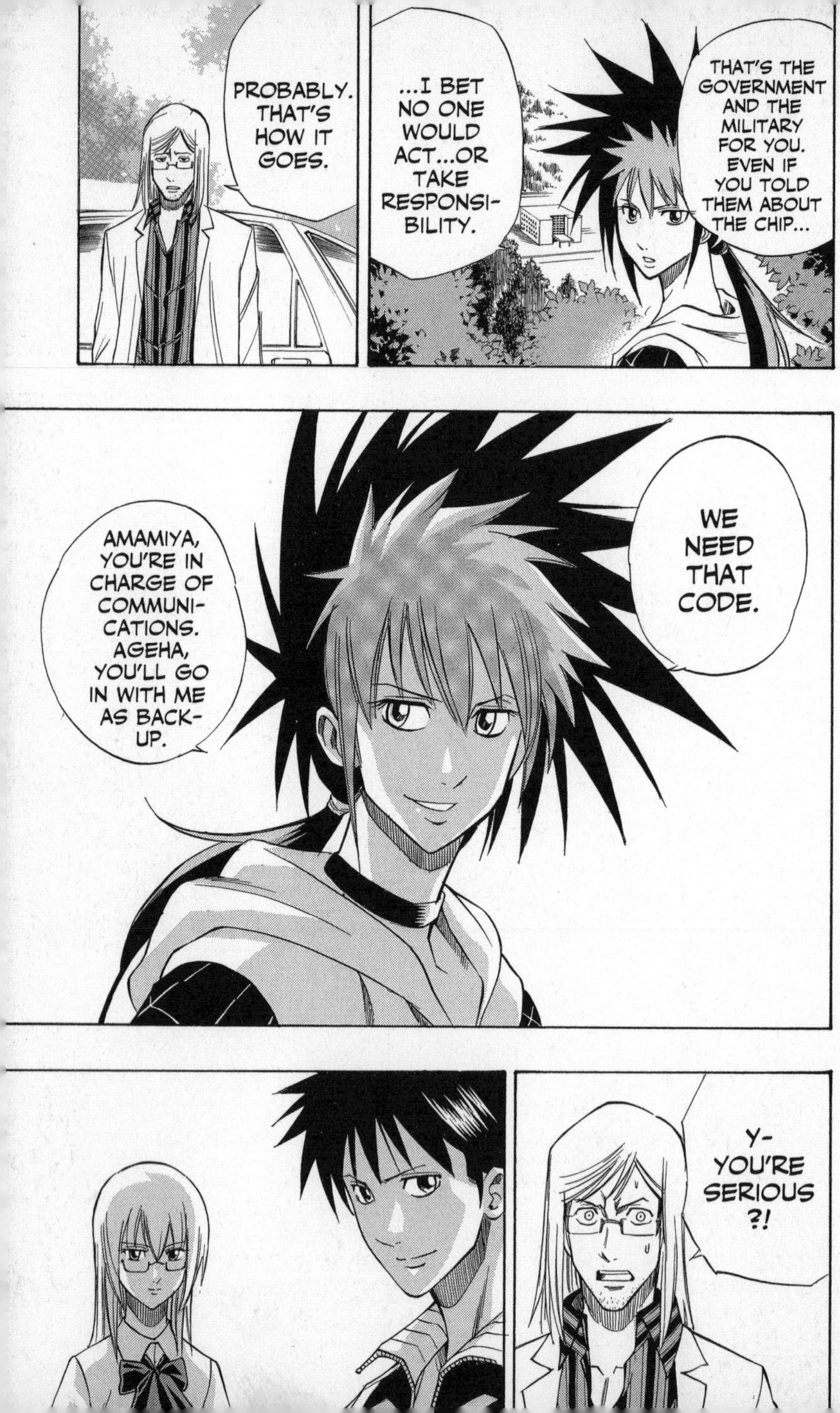
THAT'S THE GOVERNMENT AND THE MILITARY FOR YOU. EVEN IF YOU TOLD THEM ABOUT THE CHIP...
...I BET NO ONE WOULD ACT...OR TAKE RESPONSI-BILITY.
PROBABLY. THAT'S HOW IT GOES.
WE NEED THAT CODE.
AMAMIYA, YOU'RE IN CHARGE OF COMMUNI-CATIONS. AGEHA, YOU'LL GO IN WITH ME AS BACK-UP.
Y-YOU'RE SERIOUS?!

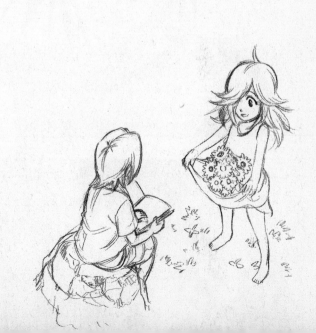

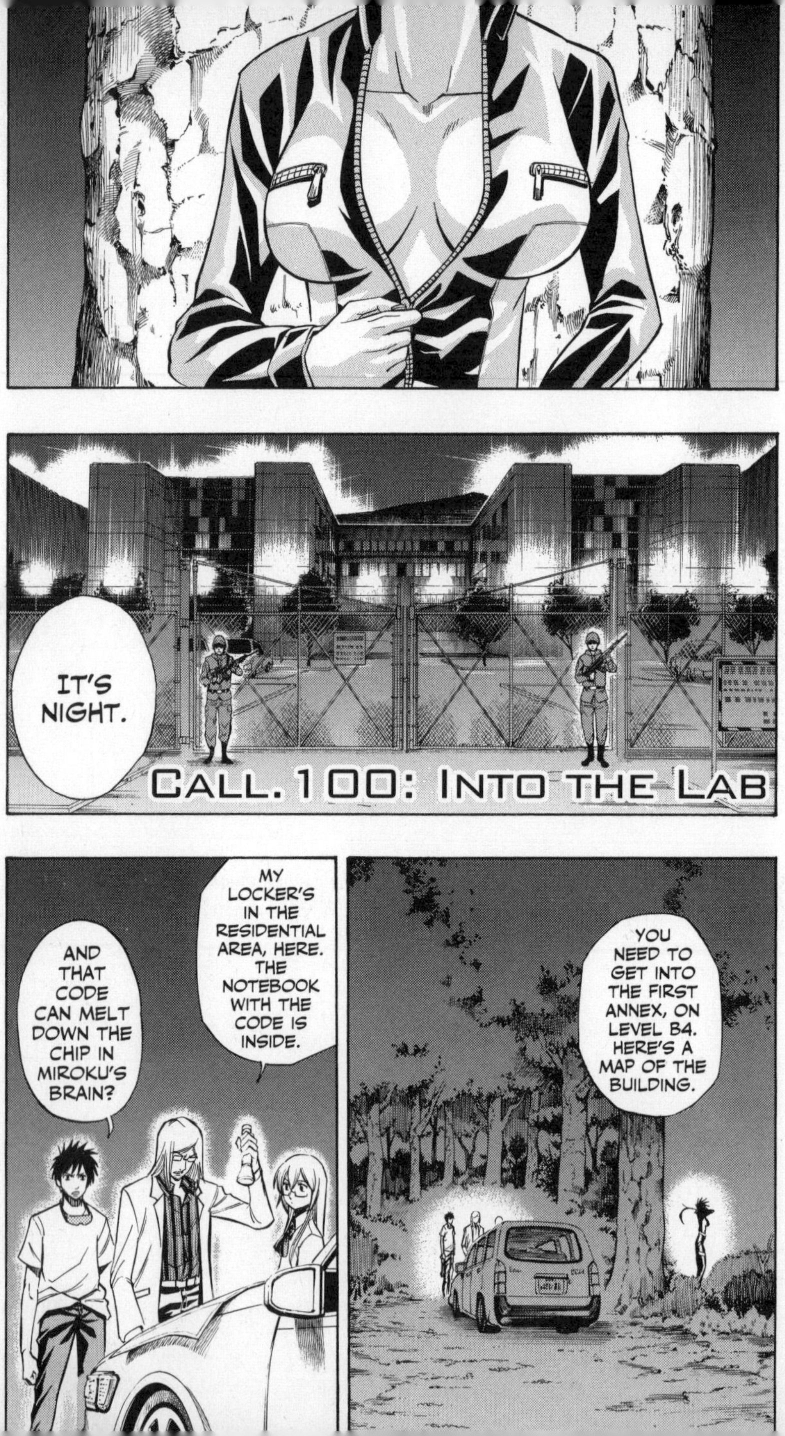
IT'S NIGHT.
CALL. 100: INTO THE LAB
YOU NEED TO GET INTO THE FIRST ANNEX, ON LEVEL B4. HERE'S A MAP OF THE BUILDING.
MY LOCKER'S IN THE RESIDENTIAL AREA, HERE. THE NOTEBOOK WITH THE CODE IS INSIDE.
AND THAT CODE CAN MELT DOWN THE CHIP IN MIROKU'S BRAIN?

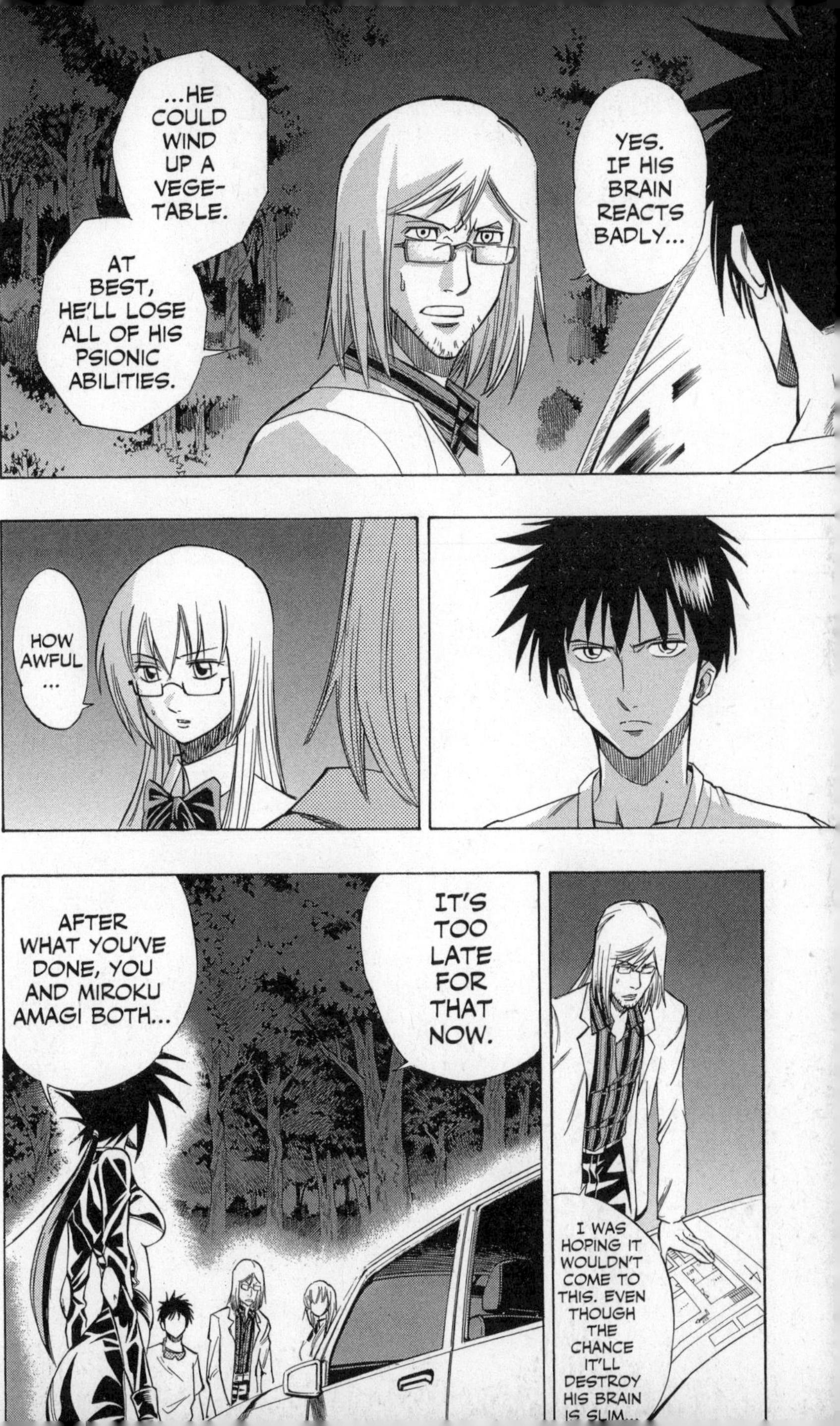
YES. IF HIS BRAIN REACTS BADLY...
...HE COULD WIND UP A VEGE- TABLE.
AT BEST, HE'LL LOSE ALL OF HIS PSIONIC ABILITIES.
HOW AWFUL ...
I WAS HOPING IT WOULDN'T COME TO THIS. EVEN THOUGH THE CHANCE IT'LL DESTROY HIS BRAIN IS SLIM...
IT'S TOO LATE FOR THAT NOW.
AFTER WHAT YOU'VE DONE, YOU AND MIROKU AMAGI BOTH...

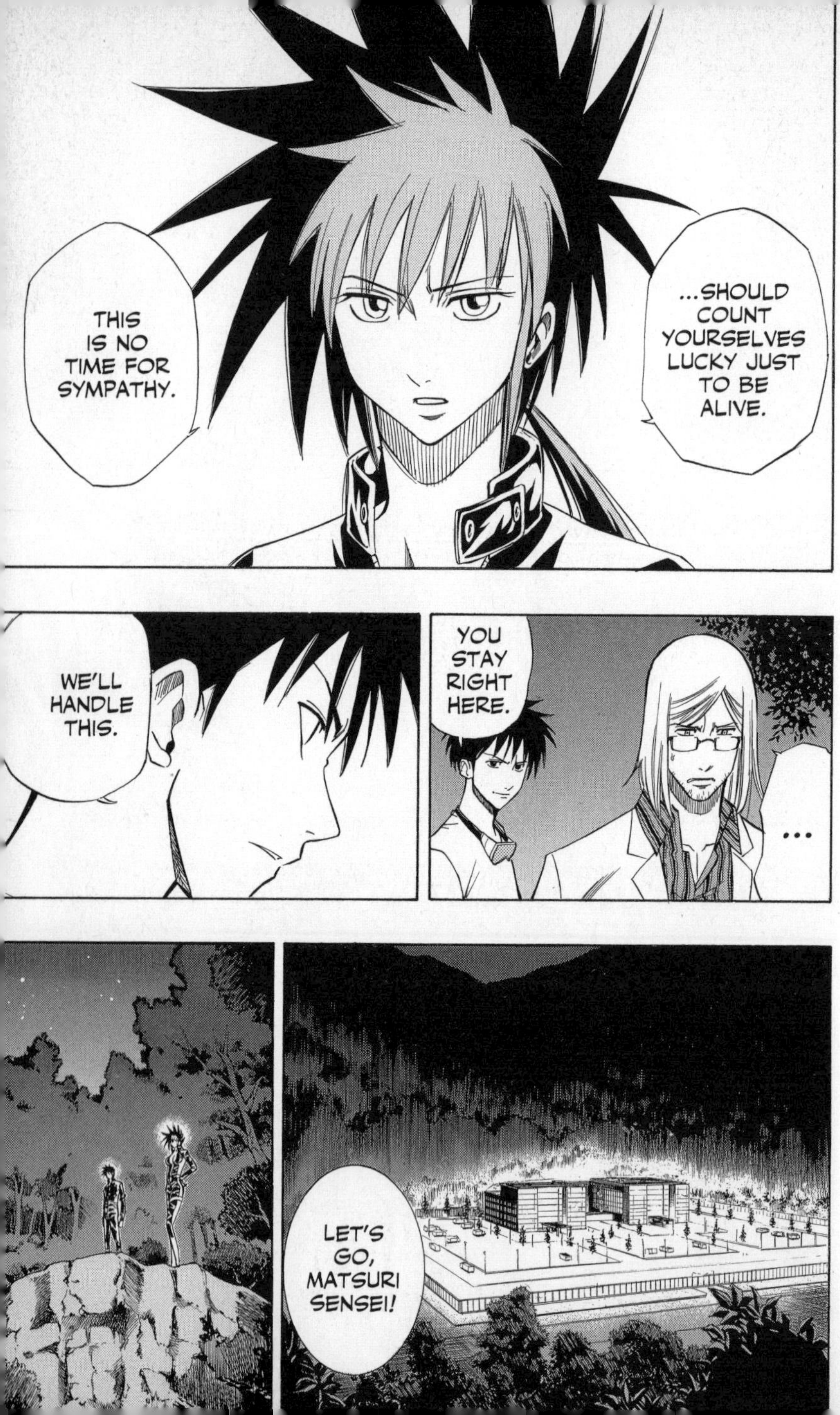
...SHOULD COUNT YOURSELVES LUCKY JUST TO BE ALIVE.
THIS IS NO TIME FOR SYMPATHY.
YOU STAY RIGHT HERE.
...
WE'LL HANDLE THIS.
LET'S GO, MATSURI SENSEI!

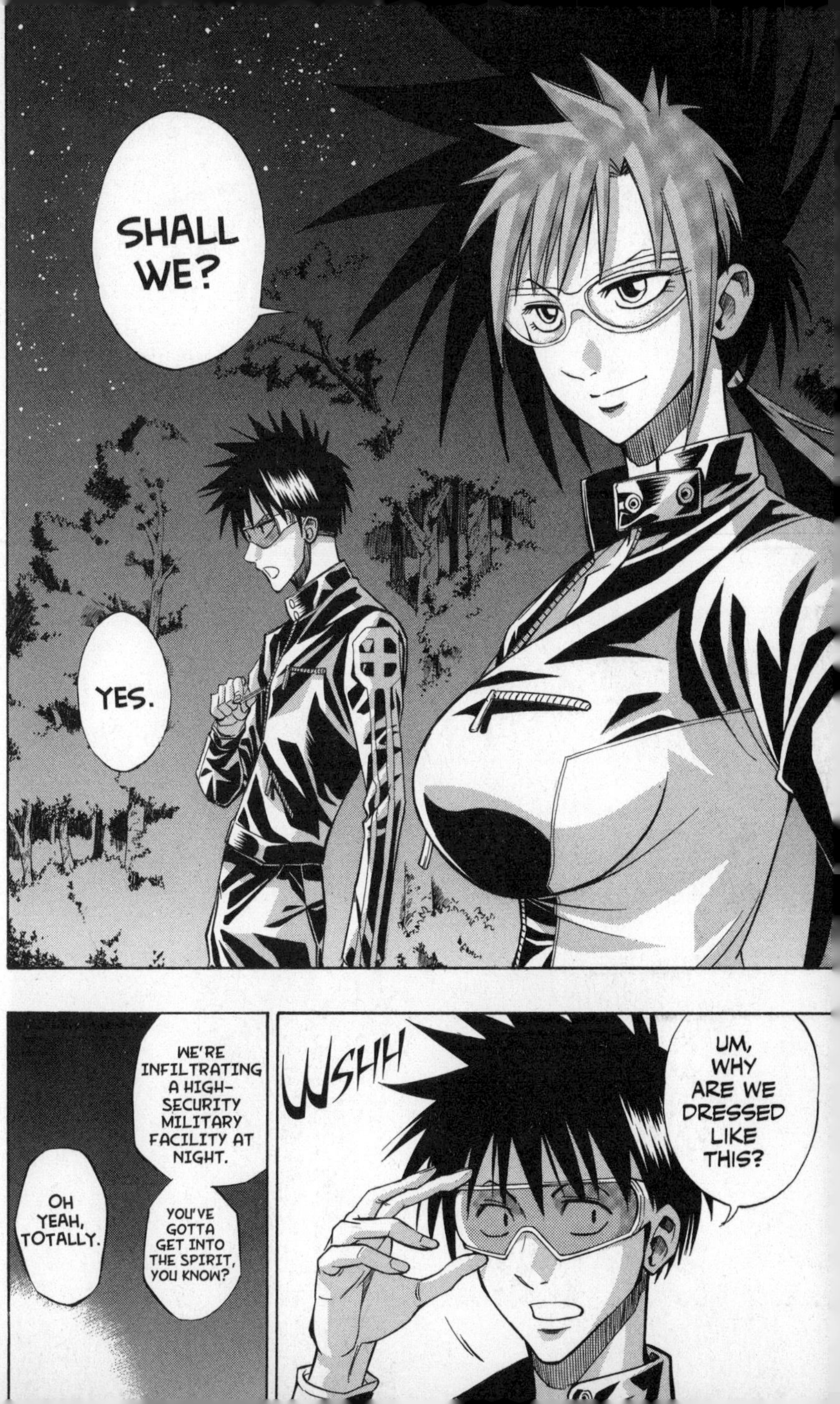
SHALL WE?
YES.
UM, WHY ARE WE DRESSED LIKE THIS?
WSHH
WE'RE INFILTRATING A HIGH-SECURITY MILITARY FACILITY AT NIGHT.
YOU'VE GOTTA GET INTO THE SPIRIT, YOU KNOW?
OH YEAH, TOTALLY.

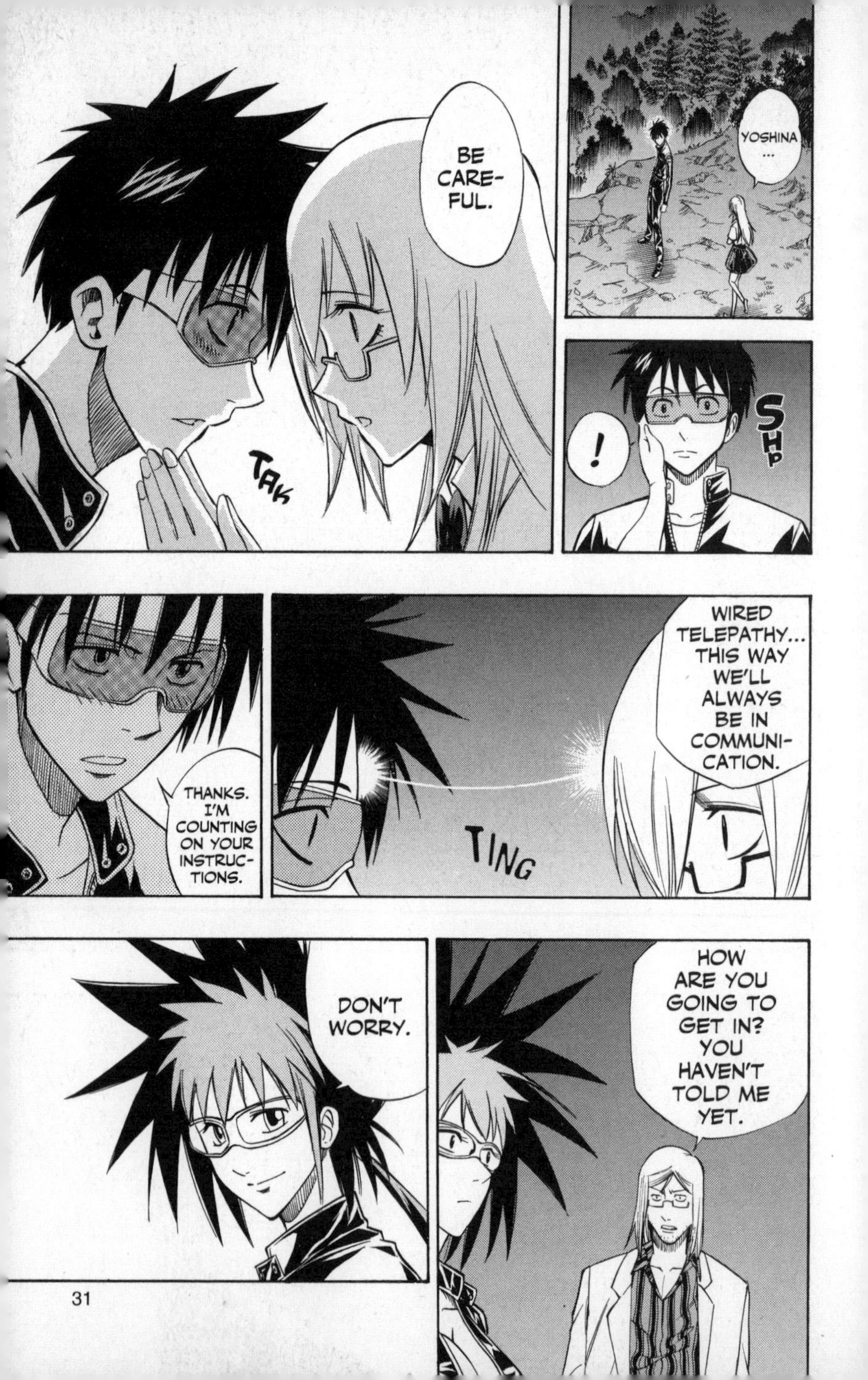
YOSHINA ...
!
SHP
BE CAREFUL.
TAK
WIRED TELEPATHY... THIS WAY WE'LL ALWAYS BE IN COMMUNICATION.
TING
THANKS. I'M COUNTING ON YOUR INSTRUCTIONS.
HOW ARE YOU GOING TO GET IN? YOU HAVEN'T TOLD ME YET.
DON'T WORRY.

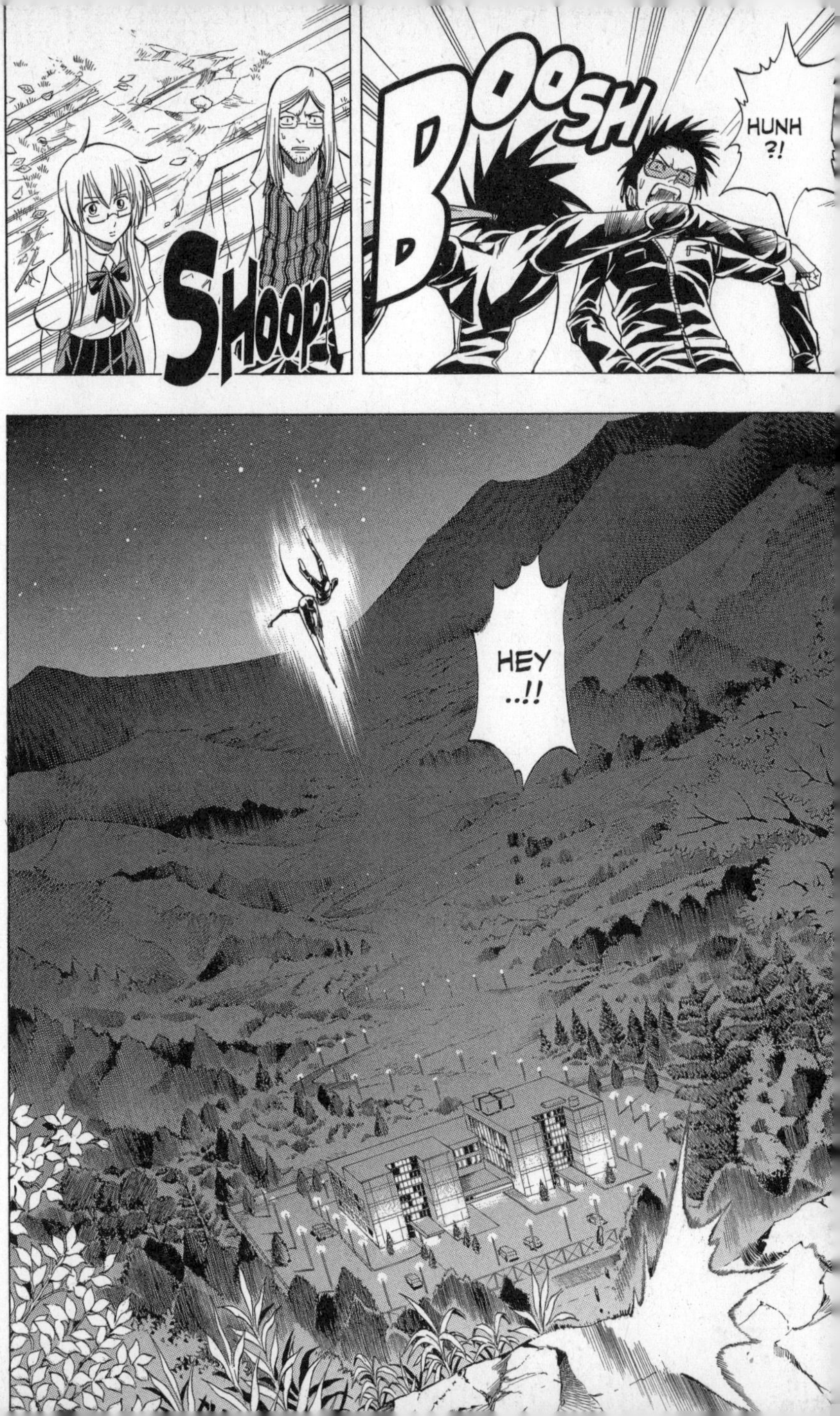
HUNH ?!
BOOSH
SHOOP
HEY ..!!

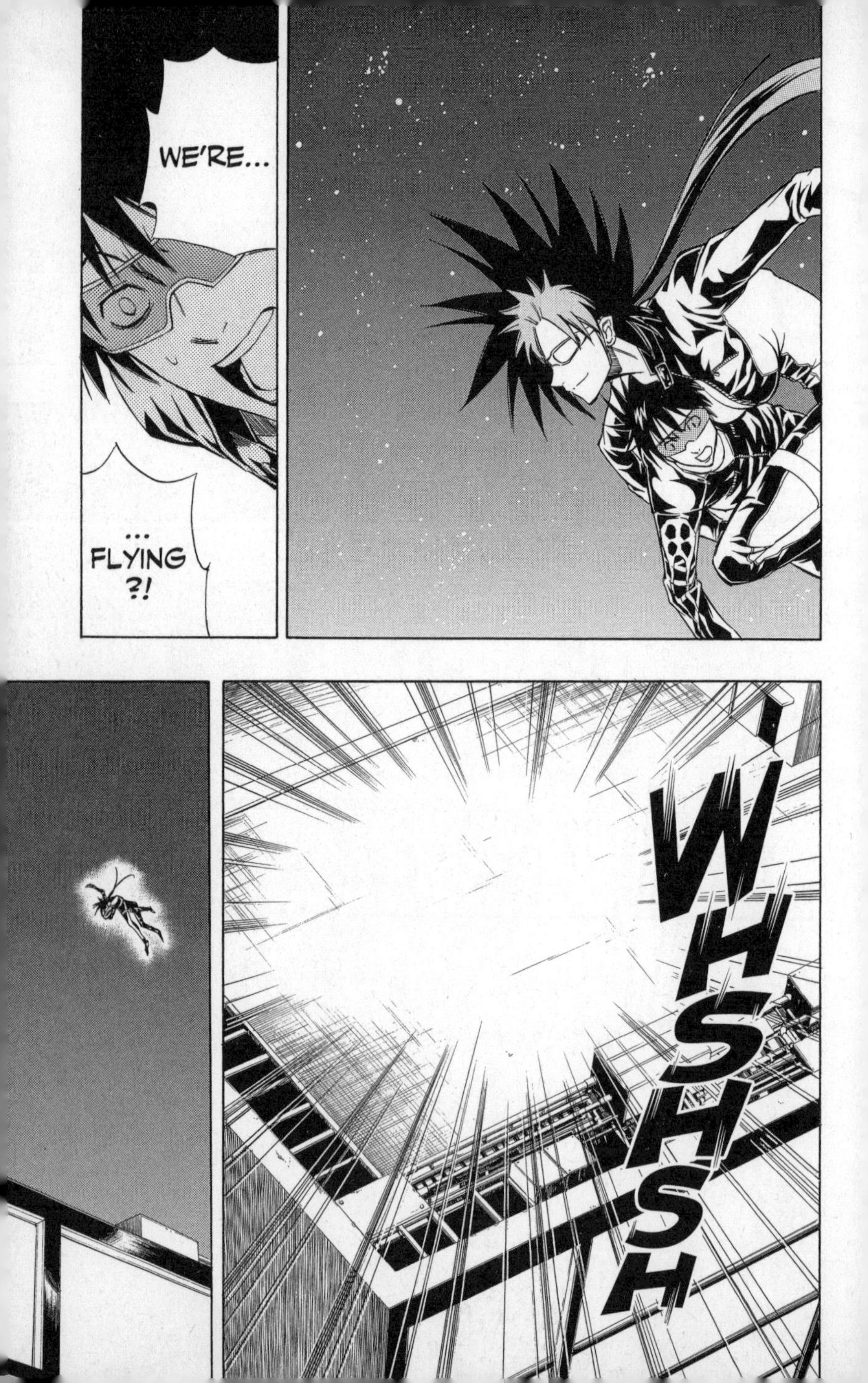
WE'RE...
...FLYING?!
WHSHSHSH

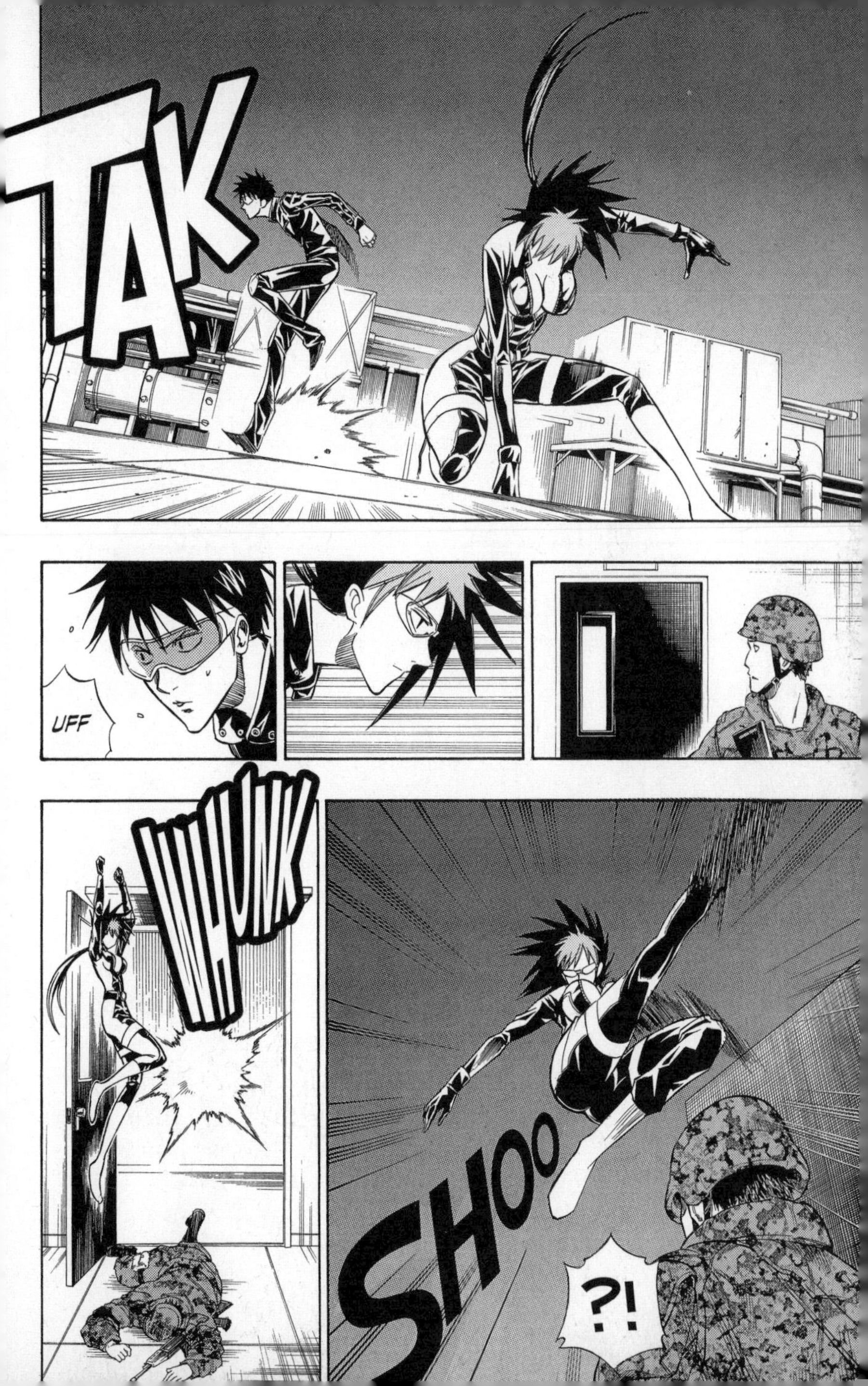
TAK
UFF
SHOO
?!
WHUNK

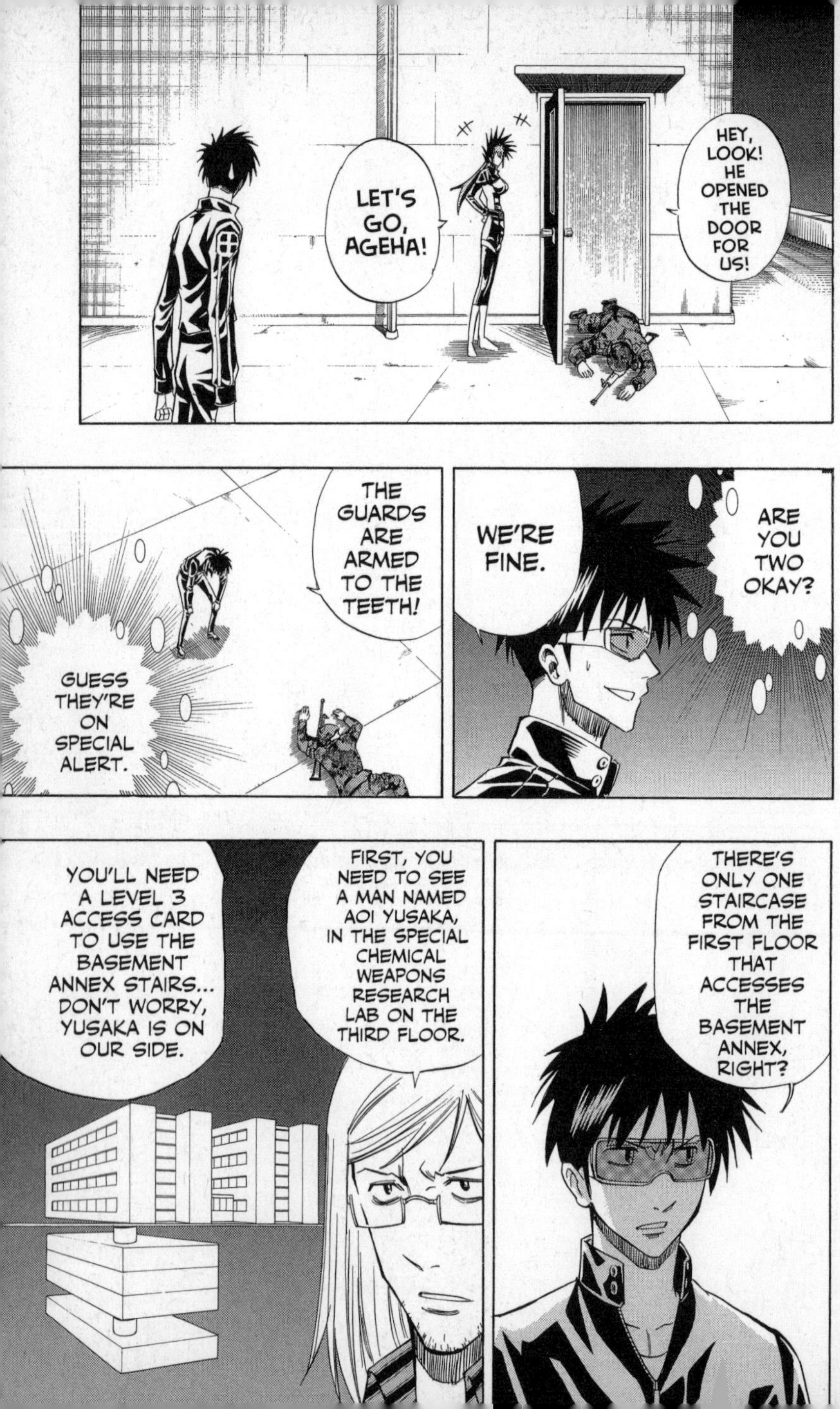
HEY, LOOK! HE OPENED THE DOOR FOR US!
LET'S GO, AGEHA!
ARE YOU TWO OKAY?
WE'RE FINE.
THE GUARDS ARE ARMED TO THE TEETH!
GUESS THEY'RE ON SPECIAL ALERT.
THERE'S ONLY ONE STAIRCASE FROM THE FIRST FLOOR THAT ACCESSES THE BASEMENT ANNEX, RIGHT?
FIRST, YOU NEED TO SEE A MAN NAMED AOI YUSAKA, IN THE SPECIAL CHEMICAL WEAPONS RESEARCH LAB ON THE THIRD FLOOR.
YOU'LL NEED A LEVEL 3 ACCESS CARD TO USE THE BASEMENT ANNEX STAIRS... DON'T WORRY, YUSAKA IS ON OUR SIDE.

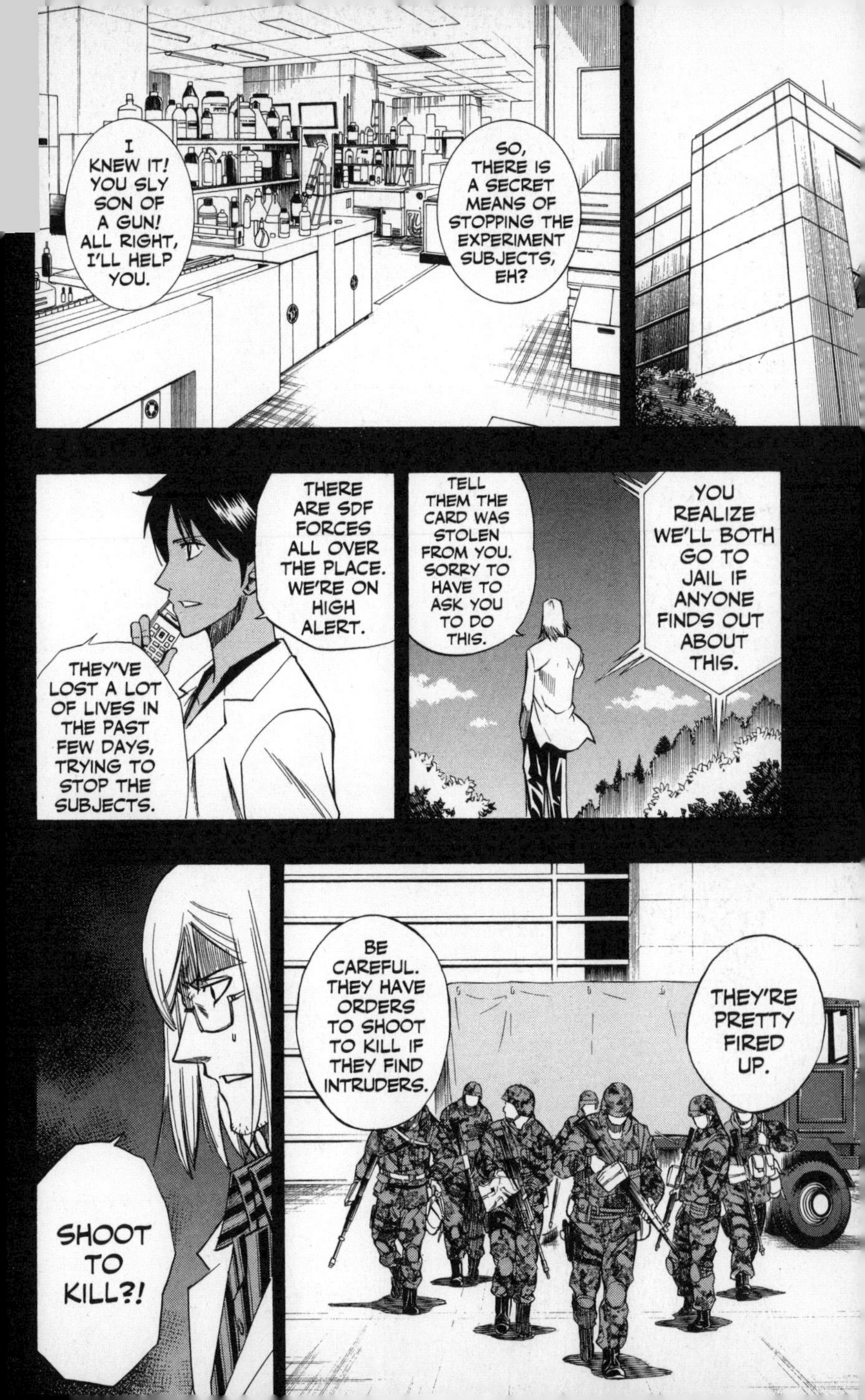
SO, THERE IS A SECRET MEANS OF STOPPING THE EXPERIMENT SUBJECTS, EH?
I KNEW IT! YOU SLY SON OF A GUN! ALL RIGHT, I'LL HELP YOU.
YOU REALIZE WE'LL BOTH GO TO JAIL IF ANYONE FINDS OUT ABOUT THIS.
TELL THEM THE CARD WAS STOLEN FROM YOU. SORRY TO HAVE TO ASK YOU TO DO THIS.
THERE ARE SDF FORCES ALL OVER THE PLACE. WE'RE ON HIGH ALERT.
THEY'VE LOST A LOT OF LIVES IN THE PAST FEW DAYS, TRYING TO STOP THE SUBJECTS.
THEY'RE PRETTY FIRED UP.
BE CAREFUL. THEY HAVE ORDERS TO SHOOT TO KILL IF THEY FIND INTRUDERS.
SHOOT TO KILL?!

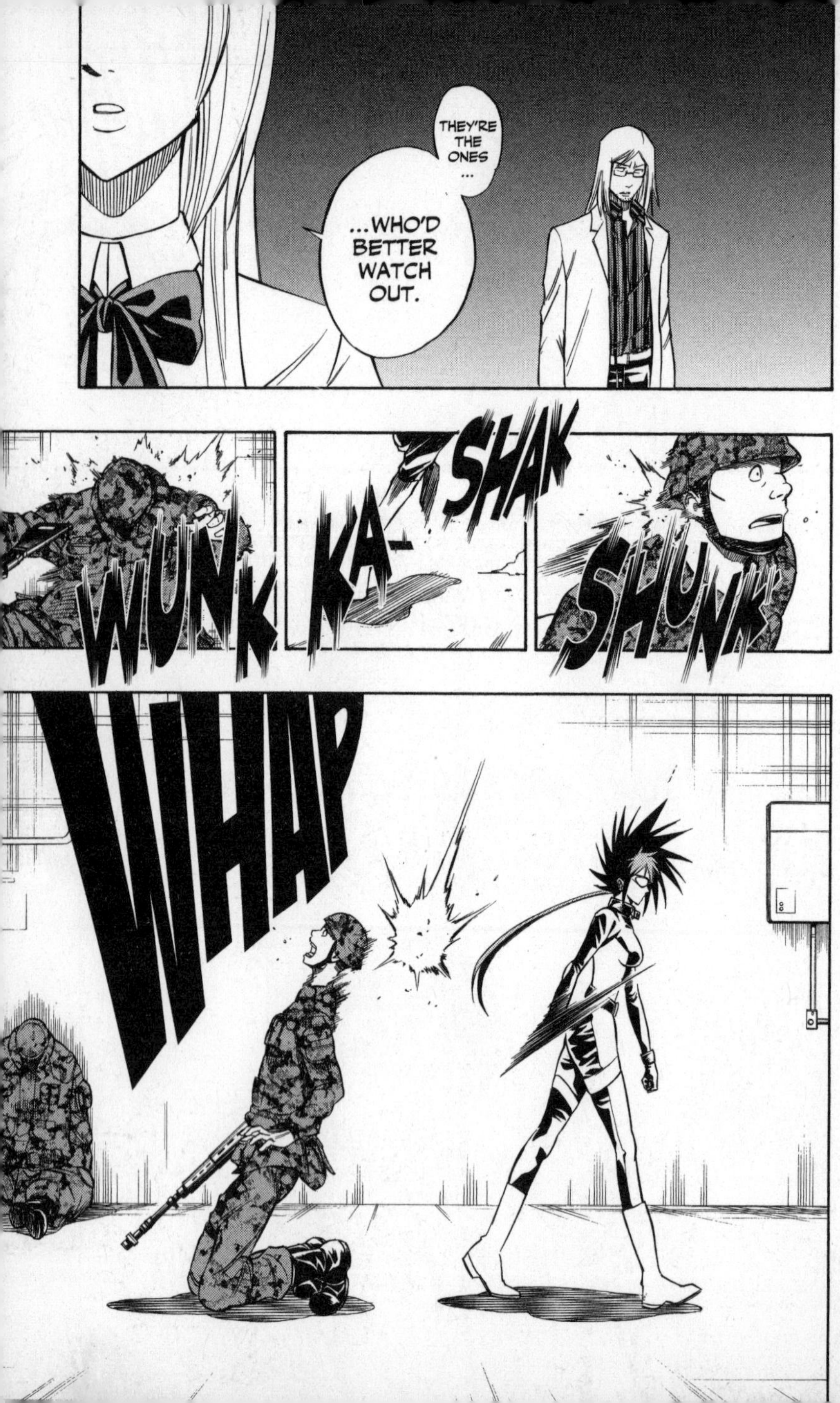
THEY'RE THE ONES...
...WHO'D BETTER WATCH OUT.
SHUNK
KA-SHAK
WUNK
WHAP

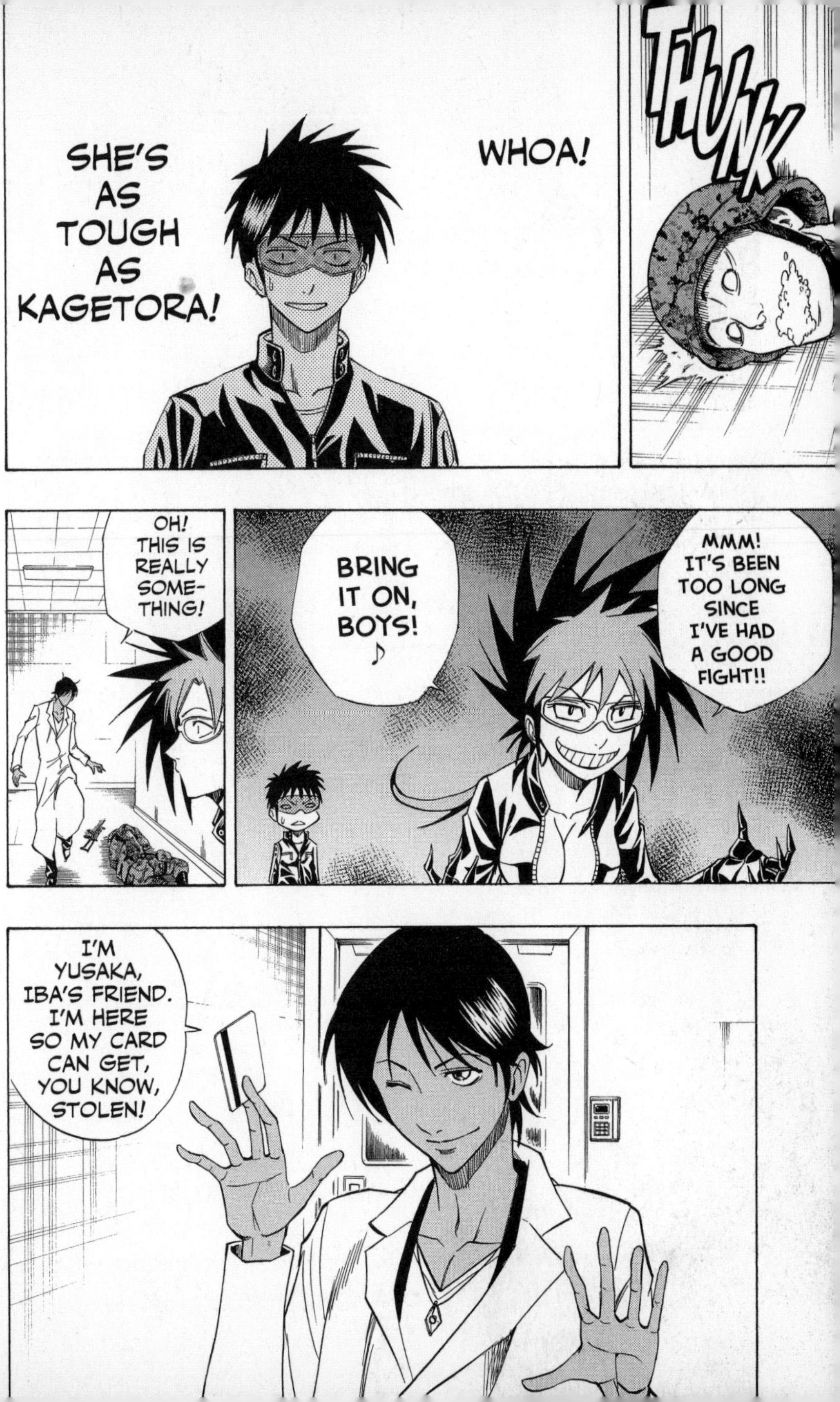
THUNK
WHOA!
SHE'S AS TOUGH AS KAGETORA!
MMM! IT'S BEEN TOO LONG SINCE I'VE HAD A GOOD FIGHT!!
BRING IT ON, BOYS! ♪
OH! THIS IS REALLY SOME-THING!
I'M YUSAKA, IBA'S FRIEND. I'M HERE SO MY CARD CAN GET, YOU KNOW, STOLEN!

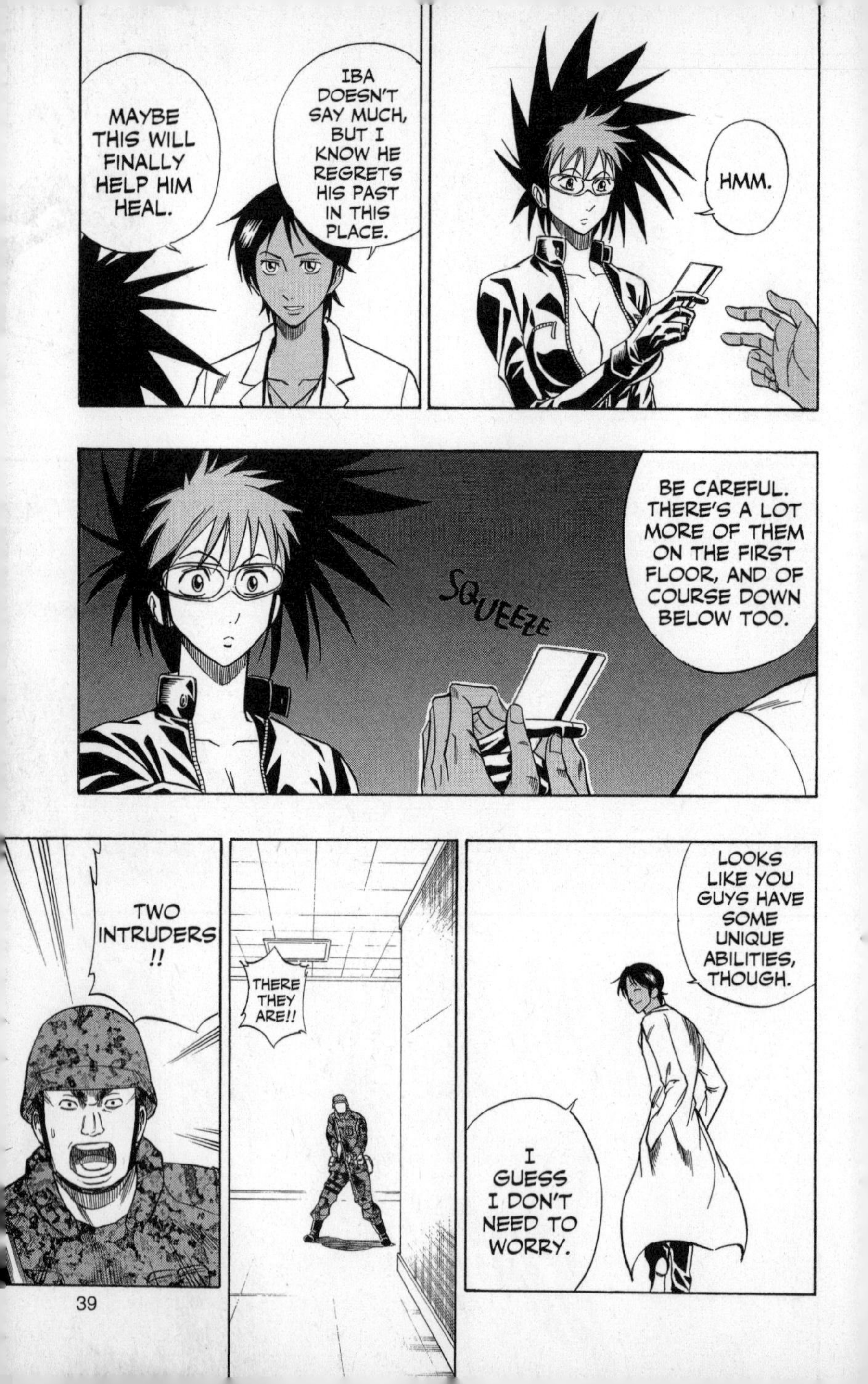
HMM.
IBA DOESN'T SAY MUCH, BUT I KNOW HE REGRETS HIS PAST IN THIS PLACE.
MAYBE THIS WILL FINALLY HELP HIM HEAL.
BE CAREFUL. THERE'S A LOT MORE OF THEM ON THE FIRST FLOOR, AND OF COURSE DOWN BELOW TOO.
SQUEEZE
LOOKS LIKE YOU GUYS HAVE SOME UNIQUE ABILITIES, THOUGH.
I GUESS I DON'T NEED TO WORRY.
THERE THEY ARE!!
TWO INTRUDERS!!

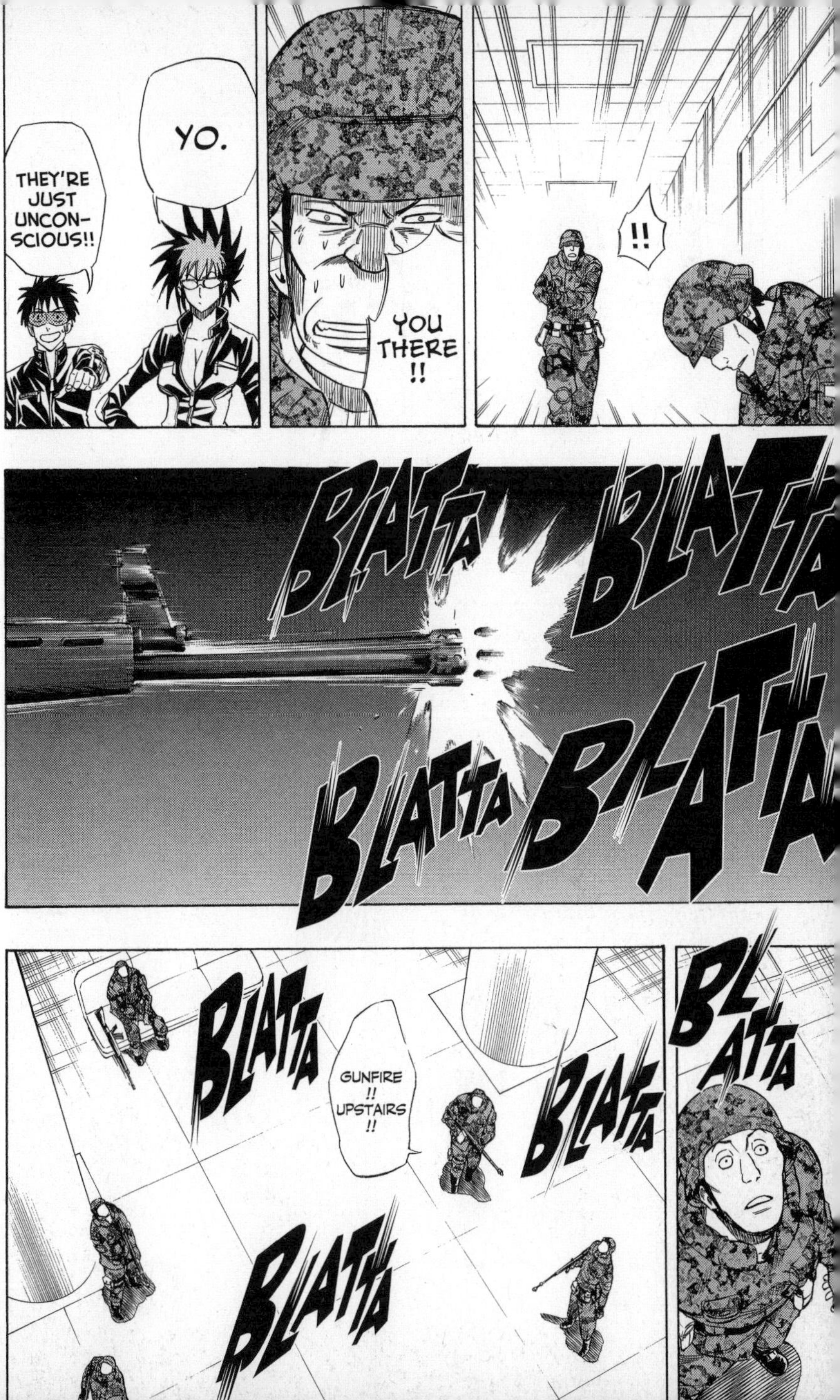
!!
YOU THERE !!
YO.
THEY'RE JUST UNCONSCIOUS!!
BLATTA
BLATTA
BLATTA
BLATTA
BLATTA
BLATTA
BLATTA
GUNFIRE !! UPSTAIRS !!
BLATTA
BLATTA

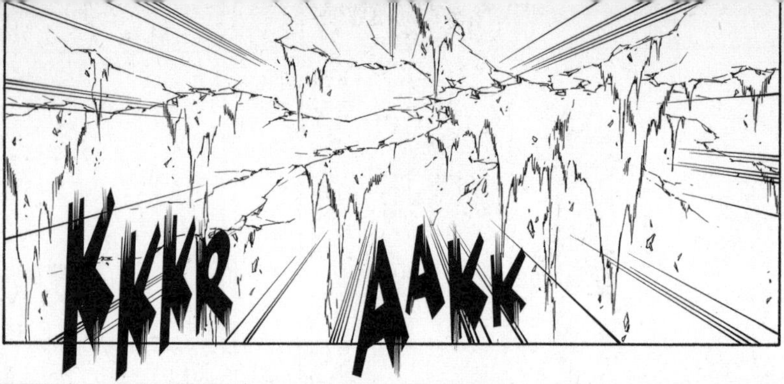
KKKR AAKK
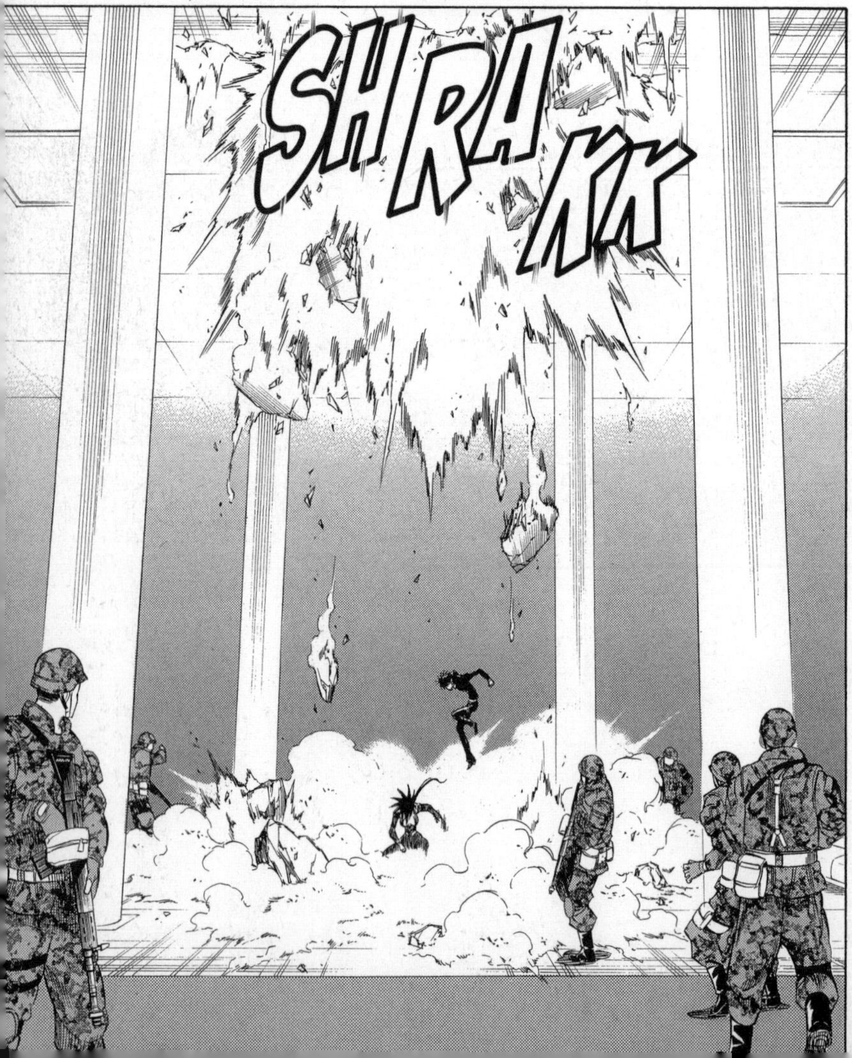
SHRANK

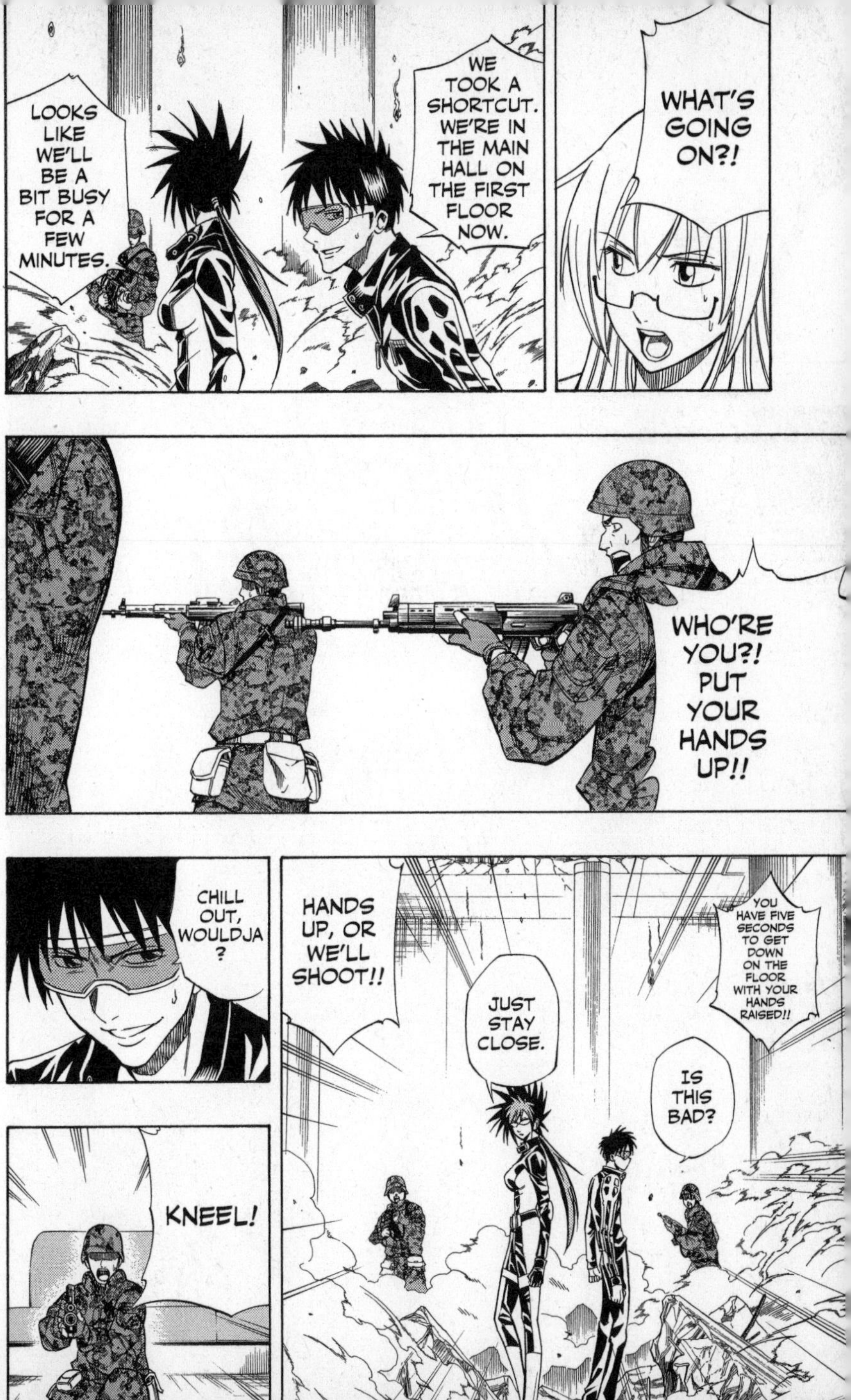
WHAT'S GOING ON?!
WE TOOK A SHORTCUT. WE'RE IN THE MAIN HALL ON THE FIRST FLOOR NOW.
LOOKS LIKE WE'LL BE A BIT BUSY FOR A FEW MINUTES.
WHO'RE YOU?! PUT YOUR HANDS UP!!
YOU HAVE FIVE SECONDS TO GET DOWN ON THE FLOOR WITH YOUR HANDS RAISED!!
HANDS UP, OR WE'LL SHOOT!!
JUST STAY CLOSE.
IS THIS BAD?
CHILL OUT, WOULDJA?
KNEEL!

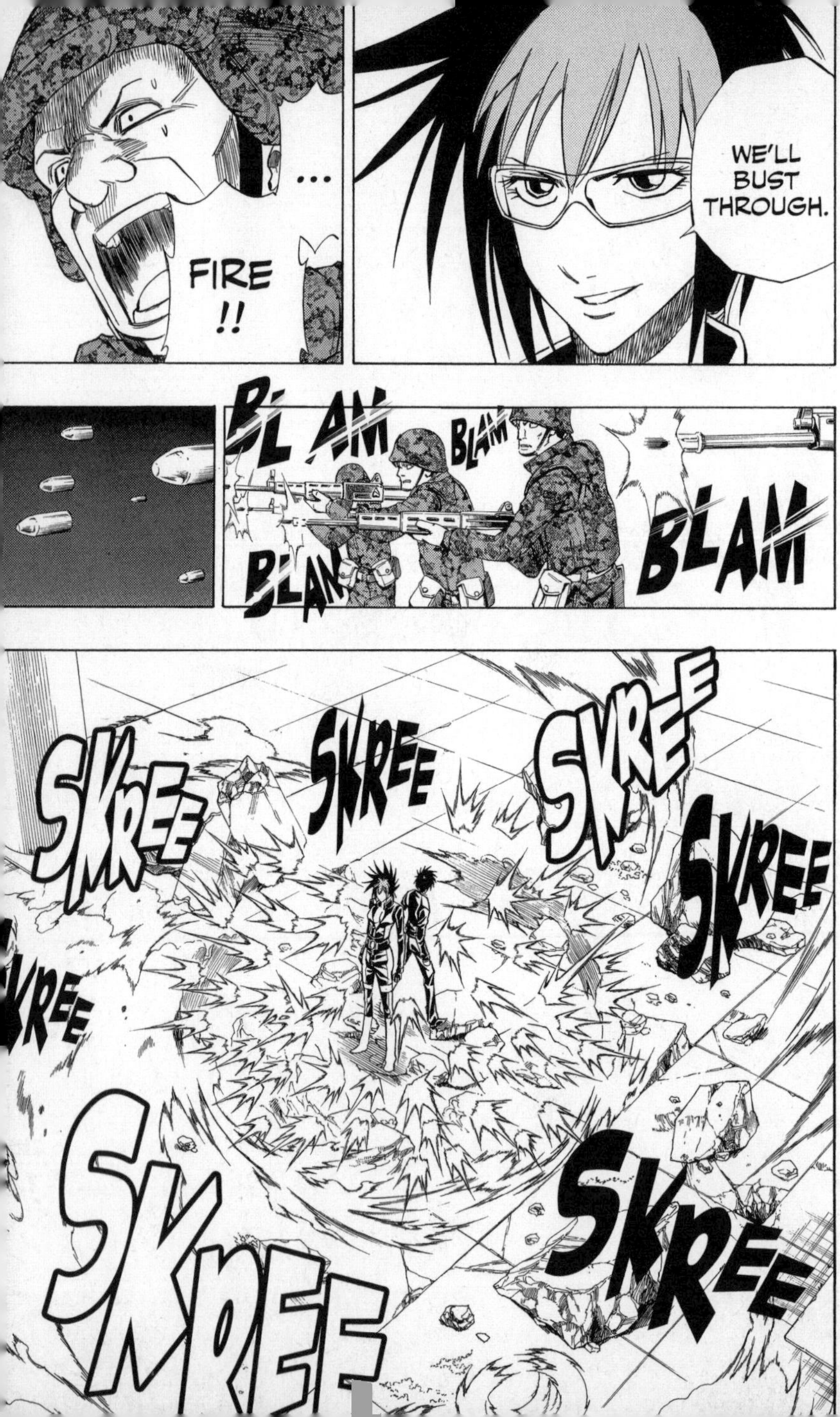
WE'LL BUST THROUGH.
...
FIRE !!
BLAM
BLAM
BLAM
BLAM
SKREE
SKREE
SKREE
SKREE
SKREE
SKREE
SKREE

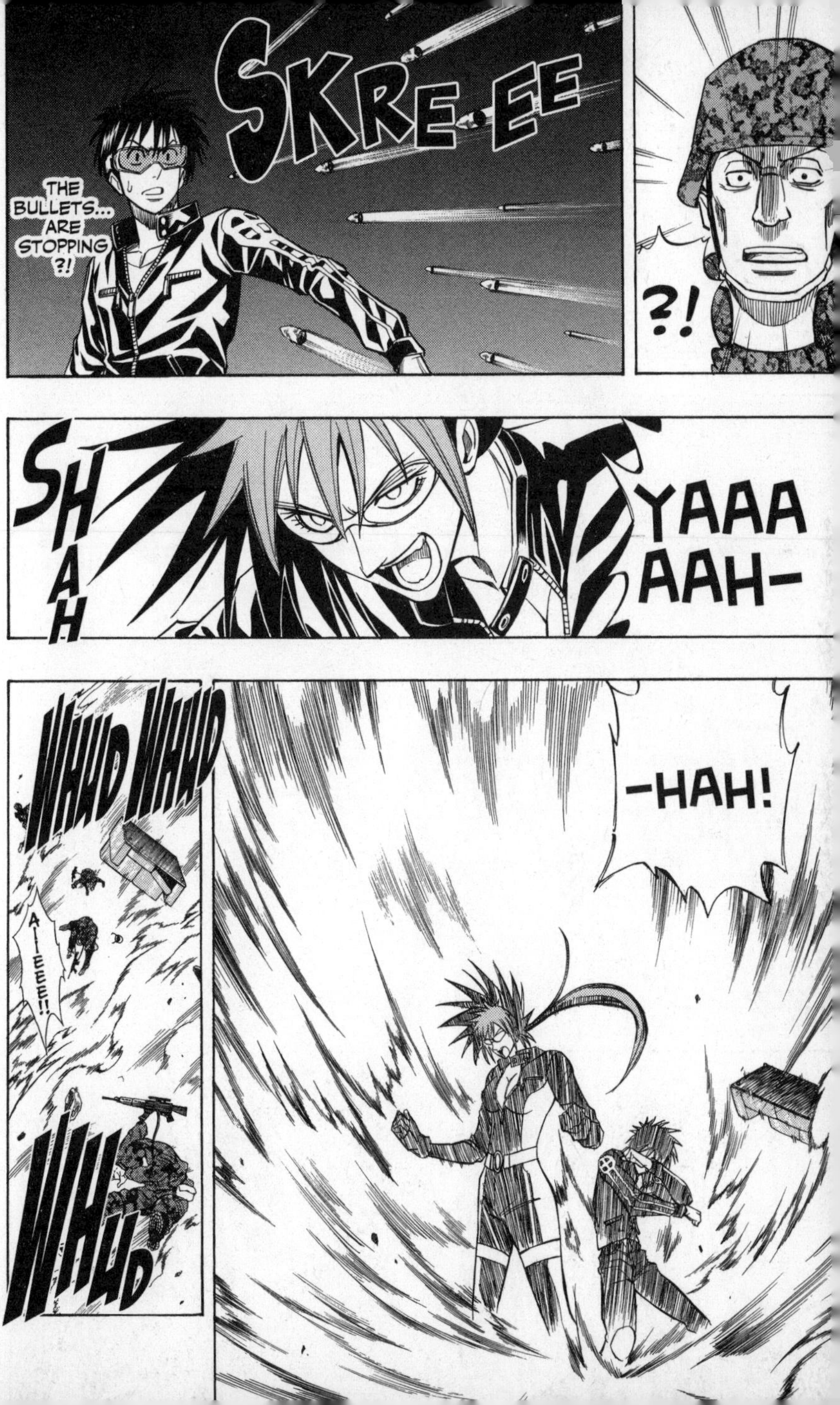
?!
SKRE-EE
THE BULLETS... ARE STOPPING ?!
YAAA AAH-
SHAH-
-HAH!
WHUD WHUD
AIIEEE!!
WHUD

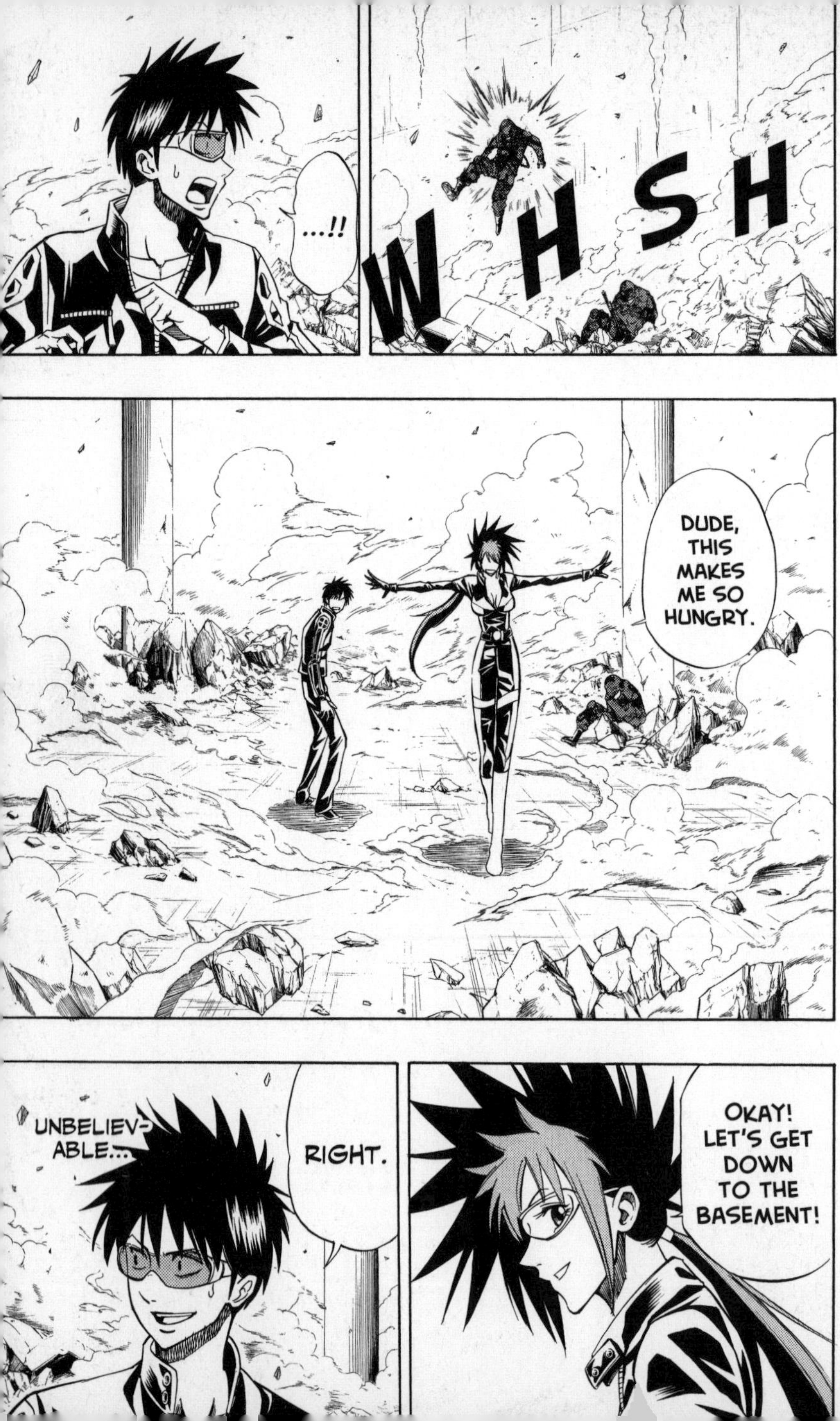
WHSH
...!!
DUDE, THIS MAKES ME SO HUNGRY.
OKAY! LET'S GET DOWN TO THE BASEMENT!
RIGHT.
UNBELIEV-ABLE...

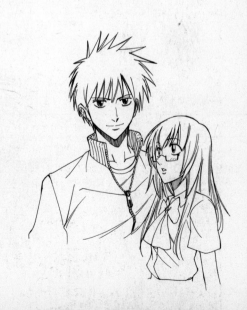

Call. 101: Virus

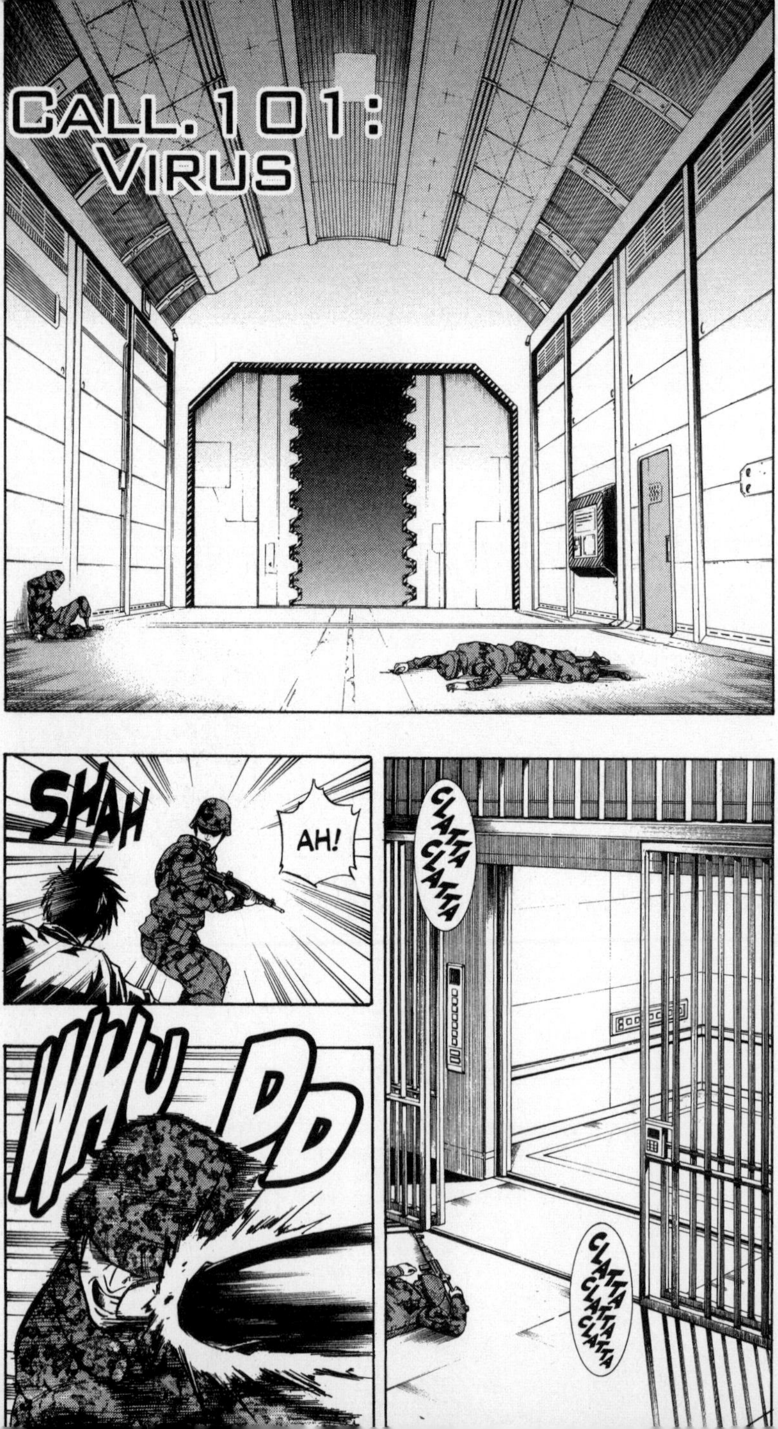
CLATTA CLATTA CLATTA
CLATTA CLATTA CLATTA
SHAH
AH!
WHU DD

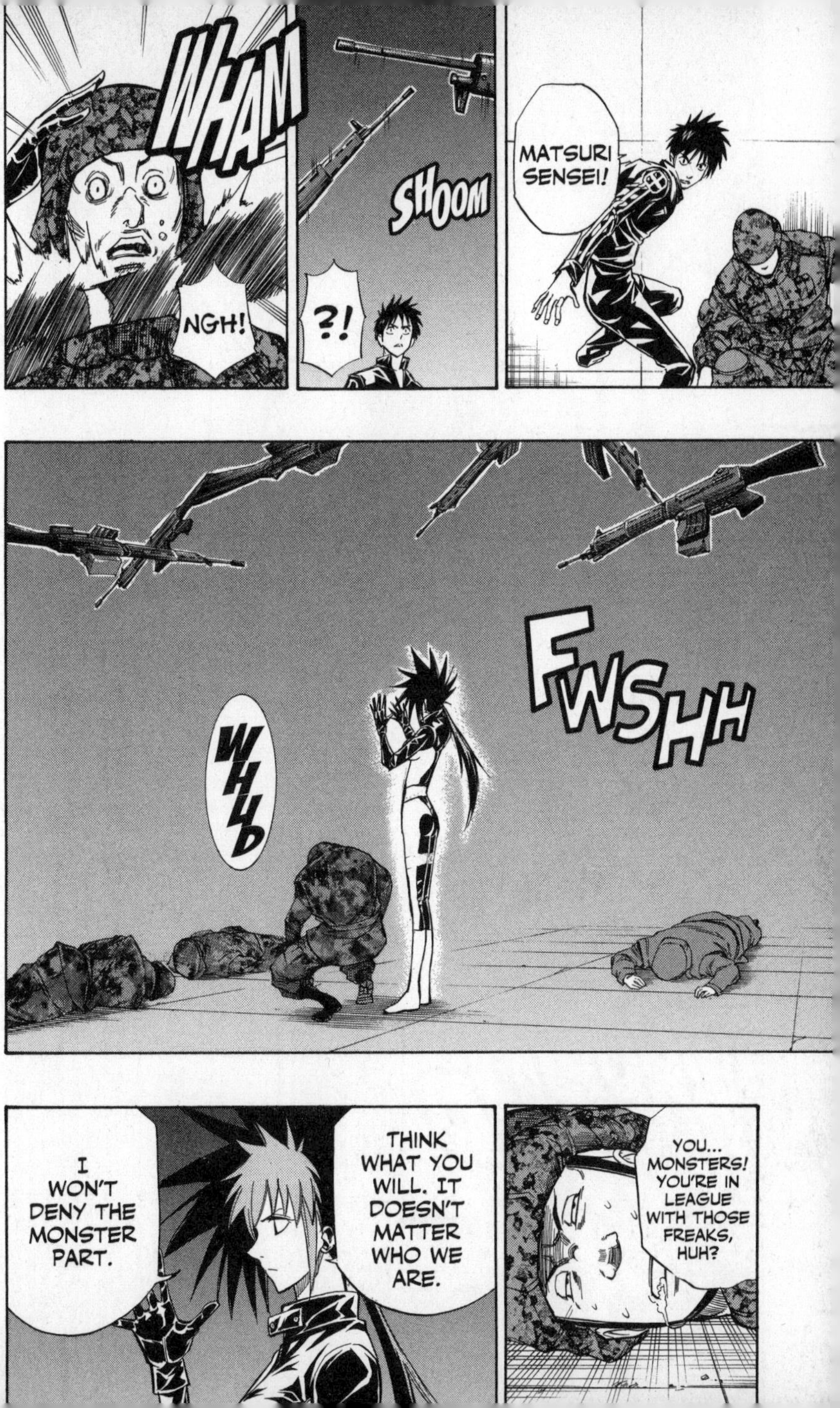
MATSURI SENSEI!
SHOOM
?!
WHAM
NGH!
FWSHH
WHUD
YOU... MONSTERS! YOU'RE IN LEAGUE WITH THOSE FREAKS, HUH?
THINK WHAT YOU WILL. IT DOESN'T MATTER WHO WE ARE.
I WON'T DENY THE MONSTER PART.

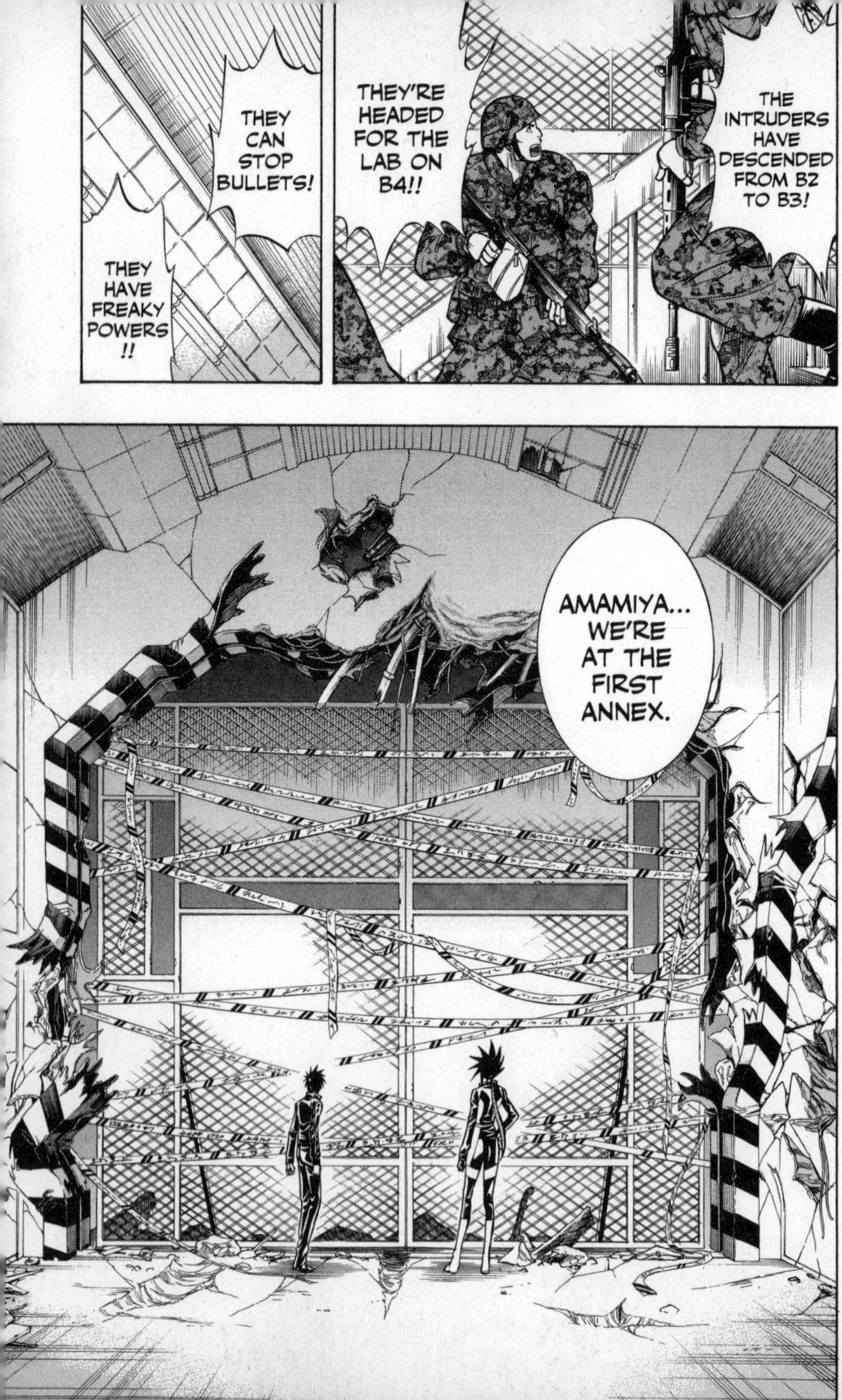
THE INTRUDERS HAVE DESCENDED FROM B2 TO B3!
THEY'RE HEADED FOR THE LAB ON B4!!
THEY CAN STOP BULLETS!
THEY HAVE FREAKY POWERS!!
AMAMIYA... WE'RE AT THE FIRST ANNEX.

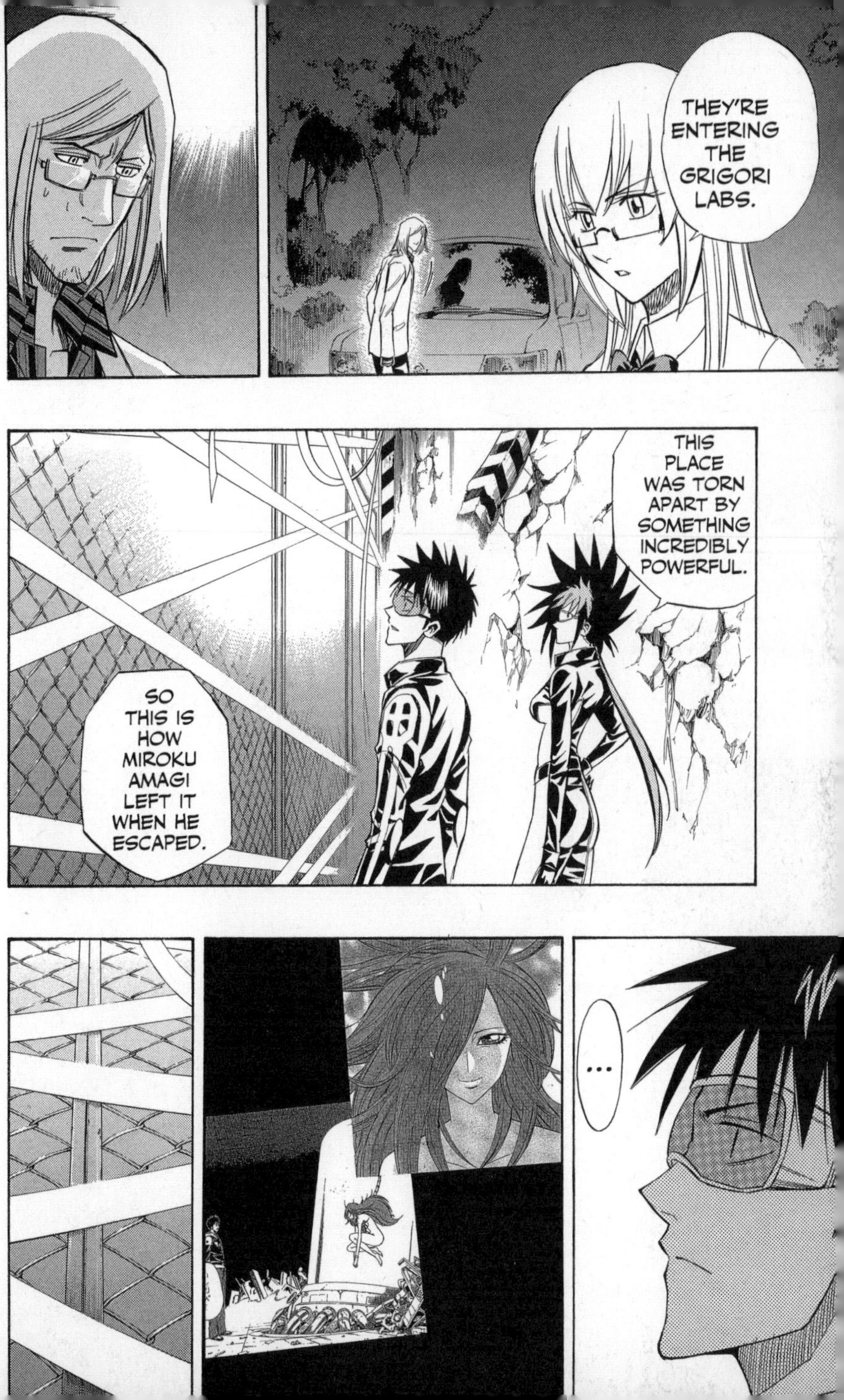
THEY'RE ENTERING THE GRIGORI LABS.
THIS PLACE WAS TORN APART BY SOMETHING INCREDIBLY POWERFUL.
SO THIS IS HOW MIROKU AMAGI LEFT IT WHEN HE ESCAPED.
...

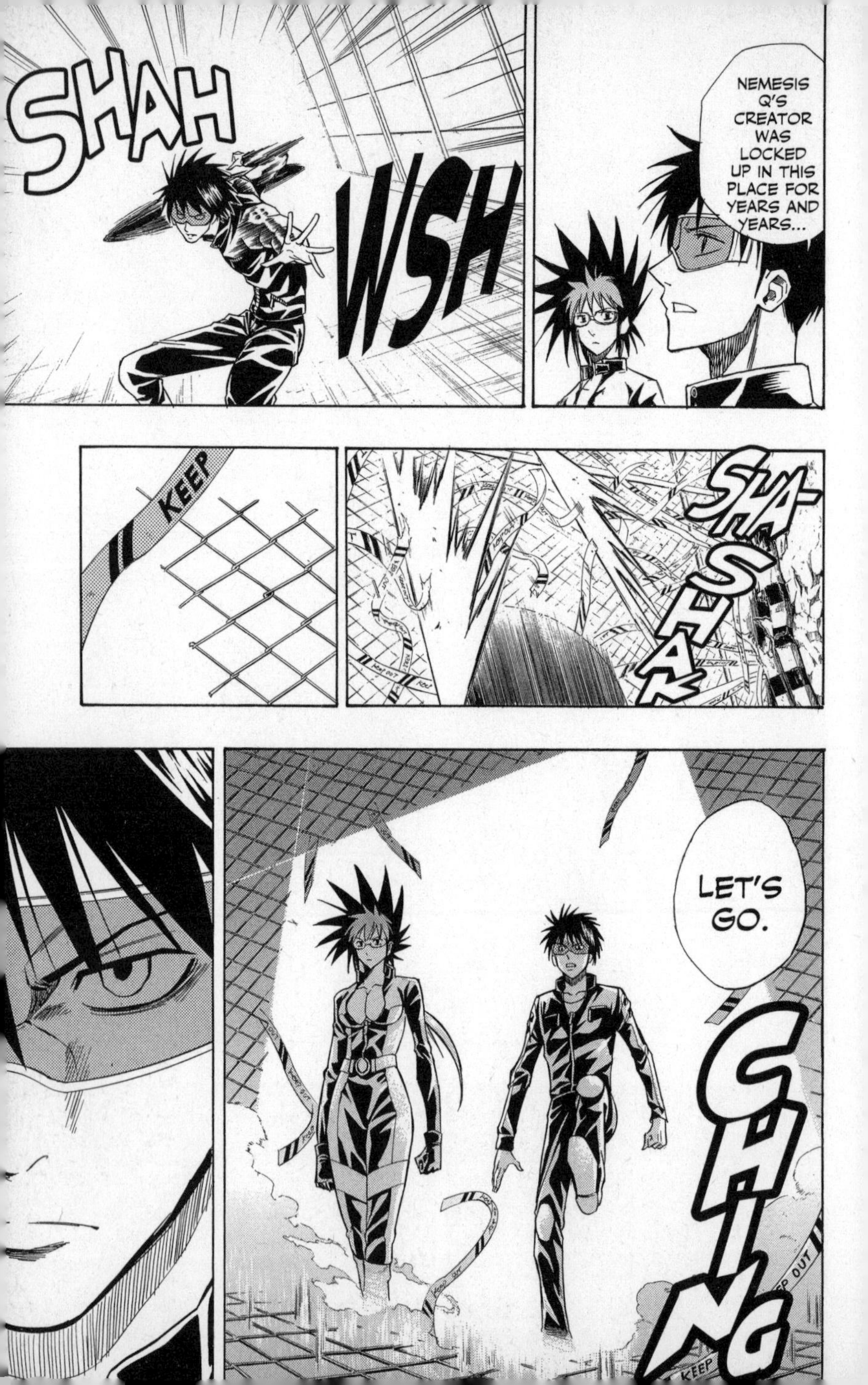
NEMESIS Q'S CREATOR WAS LOCKED UP IN THIS PLACE FOR YEARS AND YEARS...
SHAH
WSH
SHA-SHAK
KEEP
LET'S GO.
CHING

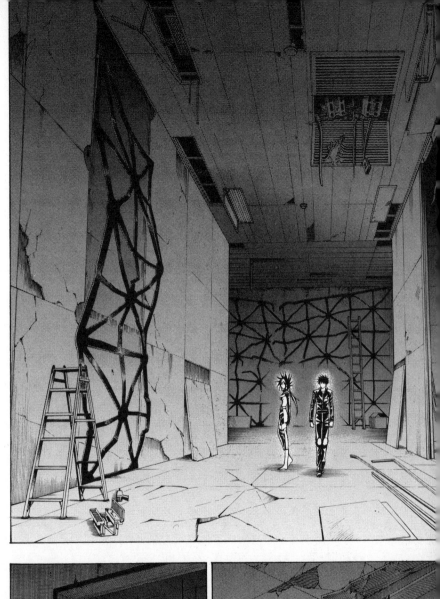
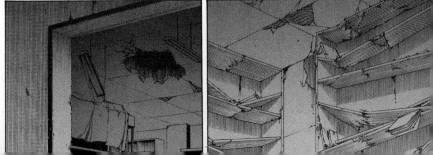

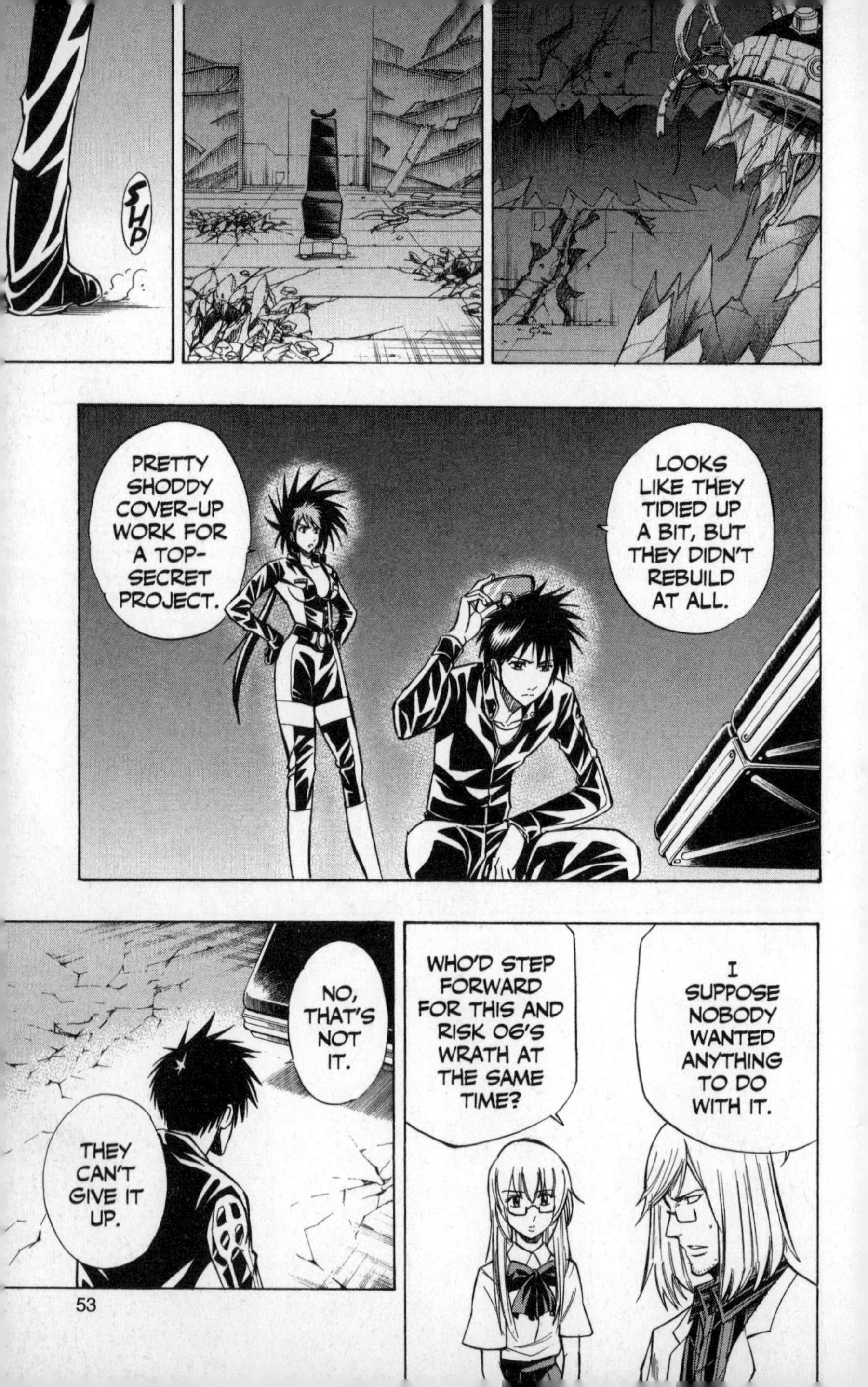
SHP
LOOKS LIKE THEY TIDIED UP A BIT, BUT THEY DIDN'T REBUILD AT ALL.
PRETTY SHODDY COVER-UP WORK FOR A TOP-SECRET PROJECT.
I SUPPOSE NOBODY WANTED ANYTHING TO DO WITH IT.
WHO'D STEP FORWARD FOR THIS AND RISK 06'S WRATH AT THE SAME TIME?
NO, THAT'S NOT IT.
THEY CAN'T GIVE IT UP.

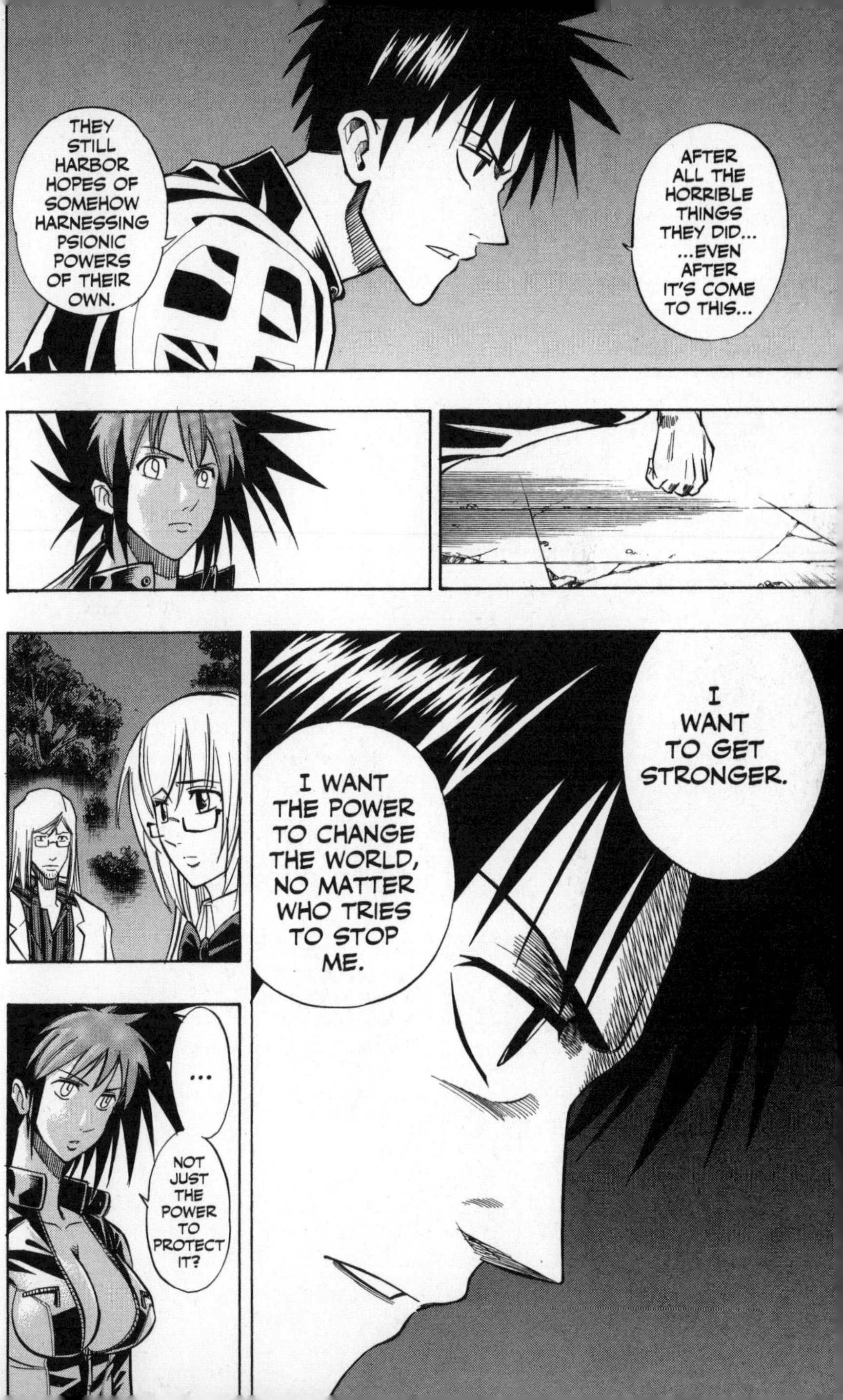
AFTER ALL THE HORRIBLE THINGS THEY DID... ...EVEN AFTER IT'S COME TO THIS...
THEY STILL HARBOR HOPES OF SOMEHOW HARNESSING PSIONIC POWERS OF THEIR OWN.
I WANT TO GET STRONGER.
I WANT THE POWER TO CHANGE THE WORLD, NO MATTER WHO TRIES TO STOP ME.
...
NOT JUST THE POWER TO PROTECT IT?

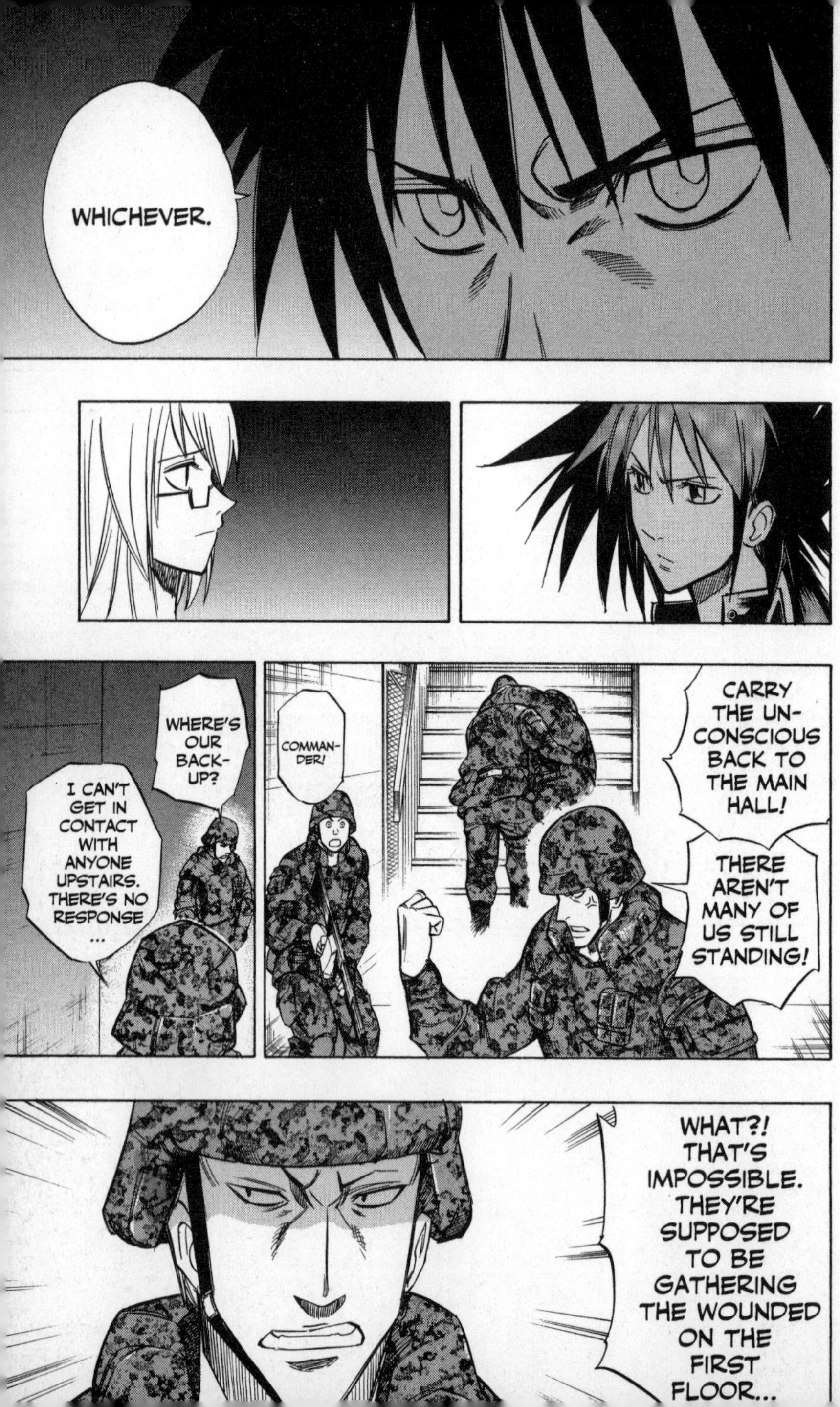
WHICHEVER.
CARRY THE UN-CONSCIOUS BACK TO THE MAIN HALL!
THERE AREN'T MANY OF US STILL STANDING!
COMMAN-DER!
WHERE'S OUR BACK-UP?
I CAN'T GET IN CONTACT WITH ANYONE UPSTAIRS. THERE'S NO RESPONSE ...
WHAT?! THAT'S IMPOSSIBLE. THEY'RE SUPPOSED TO BE GATHERING THE WOUNDED ON THE FIRST FLOOR...

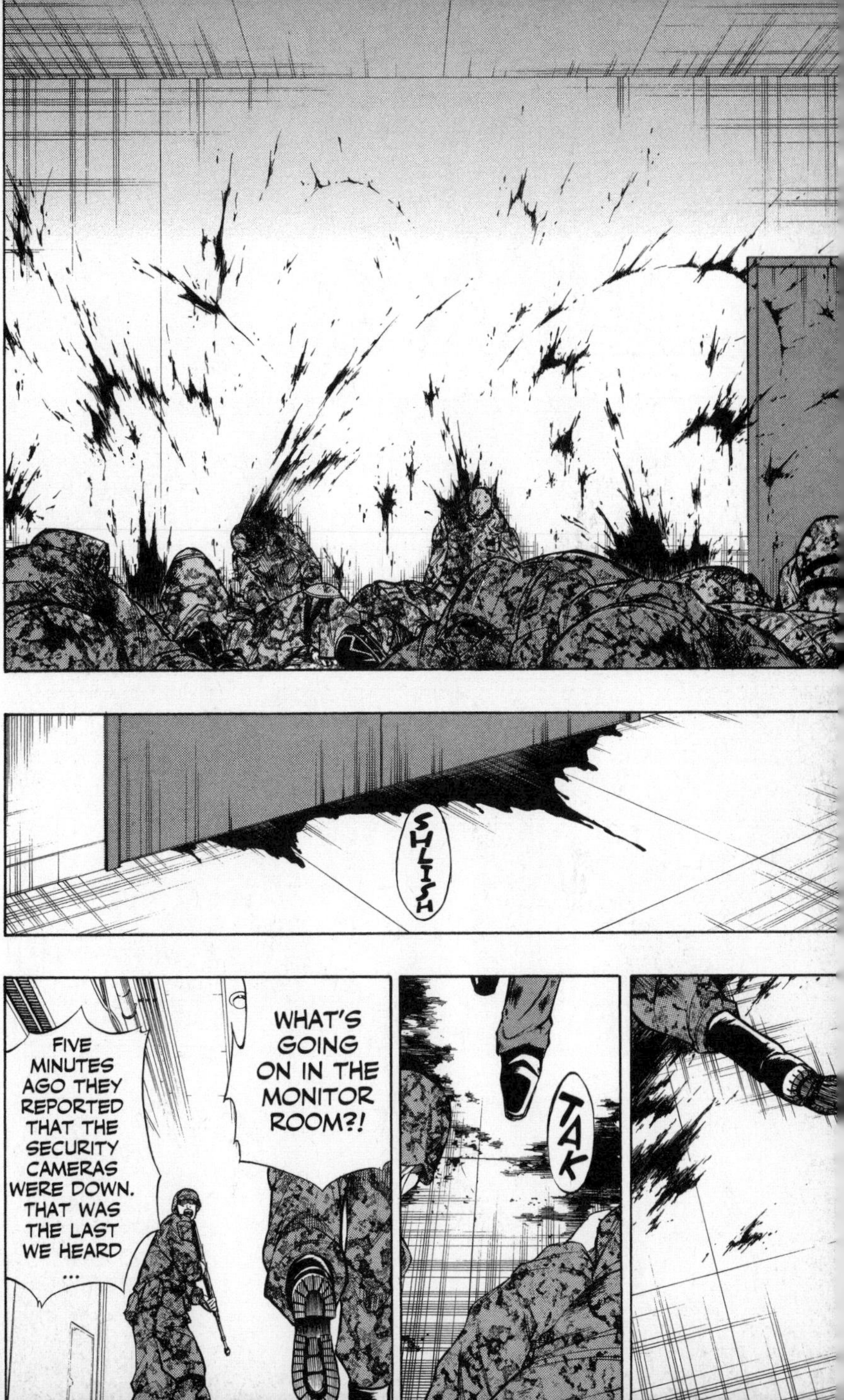
SHLISH
TAK
WHAT'S GOING ON IN THE MONITOR ROOM?!
FIVE MINUTES AGO THEY REPORTED THAT THE SECURITY CAMERAS WERE DOWN. THAT WAS THE LAST WE HEARD ...

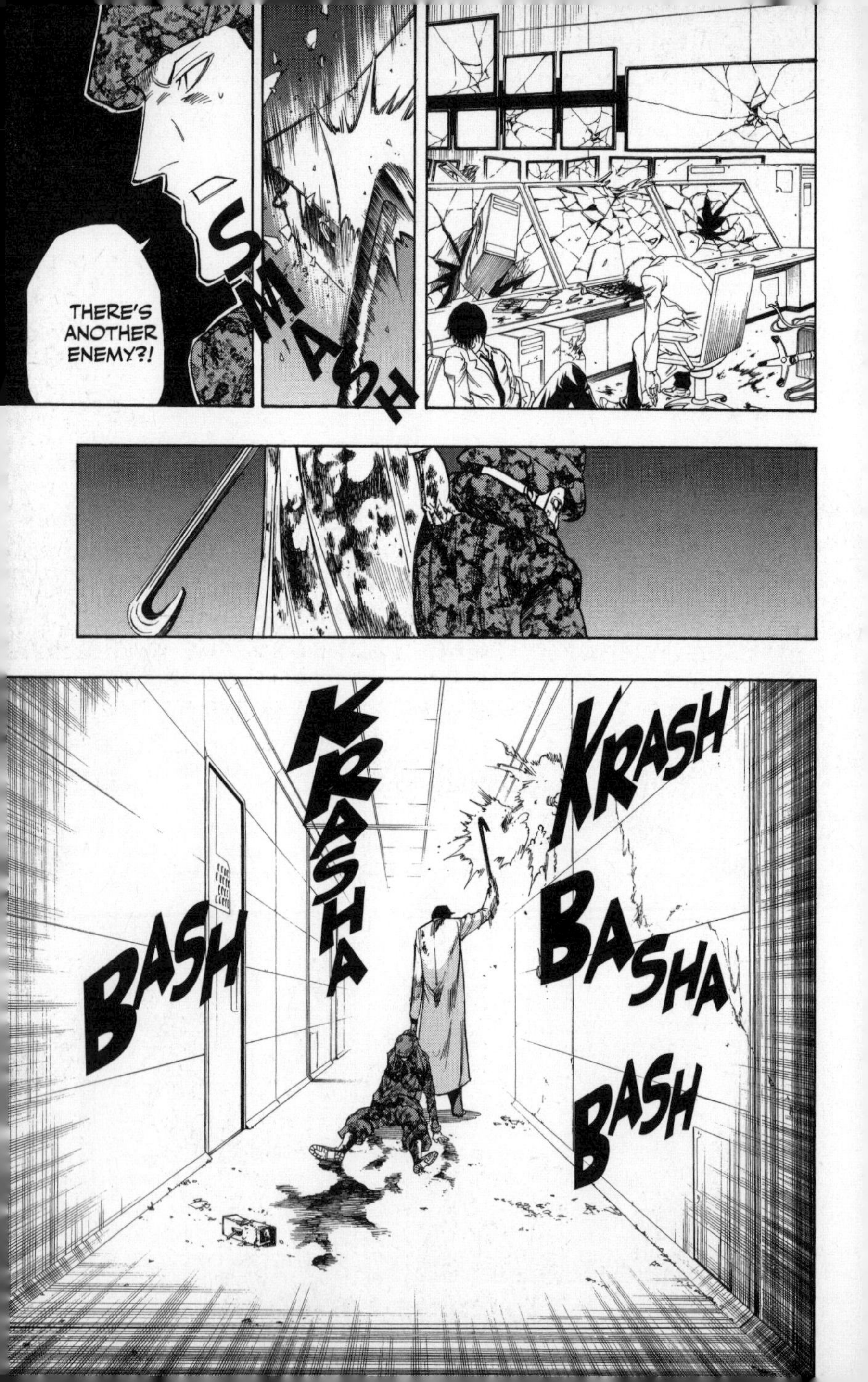
SMASH
THERE'S ANOTHER ENEMY?!
KRASH
KRASHA
BASHA
BASH
BASH

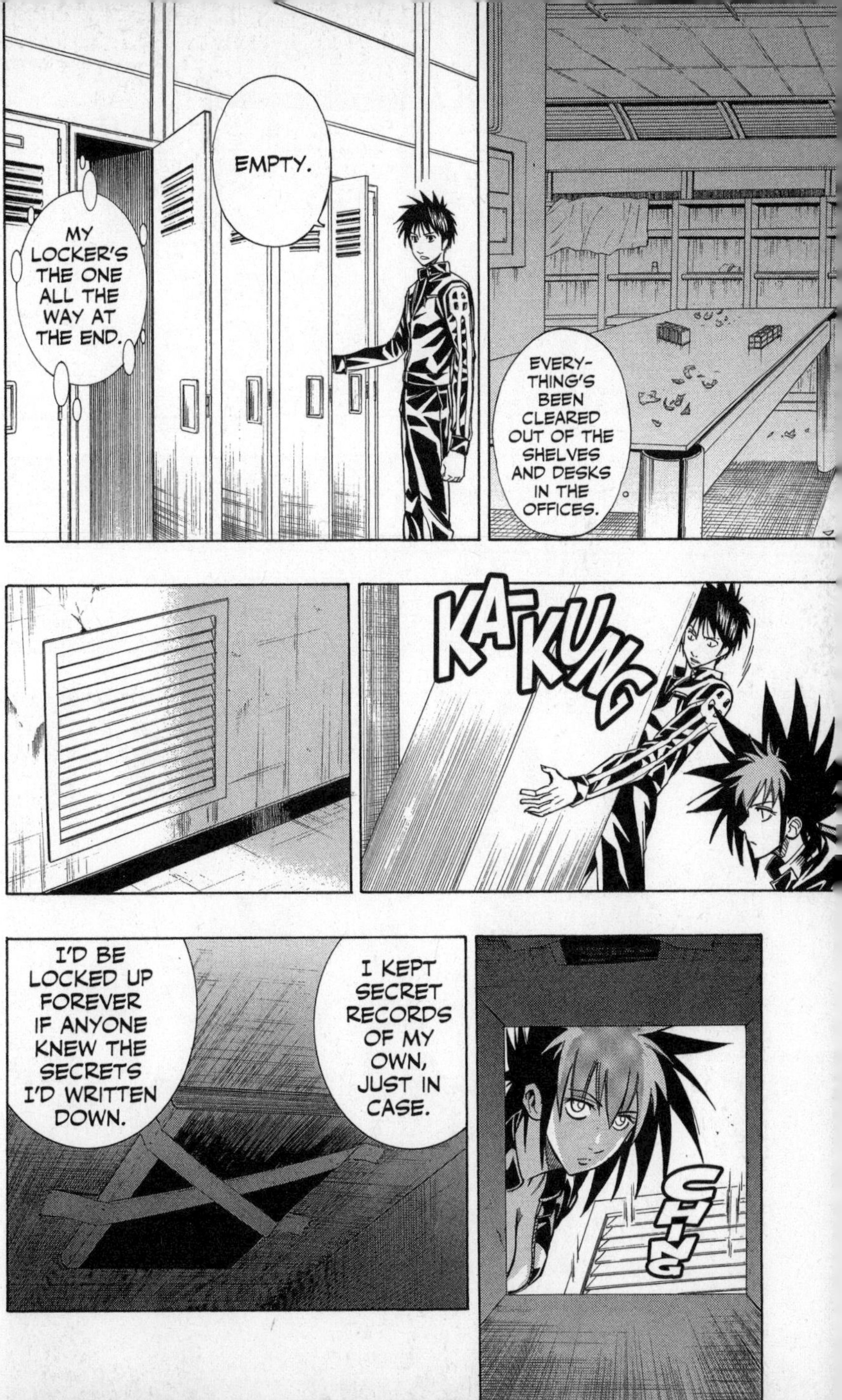
EVERYTHING'S BEEN CLEARED OUT OF THE SHELVES AND DESKS IN THE OFFICES.
EMPTY.
MY LOCKER'S THE ONE ALL THE WAY AT THE END.
KA-KUNG
CHING
I KEPT SECRET RECORDS OF MY OWN, JUST IN CASE.
I'D BE LOCKED UP FOREVER IF ANYONE KNEW THE SECRETS I'D WRITTEN DOWN.

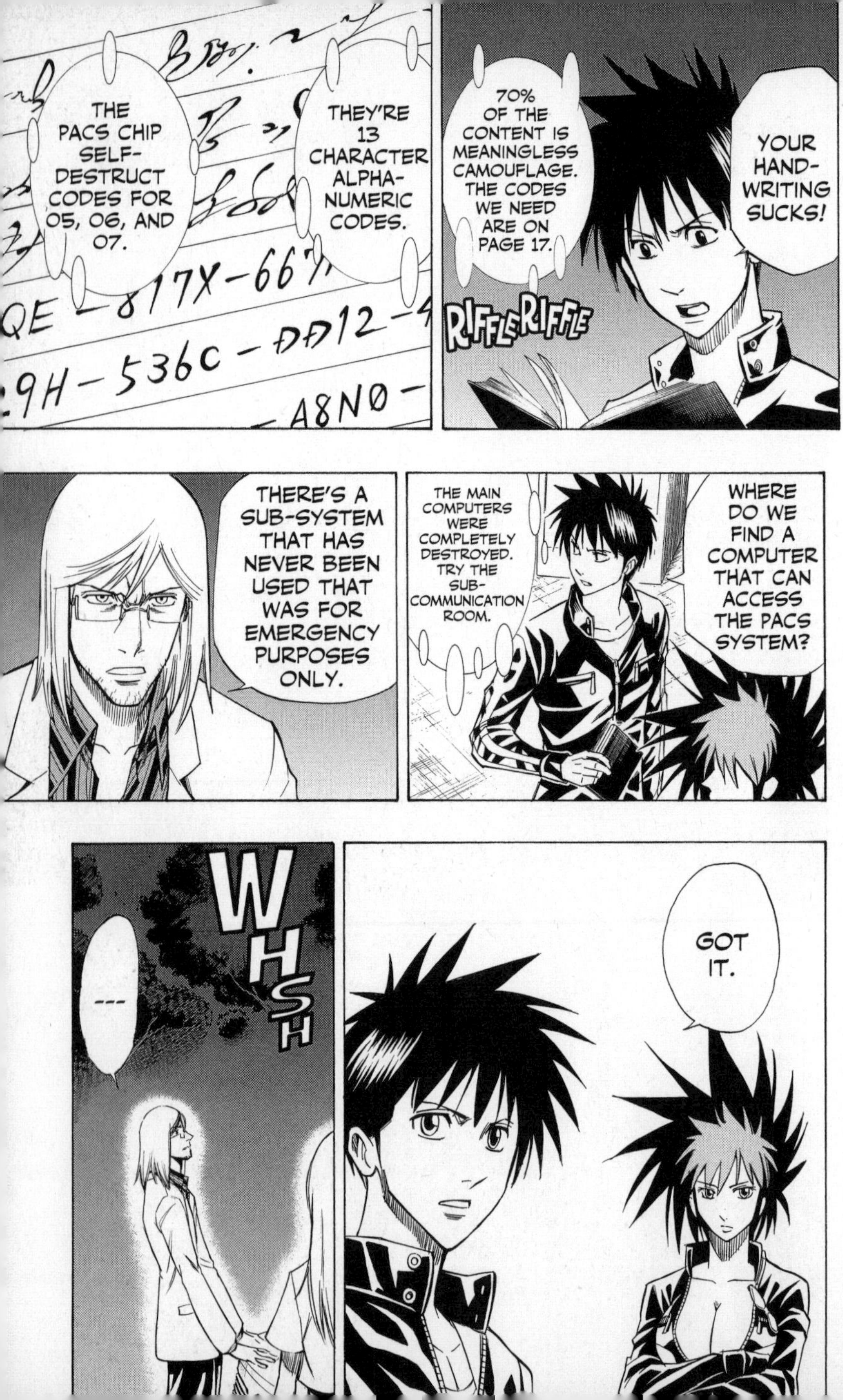
YOUR HAND-WRITING SUCKS!
70% OF THE CONTENT IS MEANINGLESS CAMOUFLAGE. THE CODES WE NEED ARE ON PAGE 17.
RIFFLERIFFLE
THEY'RE 13 CHARACTER ALPHA-NUMERIC CODES.
THE PACS CHIP SELF-DESTRUCT CODES FOR 05, 06, AND 07.
WHERE DO WE FIND A COMPUTER THAT CAN ACCESS THE PACS SYSTEM?
THE MAIN COMPUTERS WERE COMPLETELY DESTROYED. TRY THE SUB-COMMUNICATION ROOM.
THERE'S A SUB-SYSTEM THAT HAS NEVER BEEN USED THAT WAS FOR EMERGENCY PURPOSES ONLY.
GOT IT.
WHSH

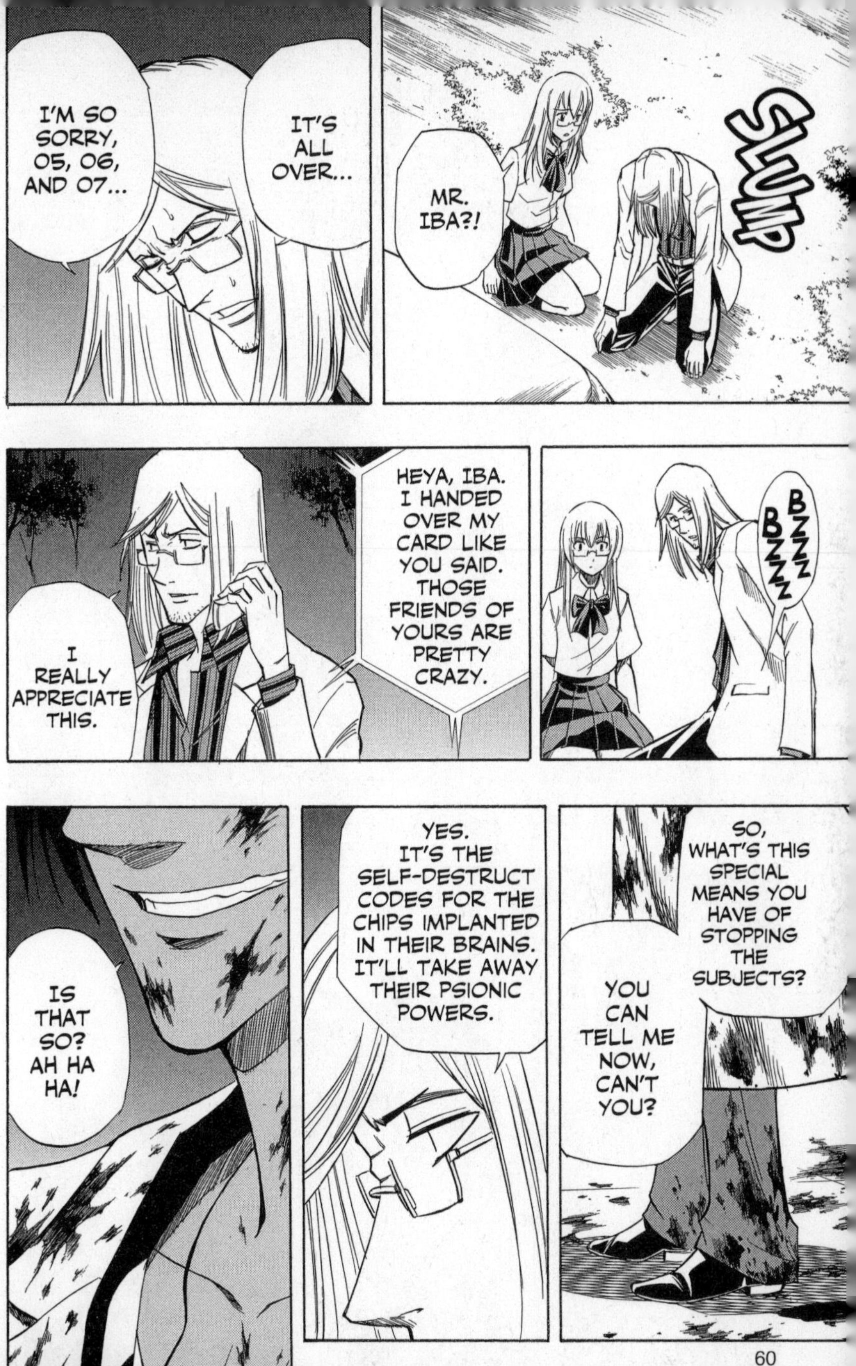
SLUMP
MR. IBA?!
IT'S ALL OVER...
I'M SO SORRY, 05, 06, AND 07...
BZZZ BZZZ
HEYA, IBA. I HANDED OVER MY CARD LIKE YOU SAID. THOSE FRIENDS OF YOURS ARE PRETTY CRAZY.
I REALLY APPRECIATE THIS.
SO, WHAT'S THIS SPECIAL MEANS YOU HAVE OF STOPPING THE SUBJECTS?
YOU CAN TELL ME NOW, CAN'T YOU?
YES. IT'S THE SELF-DESTRUCT CODES FOR THE CHIPS IMPLANTED IN THEIR BRAINS. IT'LL TAKE AWAY THEIR PSIONIC POWERS.
IS THAT SO? AH HA HA!

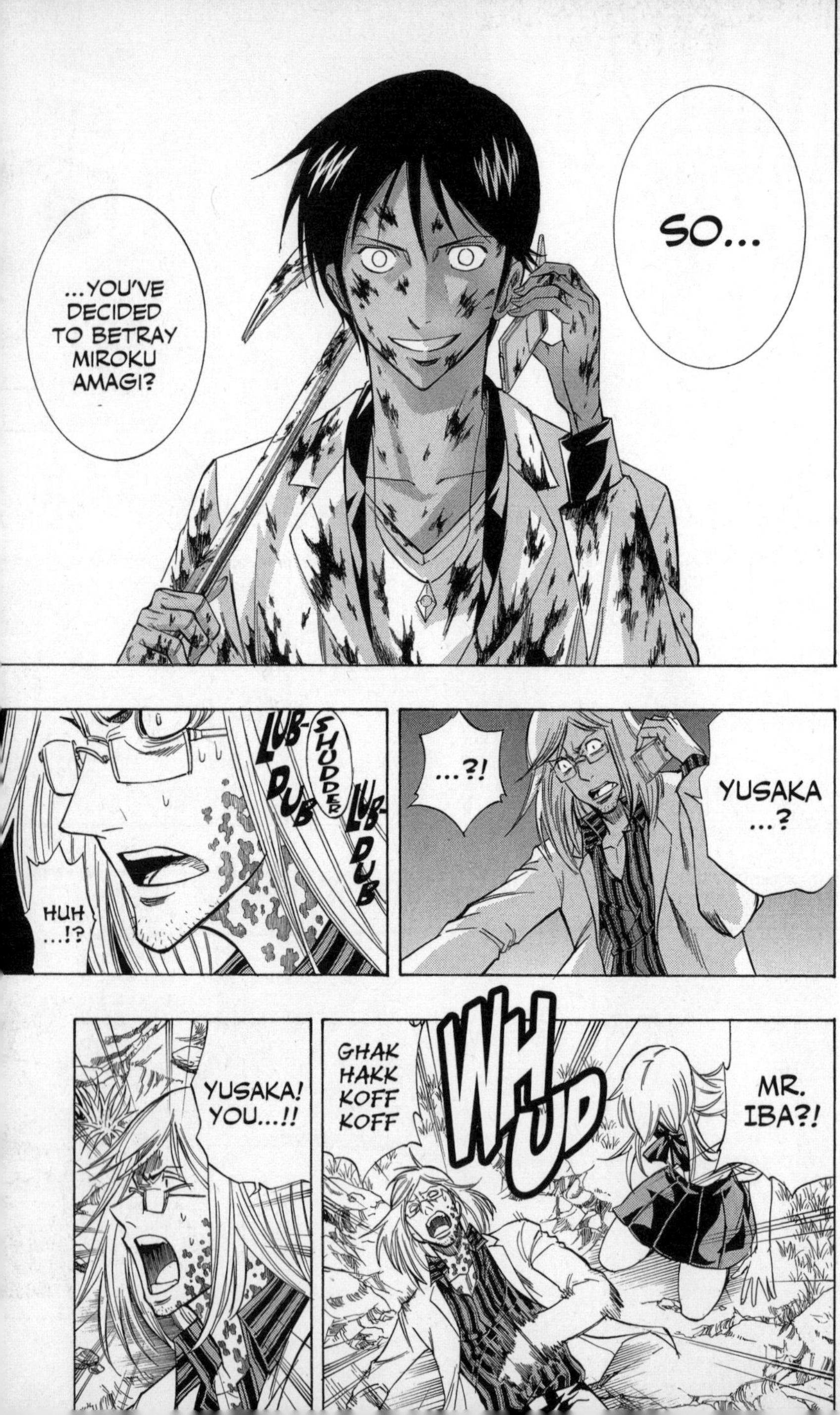
SO...
...YOU'VE DECIDED TO BETRAY MIROKU AMAGI?
YUSAKA ...?
...?!
LUB-DUB
SHUDDER
LUB-DUB
HUH ...!?
MR. IBA?!
WHUD
GHAK HAKK KOFF KOFF
YUSAKA! YOU...!!

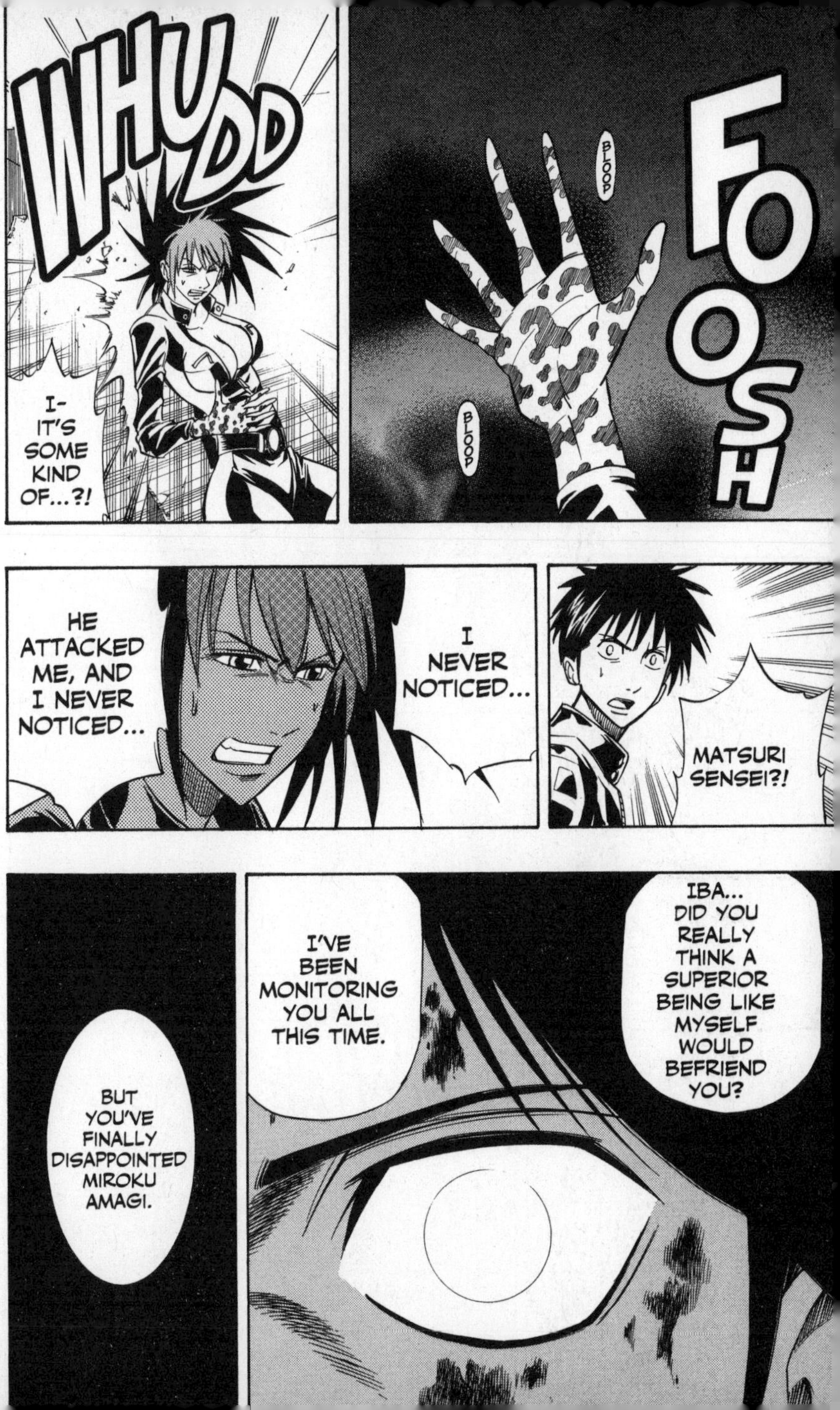
FOOSH
BLOOP
BLOOP
WHUDD
I- IT'S SOME KIND OF...?!
MATSURI SENSEI?!
I NEVER NOTICED...
HE ATTACKED ME, AND I NEVER NOTICED...
IBA... DID YOU REALLY THINK A SUPERIOR BEING LIKE MYSELF WOULD BEFRIEND YOU?
I'VE BEEN MONITORING YOU ALL THIS TIME.
BUT YOU'VE FINALLY DISAPPOINTED MIROKU AMAGI.

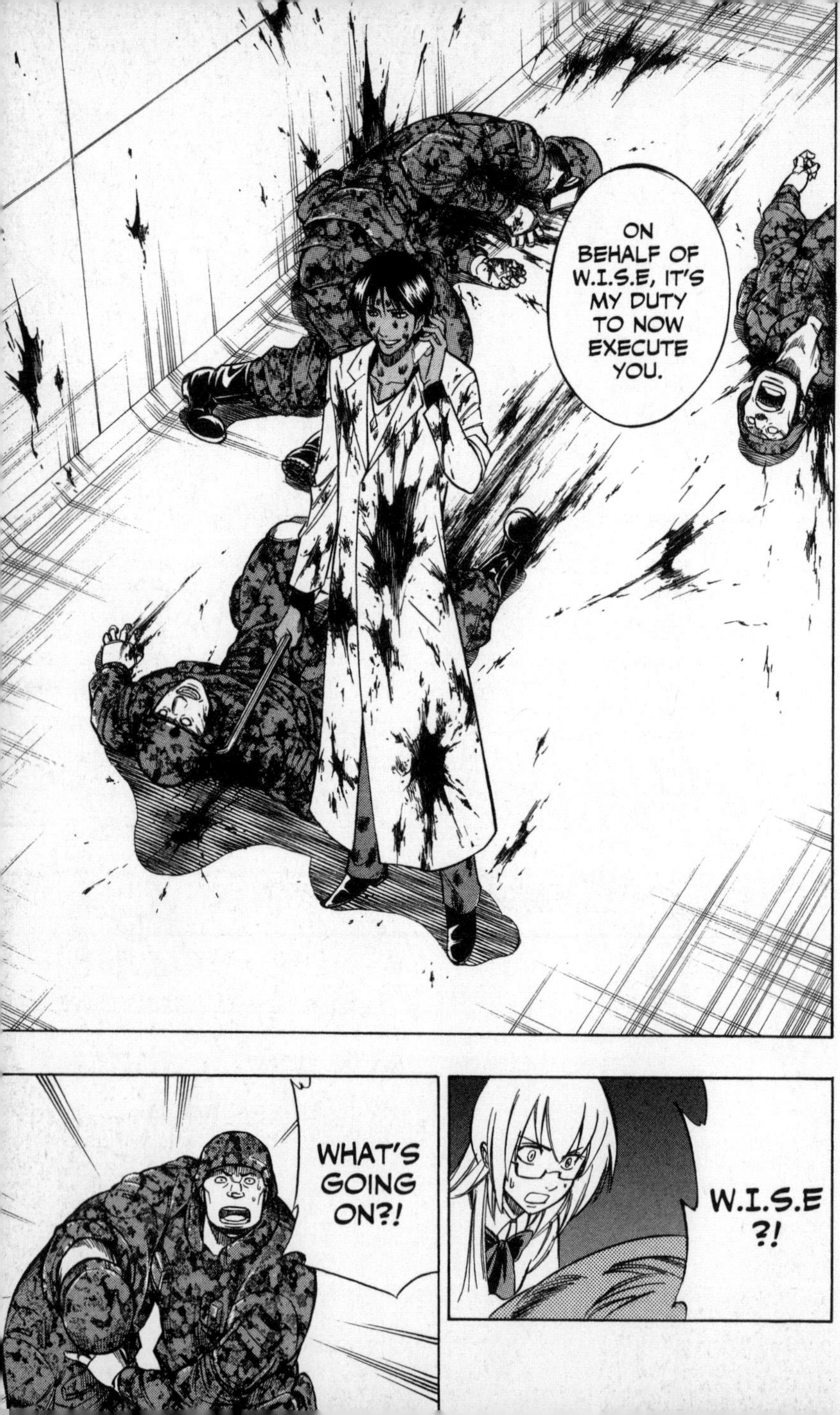
ON BEHALF OF W.I.S.E, IT'S MY DUTY TO NOW EXECUTE YOU.
W.I.S.E ?!
WHAT'S GOING ON?!

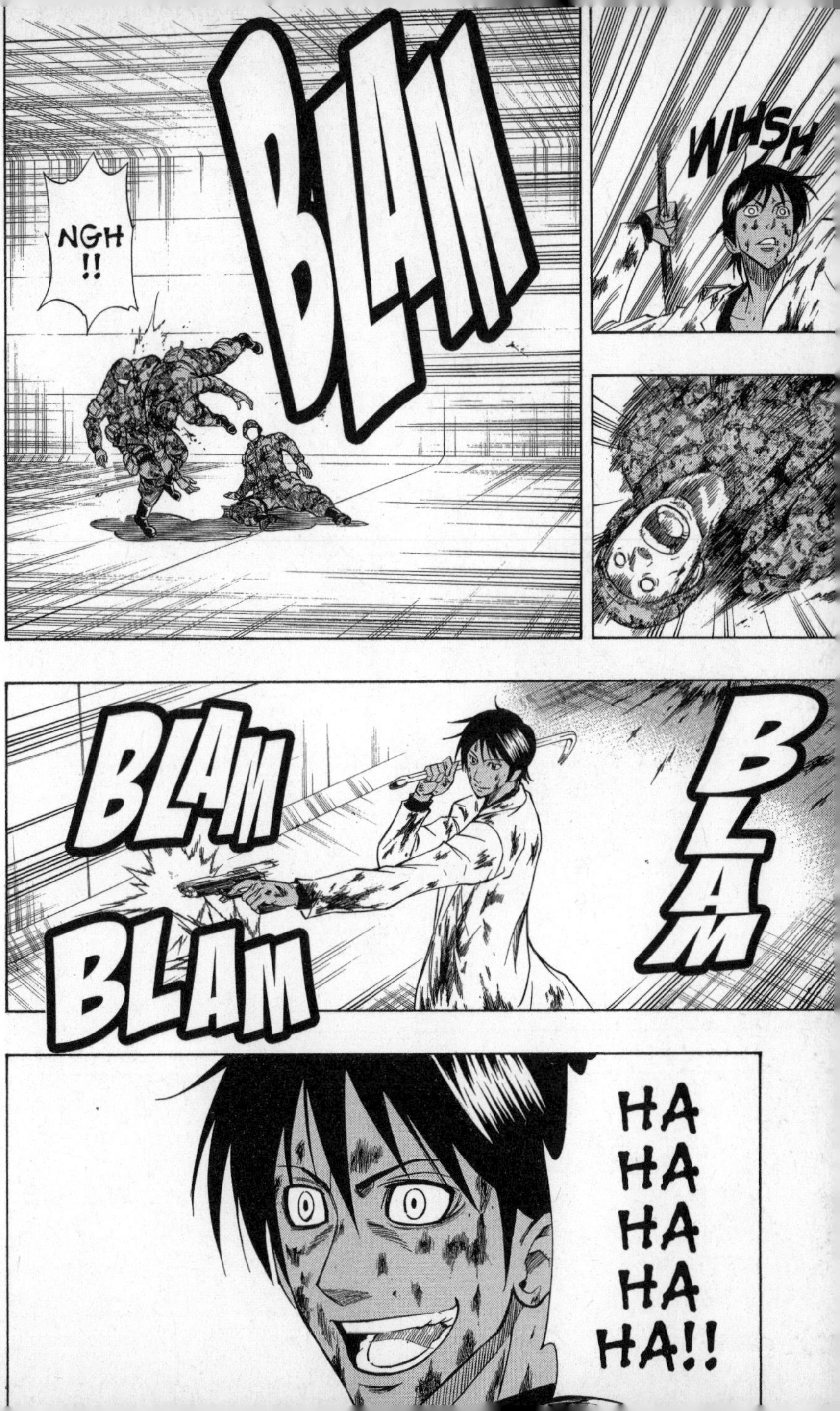
WHSH
BLAM
NGH !!
BLAM
BLAM
BLAM
HA HA HA HA HA HA!!

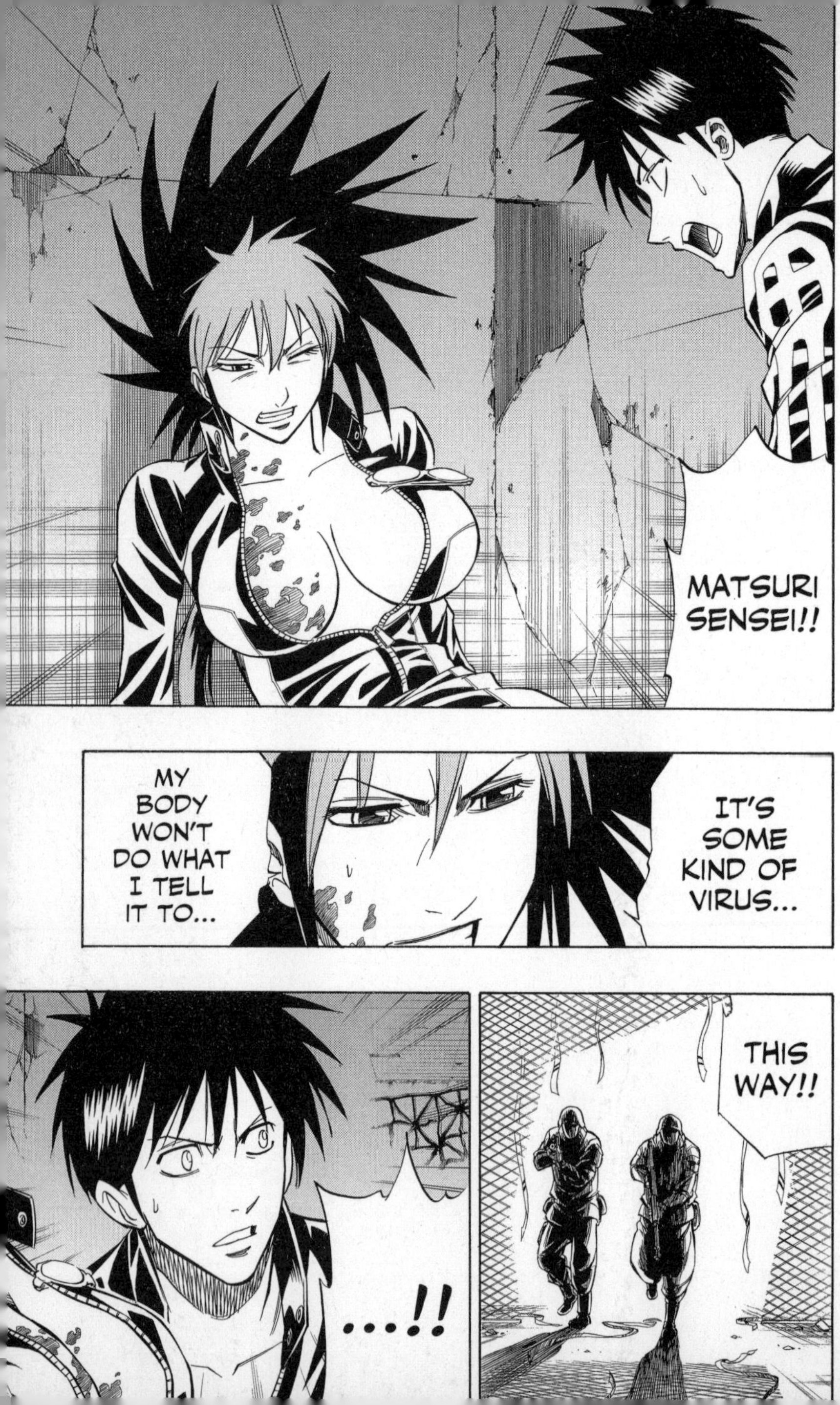
MATSURI SENSEI!!
IT'S SOME KIND OF VIRUS...
MY BODY WON'T DO WHAT I TELL IT TO...
THIS WAY!!
...!!

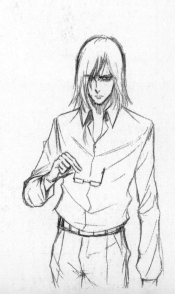

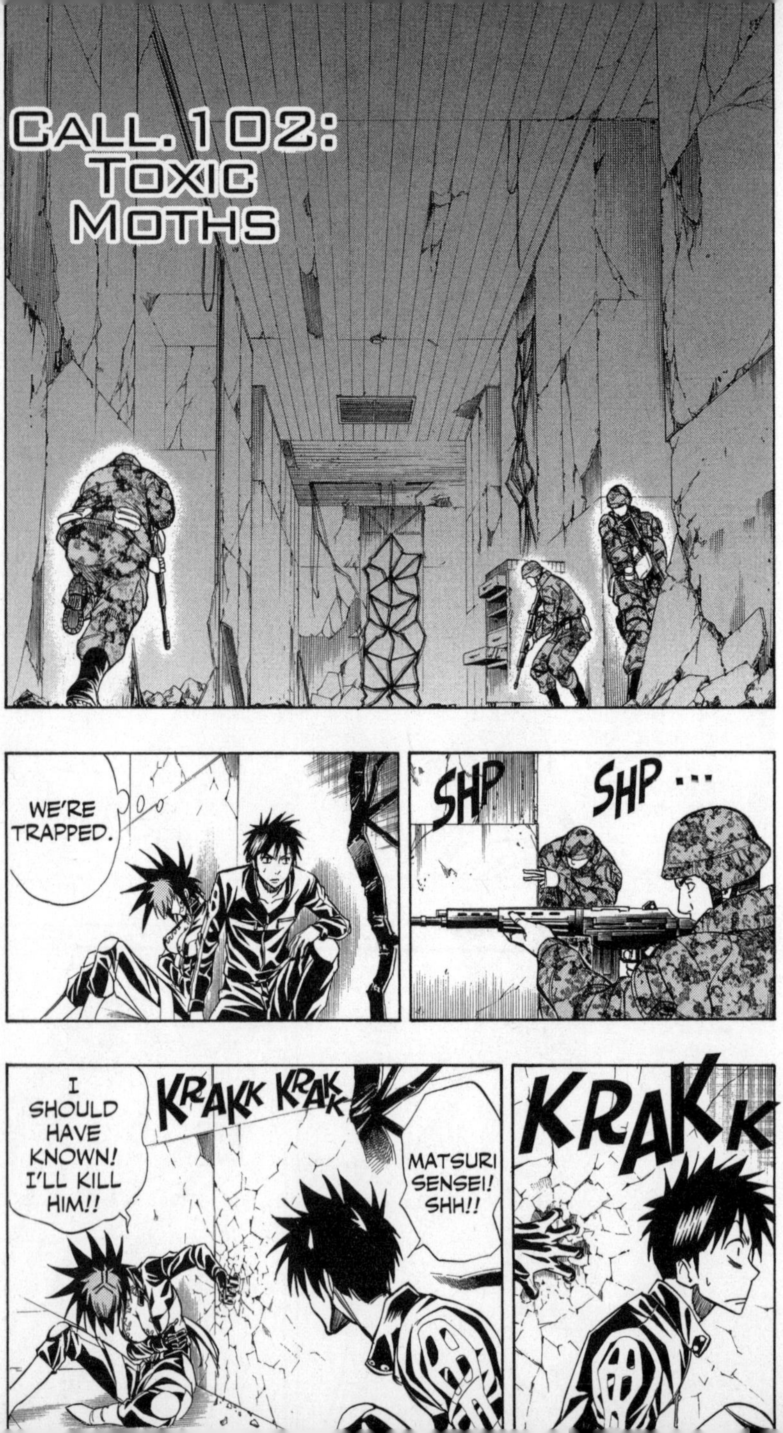
CALL. 102: TOXIC MOTHS
SHP SHP...
WE'RE TRAPPED.
KRAKK
KRAKK KRAKK
MATSURI SENSEI! SHH!!
I SHOULD HAVE KNOWN! I'LL KILL HIM!!

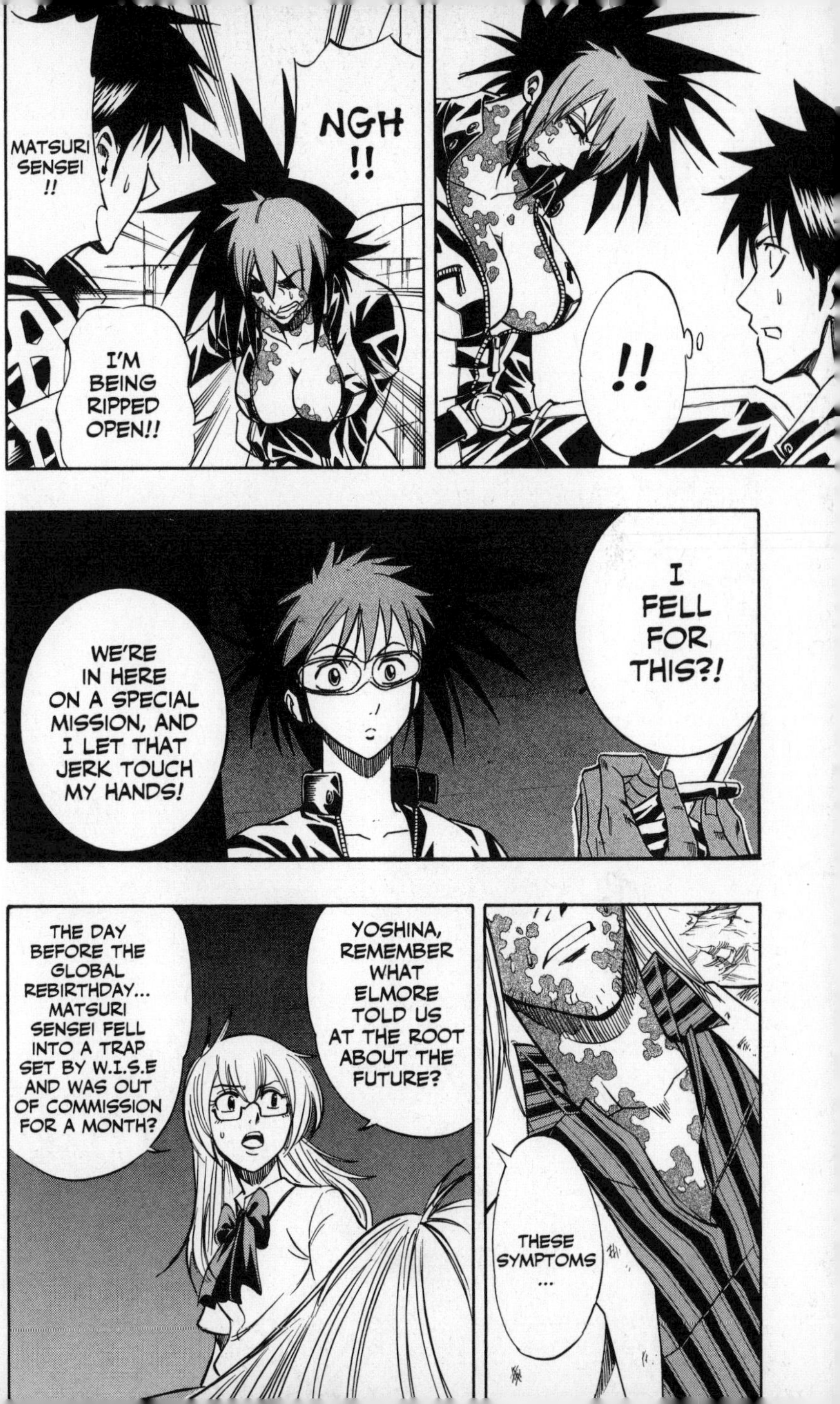
!!
NGH !!
MATSURI SENSEI !!
I'M BEING RIPPED OPEN!!
I FELL FOR THIS?!
WE'RE IN HERE ON A SPECIAL MISSION, AND I LET THAT JERK TOUCH MY HANDS!
THESE SYMPTOMS ...
YOSHINA, REMEMBER WHAT ELMORE TOLD US AT THE ROOT ABOUT THE FUTURE?
THE DAY BEFORE THE GLOBAL REBIRTHDAY... MATSURI SENSEI FELL INTO A TRAP SET BY W.I.S.E AND WAS OUT OF COMMISSION FOR A MONTH?

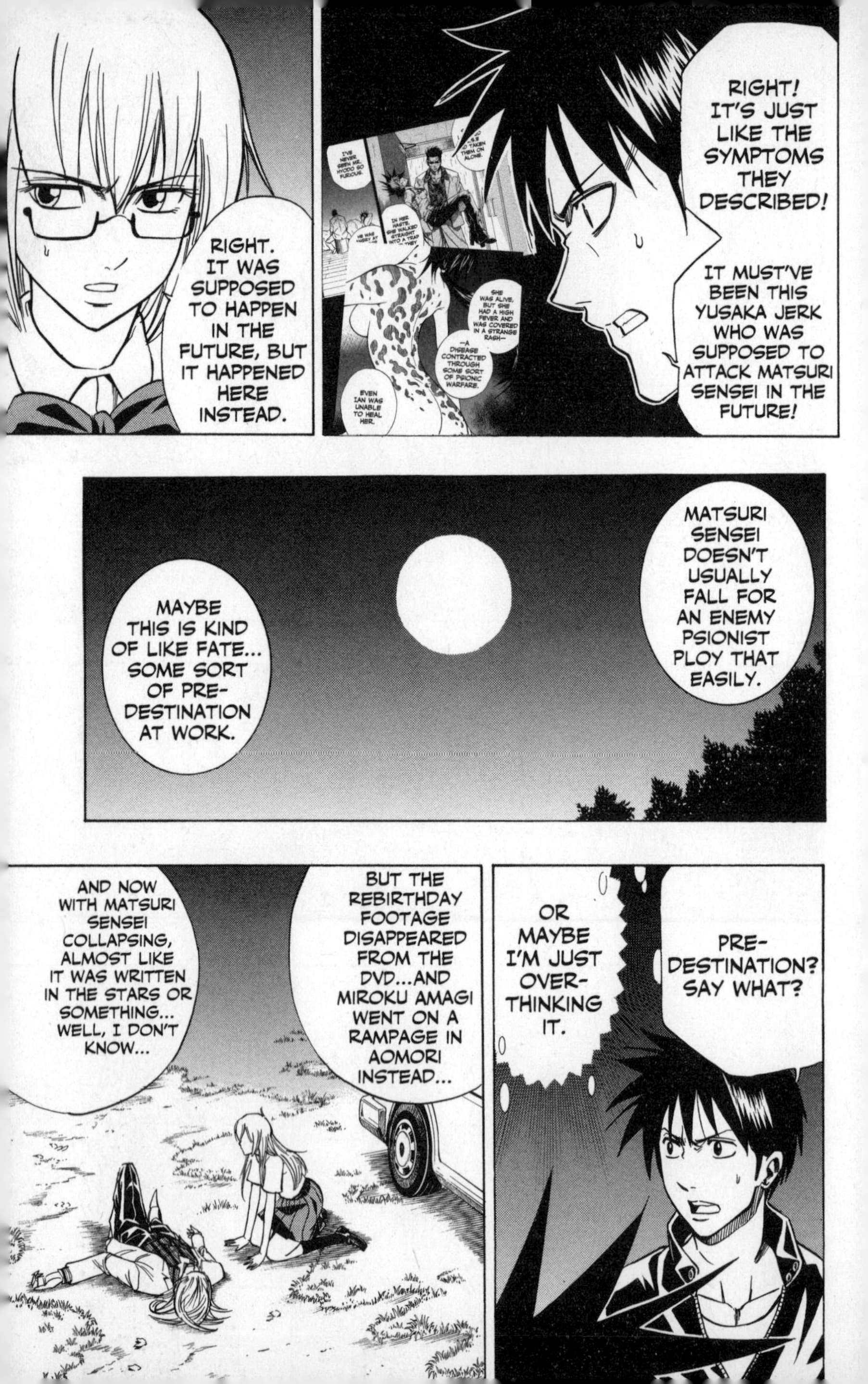
RIGHT! IT'S JUST LIKE THE SYMPTOMS THEY DESCRIBED!
IT MUST'VE BEEN THIS YUSAKA JERK WHO WAS SUPPOSED TO ATTACK MATSURI SENSEI IN THE FUTURE!
I'VE NEVER SEEN MR. HYODO SO FURIOUS.
SHE WAS ALIVE, BUT SHE HAD A HIGH FEVER AND WAS COVERED IN A STRANGE RASH—
—A DISEASE CONTRACTED THROUGH SOME SORT OF PSIONIC WARFARE.
EVEN IAN WAS UNABLE TO HEAL HER.
RIGHT. IT WAS SUPPOSED TO HAPPEN IN THE FUTURE, BUT IT HAPPENED HERE INSTEAD.
MATSURI SENSEI DOESN'T USUALLY FALL FOR AN ENEMY PSIONIST PLOY THAT EASILY.
MAYBE THIS IS KIND OF LIKE FATE... SOME SORT OF PRE-DESTINATION AT WORK.
PRE-DESTINATION? SAY WHAT?
OR MAYBE I'M JUST OVER-THINKING IT.
BUT THE REBIRTHDAY FOOTAGE DISAPPEARED FROM THE DVD...AND MIROKU AMAGI WENT ON A RAMPAGE IN AOMORI INSTEAD...
AND NOW WITH MATSURI SENSEI COLLAPSING, ALMOST LIKE IT WAS WRITTEN IN THE STARS OR SOMETHING... WELL, I DON'T KNOW...

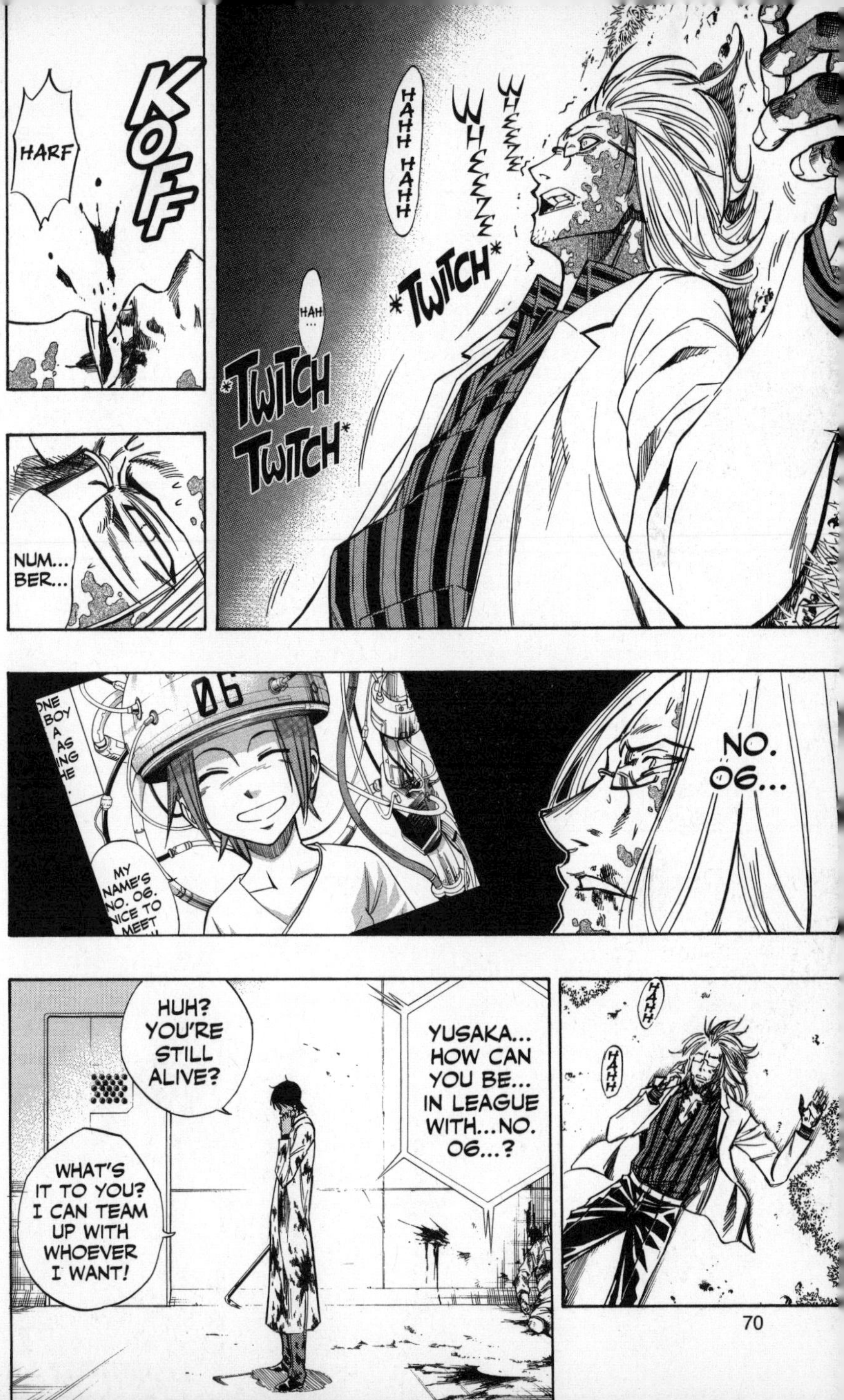
WHEEZE
WHEEZE
HAHH HAHH
TWITCH
HAH...
TWITCH TWITCH
KOFF
HARF
NUM... BER...
NO. 06...
MY NAME'S NO. 06. NICE TO
HAHH
HAHH
YUSAKA... HOW CAN YOU BE... IN LEAGUE WITH...NO. 06...?
HUH? YOU'RE STILL ALIVE?
WHAT'S IT TO YOU? I CAN TEAM UP WITH WHOEVER I WANT!

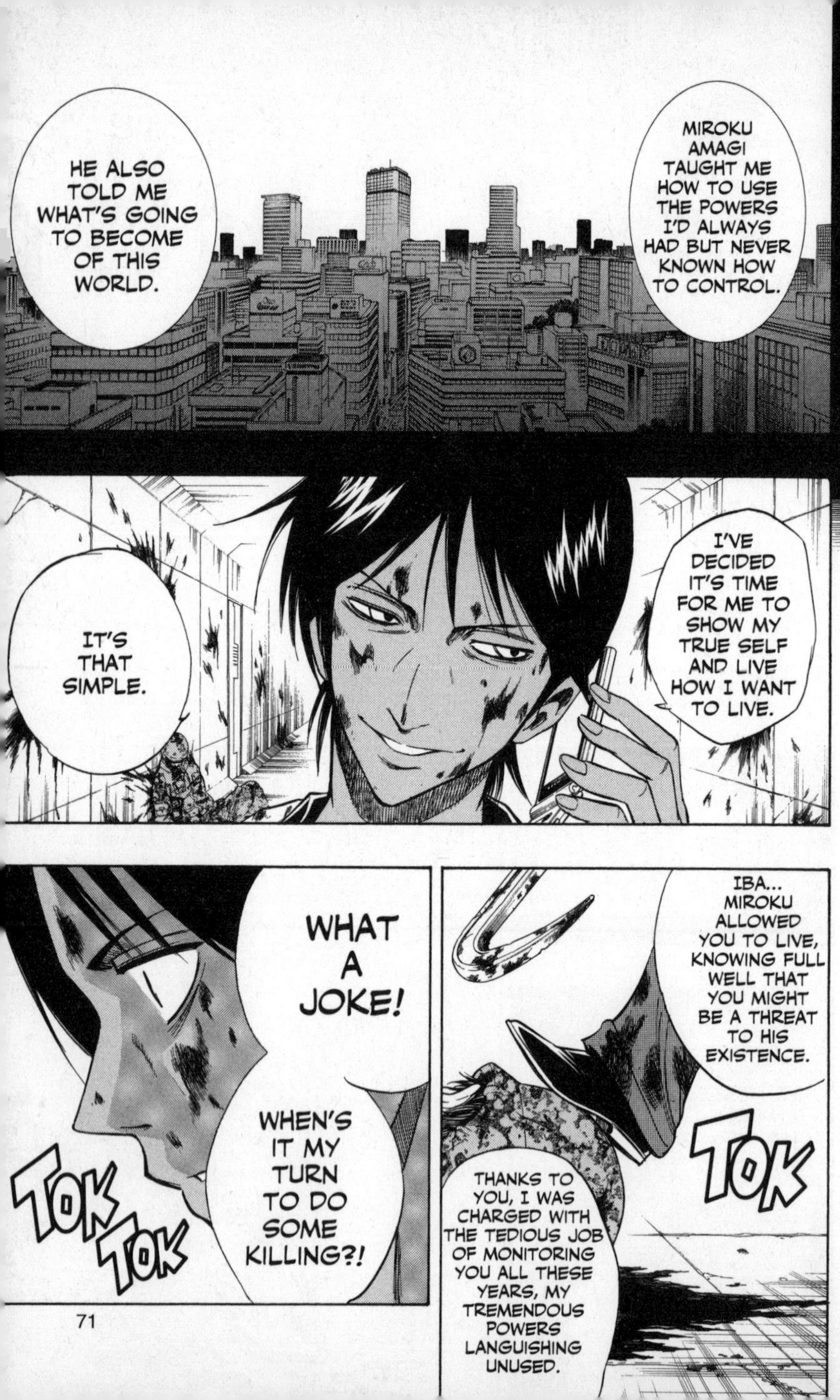
MIROKU AMAGI TAUGHT ME HOW TO USE THE POWERS I'D ALWAYS HAD BUT NEVER KNOWN HOW TO CONTROL.
HE ALSO TOLD ME WHAT'S GOING TO BECOME OF THIS WORLD.
I'VE DECIDED IT'S TIME FOR ME TO SHOW MY TRUE SELF AND LIVE HOW I WANT TO LIVE.
IT'S THAT SIMPLE.
IBA... MIROKU ALLOWED YOU TO LIVE, KNOWING FULL WELL THAT YOU MIGHT BE A THREAT TO HIS EXISTENCE.
TOK
THANKS TO YOU, I WAS CHARGED WITH THE TEDIOUS JOB OF MONITORING YOU ALL THESE YEARS, MY TREMENDOUS POWERS LANGUISHING UNUSED.
WHAT A JOKE!
WHEN'S IT MY TURN TO DO SOME KILLING?!
TOK TOK

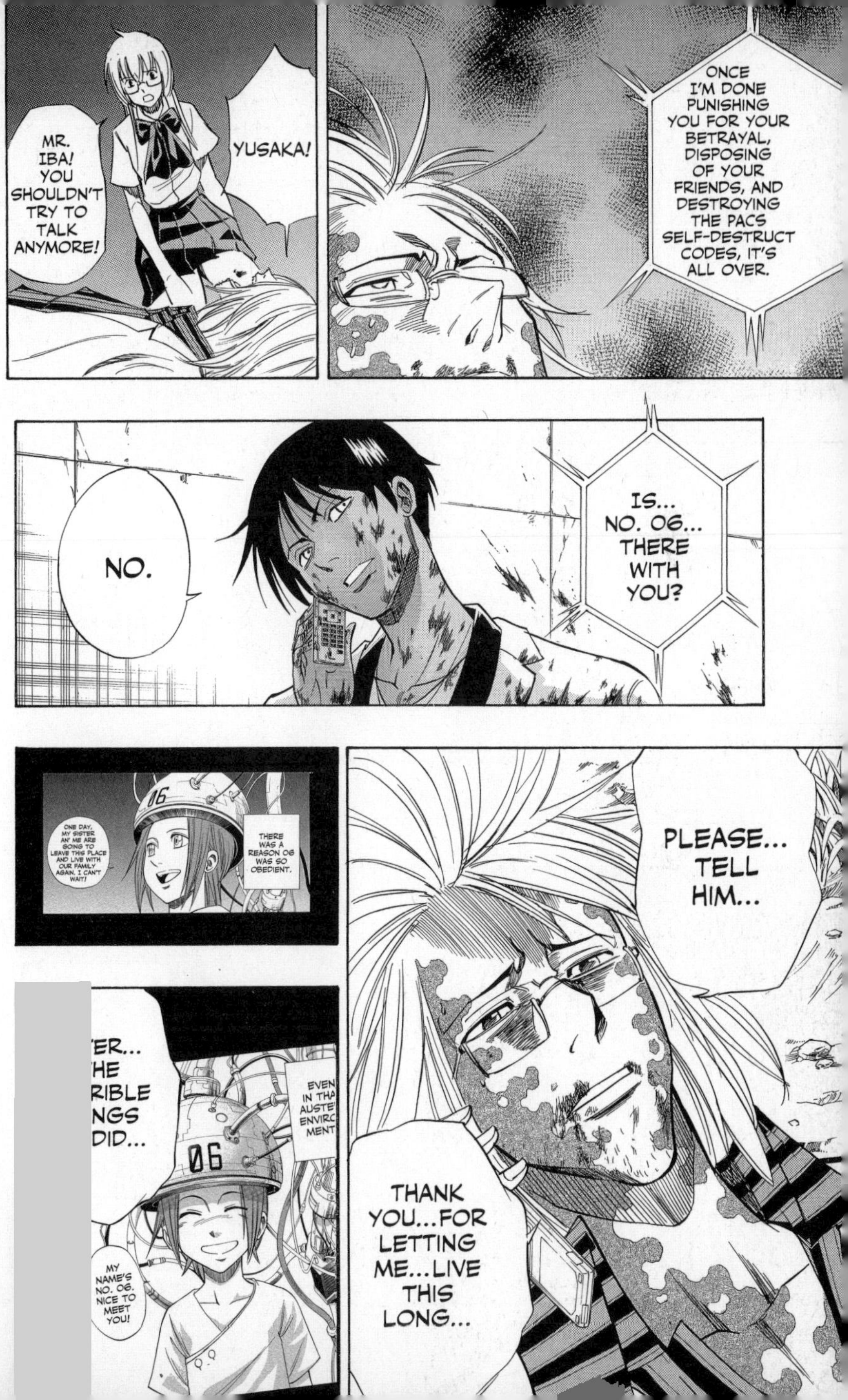
ONCE I'M DONE PUNISHING YOU FOR YOUR BETRAYAL, DISPOSING OF YOUR FRIENDS, AND DESTROYING THE PACS SELF-DESTRUCT CODES, IT'S ALL OVER.
YUSAKA!
MR. IBA! YOU SHOULDN'T TRY TO TALK ANYMORE!
IS... NO. 06... THERE WITH YOU?
NO.
PLEASE... TELL HIM...
THANK YOU...FOR LETTING ME...LIVE THIS LONG...
THERE WAS A REASON 06 WAS SO OBEDIENT.
ONE DAY, MY SISTER AN' ME ARE GOING TO LEAVE THIS PLACE AND LIVE WITH OUR FAMILY AGAIN. I CAN'T WAIT!
EVEN IN THA AUSTE ENVIRO MENT
TER... THE RIBLE NGS DID...
MY NAME'S NO. 06. NICE TO MEET YOU!

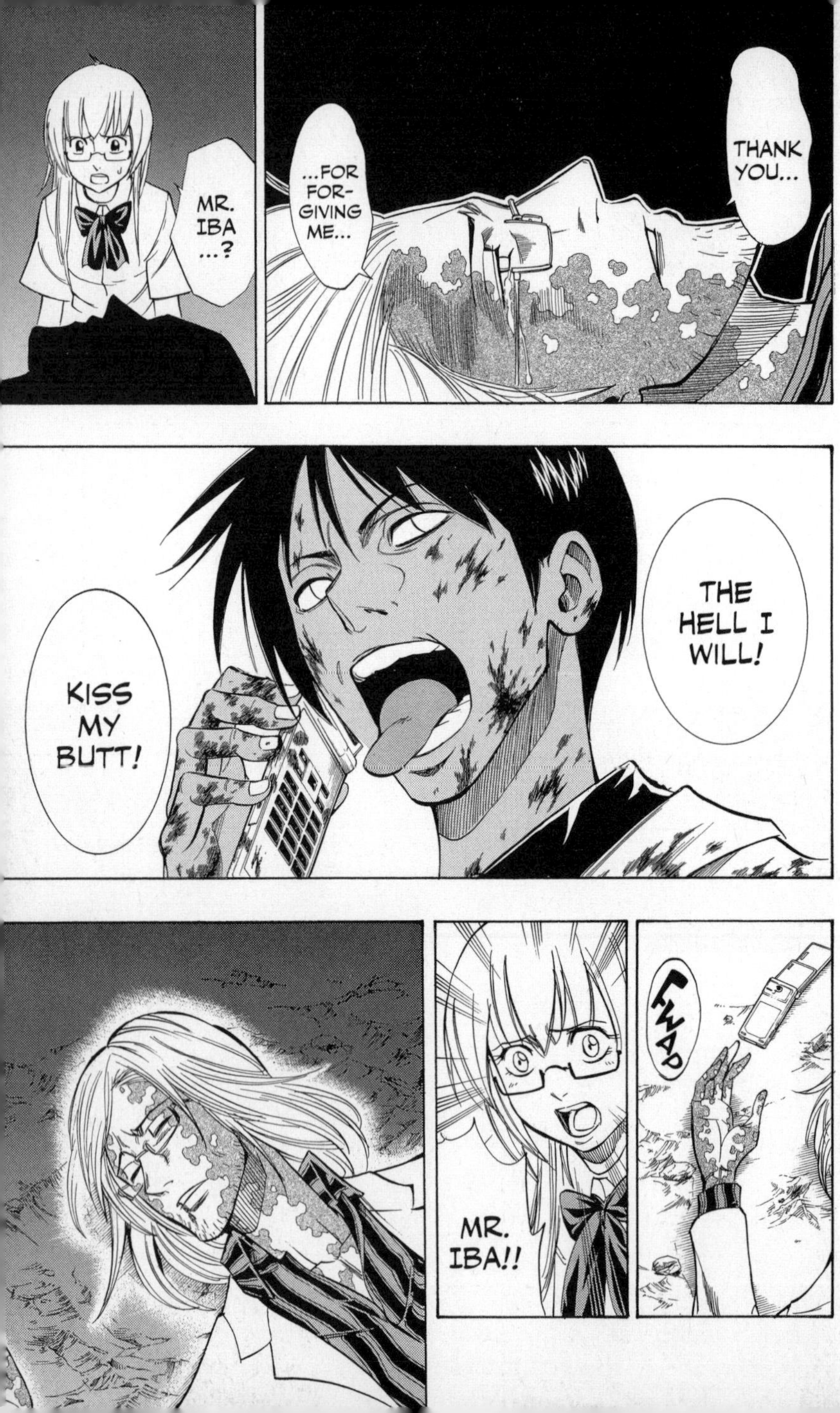
THANK YOU...
...FOR FOR-GIVING ME...
MR. IBA ...?
THE HELL I WILL!
KISS MY BUTT!
FWAP
MR. IBA!!

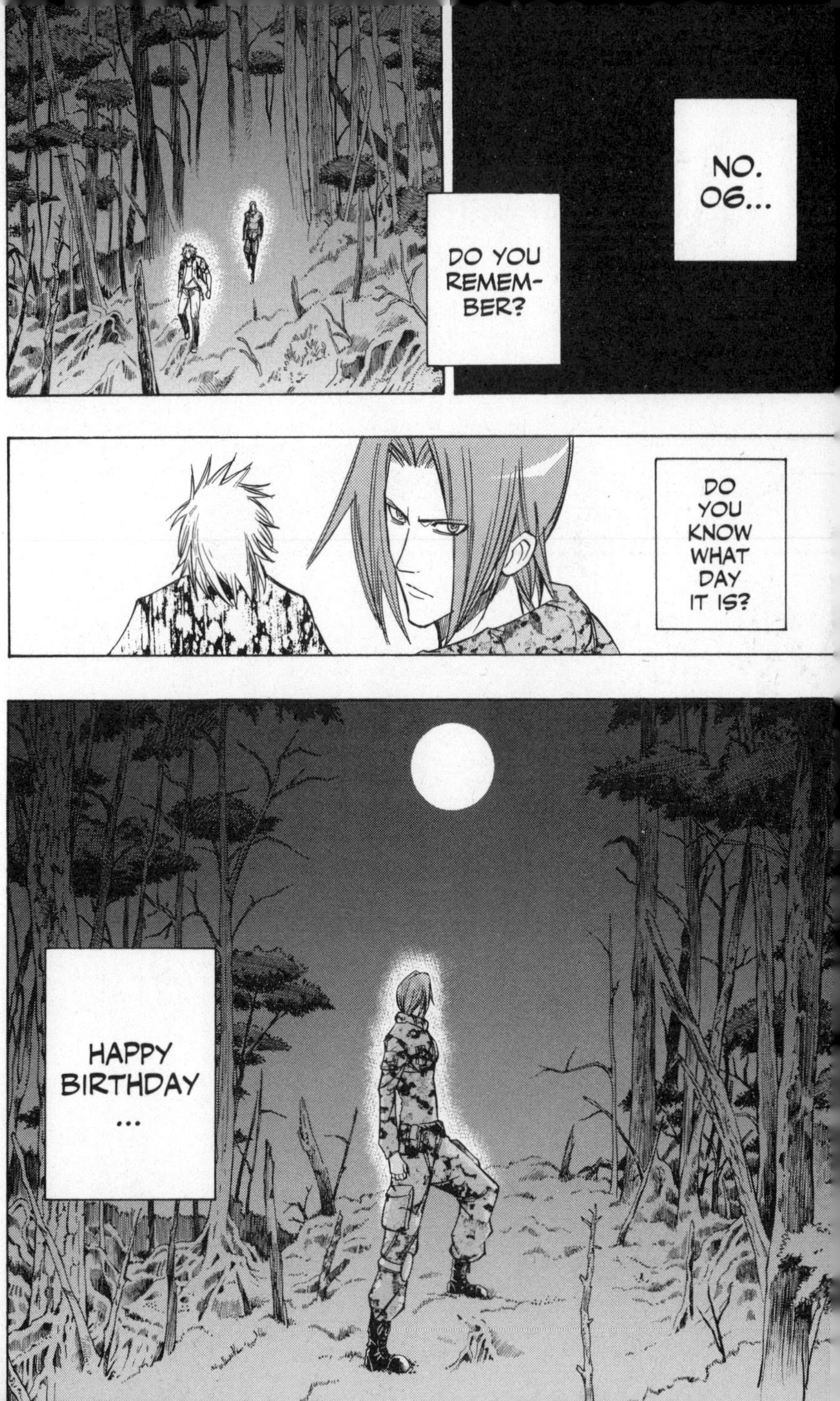
NO. 06...
DO YOU REMEMBER?
DO YOU KNOW WHAT DAY IT IS?
HAPPY BIRTHDAY ...

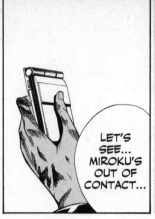

LET'S SEE... MIROKU'S OUT OF CONTACT...

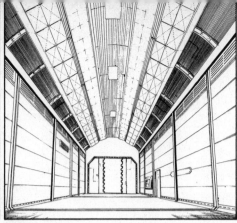

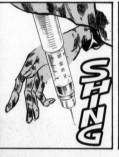

SHING

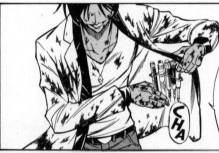

CHA

GUESS I HAVE CARTE BLANCHE TO DO WHATEVER I WANT!

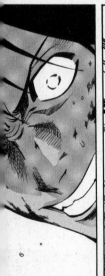

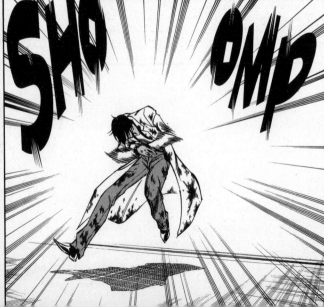

SHO

OMID

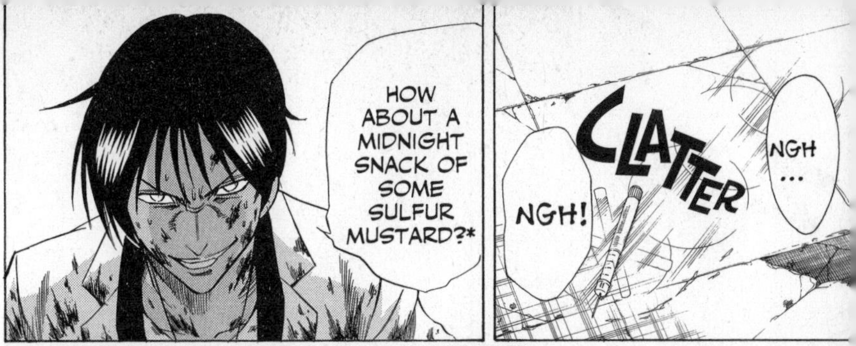
NGH ...
CLATTER
NGH!
HOW ABOUT A MIDNIGHT SNACK OF SOME SULFUR MUSTARD?*

*A BLISTER AGENT THAT CAUSES SEVERE BURNING OF THE EYES AND SKIN

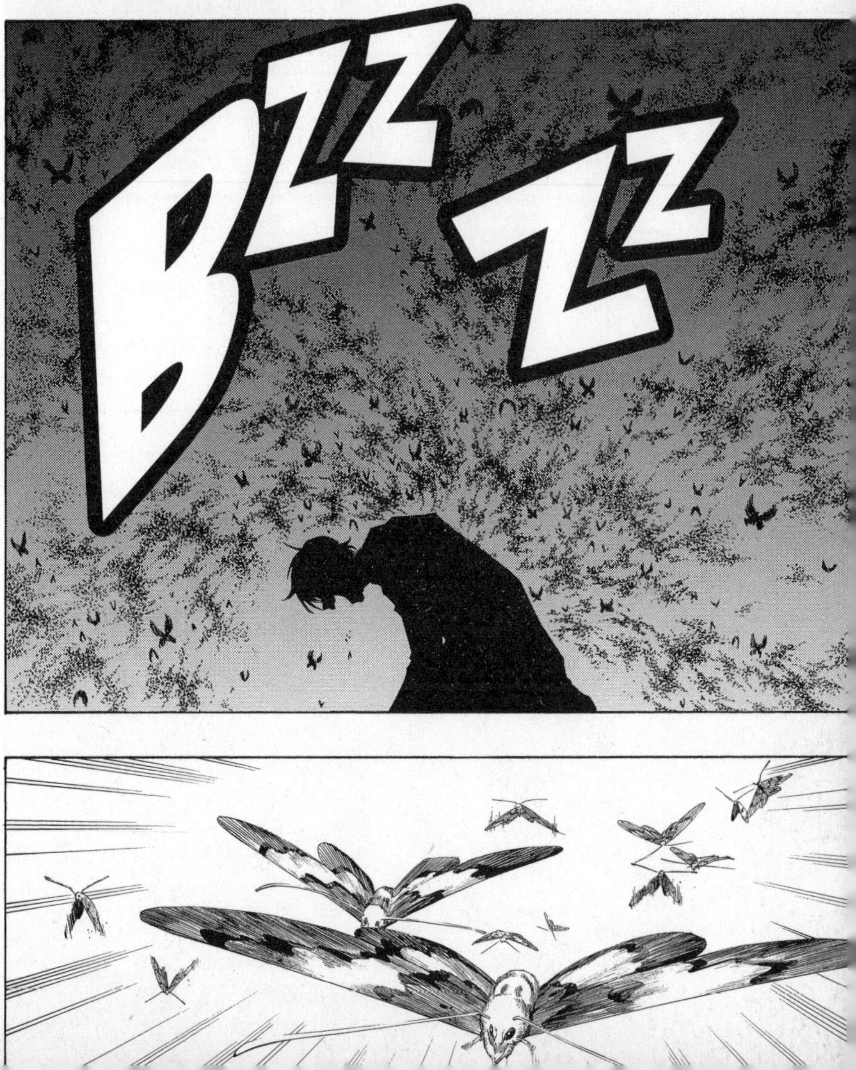
BZZZ-ZZZ

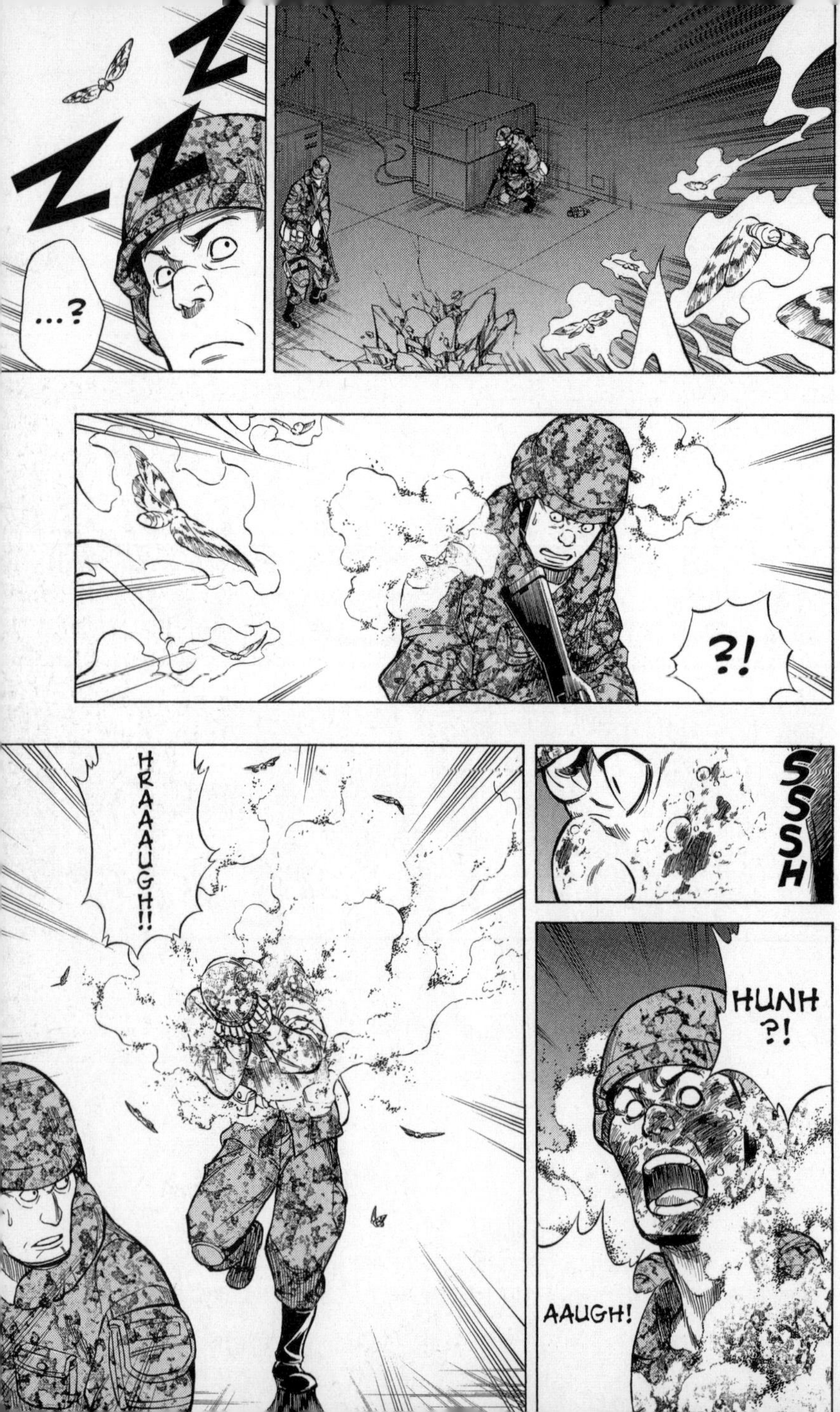
ZZZ
...?
?!
SSSH
HUNH ?!
AAUGH!
HRAAAUGH!!

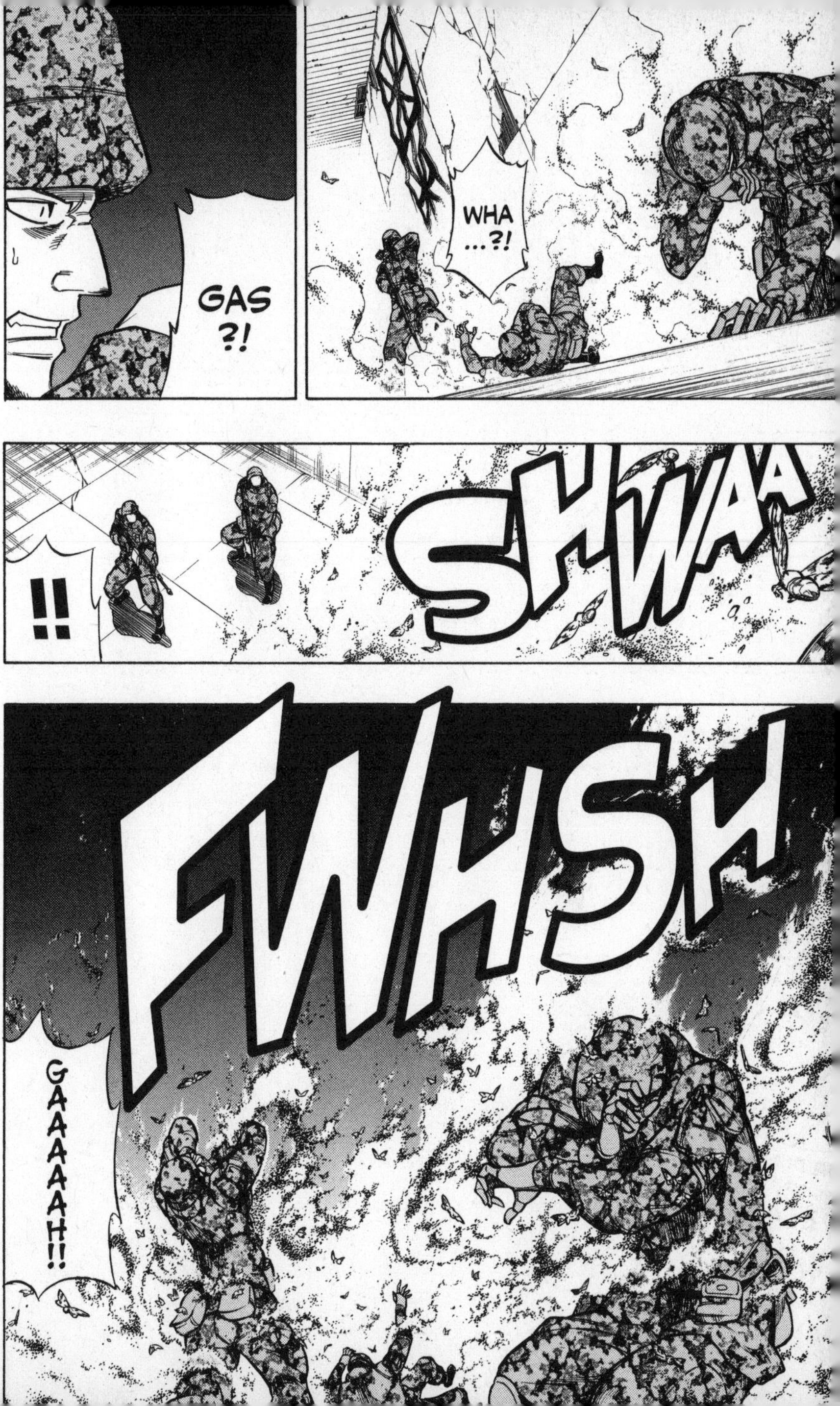
WHA ...?!
GAS ?!
SHWAA
!!
FWSH
GAAAAAAH!!

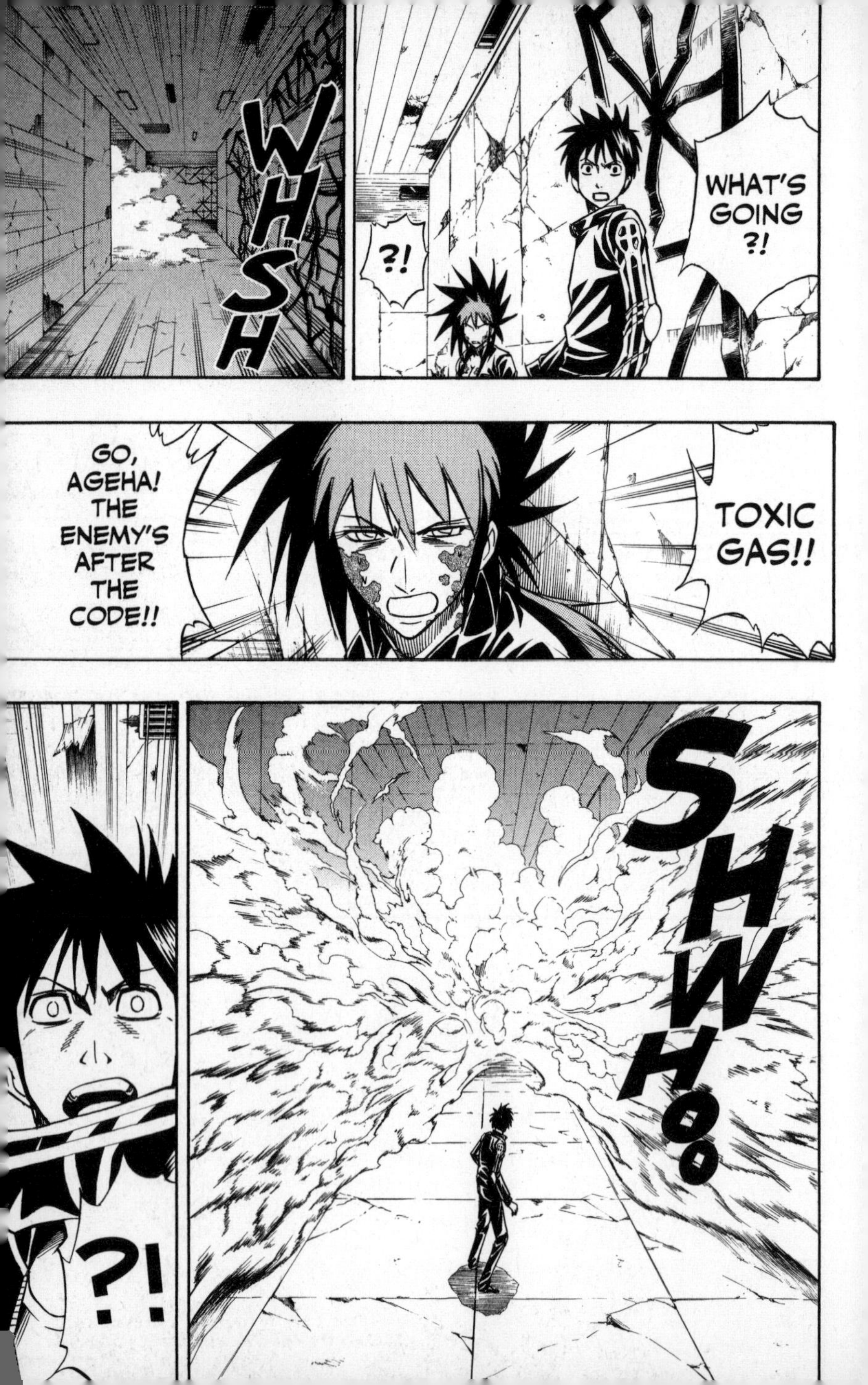
WHAT'S GOING ?!
?!
WHSH
TOXIC GAS!!
GO, AGEHA! THE ENEMY'S AFTER THE CODE!!
SHWHOO
?!

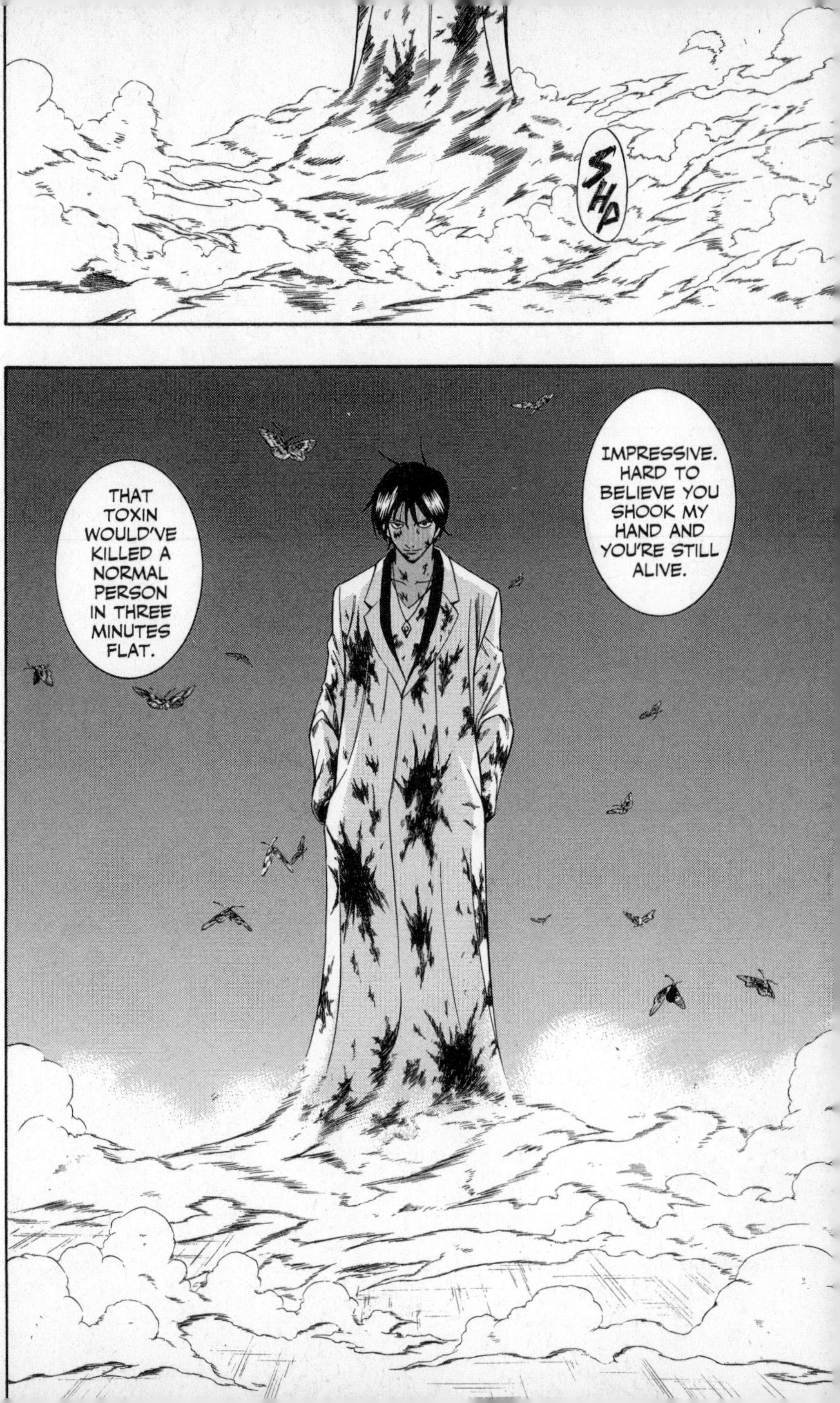
SHP
IMPRESSIVE. HARD TO BELIEVE YOU SHOOK MY HAND AND YOU'RE STILL ALIVE.
THAT TOXIN WOULD'VE KILLED A NORMAL PERSON IN THREE MINUTES FLAT.

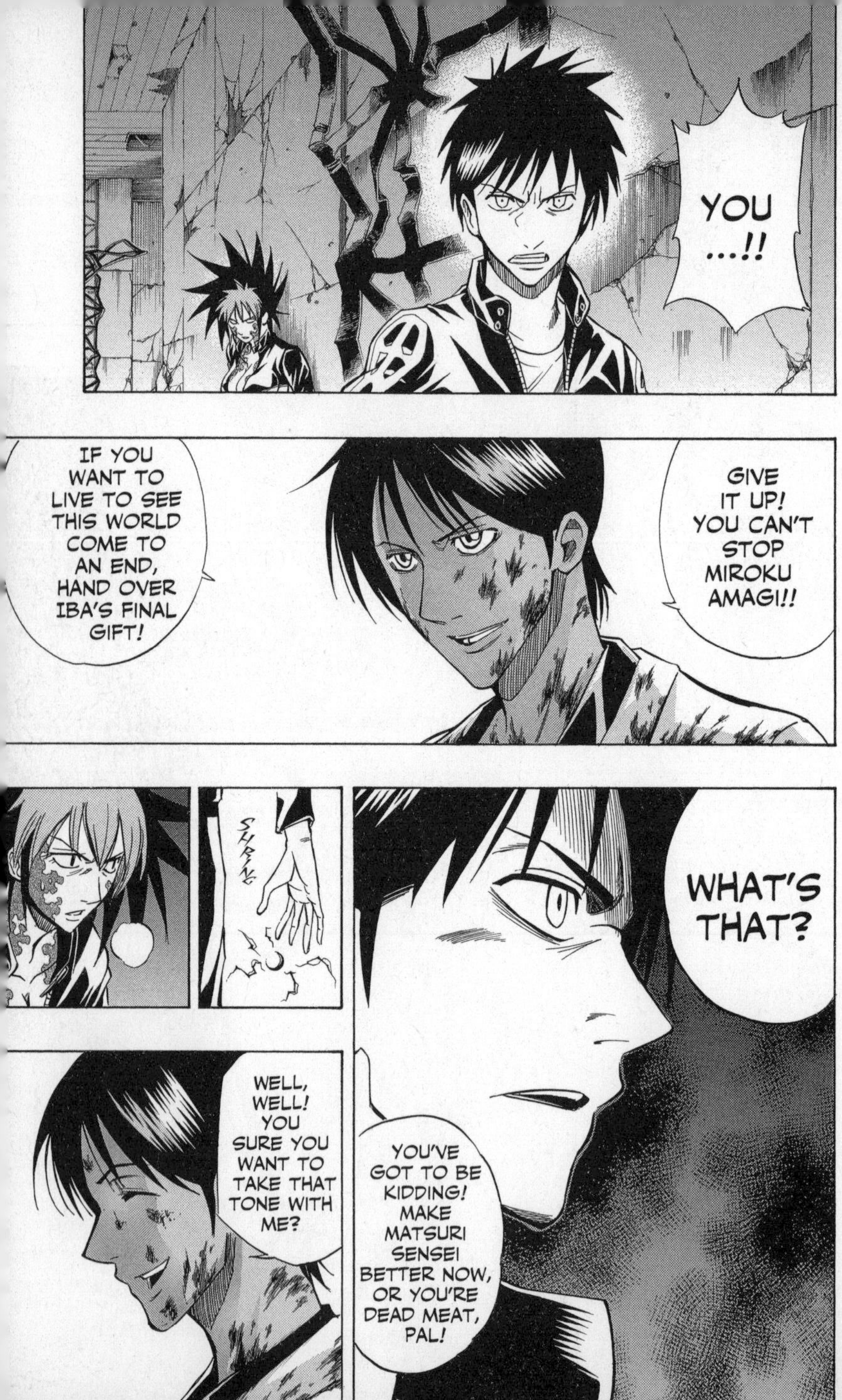
YOU ...!!
GIVE IT UP! YOU CAN'T STOP MIROKU AMAGI!!
IF YOU WANT TO LIVE TO SEE THIS WORLD COME TO AN END, HAND OVER IBA'S FINAL GIFT!
WHAT'S THAT?
YOU'VE GOT TO BE KIDDING! MAKE MATSURI SENSEI BETTER NOW, OR YOU'RE DEAD MEAT, PAL!
SHRING
WELL, WELL! YOU SURE YOU WANT TO TAKE THAT TONE WITH ME?

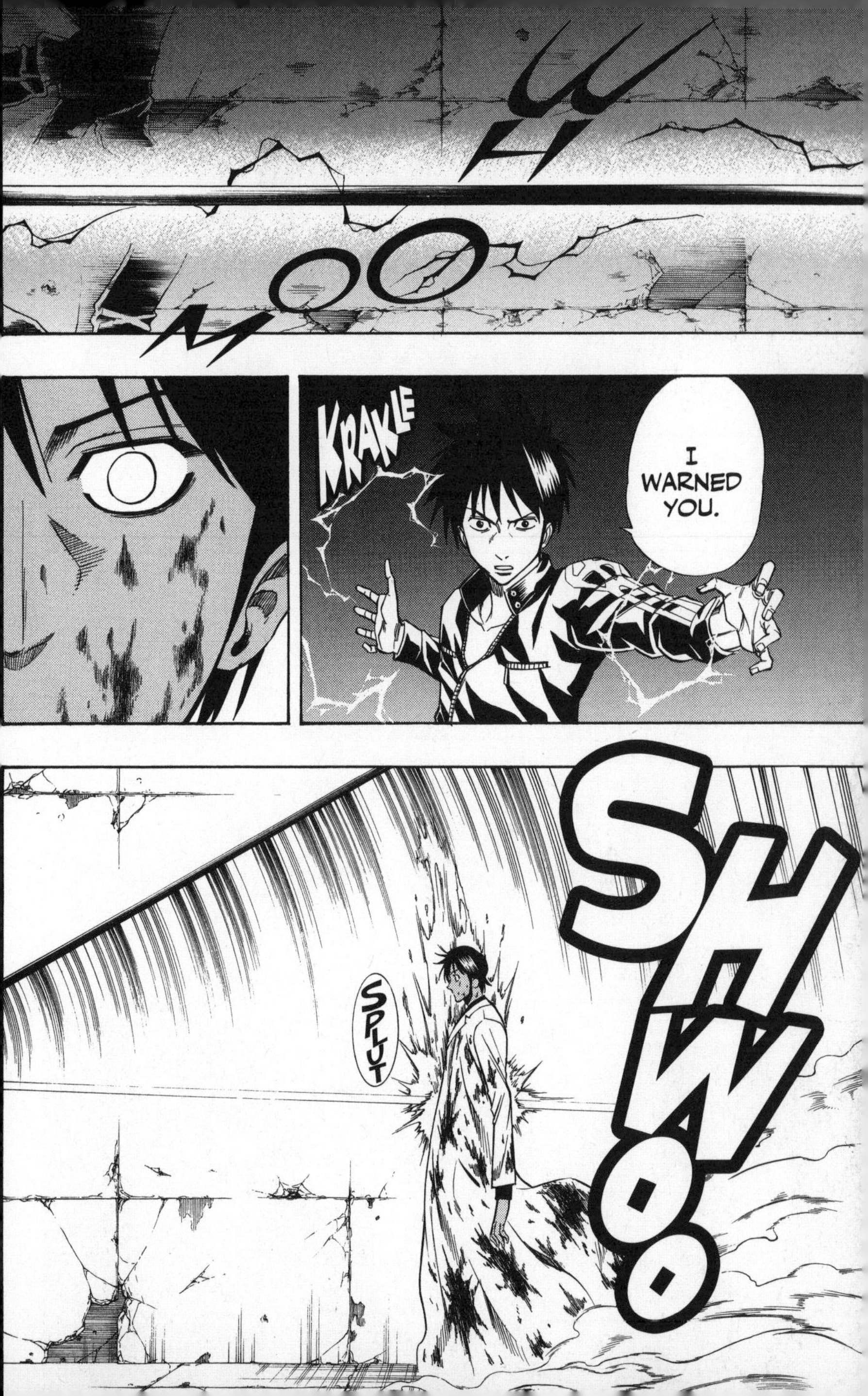
WH
OOM
KRAKLE
I WARNED YOU.
SHWOO
SPLUT

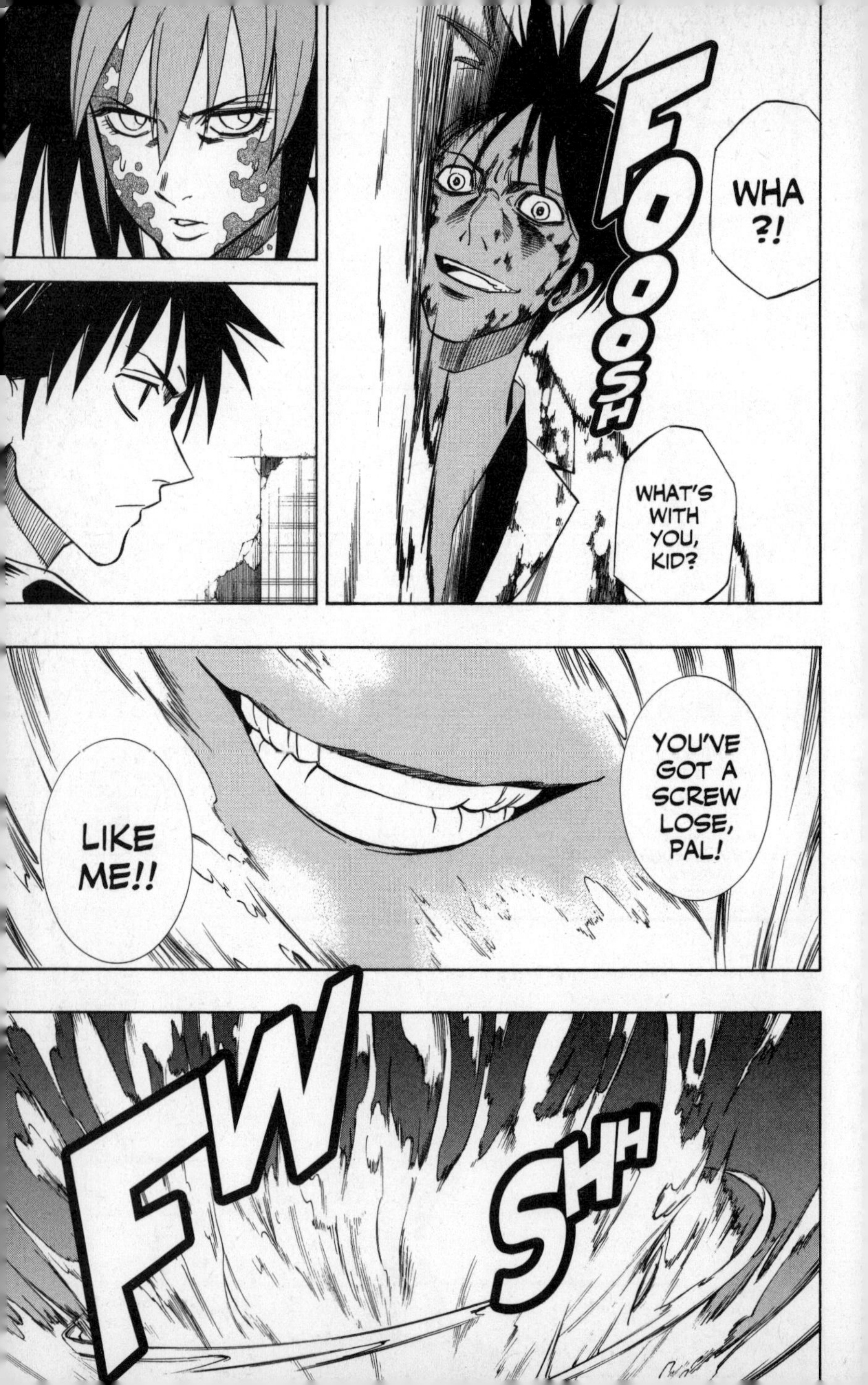
WHA ?!
FOOOOSH
WHAT'S WITH YOU, KID?
YOU'VE GOT A SCREW LOSE, PAL!
LIKE ME!!
FWSHH

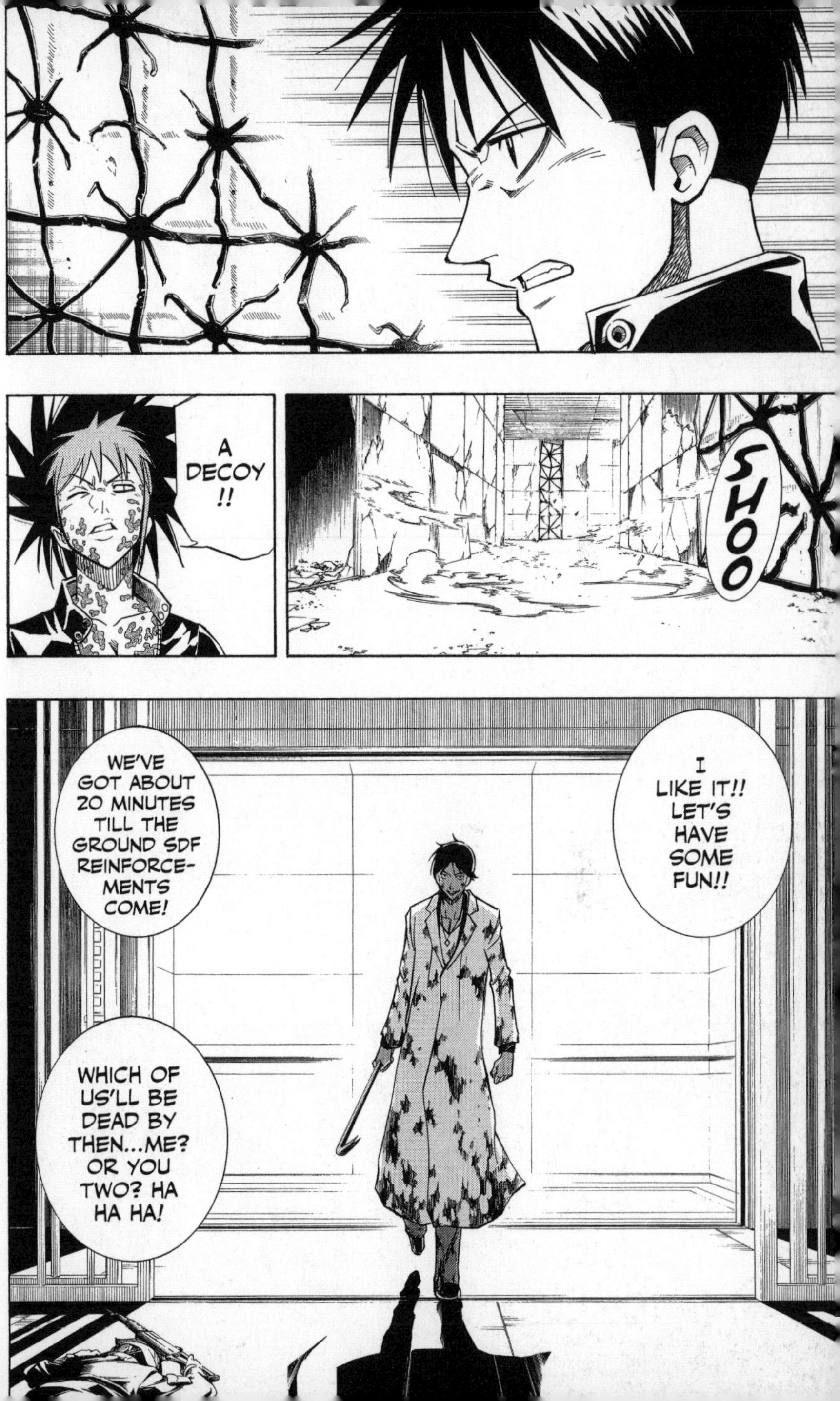
SHOO
A DECOY!!
I LIKE IT!! LET'S HAVE SOME FUN!!
WE'VE GOT ABOUT 20 MINUTES TILL THE GROUND SDF REINFORCE-MENTS COME!
WHICH OF US'LL BE DEAD BY THEN...ME? OR YOU TWO? HA HA HA!

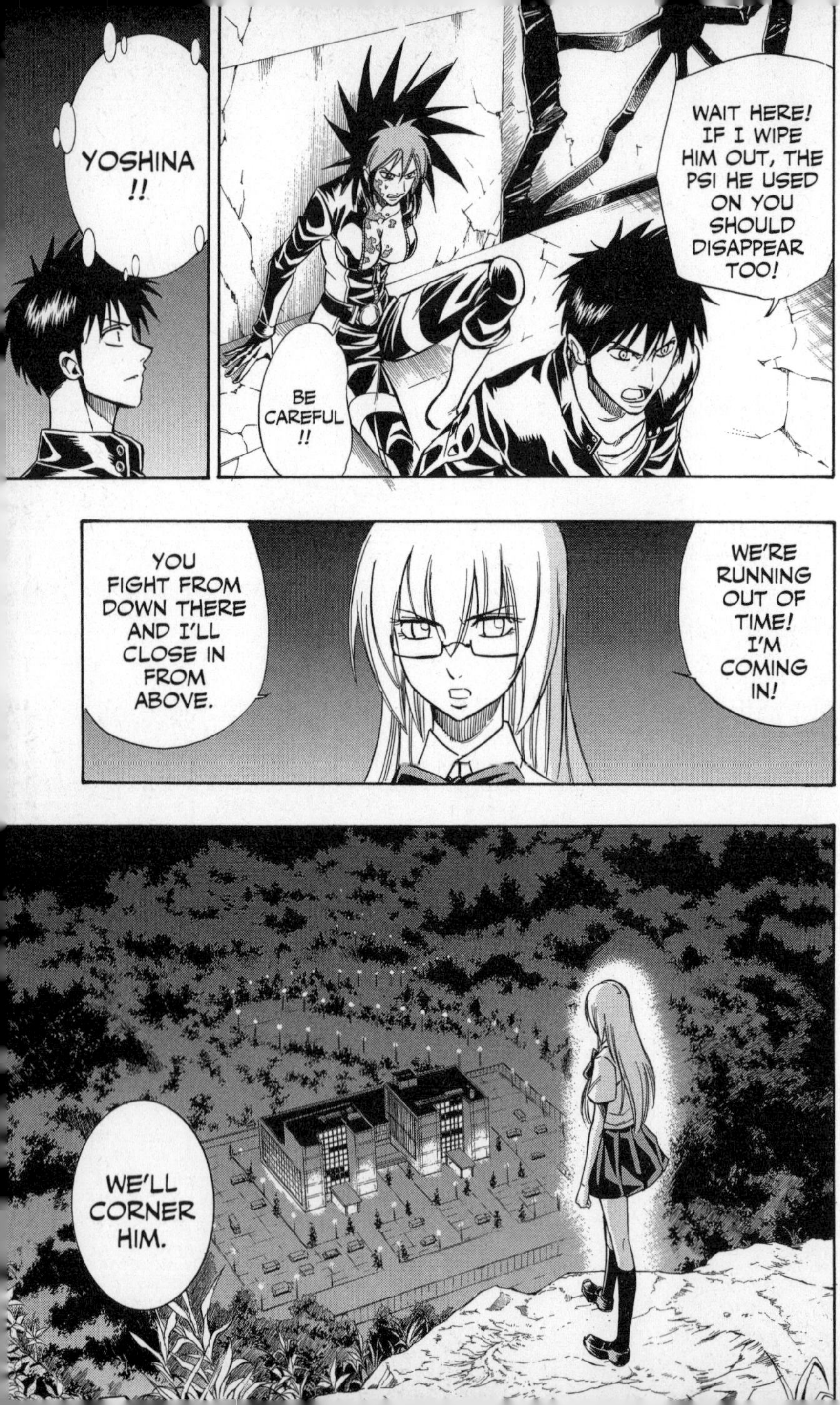
WAIT HERE! IF I WIPE HIM OUT, THE PSI HE USED ON YOU SHOULD DISAPPEAR TOO!
BE CAREFUL!!
YOSHINA!!
WE'RE RUNNING OUT OF TIME! I'M COMING IN!
YOU FIGHT FROM DOWN THERE AND I'LL CLOSE IN FROM ABOVE.
WE'LL CORNER HIM.

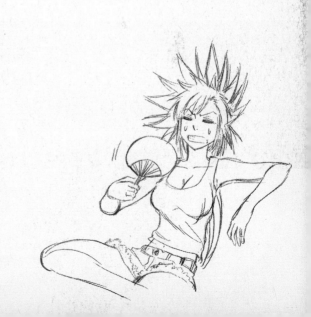

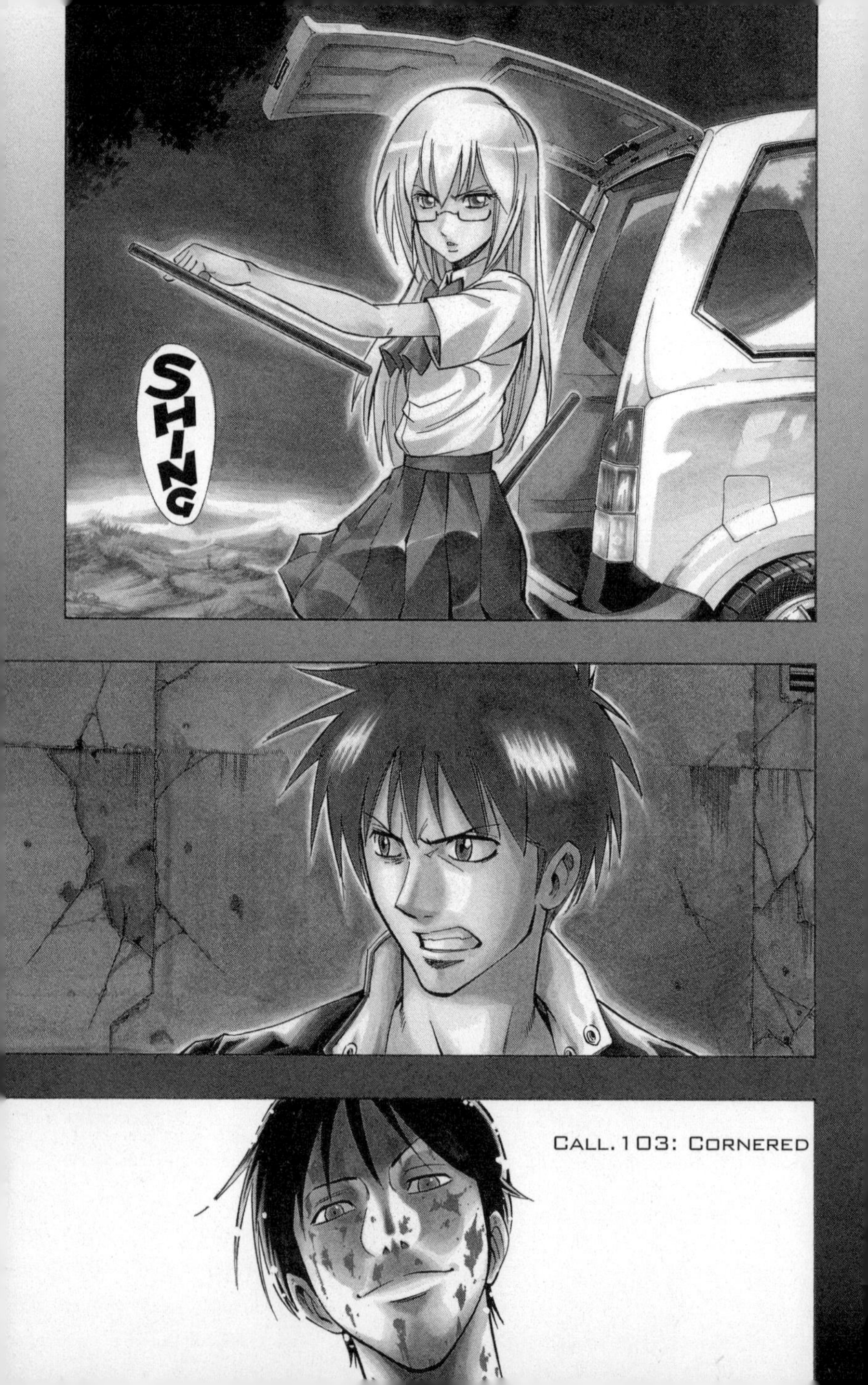
SHING
CALL. 103: CORNERED

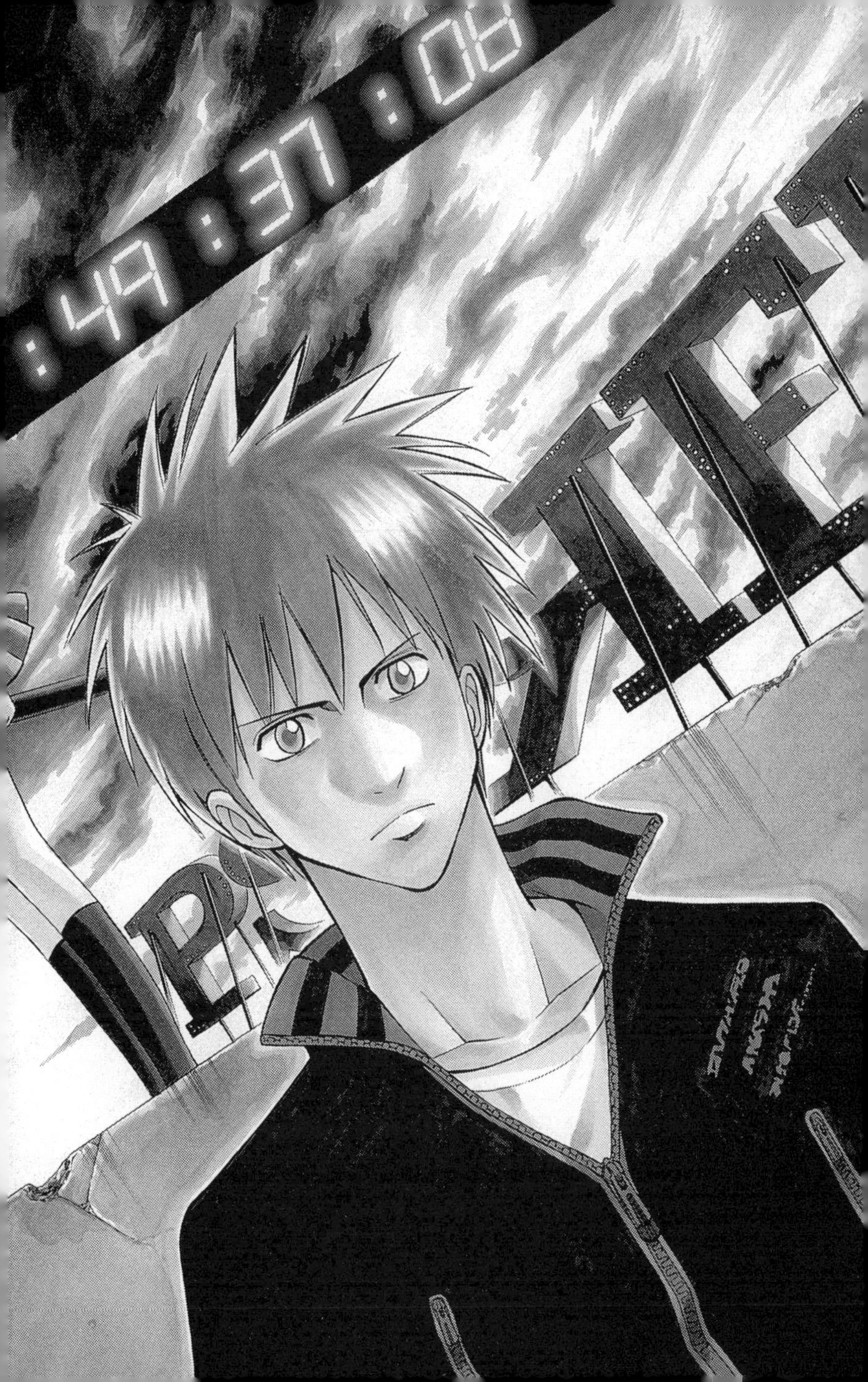
:49:37:08

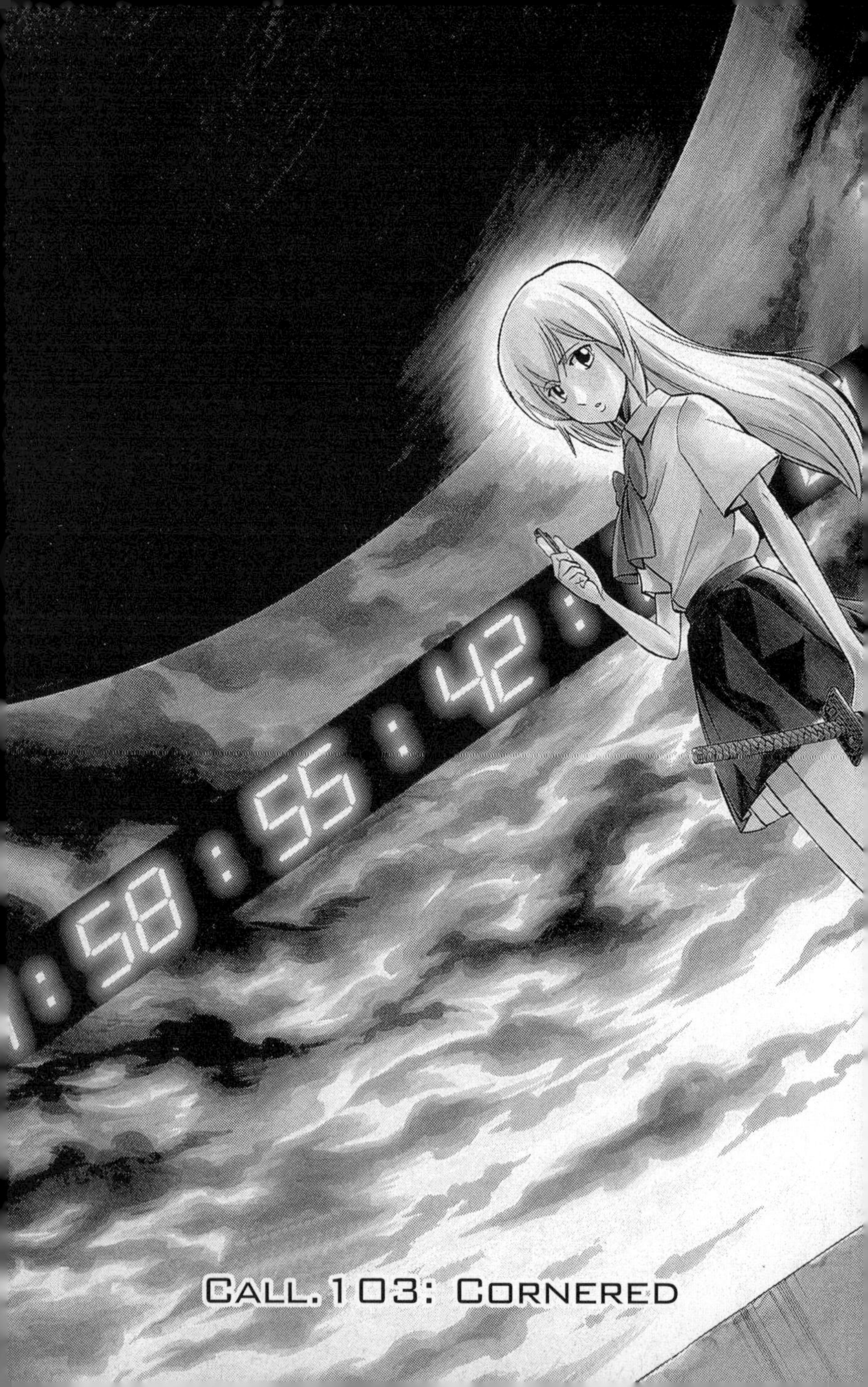
58 : 55 : 42

CALL. 103: CORNERED

PSYREN
サイレン

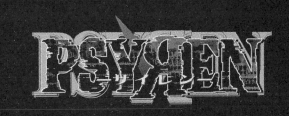

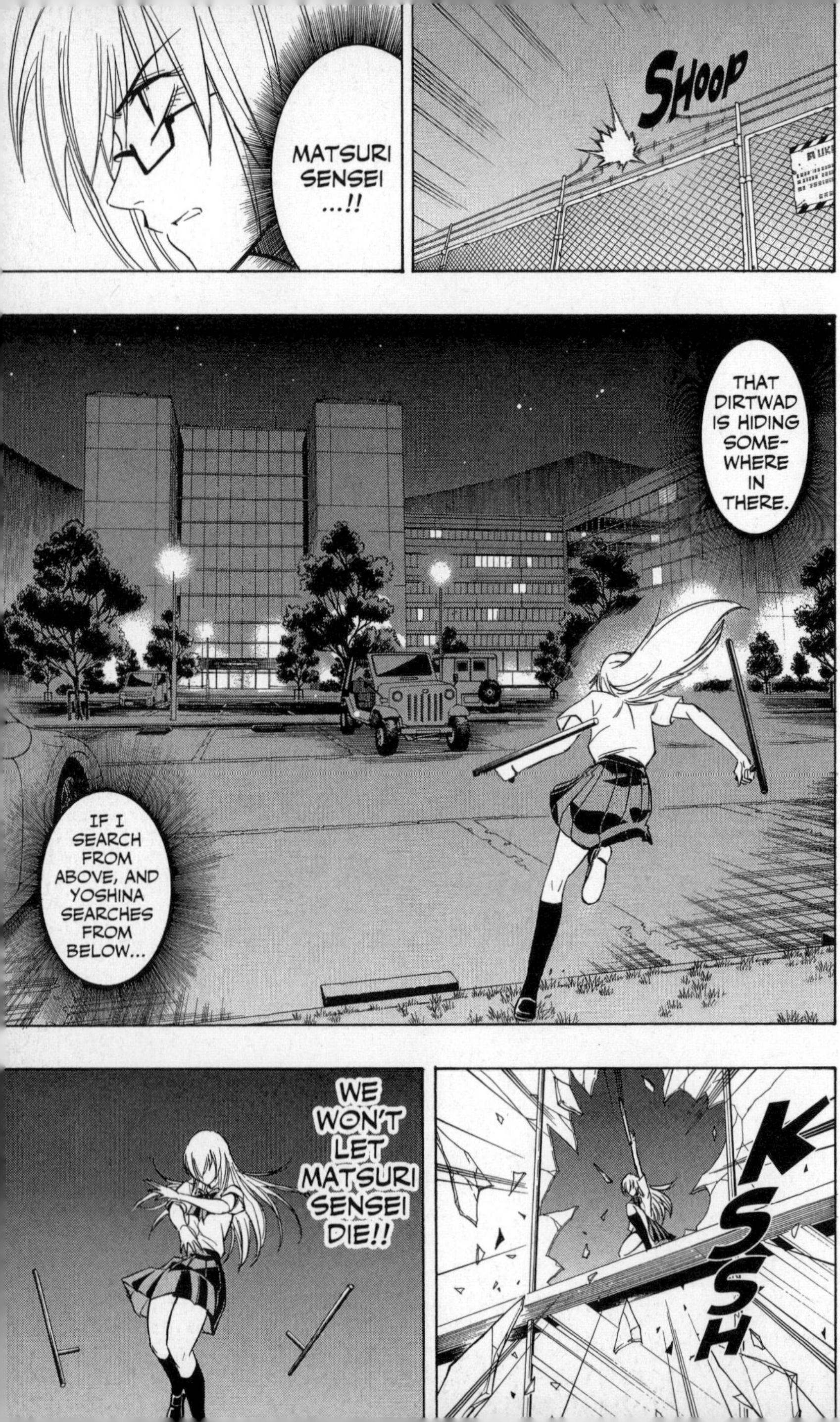
SHOOP
MATSURI SENSEI ...!!
THAT DIRTWAD IS HIDING SOME-WHERE IN THERE.
IF I SEARCH FROM ABOVE, AND YOSHINA SEARCHES FROM BELOW...
KSSH
WE WON'T LET MATSURI SENSEI DIE!!

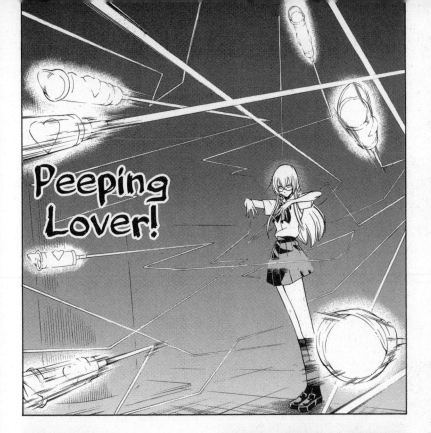

Peeping Lover!
BLOOP
YUSAKA ...!!
NO MATTER WHERE YOU HIDE...
I'LL HUNT YOU DOWN!!

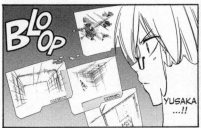

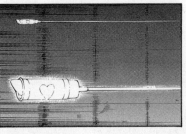

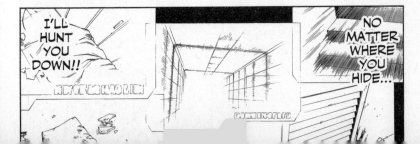

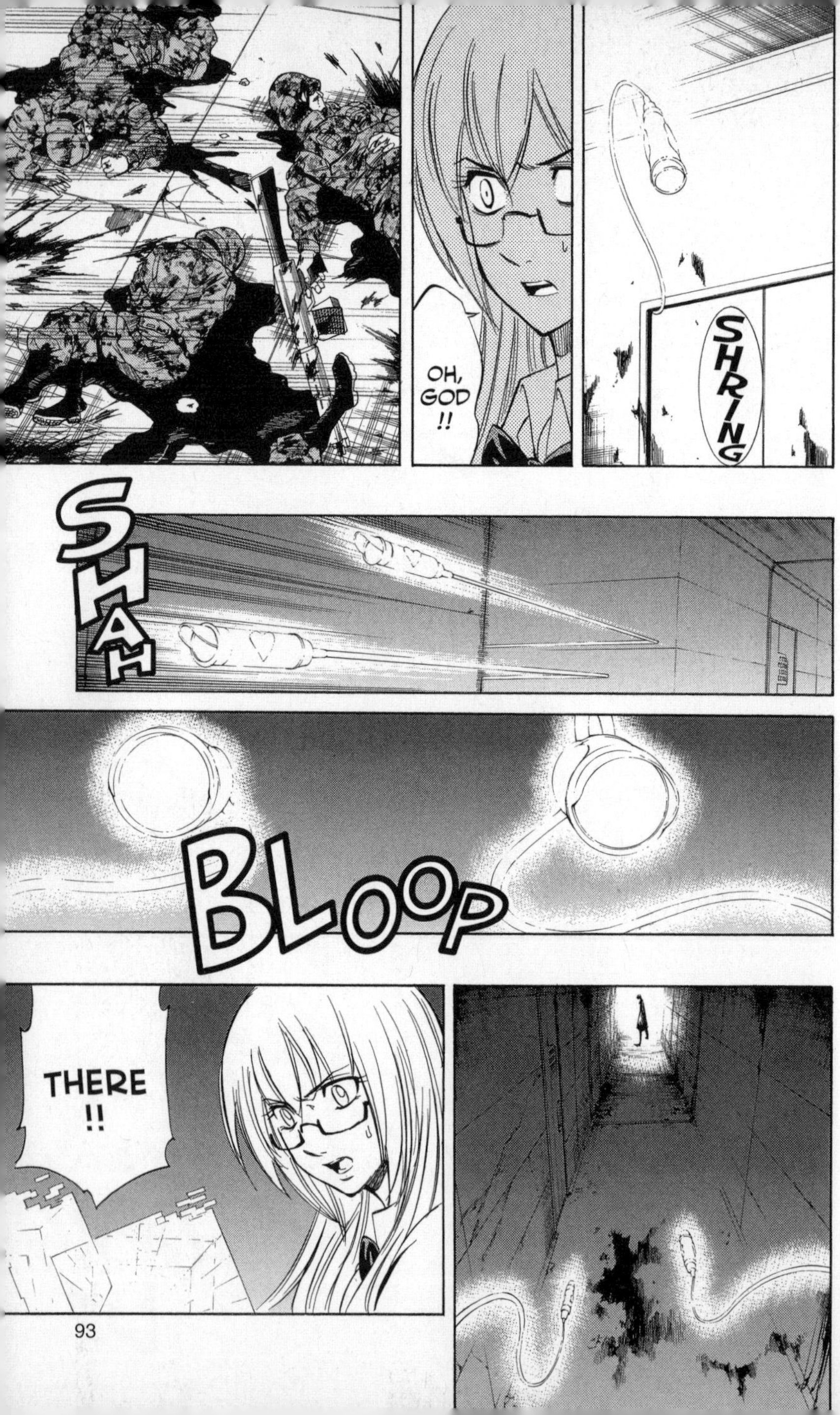
SHRING
OH, GOD !!
SHAH
BLOOP
THERE !!

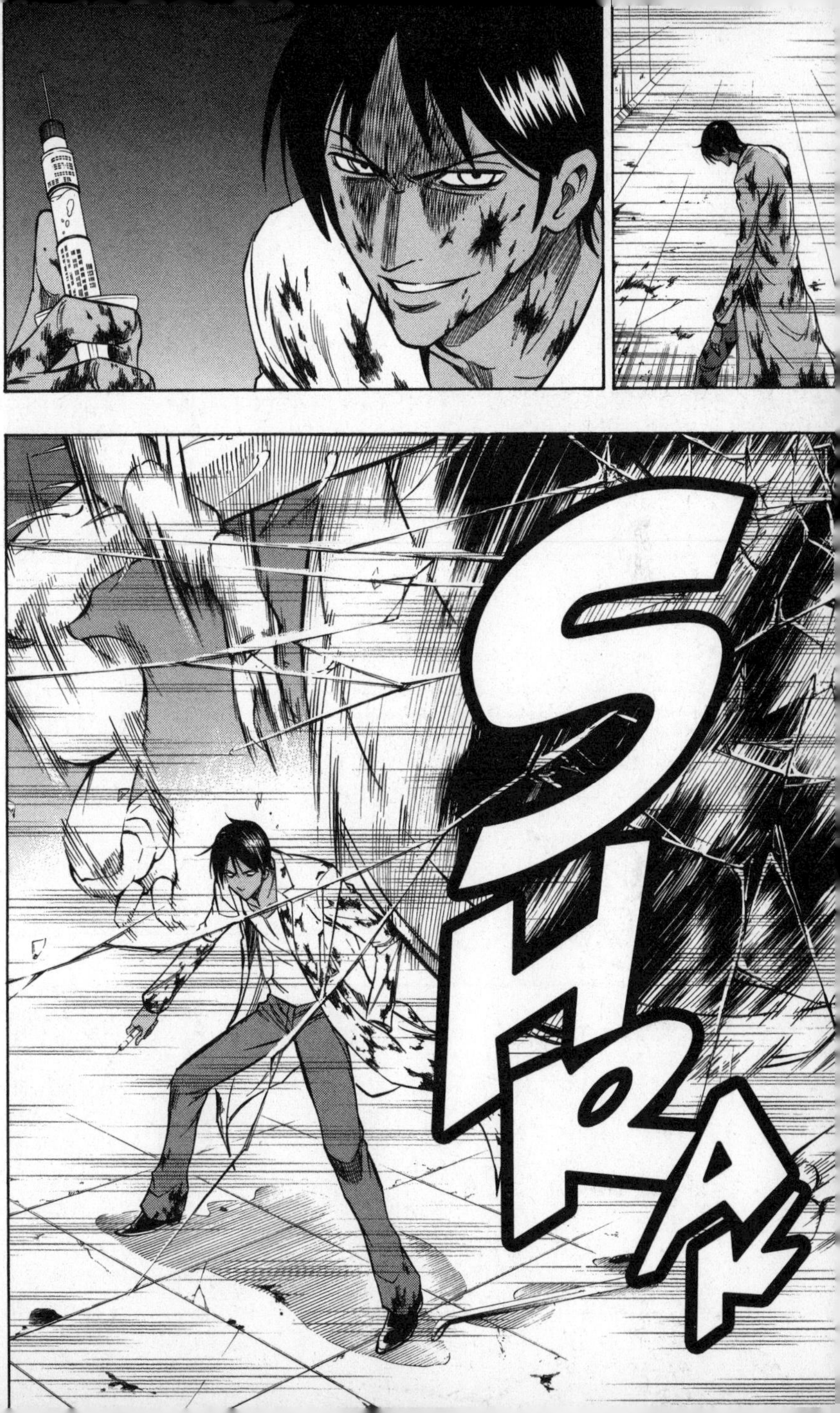
SHRAK

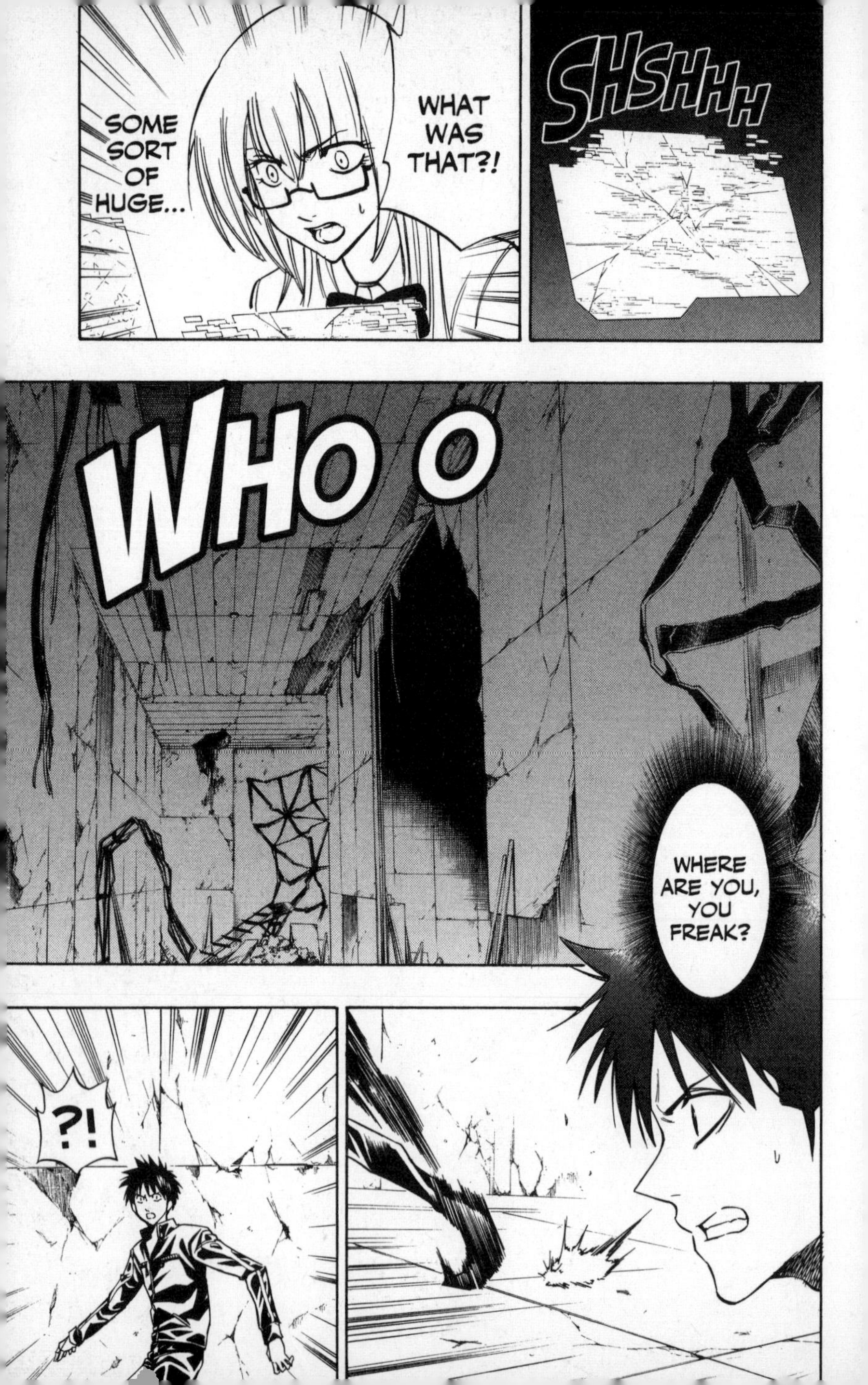
SHSHHH
WHAT WAS THAT?!
SOME SORT OF HUGE...
WHO O
WHERE ARE YOU, YOU FREAK?
?!

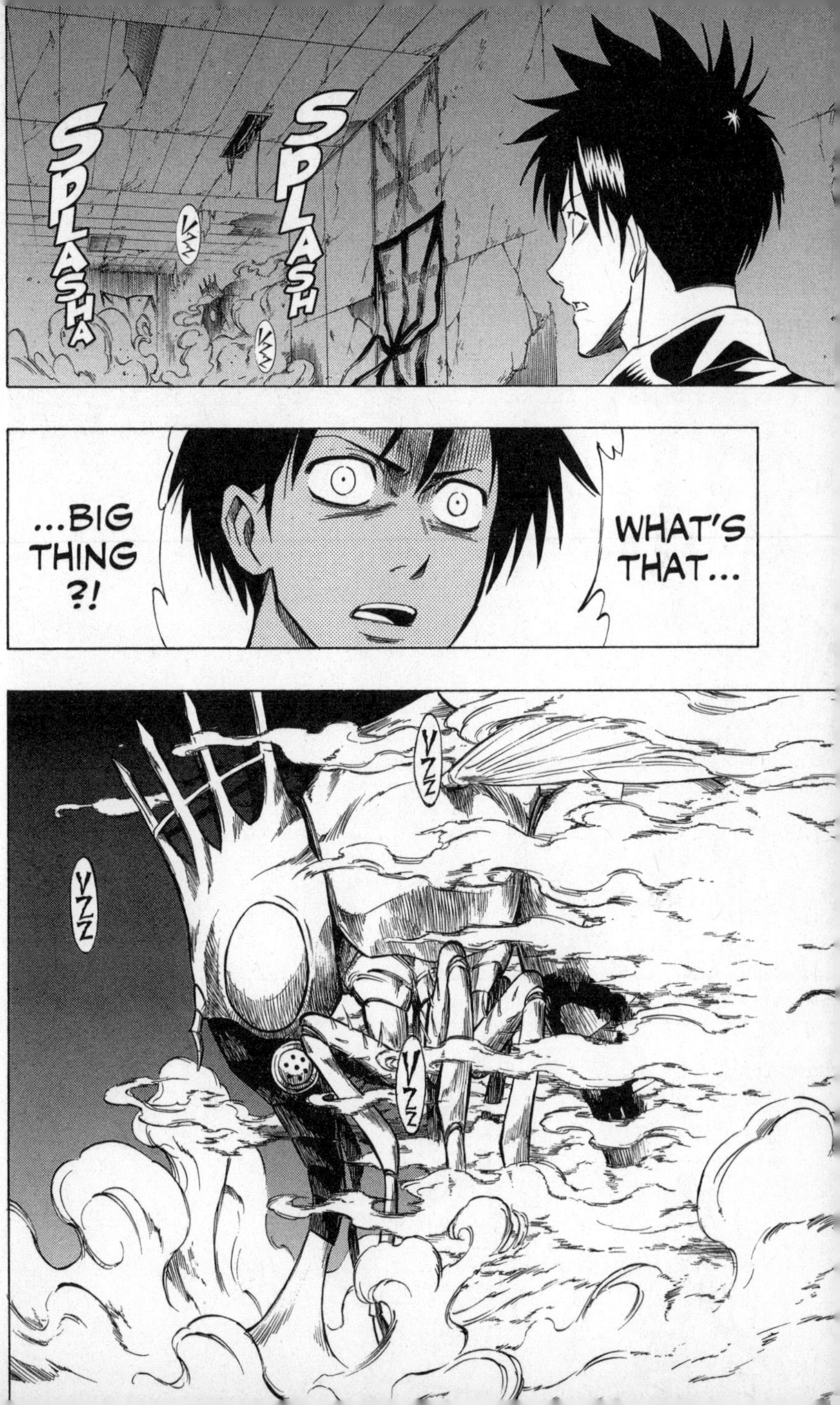
SPLASH
VZZ
VZZ
SPLASHA
WHAT'S THAT...
...BIG THING ?!
VZZ
VZZ
VZZ

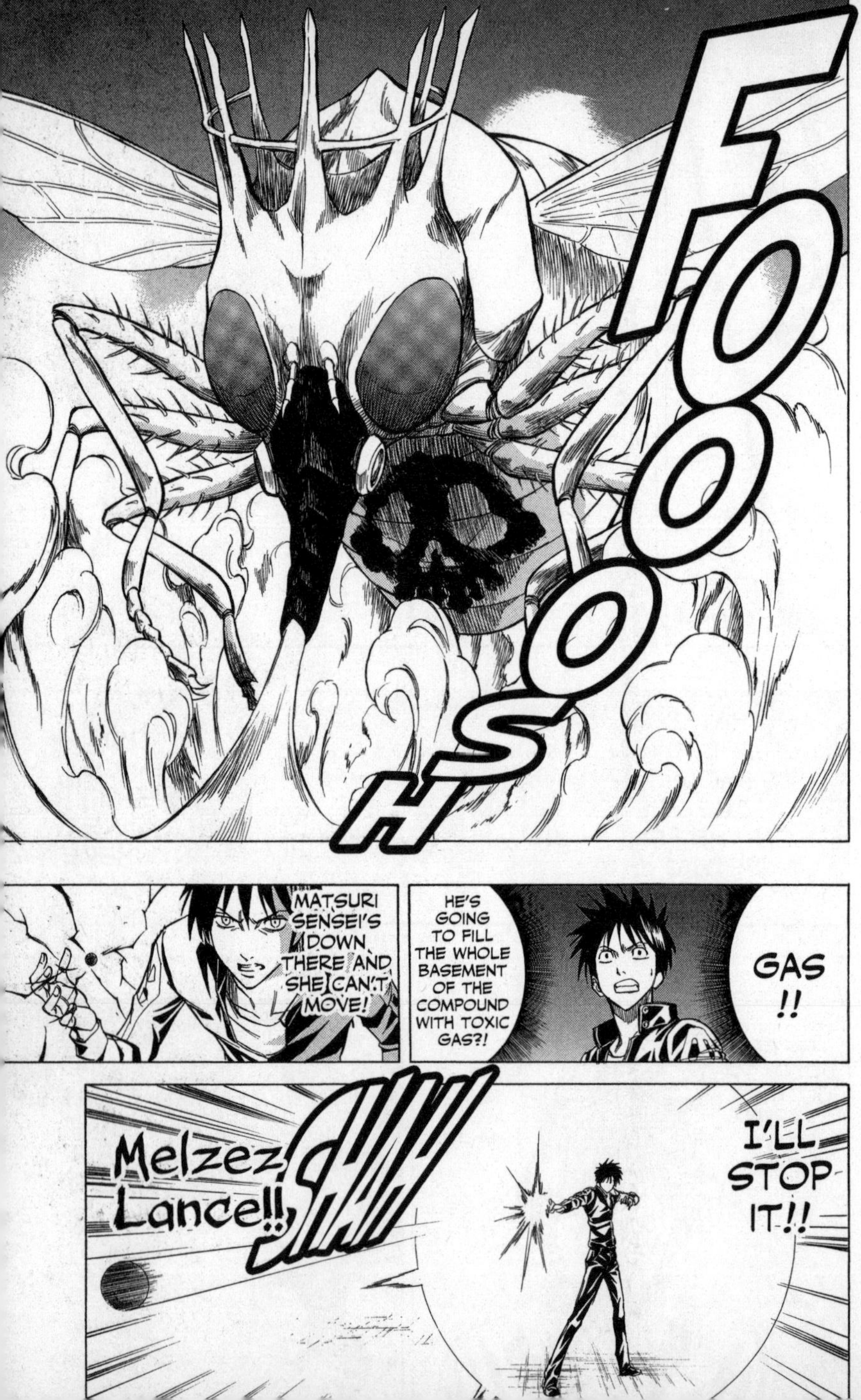
FOOOSH
GAS !!
HE'S GOING TO FILL THE WHOLE BASEMENT OF THE COMPOUND WITH TOXIC GAS?!
MATSURI SENSEI'S DOWN THERE AND SHE CAN'T MOVE!
I'LL STOP IT!!
Melzez Lance!!

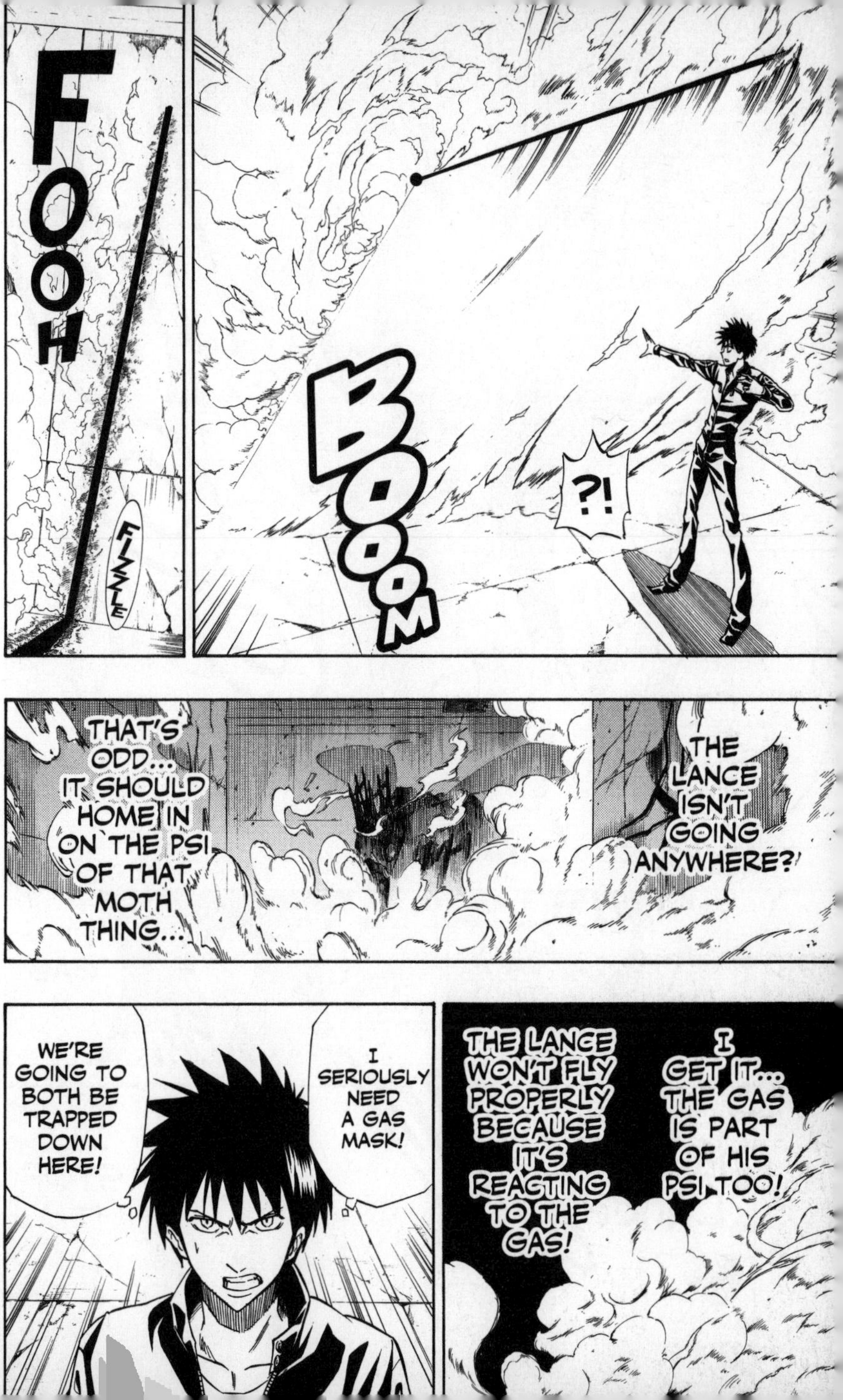
BOOM
?!
FOOH
FIZZLE
THE LANCE ISN'T GOING ANYWHERE?
THAT'S ODD... IT SHOULD HOME IN ON THE PSI OF THAT MOTH THING...
I GET IT... THE GAS IS PART OF HIS PSI TOO!
THE LANCE WON'T FLY PROPERLY BECAUSE IT'S REACTING TO THE GAS!
I SERIOUSLY NEED A GAS MASK!
WE'RE GOING TO BOTH BE TRAPPED DOWN HERE!

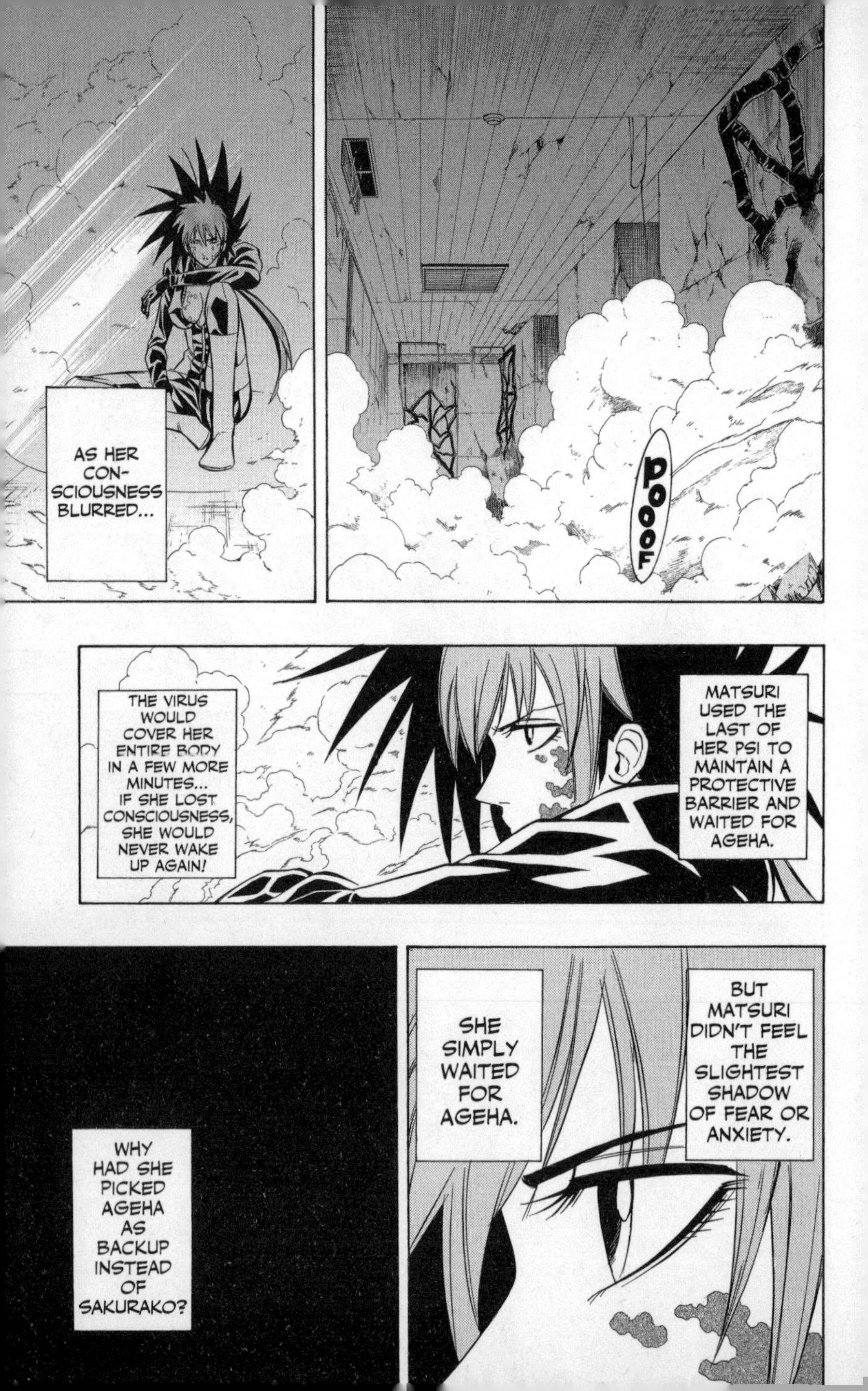
POOOF
AS HER CONSCIOUSNESS BLURRED...
MATSURI USED THE LAST OF HER PSI TO MAINTAIN A PROTECTIVE BARRIER AND WAITED FOR AGEHA.
THE VIRUS WOULD COVER HER ENTIRE BODY IN A FEW MORE MINUTES... IF SHE LOST CONSCIOUSNESS, SHE WOULD NEVER WAKE UP AGAIN!
BUT MATSURI DIDN'T FEEL THE SLIGHTEST SHADOW OF FEAR OR ANXIETY.
SHE SIMPLY WAITED FOR AGEHA.
WHY HAD SHE PICKED AGEHA AS BACKUP INSTEAD OF SAKURAKO?

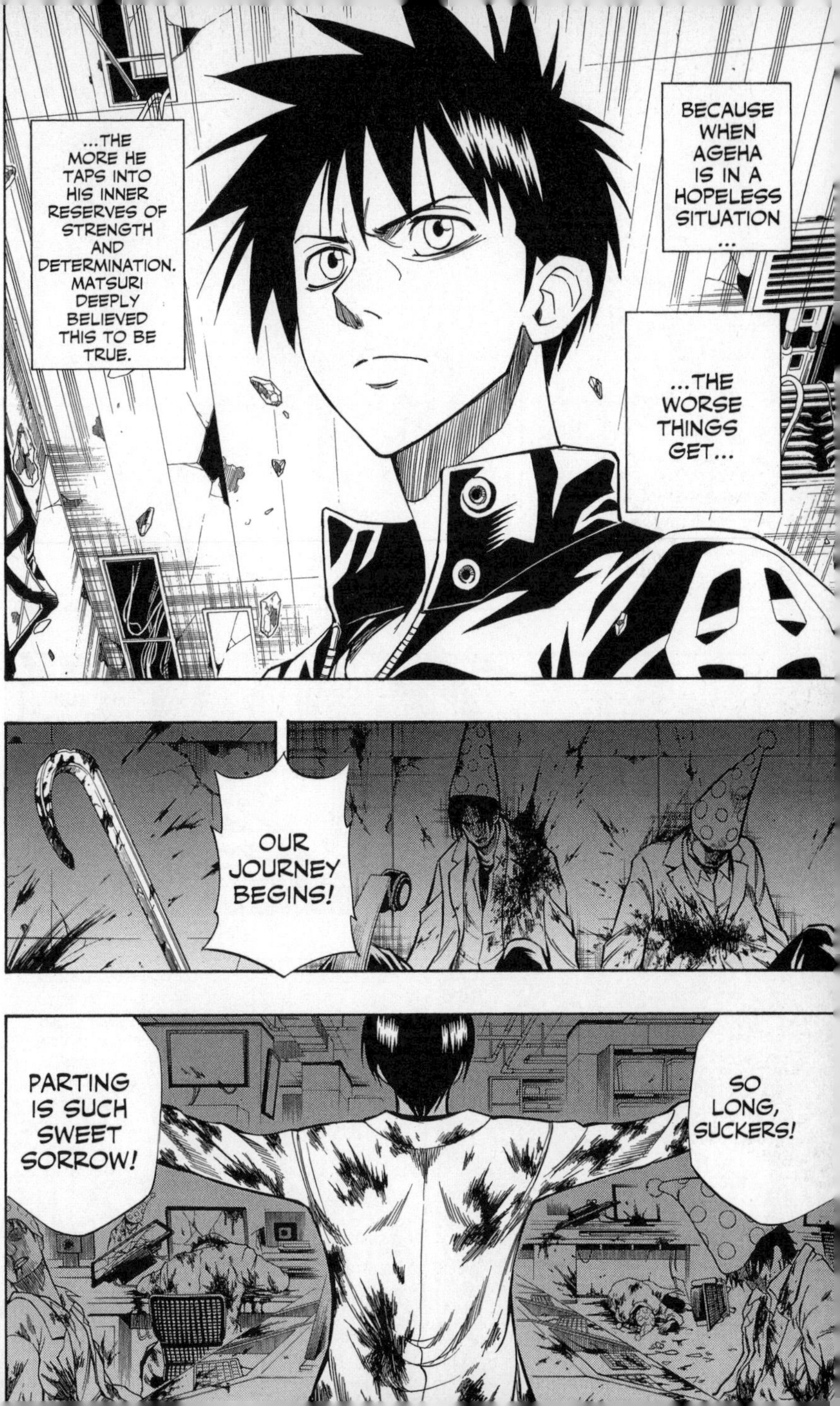
BECAUSE WHEN AGEHA IS IN A HOPELESS SITUATION ...
...THE WORSE THINGS GET...
...THE MORE HE TAPS INTO HIS INNER RESERVES OF STRENGTH AND DETERMINATION. MATSURI DEEPLY BELIEVED THIS TO BE TRUE.
OUR JOURNEY BEGINS!
SO LONG, SUCKERS!
PARTING IS SUCH SWEET SORROW!

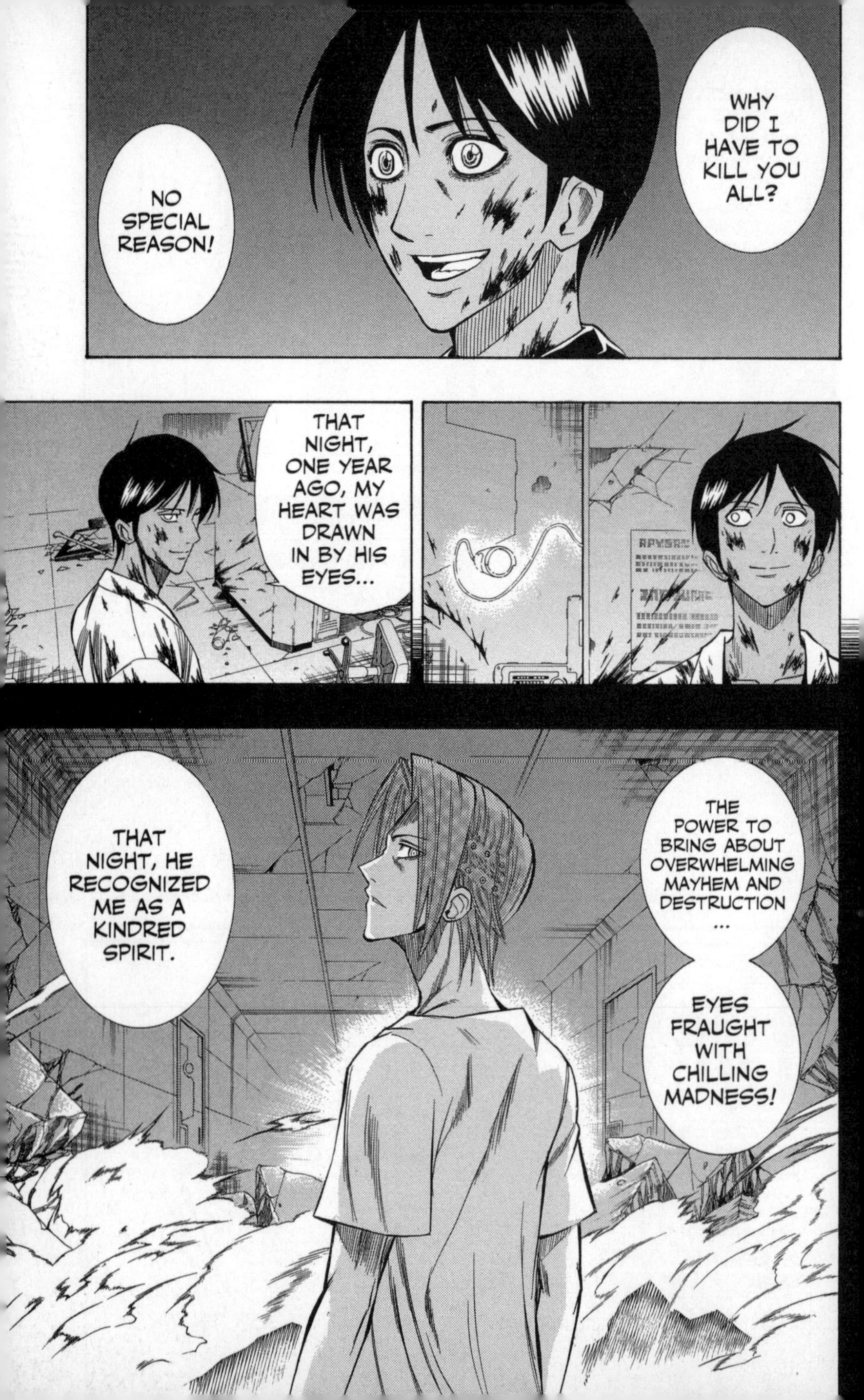
WHY DID I HAVE TO KILL YOU ALL?
NO SPECIAL REASON!
THAT NIGHT, ONE YEAR AGO, MY HEART WAS DRAWN IN BY HIS EYES...
THE POWER TO BRING ABOUT OVERWHELMING MAYHEM AND DESTRUCTION ...
EYES FRAUGHT WITH CHILLING MADNESS!
THAT NIGHT, HE RECOGNIZED ME AS A KINDRED SPIRIT.

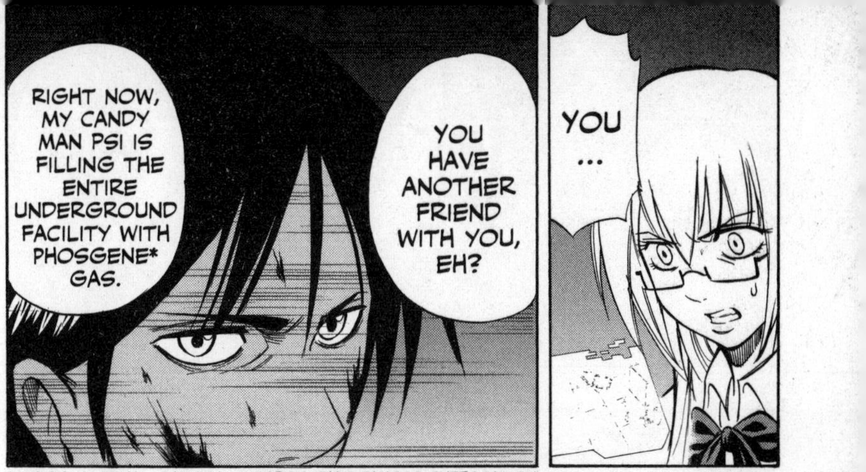
YOU ...
YOU HAVE ANOTHER FRIEND WITH YOU, EH?
RIGHT NOW, MY CANDY MAN PSI IS FILLING THE ENTIRE UNDERGROUND FACILITY WITH PHOSGENE* GAS.

*A HIGHLY LETHAL CHEMICAL WEAPON THAT CAUSES SUFFOCATION.

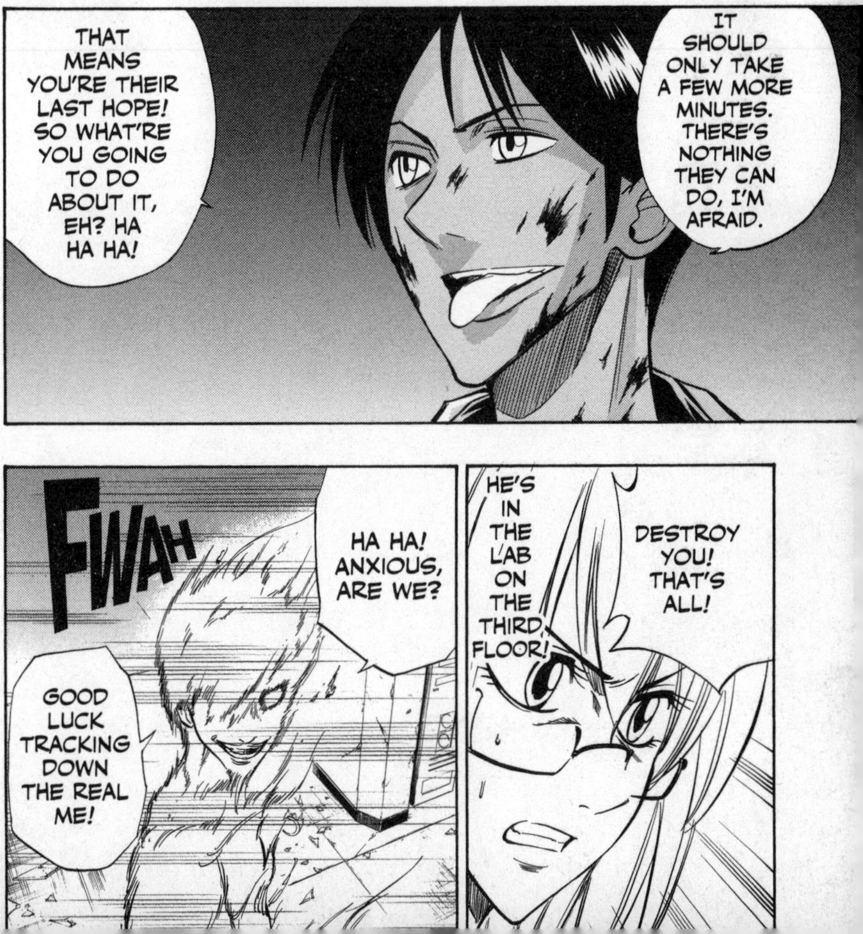
IT SHOULD ONLY TAKE A FEW MORE MINUTES. THERE'S NOTHING THEY CAN DO, I'M AFRAID.
THAT MEANS YOU'RE THEIR LAST HOPE! SO WHAT'RE YOU GOING TO DO ABOUT IT, EH? HA HA HA!
DESTROY YOU! THAT'S ALL!
HE'S IN THE LAB ON THE THIRD FLOOR!
HA HA! ANXIOUS, ARE WE?
FWAH
GOOD LUCK TRACKING DOWN THE REAL ME!

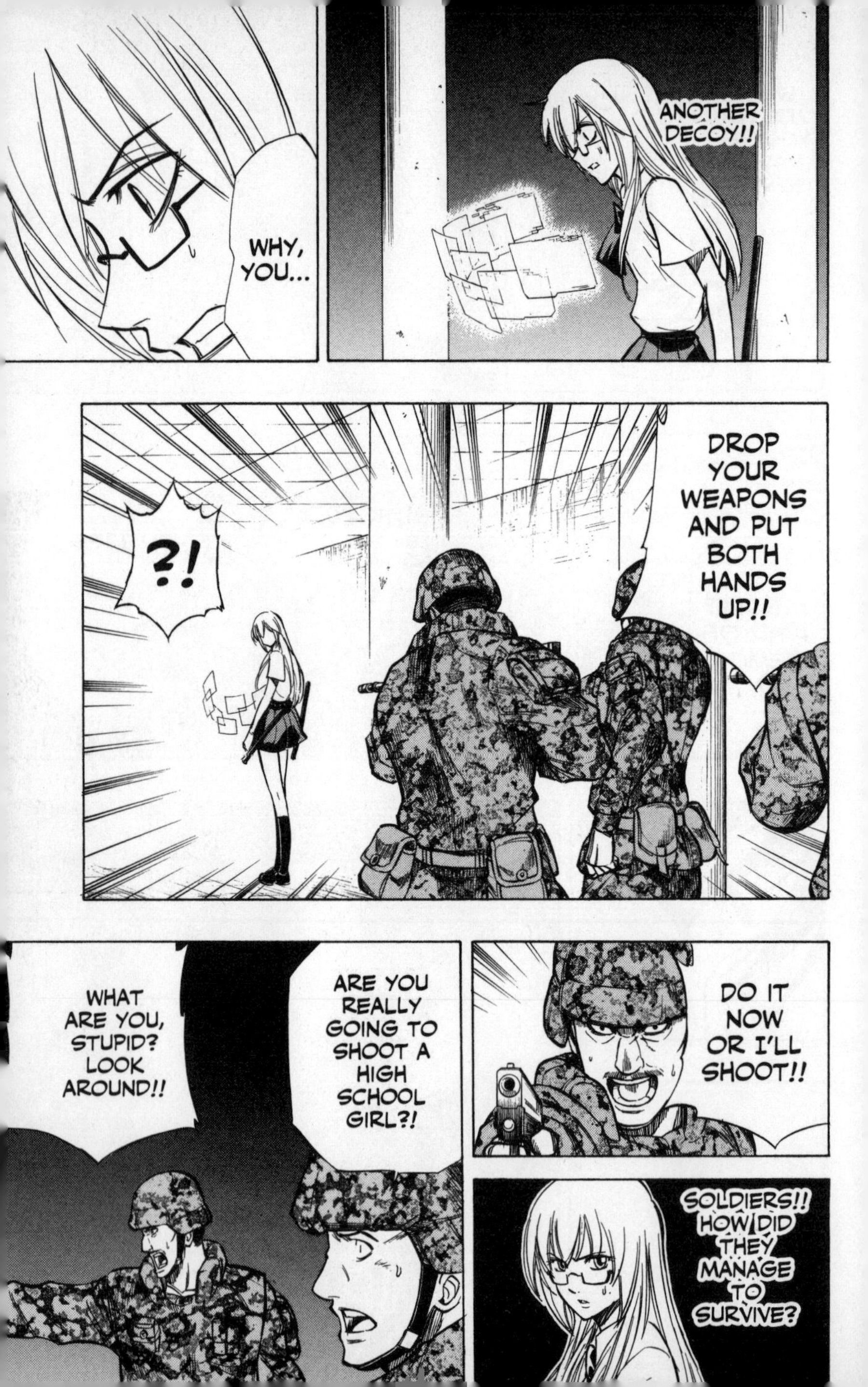
ANOTHER DECOY!!
WHY, YOU...
DROP YOUR WEAPONS AND PUT BOTH HANDS UP!!
?!
DO IT NOW OR I'LL SHOOT!!
SOLDIERS!! HOW DID THEY MANAGE TO SURVIVE?
ARE YOU REALLY GOING TO SHOOT A HIGH SCHOOL GIRL?!
WHAT ARE YOU, STUPID? LOOK AROUND!!

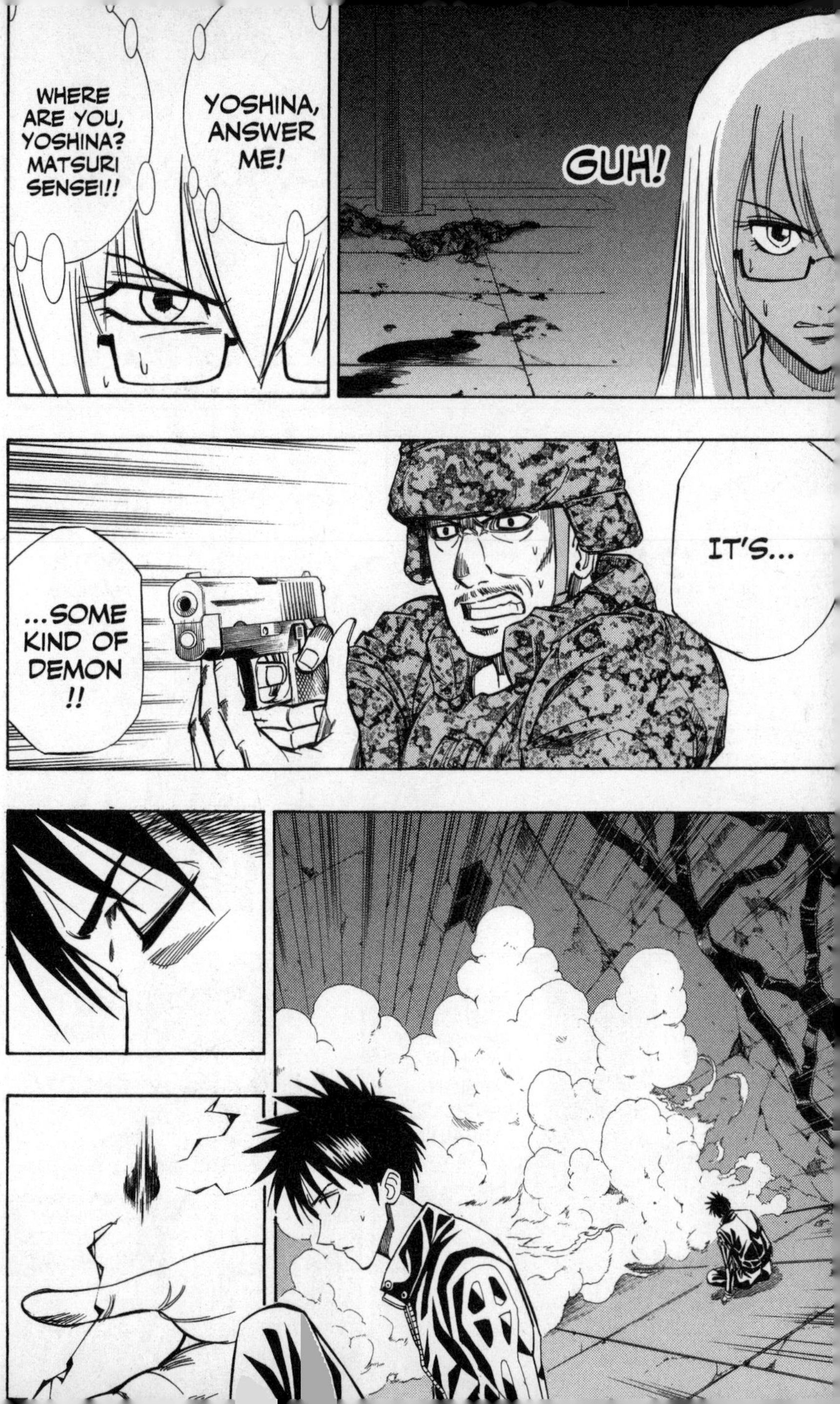
GUH!
YOSHINA, ANSWER ME!
WHERE ARE YOU, YOSHINA? MATSURI SENSEI!!
IT'S...
...SOME KIND OF DEMON !!

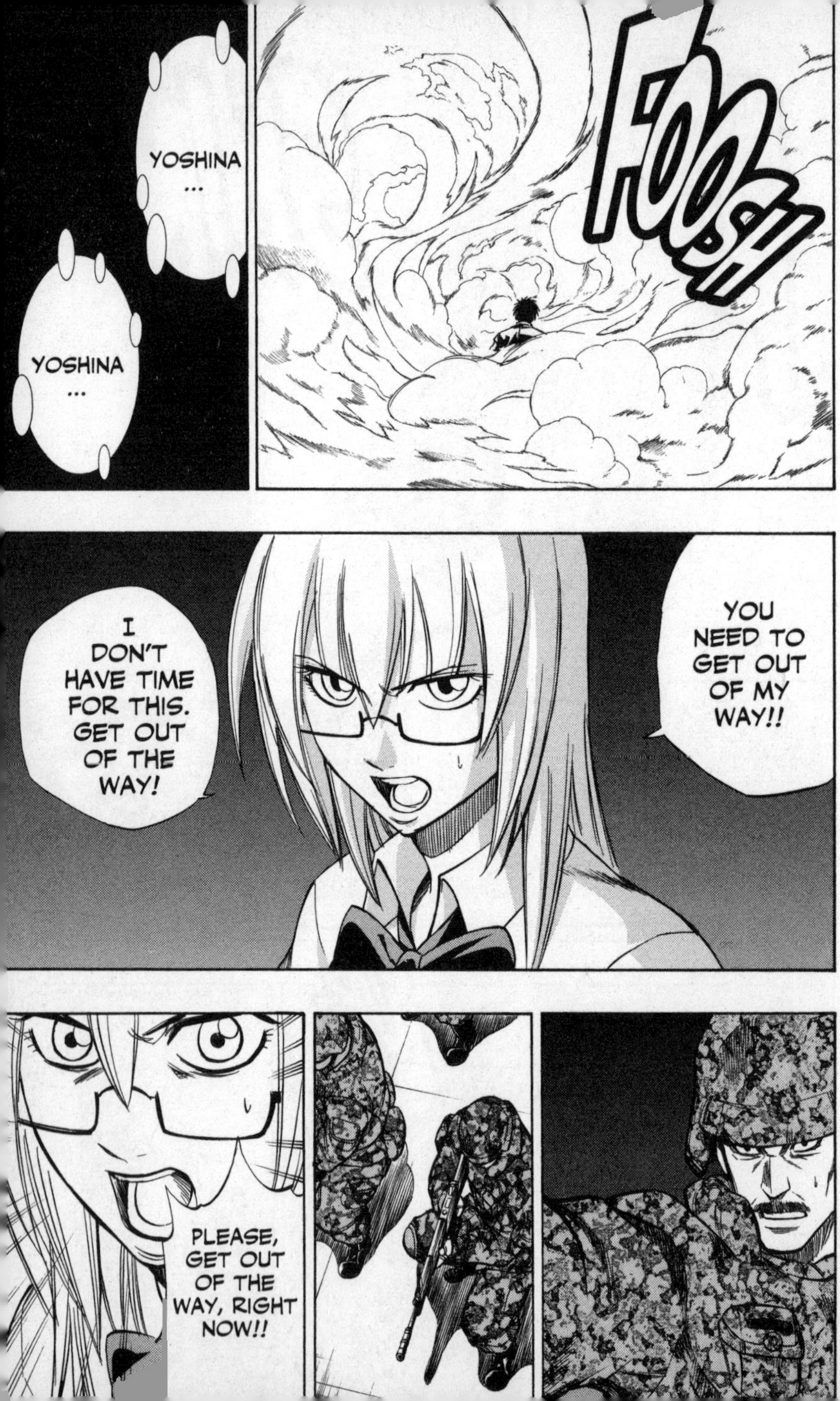
FOOSH
YOSHINA ...
YOSHINA ...
YOU NEED TO GET OUT OF MY WAY!!
I DON'T HAVE TIME FOR THIS. GET OUT OF THE WAY!
PLEASE, GET OUT OF THE WAY, RIGHT NOW!!

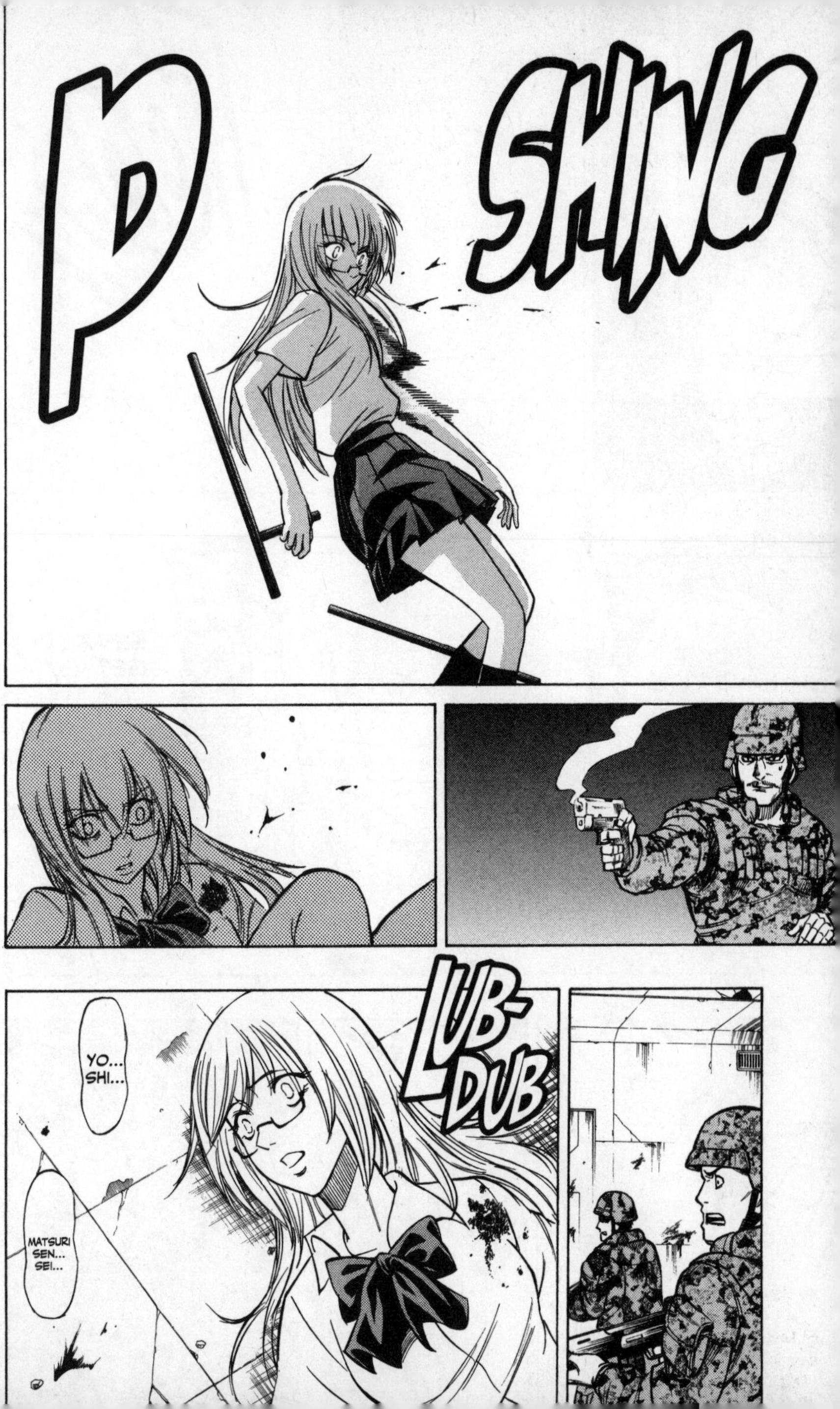
PSHING
LUB-DUB
YO... SHI...
MATSURI SEN... SEI...

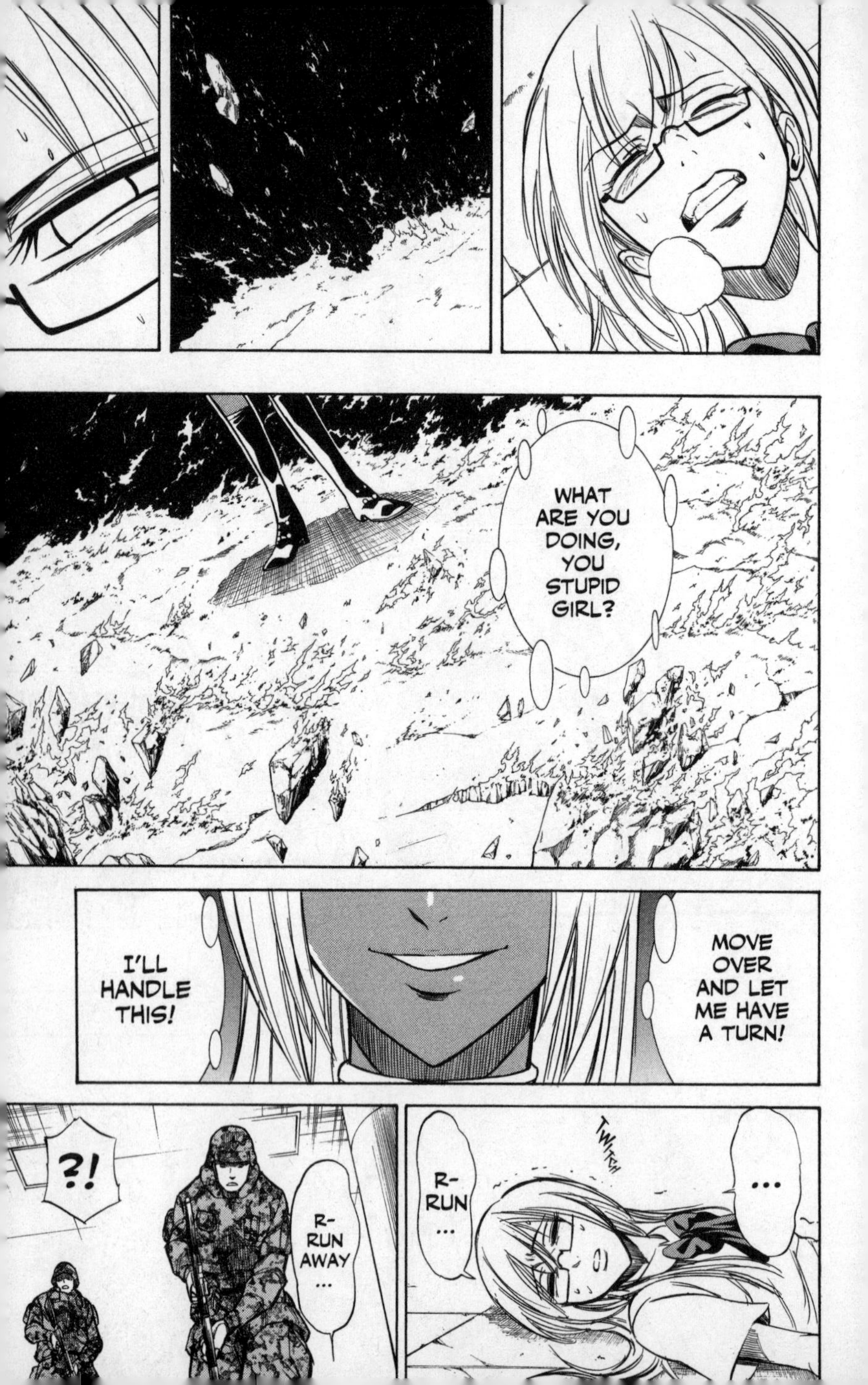
WHAT ARE YOU DOING, YOU STUPID GIRL?
MOVE OVER AND LET ME HAVE A TURN!
I'LL HANDLE THIS!
...
TWITCH
R-RUN ...
R-RUN AWAY ...
?!

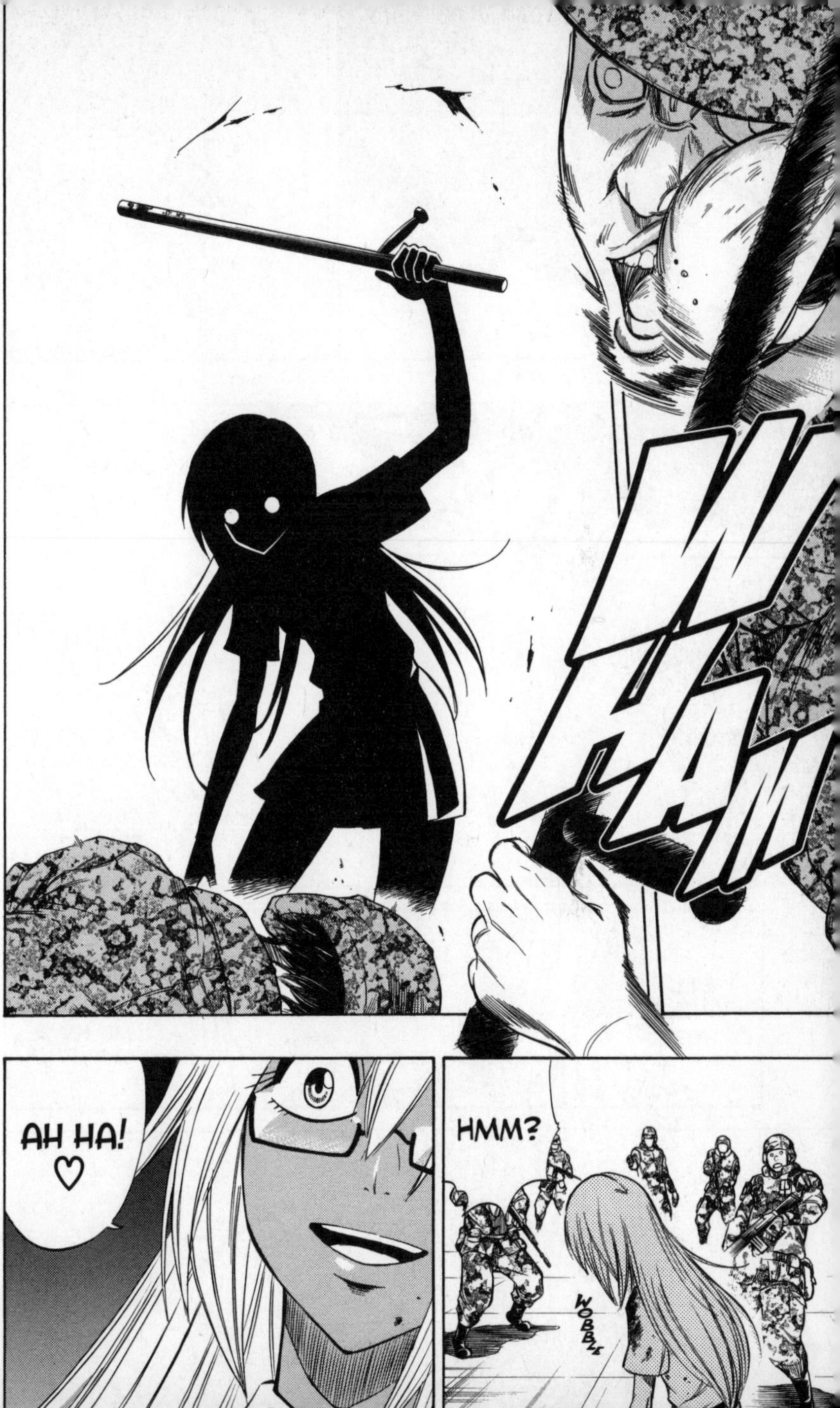

HAM
HMM?
WOBBLE
AH HA! ♡

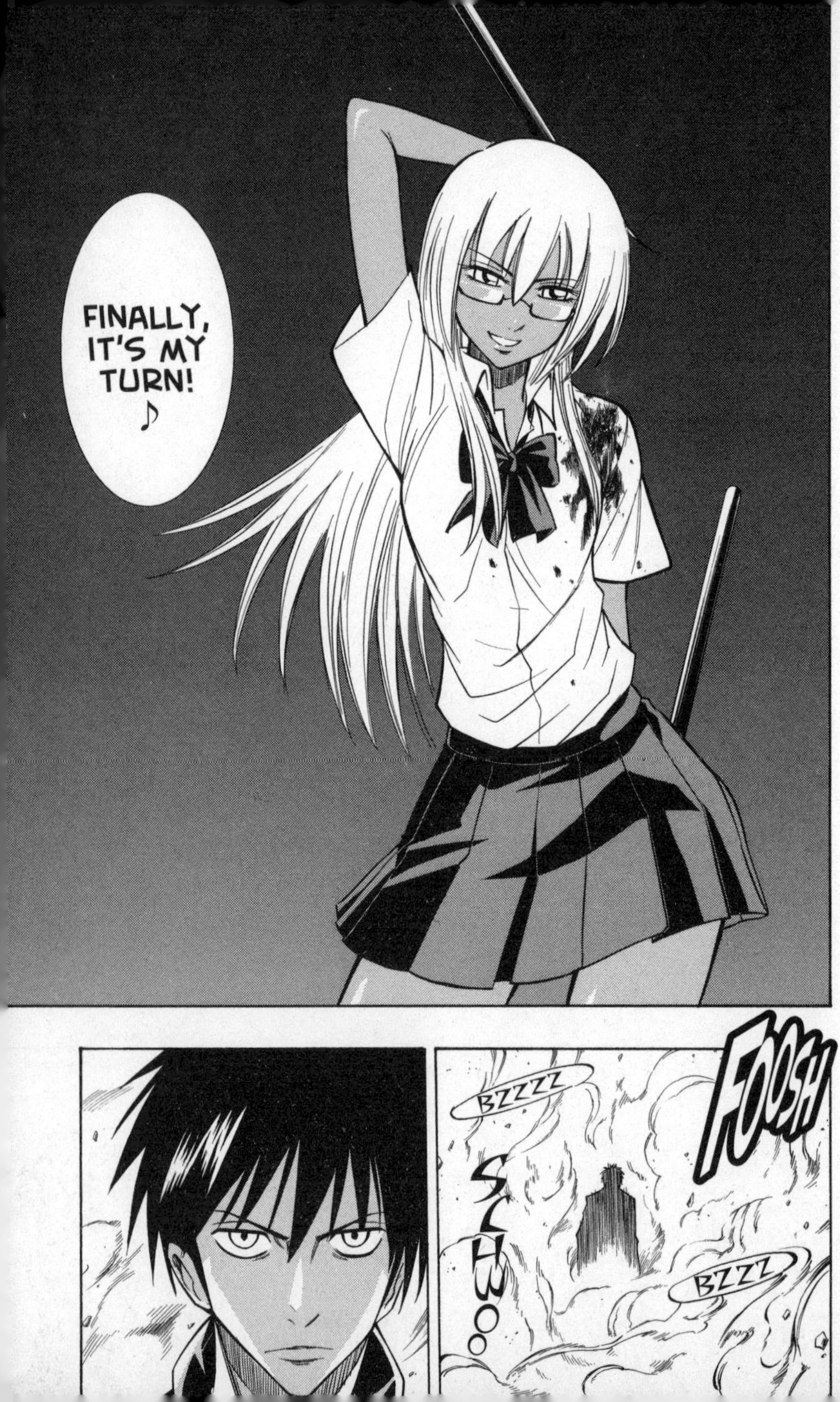
FINALLY, IT'S MY TURN! ♪
FOOSH
BZZZZ
SCHWOO
BZZZ

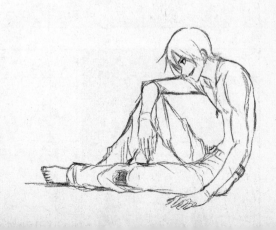

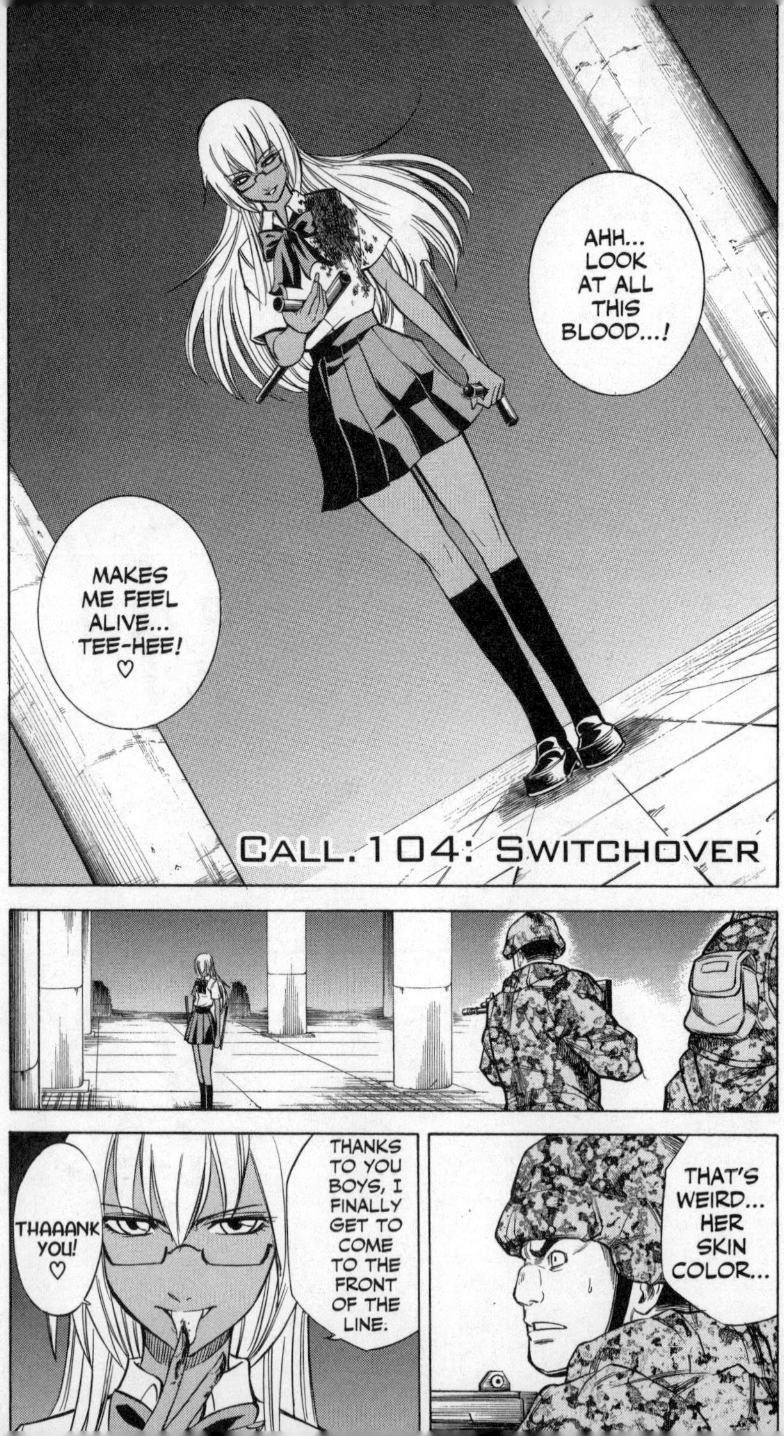
AHH... LOOK AT ALL THIS BLOOD...!
MAKES ME FEEL ALIVE... TEE-HEE! ♡
CALL. 104: SWITCHOVER
THAT'S WEIRD... HER SKIN COLOR...
THANKS TO YOU BOYS, I FINALLY GET TO COME TO THE FRONT OF THE LINE.
THAAANK YOU! ♡

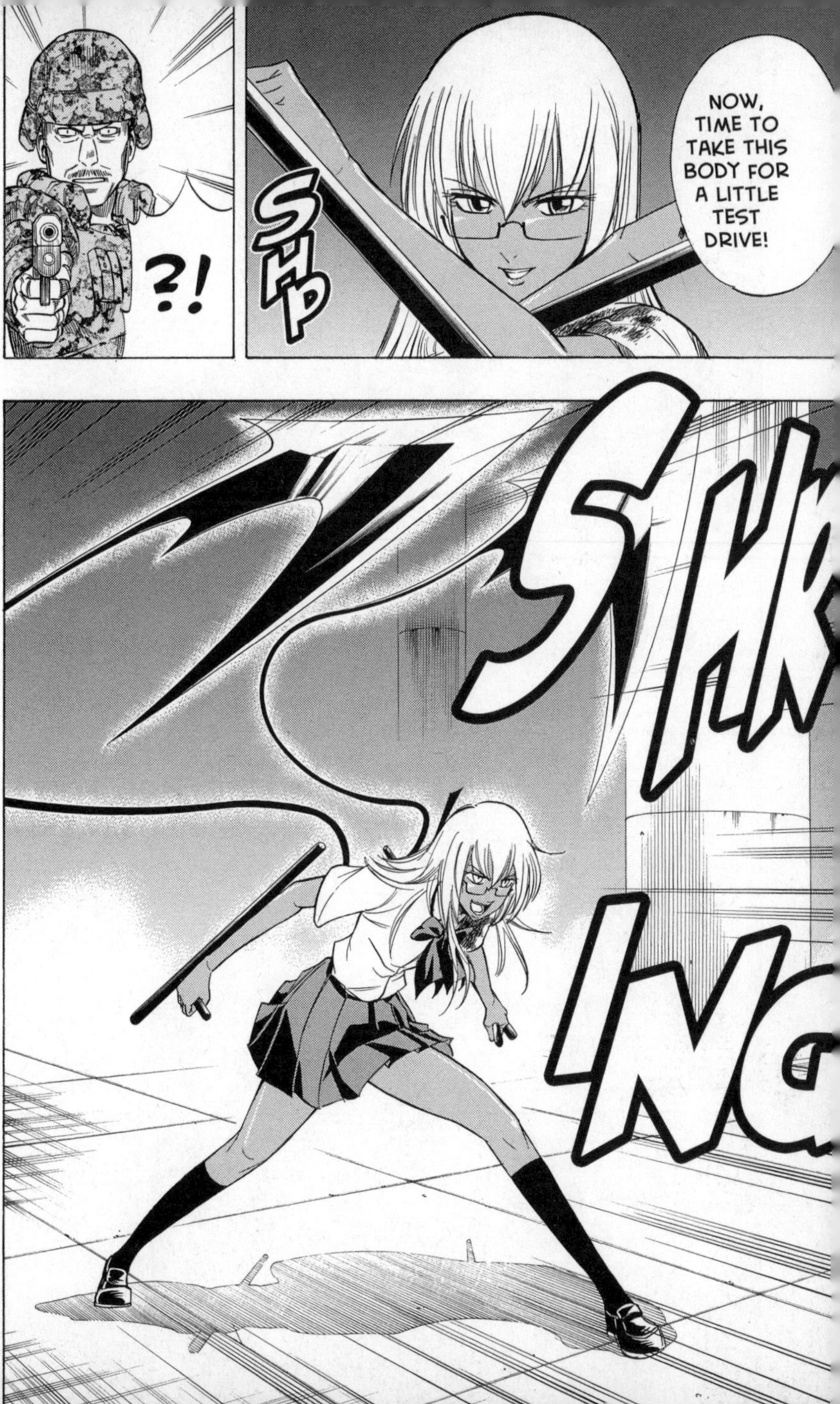
NOW, TIME TO TAKE THIS BODY FOR A LITTLE TEST DRIVE!
SHP
?!

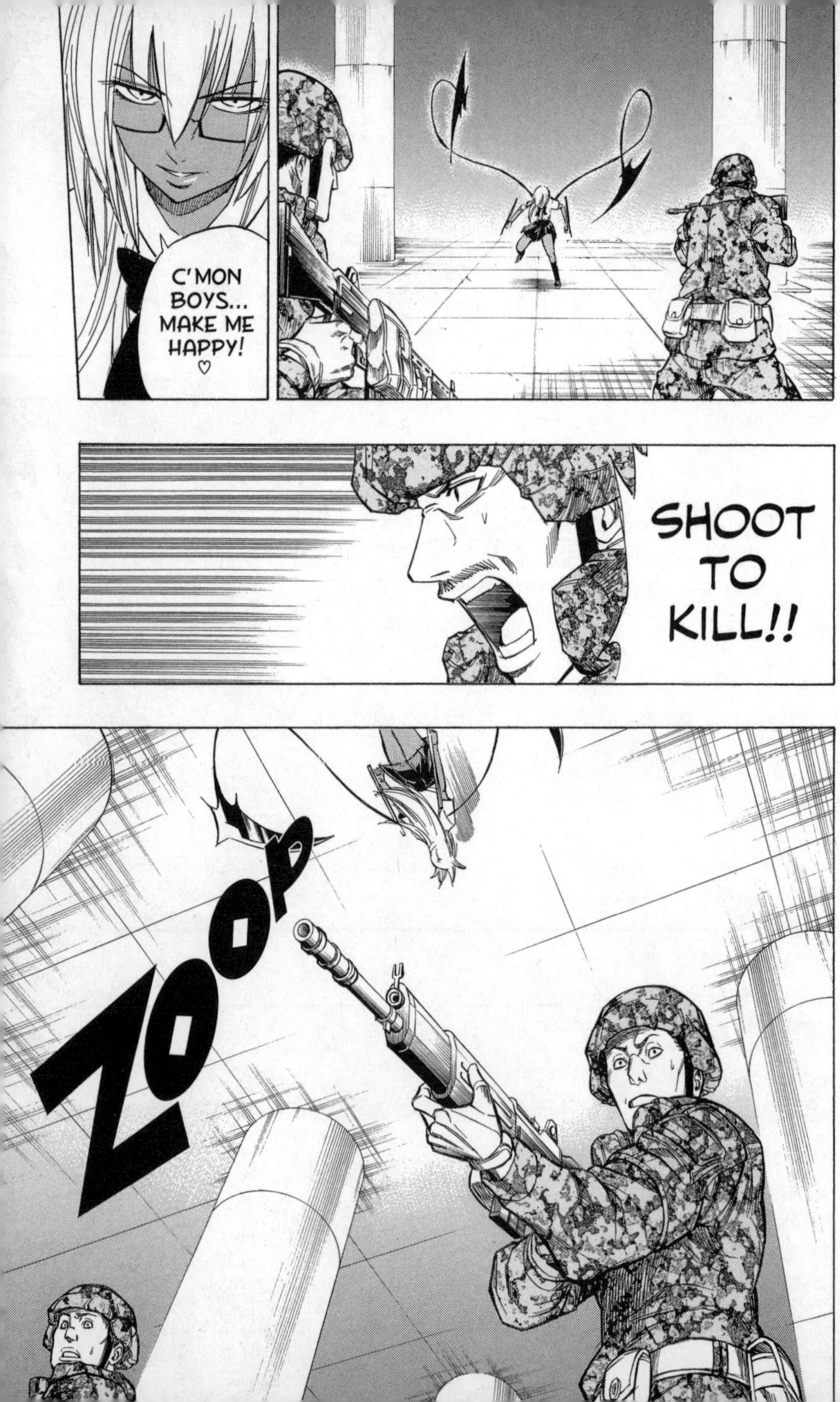
C'MON BOYS... MAKE ME HAPPY! ♡
SHOOT TO KILL!!
ZOOOP

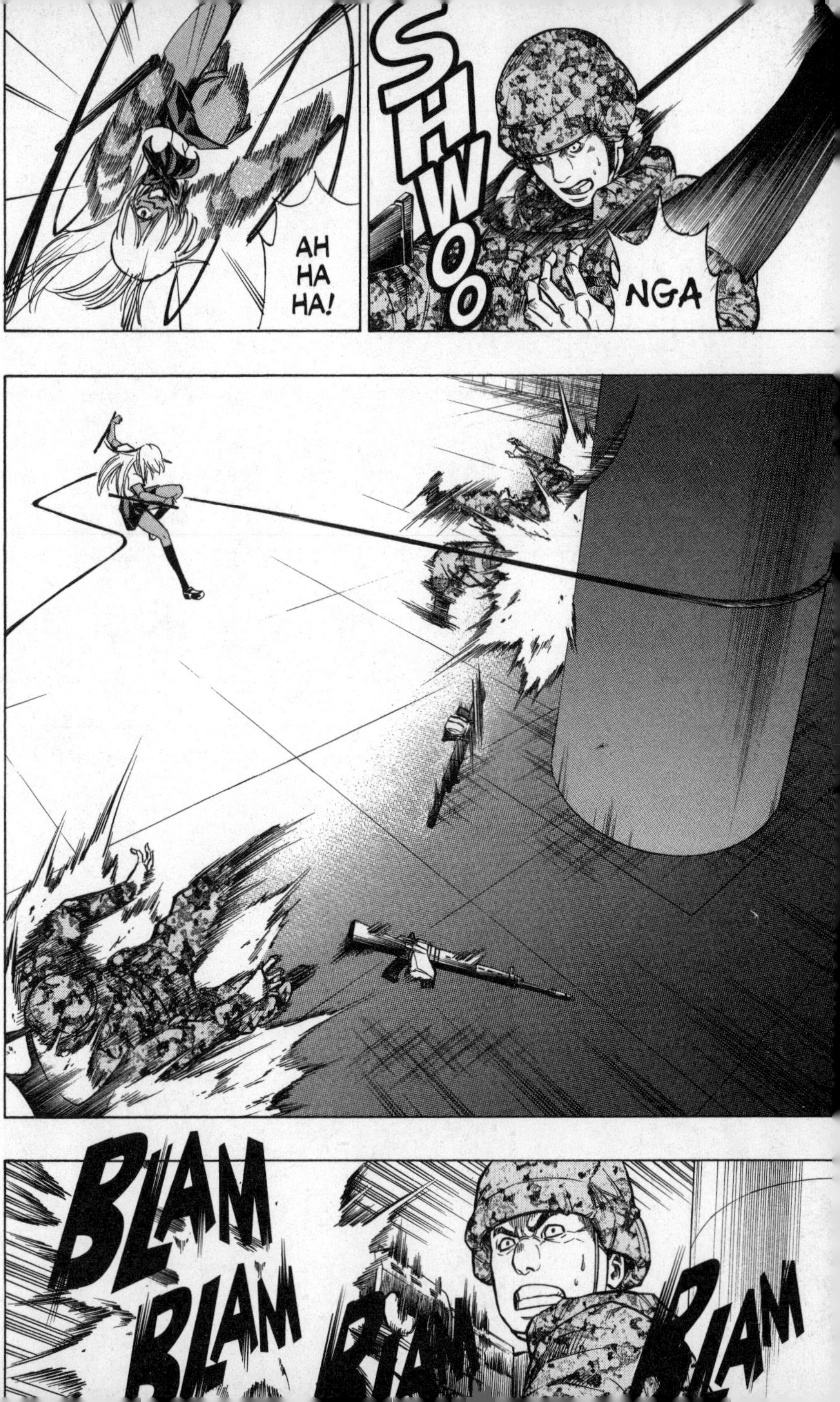
SHWOO
NGA
AH HA HA!
BLAM
BLAM
BLAM
BLAM
BLAM

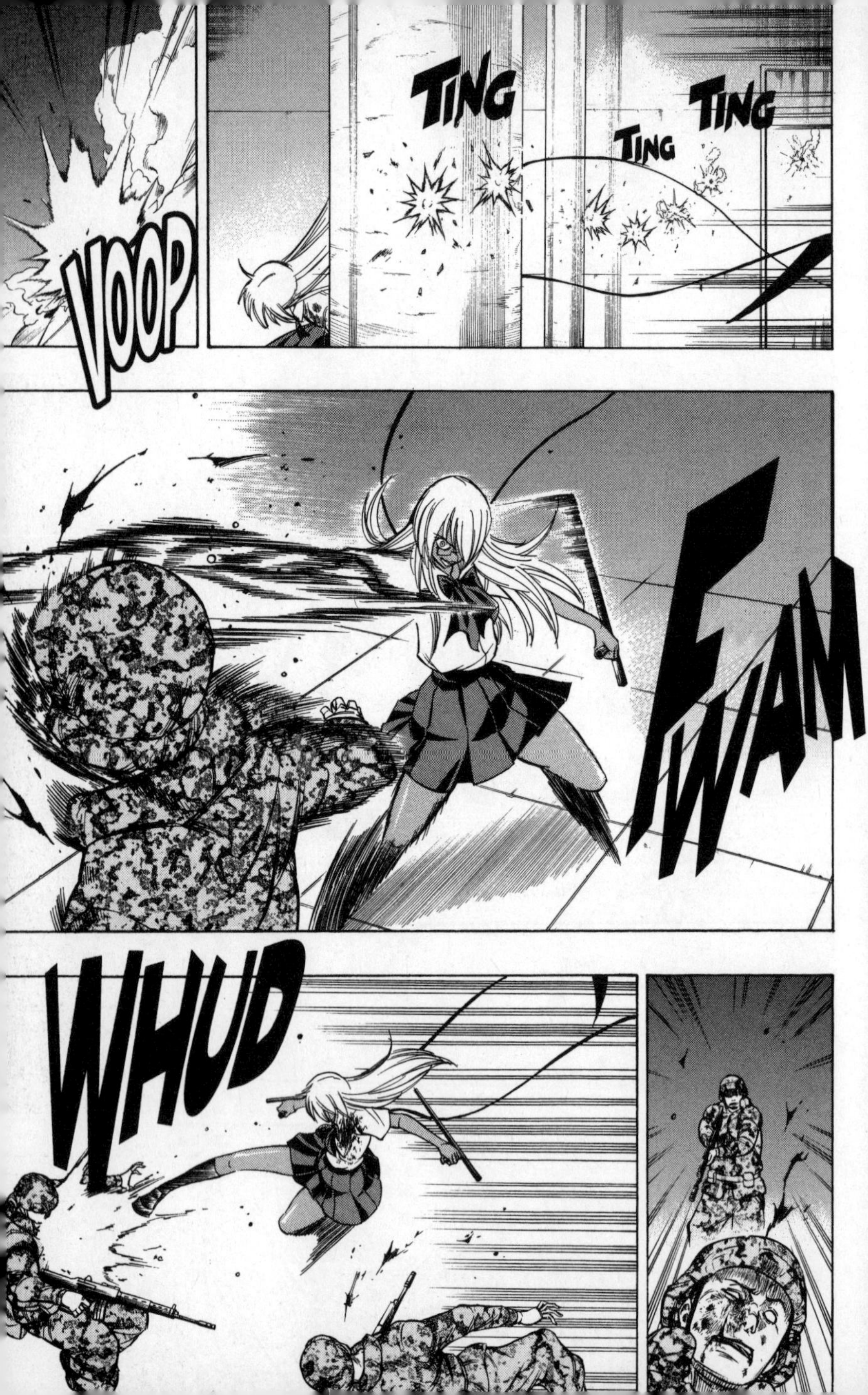
TING
TING
TING
VOOP
FWAM
WHUD

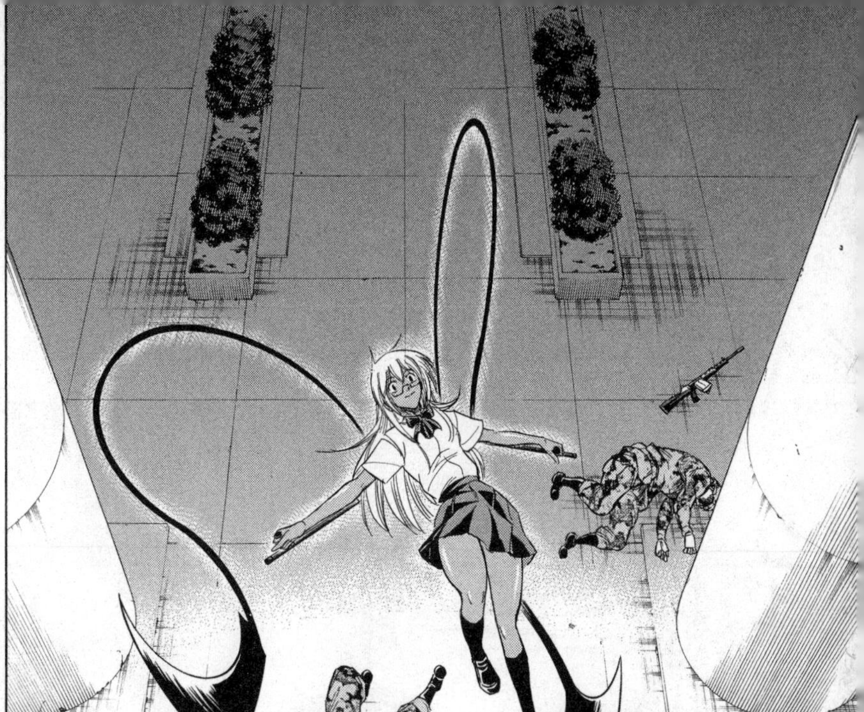
SHOOP
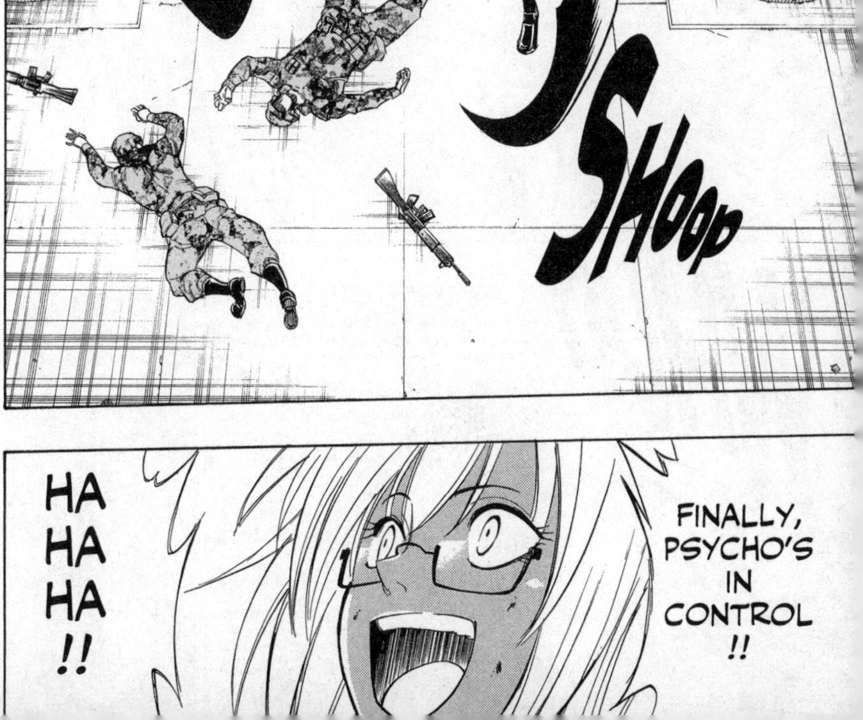
FINALLY, PSYCHO'S IN CONTROL!!
HA HA HA!!

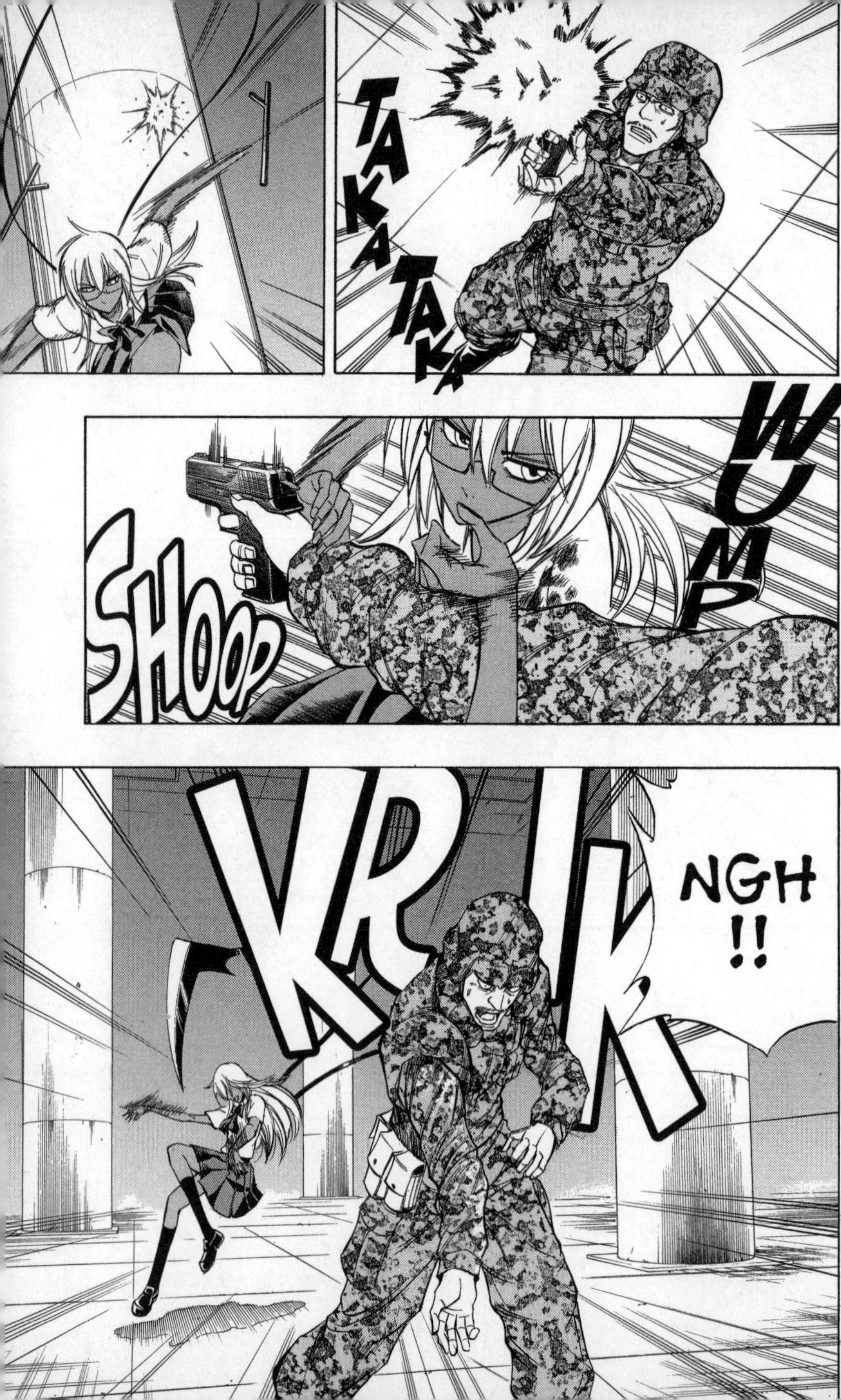
TAKA TAKA
WUMP
SHOOP
NGH!!
KRIK

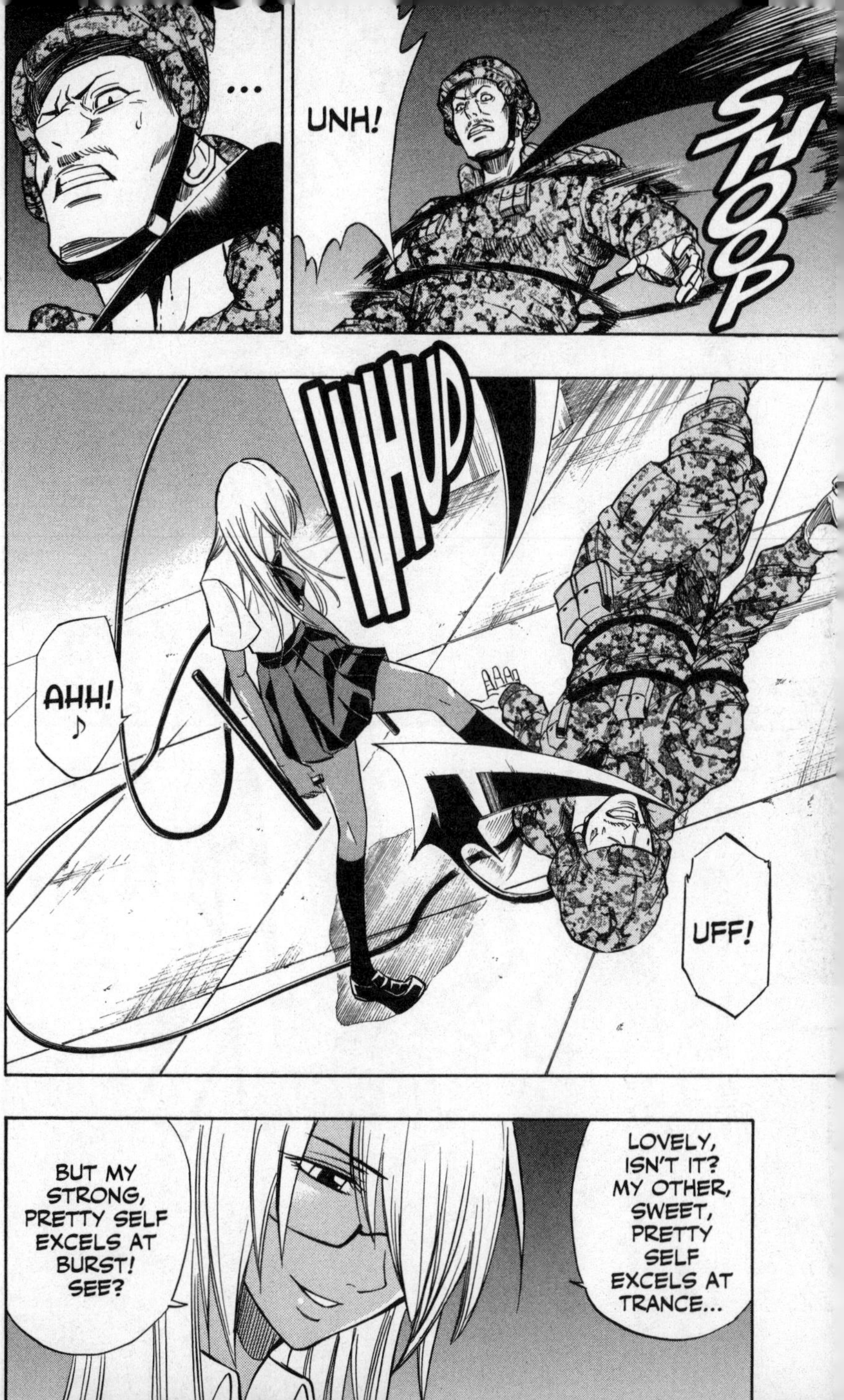
SHOOP
UNH!
...
WHUD
UFF!
AHH! ♪
LOVELY, ISN'T IT? MY OTHER, SWEET, PRETTY SELF EXCELS AT TRANCE...
BUT MY STRONG, PRETTY SELF EXCELS AT BURST! SEE?

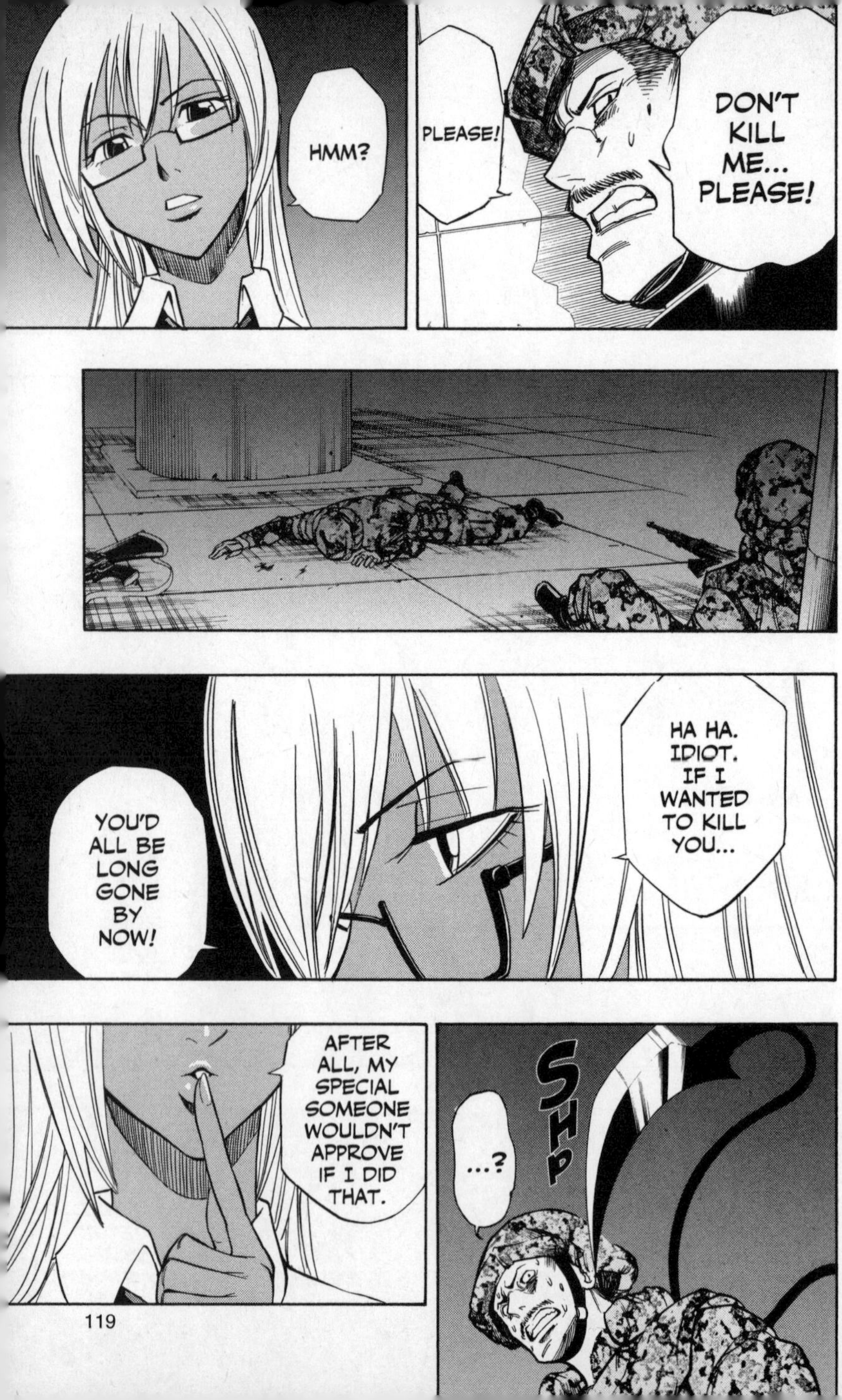
DON'T KILL ME... PLEASE!
PLEASE!
HMM?
HA HA. IDIOT. IF I WANTED TO KILL YOU...
YOU'D ALL BE LONG GONE BY NOW!
SHP
...?
AFTER ALL, MY SPECIAL SOMEONE WOULDN'T APPROVE IF I DID THAT.

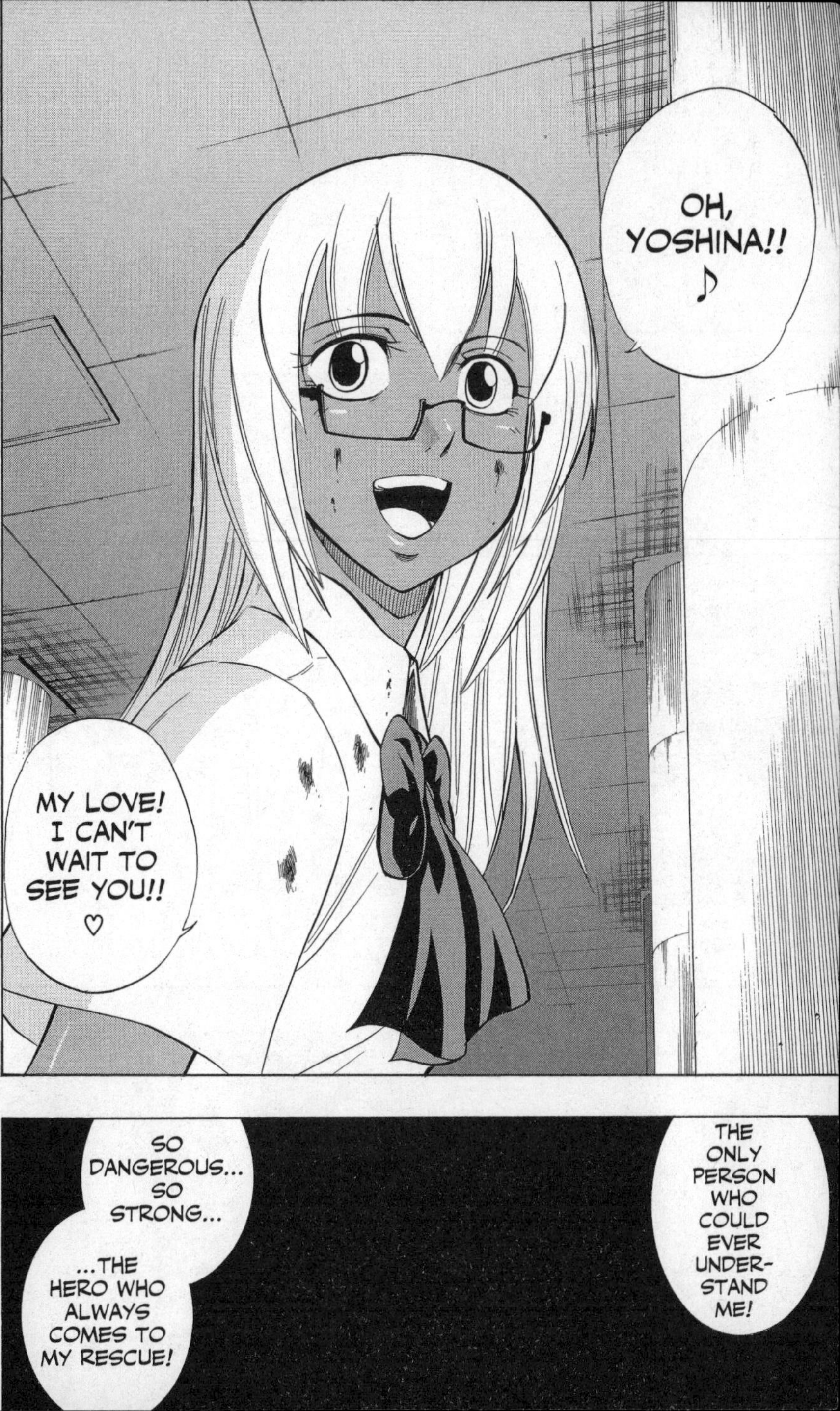
OH, YOSHINA!! ♪
MY LOVE! I CAN'T WAIT TO SEE YOU!! ♡
THE ONLY PERSON WHO COULD EVER UNDER-STAND ME!
SO DANGEROUS... SO STRONG...
...THE HERO WHO ALWAYS COMES TO MY RESCUE!

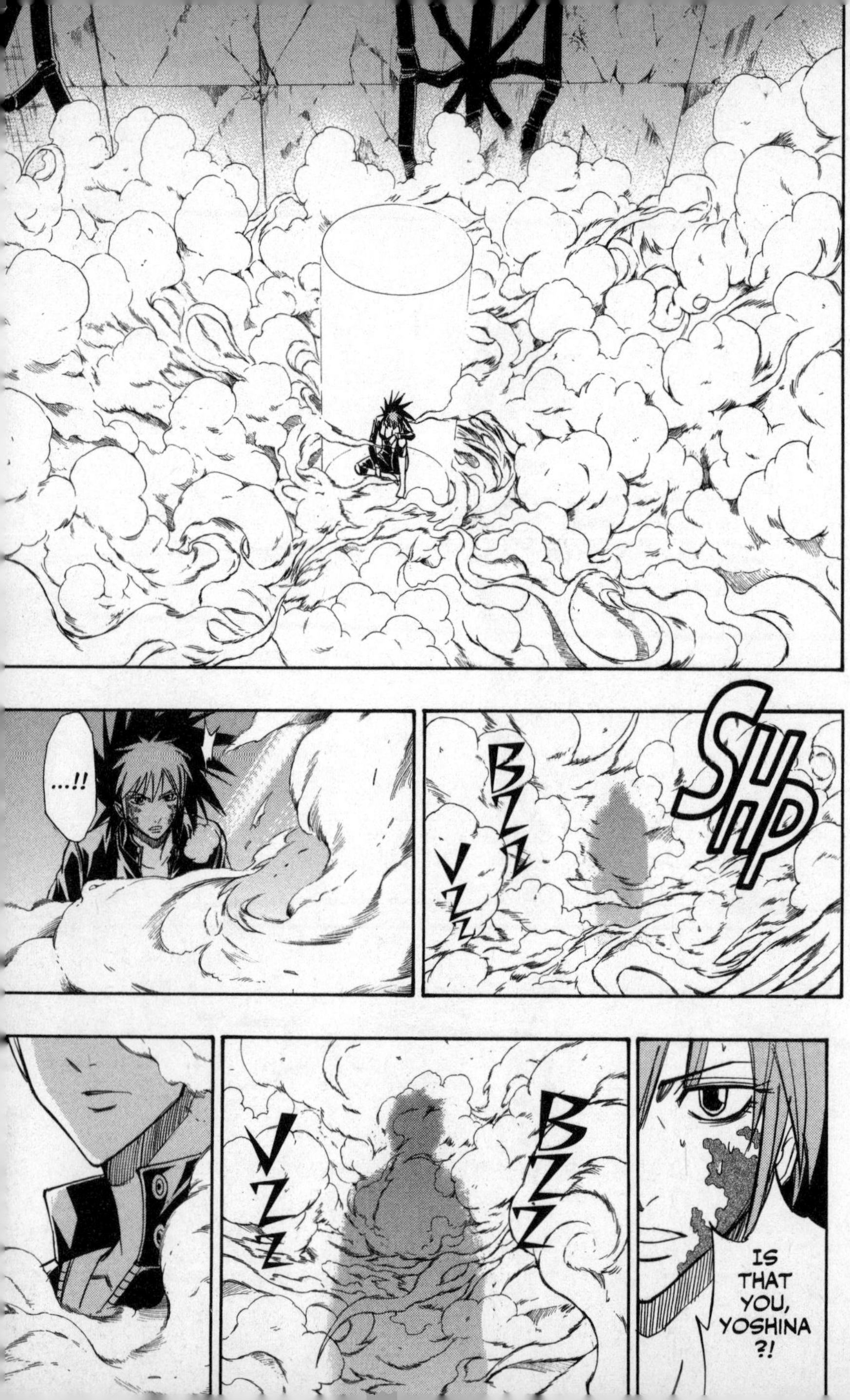
SHP
BZZ
VZZZ
...!!
IS THAT YOU, YOSHINA ?!
BZZZ
VZZZ

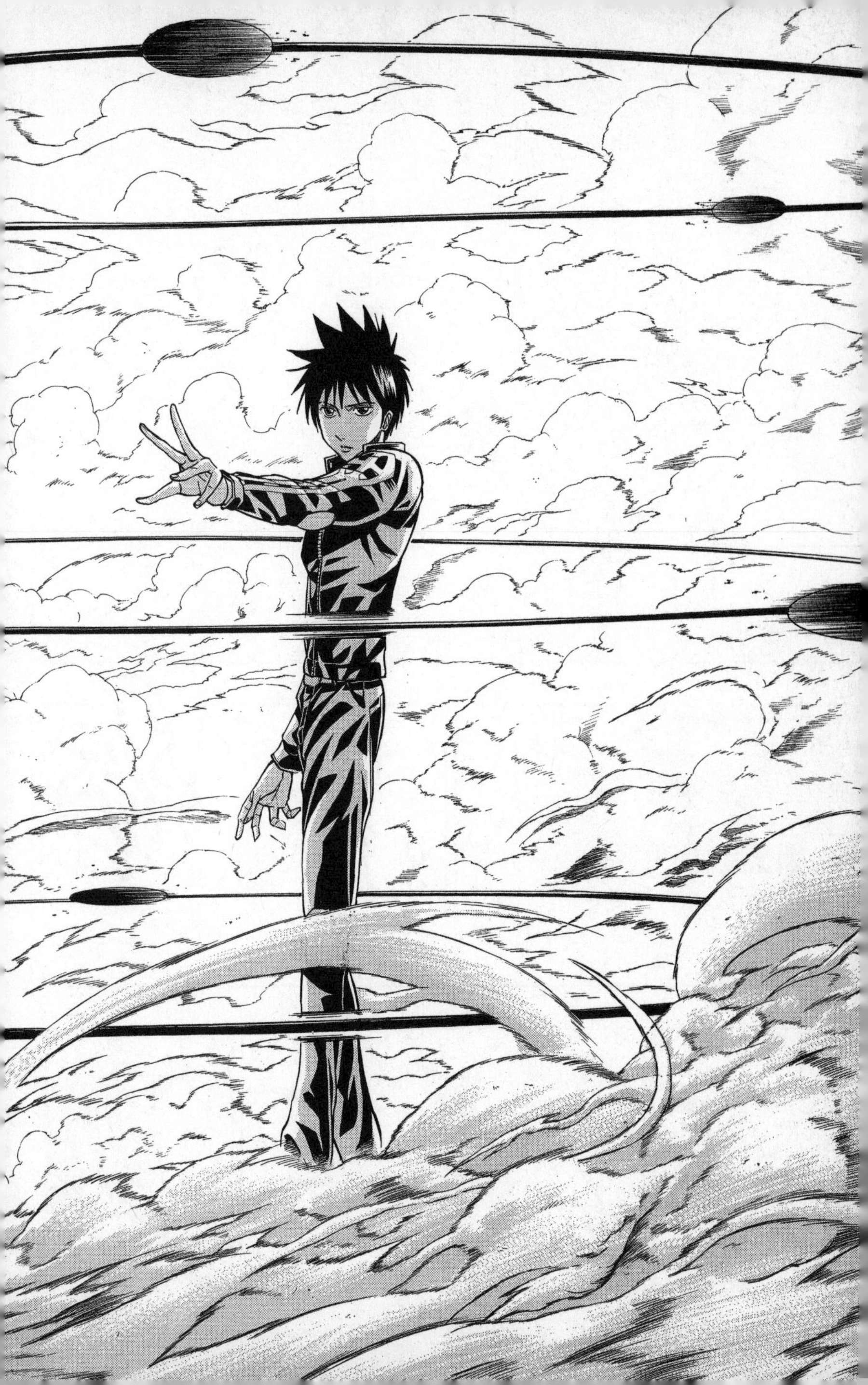

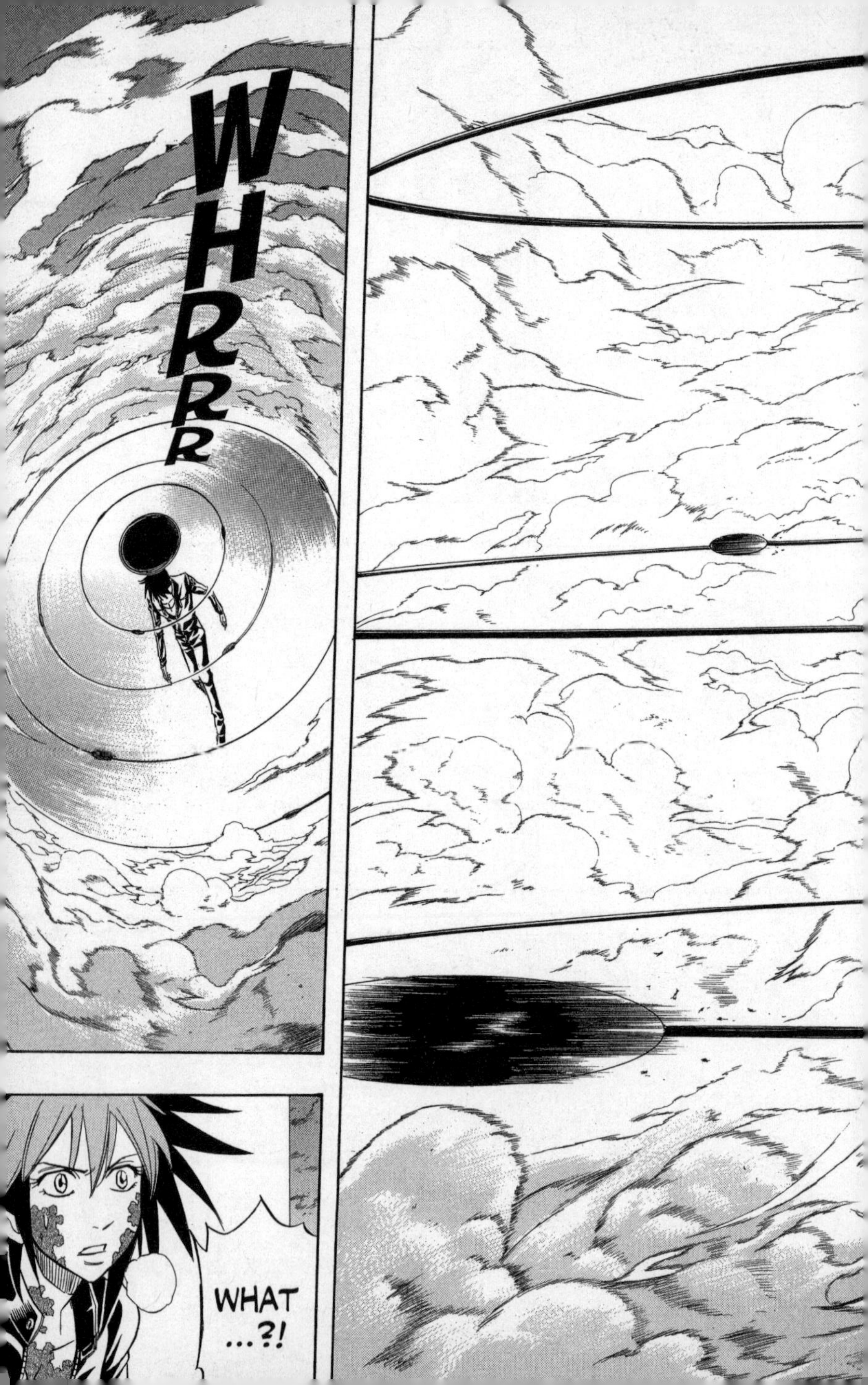
WHRRR
WHAT ...?!

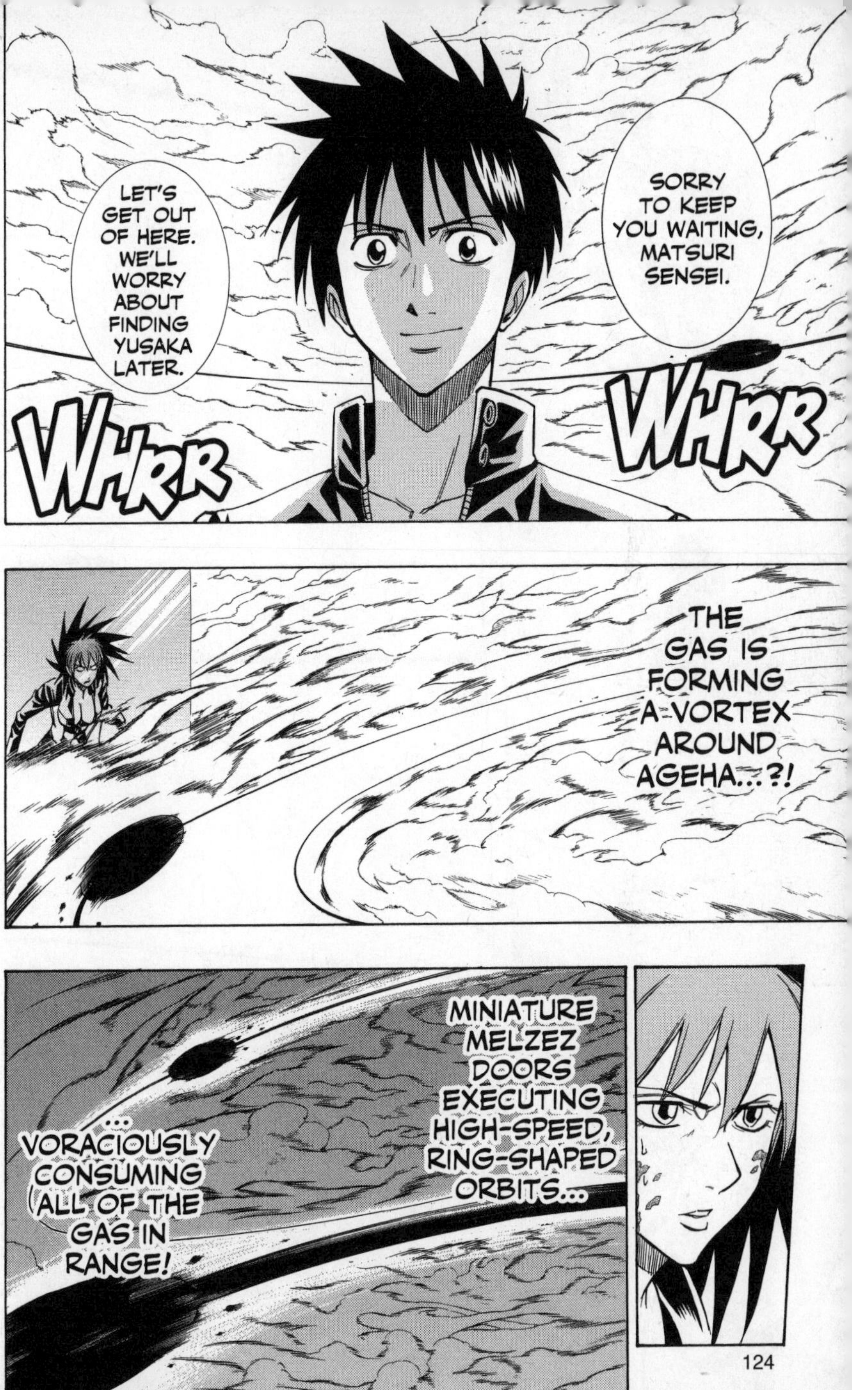
SORRY TO KEEP YOU WAITING, MATSURI SENSEI.
LET'S GET OUT OF HERE. WE'LL WORRY ABOUT FINDING YUSAKA LATER.
WHRR
WHRR
THE GAS IS FORMING A VORTEX AROUND AGEHA...?!
MINIATURE MELZEZ DOORS EXECUTING HIGH-SPEED, RING-SHAPED ORBITS...
...VORACIOUSLY CONSUMING ALL OF THE GAS IN RANGE!

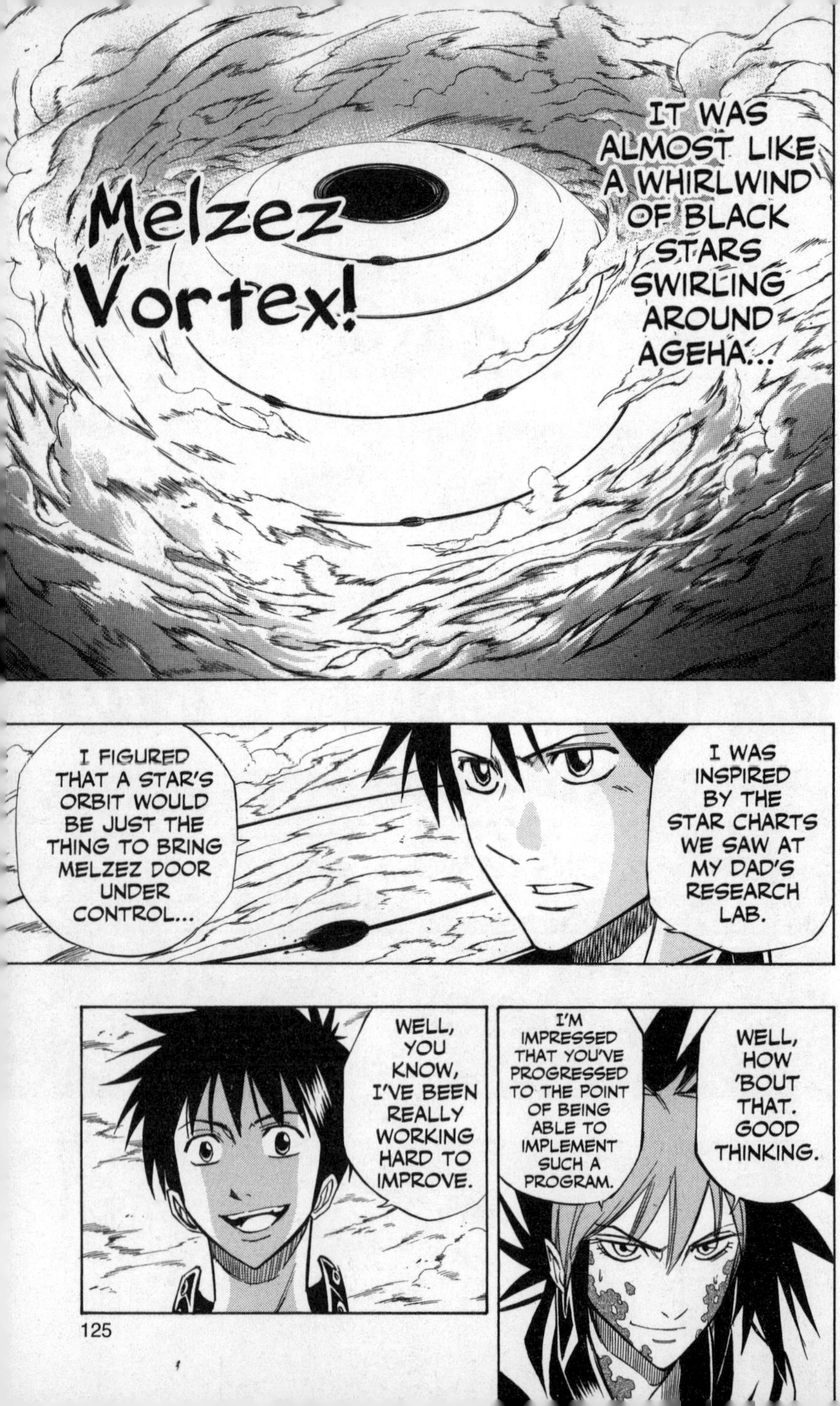
IT WAS ALMOST LIKE A WHIRLWIND OF BLACK STARS SWIRLING AROUND AGEHA...
Melzez Vortex!
I WAS INSPIRED BY THE STAR CHARTS WE SAW AT MY DAD'S RESEARCH LAB.
I FIGURED THAT A STAR'S ORBIT WOULD BE JUST THE THING TO BRING MELZEZ DOOR UNDER CONTROL...
WELL, HOW 'BOUT THAT. GOOD THINKING.
I'M IMPRESSED THAT YOU'VE PROGRESSED TO THE POINT OF BEING ABLE TO IMPLEMENT SUCH A PROGRAM.
WELL, YOU KNOW, I'VE BEEN REALLY WORKING HARD TO IMPROVE.

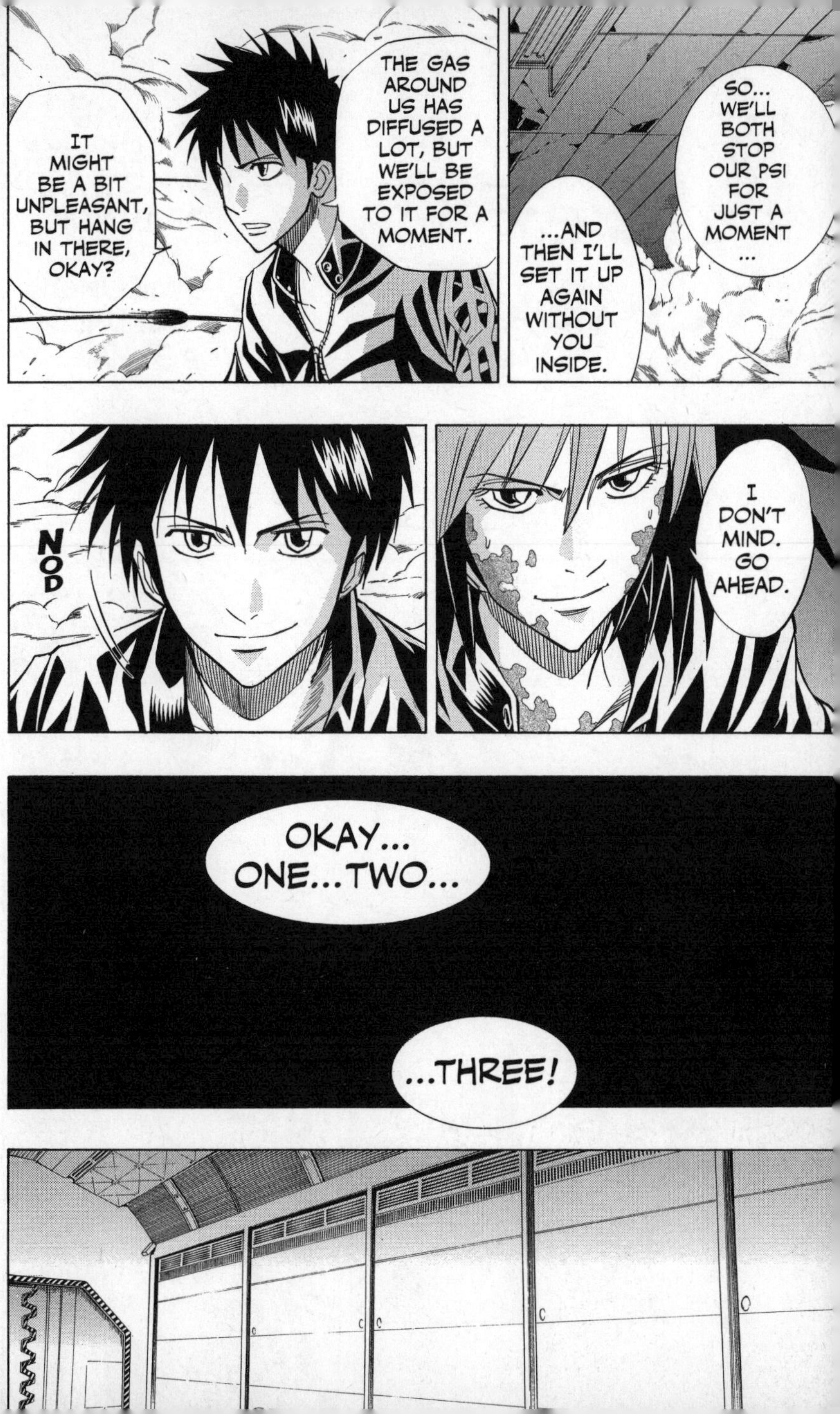
SO... WE'LL BOTH STOP OUR PSI FOR JUST A MOMENT ...
...AND THEN I'LL SET IT UP AGAIN WITHOUT YOU INSIDE.
THE GAS AROUND US HAS DIFFUSED A LOT, BUT WE'LL BE EXPOSED TO IT FOR A MOMENT.
IT MIGHT BE A BIT UNPLEASANT, BUT HANG IN THERE, OKAY?
I DON'T MIND. GO AHEAD.
NOD
OKAY... ONE...TWO...
...THREE!

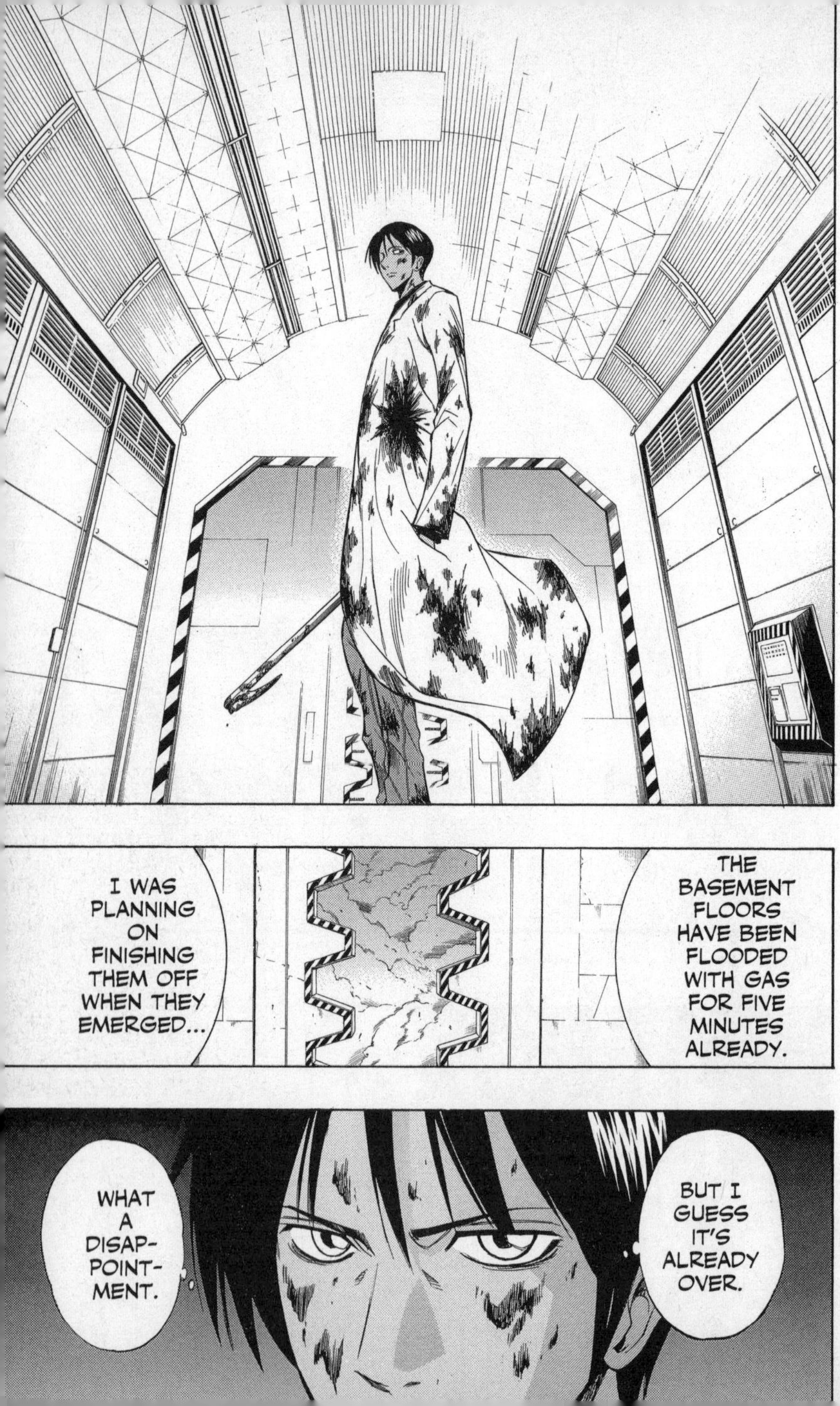
THE BASEMENT FLOORS HAVE BEEN FLOODED WITH GAS FOR FIVE MINUTES ALREADY.
I WAS PLANNING ON FINISHING THEM OFF WHEN THEY EMERGED...
BUT I GUESS IT'S ALREADY OVER.
WHAT A DISAP-POINT-MENT.

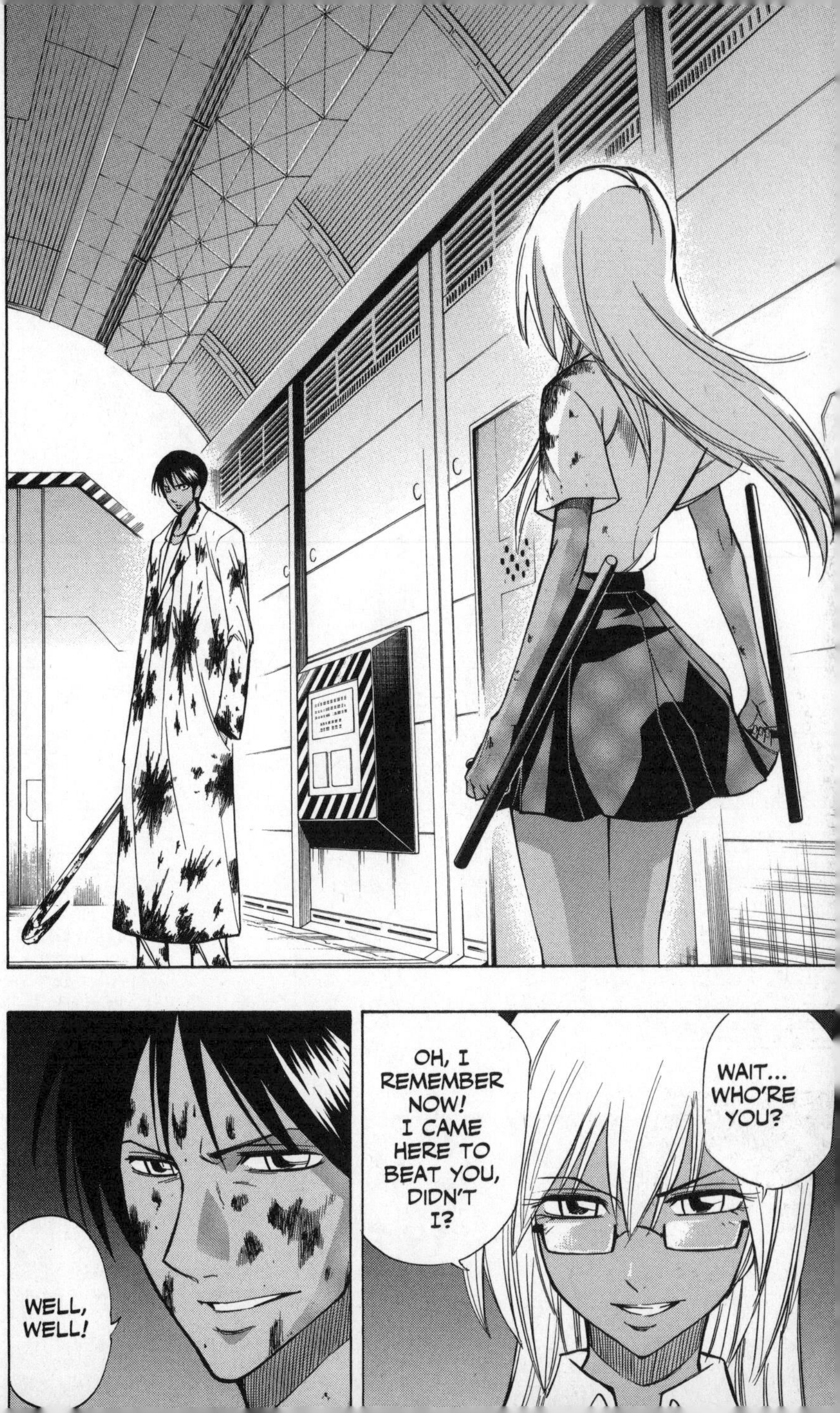
WAIT... WHO'RE YOU?
OH, I REMEMBER NOW! I CAME HERE TO BEAT YOU, DIDN'T I?
WELL, WELL!

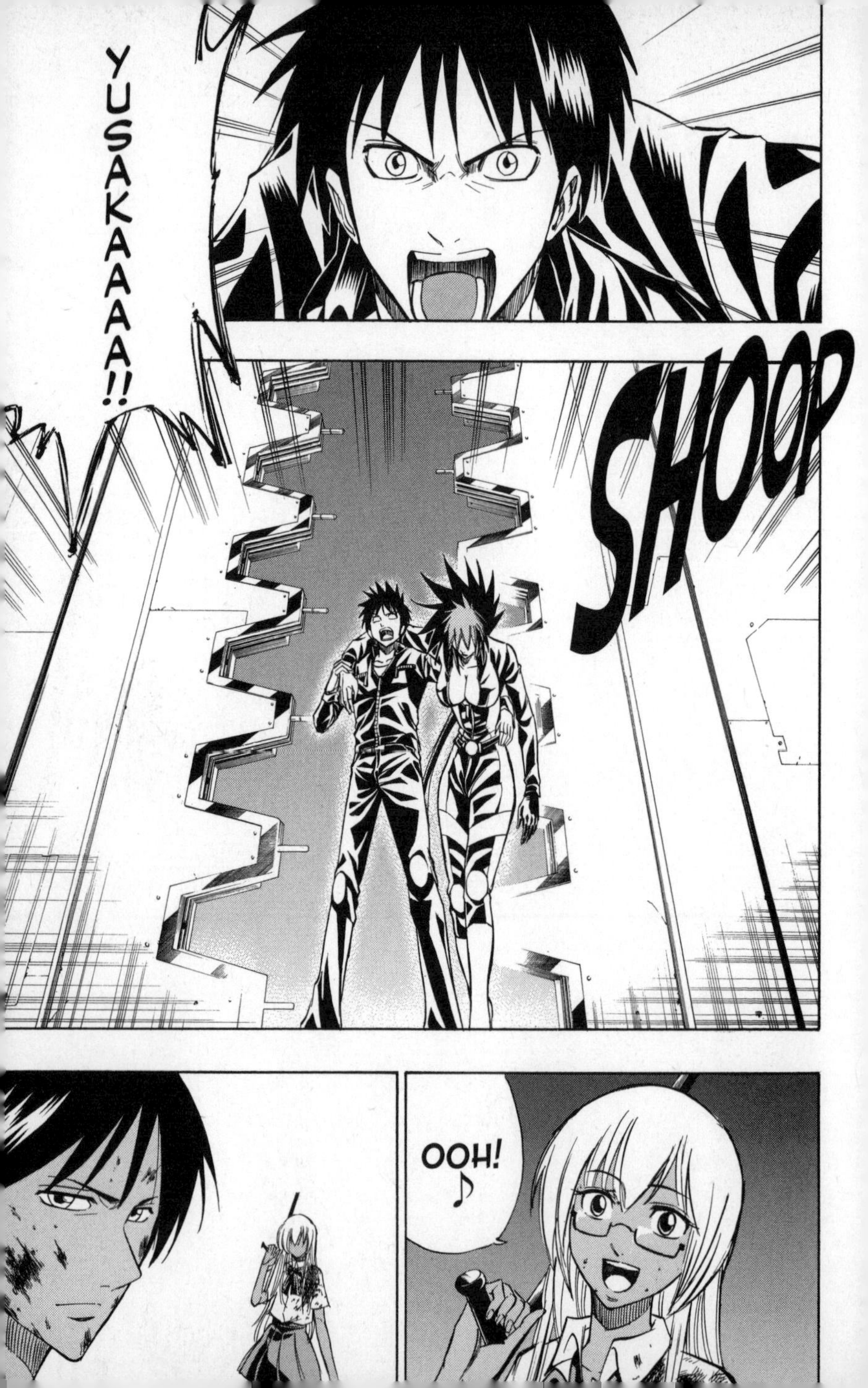
YUSAKAAAAAA!!
SHOOP
OOH! ♪

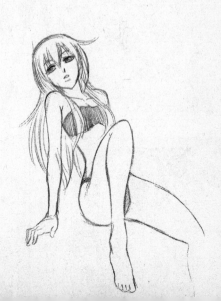

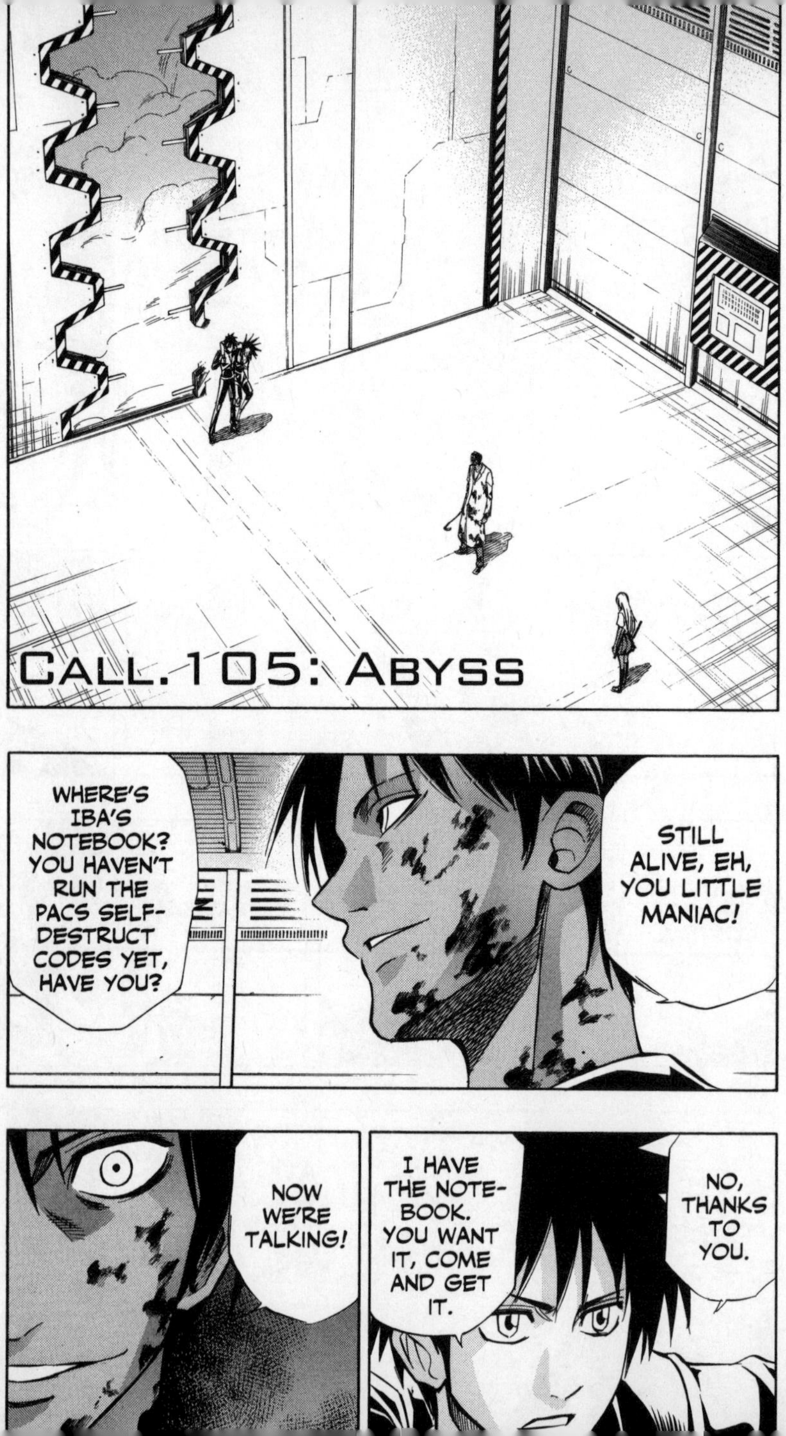
CALL. 105: ABYSS
STILL ALIVE, EH, YOU LITTLE MANIAC!
WHERE'S IBA'S NOTEBOOK? YOU HAVEN'T RUN THE PACS SELF-DESTRUCT CODES YET, HAVE YOU?
NO, THANKS TO YOU.
I HAVE THE NOTE-BOOK. YOU WANT IT, COME AND GET IT.
NOW WE'RE TALKING!

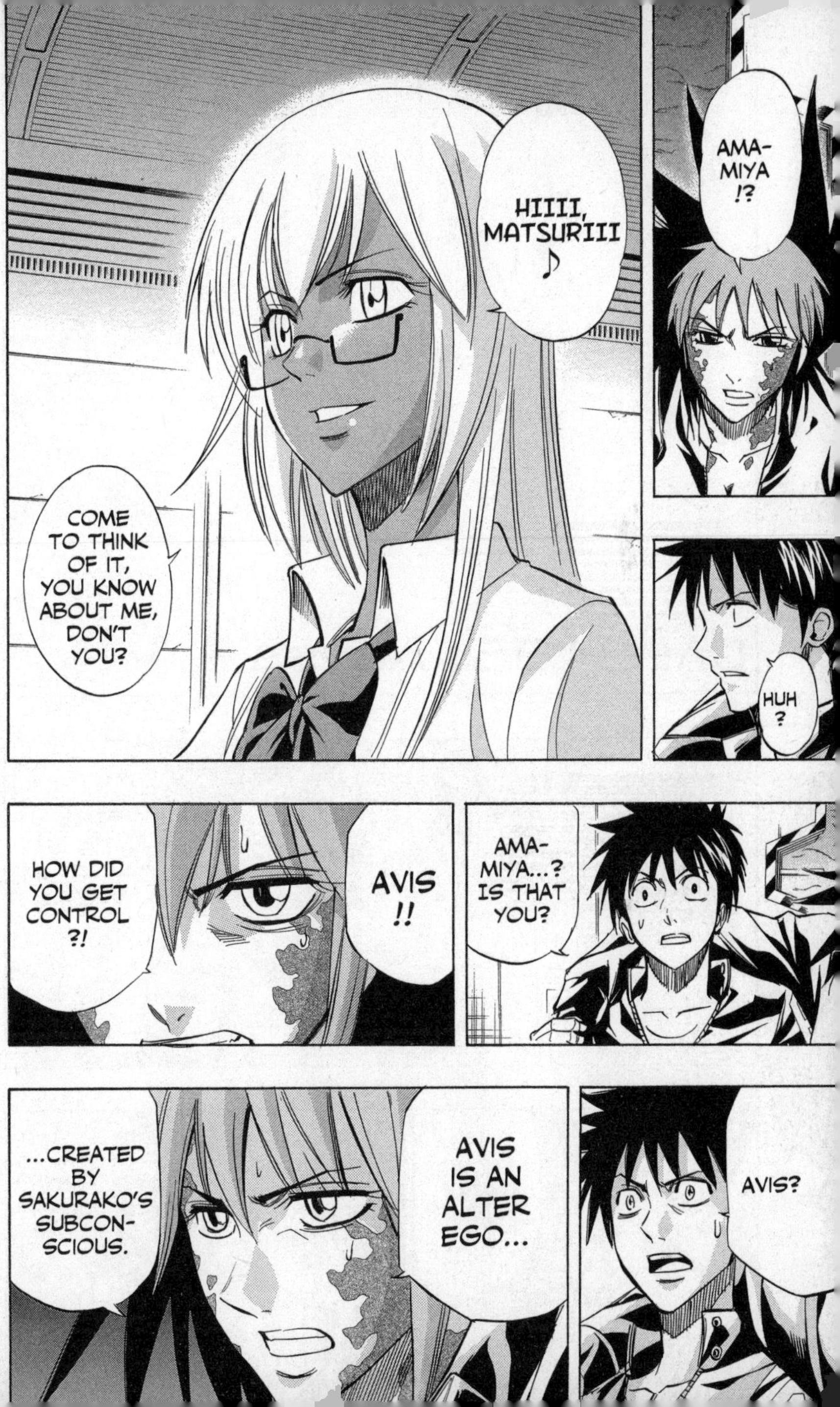
AMA-MIYA !?
HUH ?
HIIII, MATSURIII ♪
COME TO THINK OF IT, YOU KNOW ABOUT ME, DON'T YOU?
AMA-MIYA...? IS THAT YOU?
AVIS !!
HOW DID YOU GET CONTROL ?!
AVIS?
AVIS IS AN ALTER EGO...
...CREATED BY SAKURAKO'S SUBCONSCIOUS.

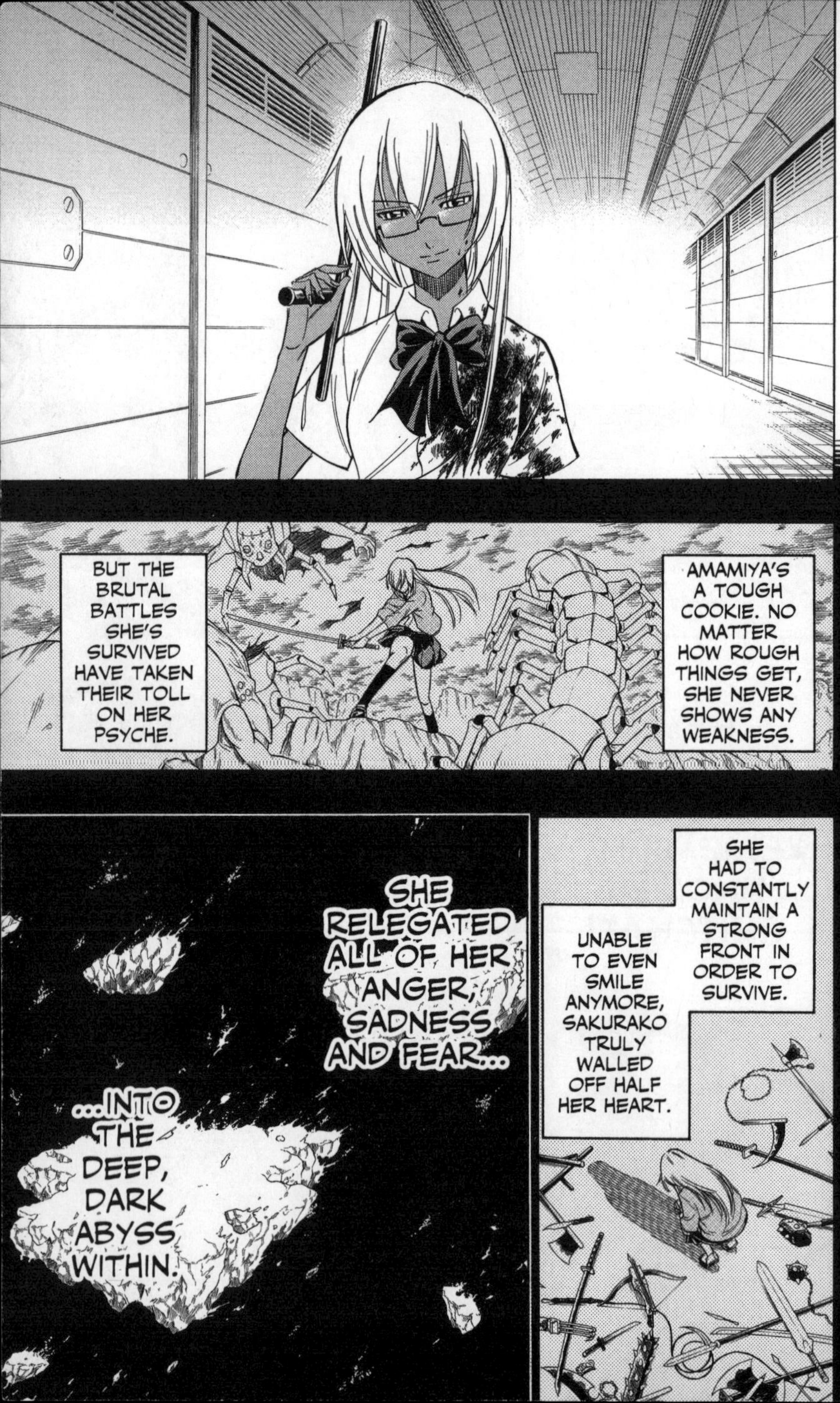
AMAMIYA'S A TOUGH COOKIE. NO MATTER HOW ROUGH THINGS GET, SHE NEVER SHOWS ANY WEAKNESS.
BUT THE BRUTAL BATTLES SHE'S SURVIVED HAVE TAKEN THEIR TOLL ON HER PSYCHE.
SHE HAD TO CONSTANTLY MAINTAIN A STRONG FRONT IN ORDER TO SURVIVE.
UNABLE TO EVEN SMILE ANYMORE, SAKURAKO TRULY WALLED OFF HALF HER HEART.
SHE RELEGATED ALL OF HER ANGER, SADNESS AND FEAR...
...INTO THE DEEP, DARK ABYSS WITHIN.

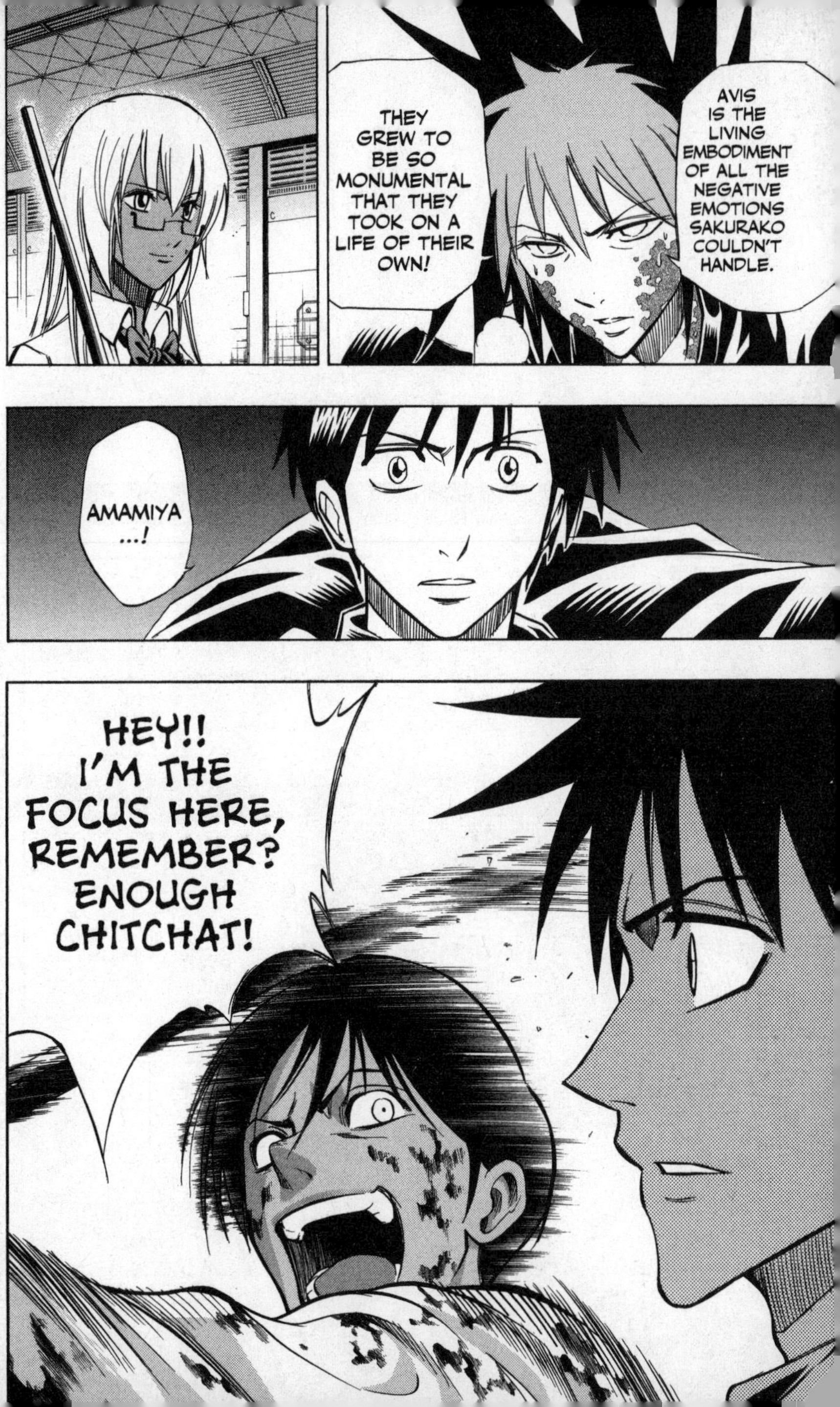
AVIS IS THE LIVING EMBODIMENT OF ALL THE NEGATIVE EMOTIONS SAKURAKO COULDN'T HANDLE.
THEY GREW TO BE SO MONUMENTAL THAT THEY TOOK ON A LIFE OF THEIR OWN!
AMAMIYA ...!
HEY!! I'M THE FOCUS HERE, REMEMBER? ENOUGH CHITCHAT!

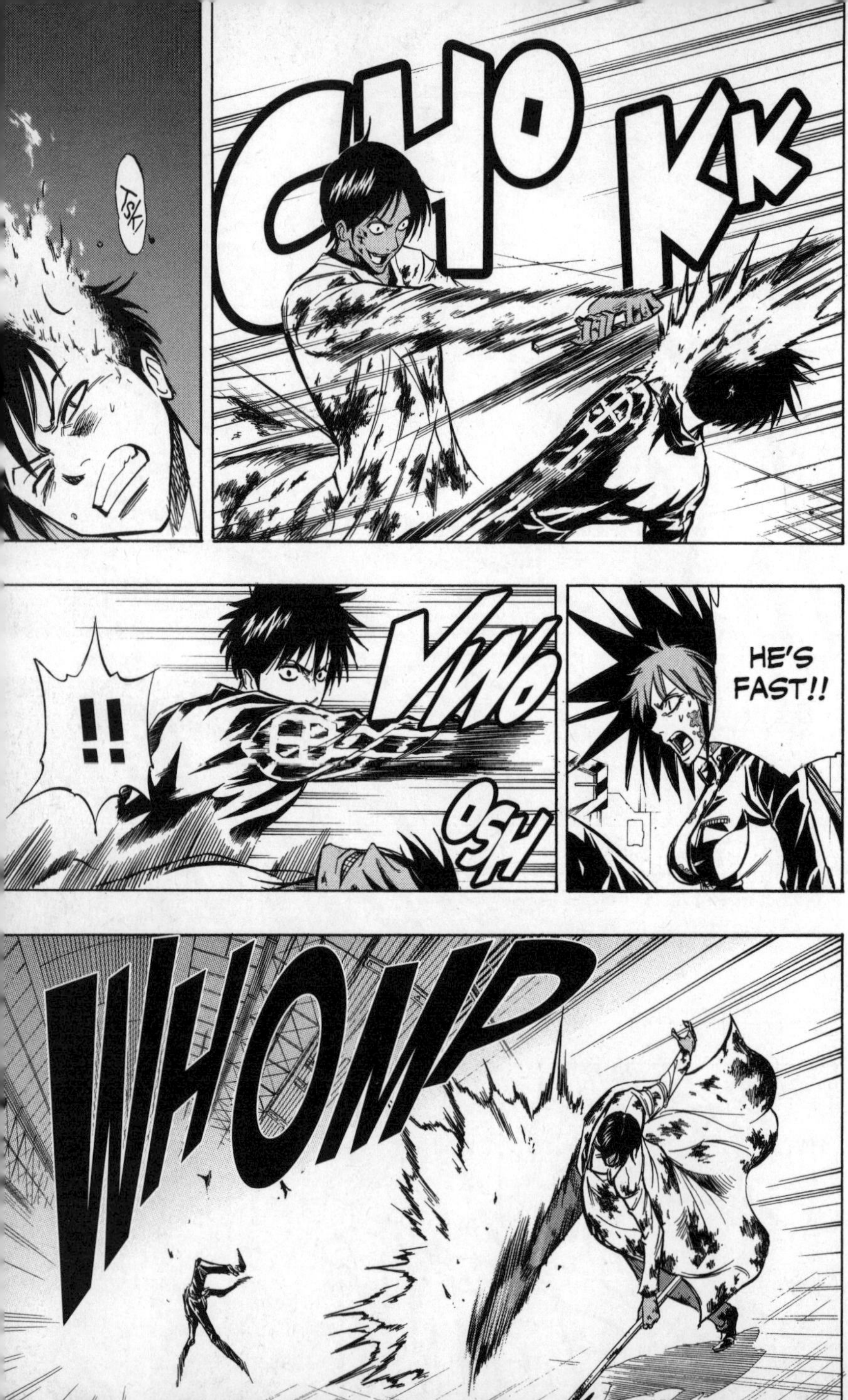
CHOKK
TSK!
HE'S FAST!!
VWOOSH
!!
WHOMP

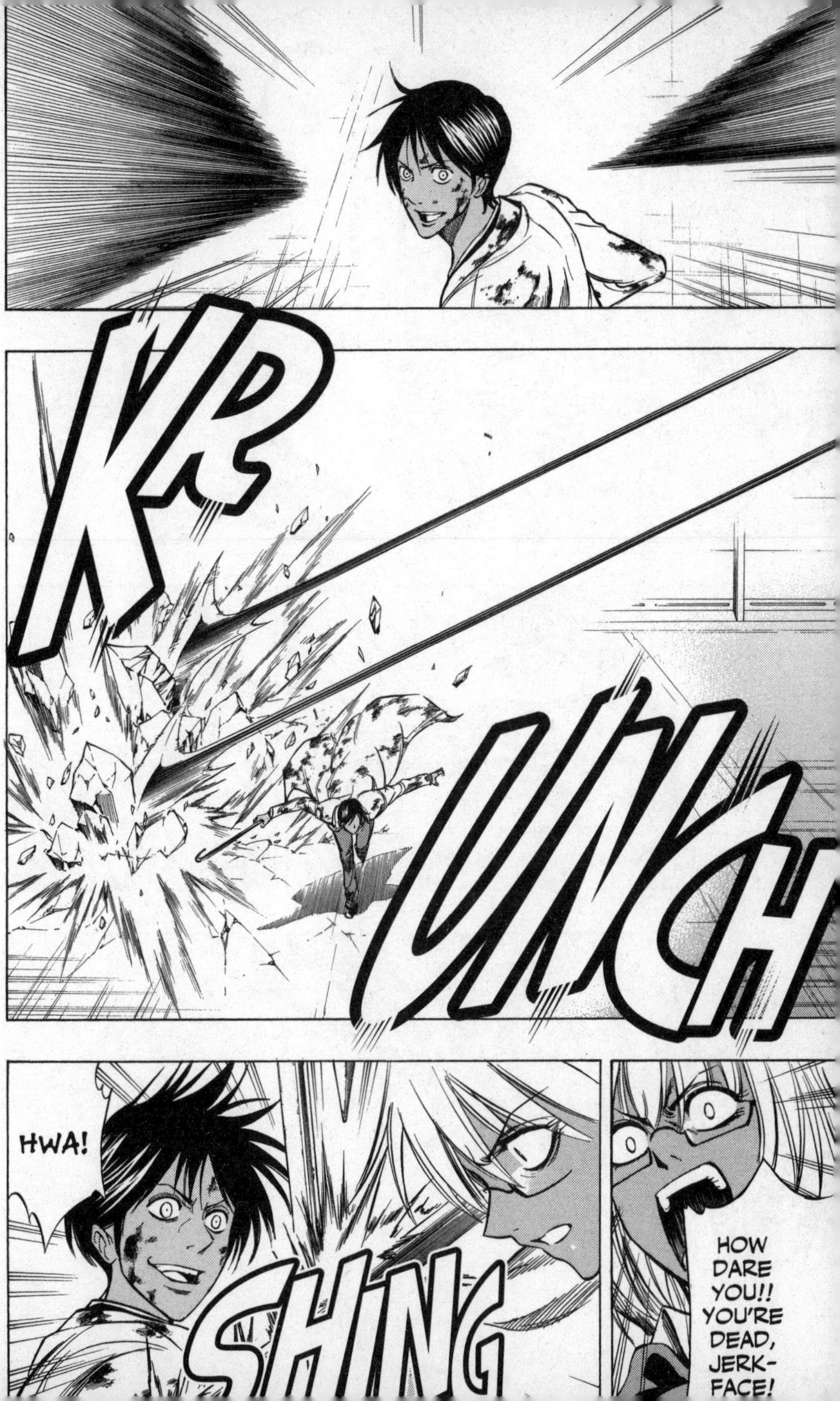
KRUNCH
HOW DARE YOU!! YOU'RE DEAD, JERK-FACE!
HWA!
SHING

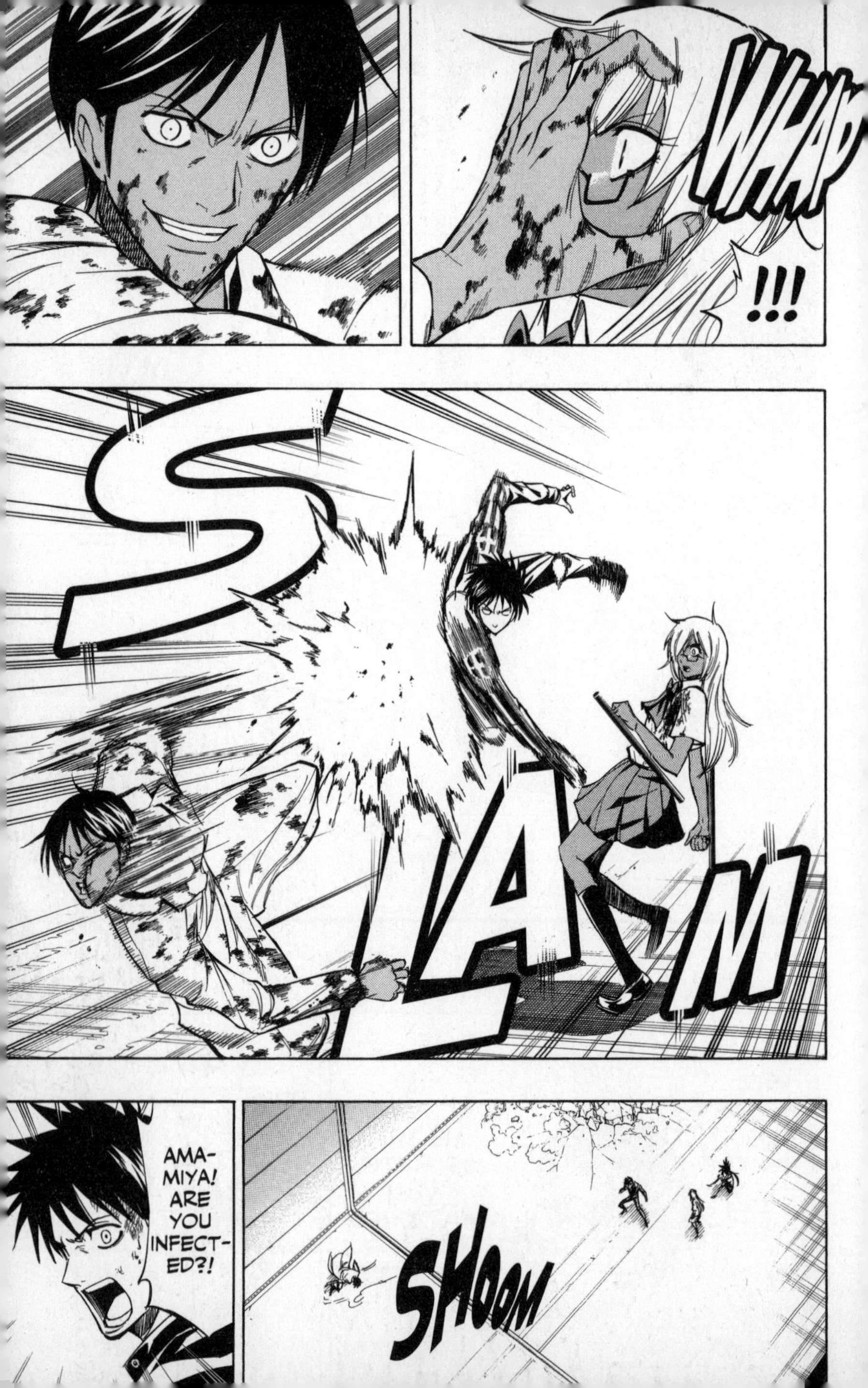
WHAP
!!!
SLAM
SHOOM
AMA-MIYA! ARE YOU INFECT-ED?!

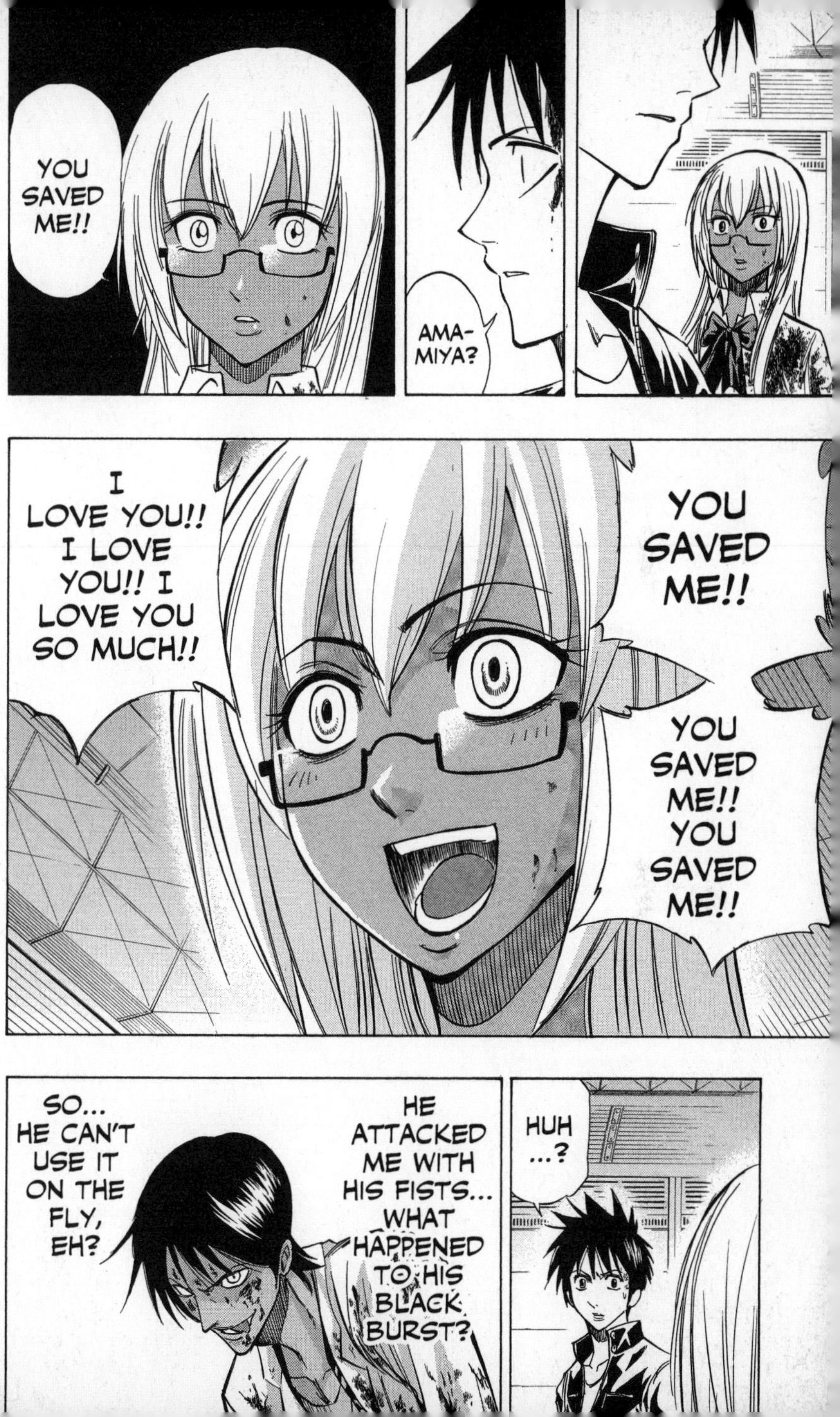
AMA-MIYA?
YOU SAVED ME!!
YOU SAVED ME!!
YOU SAVED ME!! YOU SAVED ME!!
I LOVE YOU!! I LOVE YOU!! I LOVE YOU SO MUCH!!
HUH ...?
HE ATTACKED ME WITH HIS FISTS... WHAT HAPPENED TO HIS BLACK BURST?
SO... HE CAN'T USE IT ON THE FLY, EH?

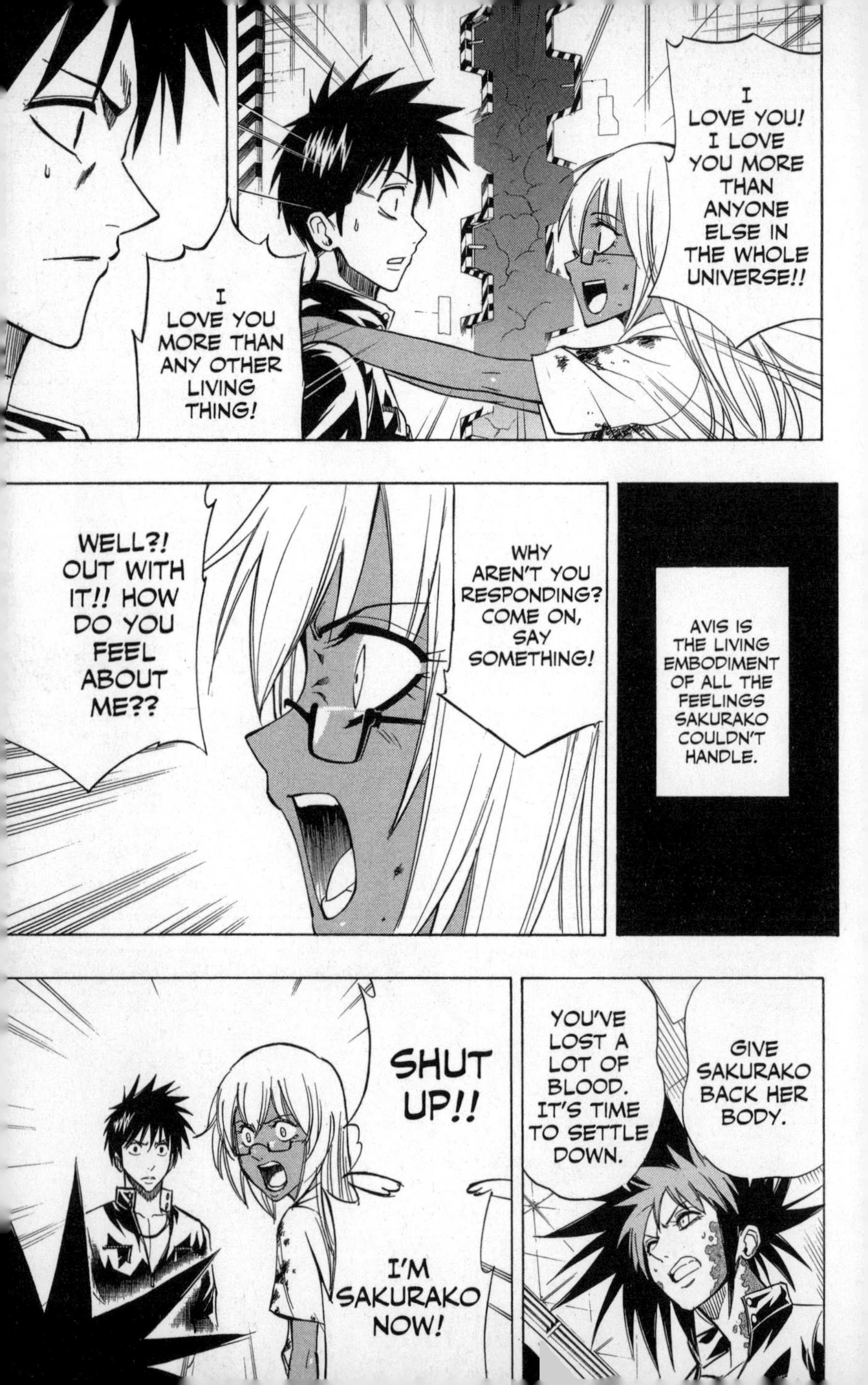
I LOVE YOU! I LOVE YOU MORE THAN ANYONE ELSE IN THE WHOLE UNIVERSE!!
I LOVE YOU MORE THAN ANY OTHER LIVING THING!
AVIS IS THE LIVING EMBODIMENT OF ALL THE FEELINGS SAKURAKO COULDN'T HANDLE.
WHY AREN'T YOU RESPONDING? COME ON, SAY SOMETHING!
WELL?! OUT WITH IT!! HOW DO YOU FEEL ABOUT ME??
GIVE SAKURAKO BACK HER BODY.
YOU'VE LOST A LOT OF BLOOD. IT'S TIME TO SETTLE DOWN.
SHUT UP!!
I'M SAKURAKO NOW!

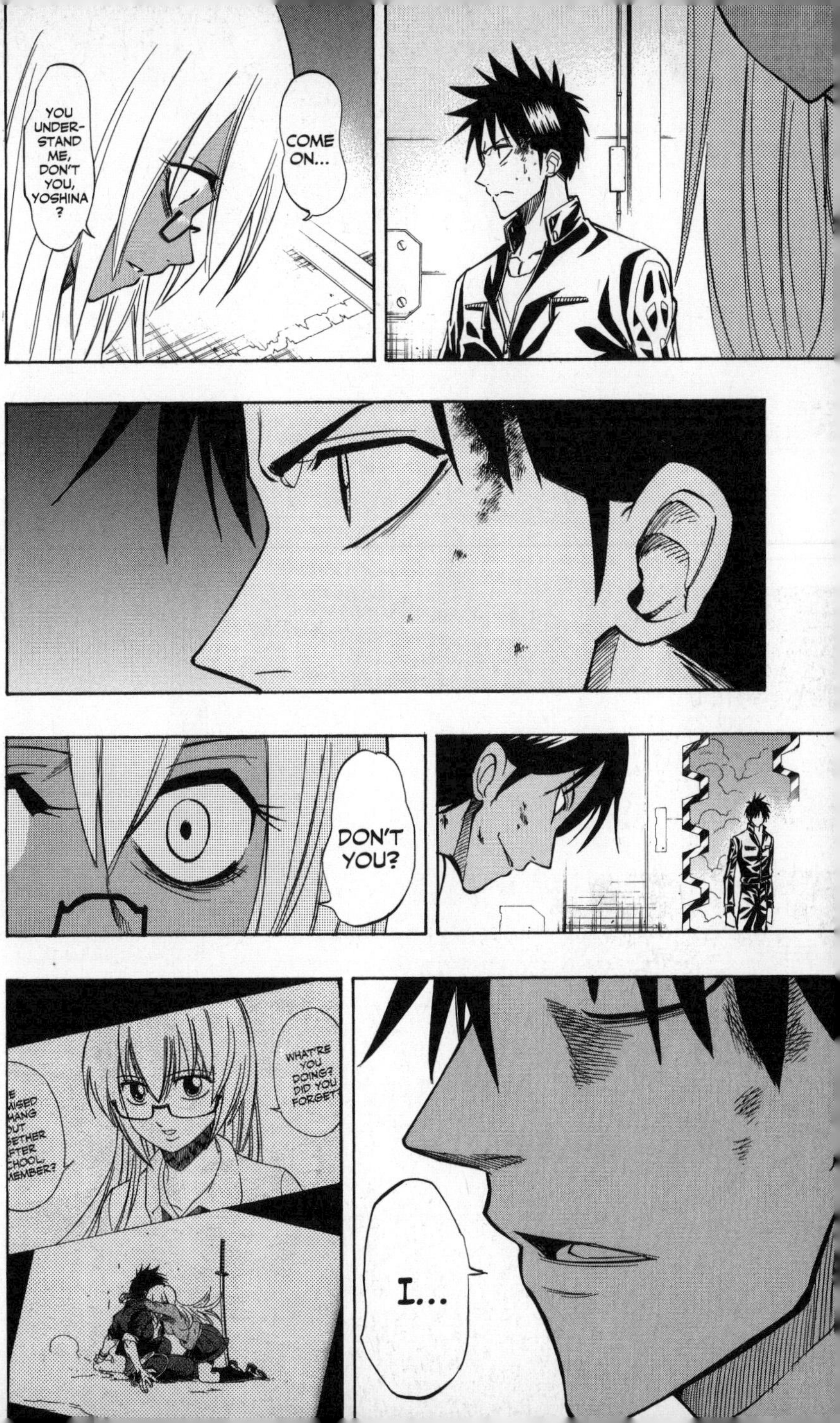
COME ON...
YOU UNDERSTAND ME, DON'T YOU, YOSHINA?
DON'T YOU?
I...
WHAT'RE YOU DOING? DID YOU FORGET?

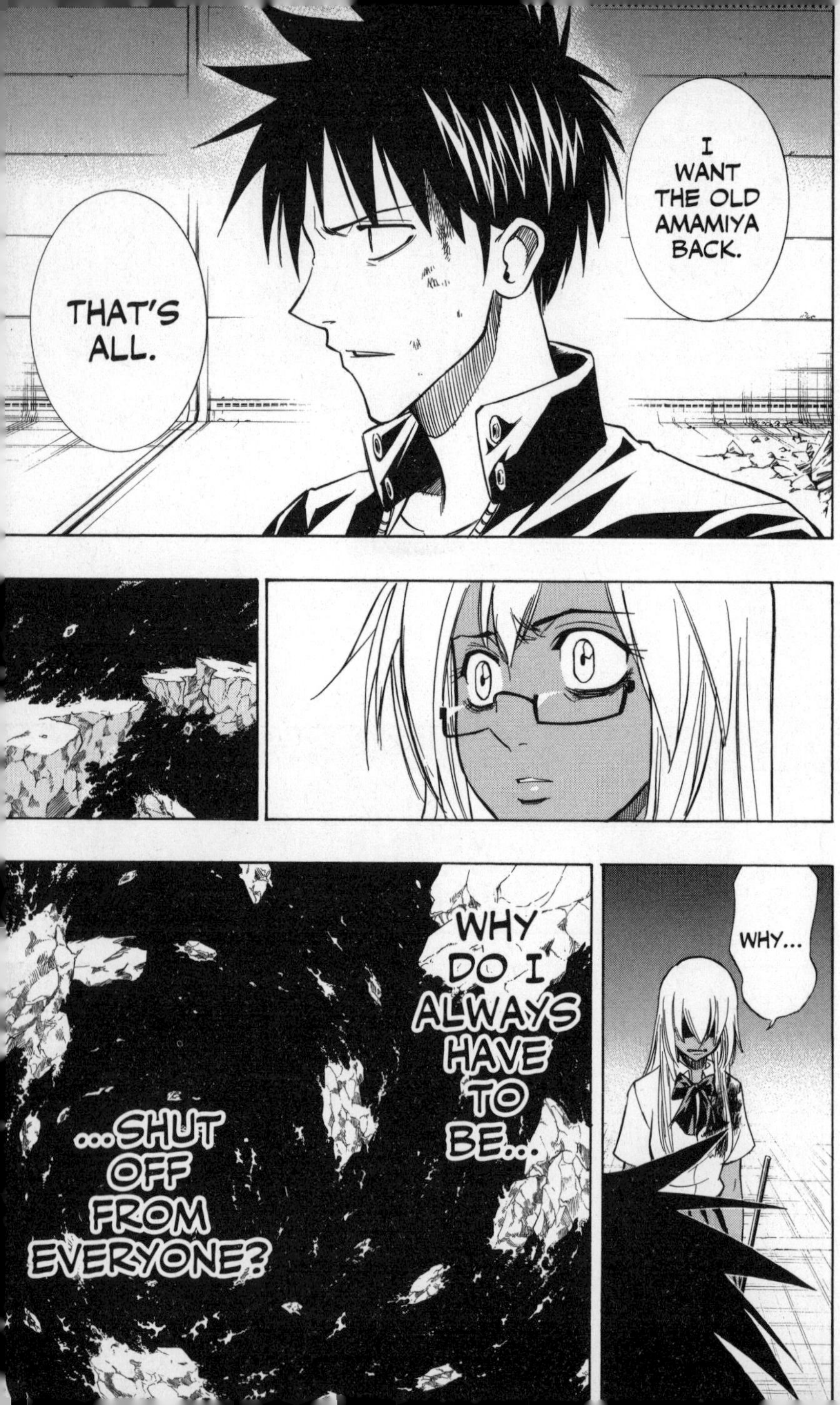
I WANT THE OLD AMAMIYA BACK.
THAT'S ALL.
WHY...
WHY DO I ALWAYS HAVE TO BE...
...SHUT OFF FROM EVERYONE?

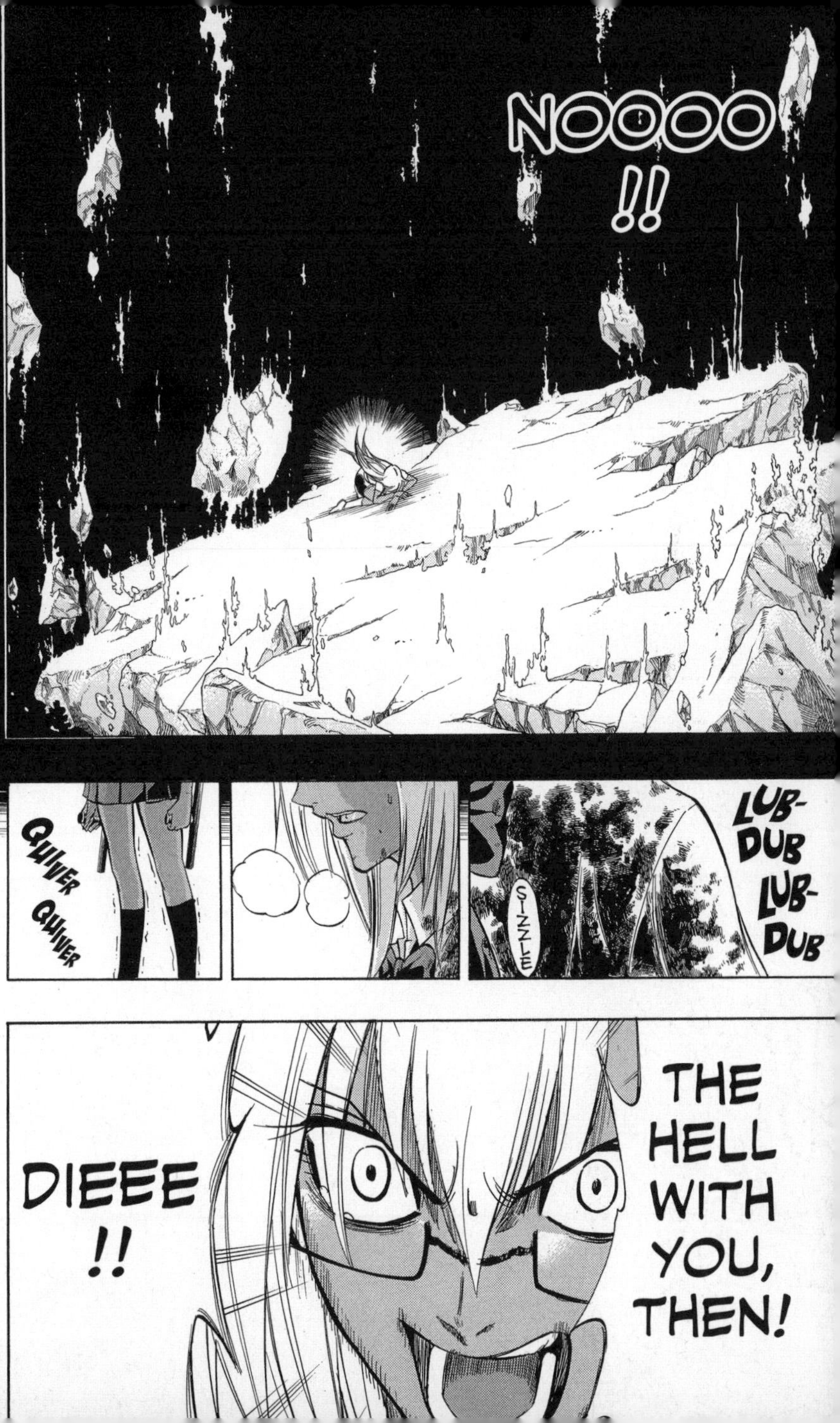
NOOOO!!
LUB-DUB LUB-DUB
SIZZLE
QUIVER QUIVER
THE HELL WITH YOU, THEN!
DIEEE!!

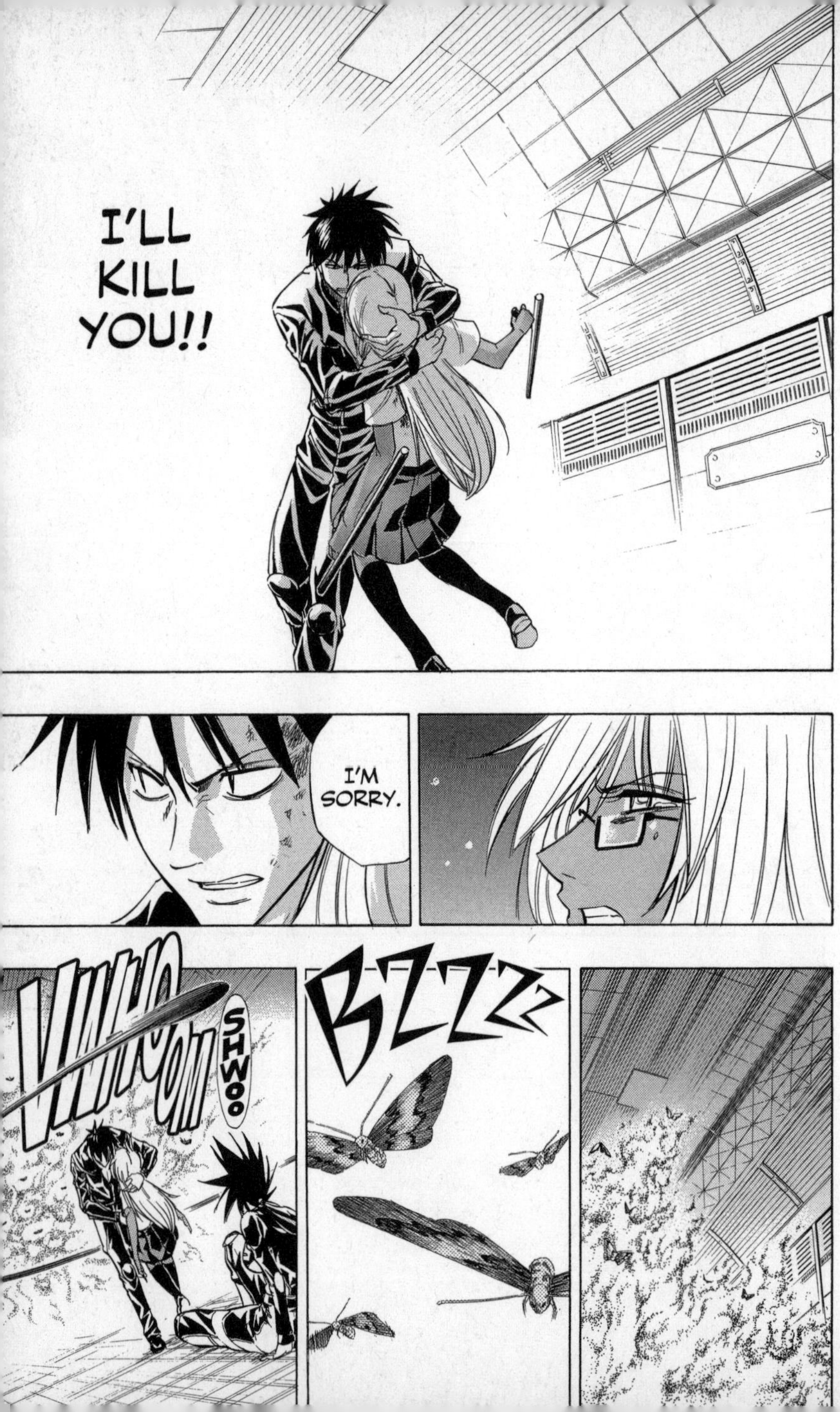
I'LL KILL YOU!!
I'M SORRY.
VWHOOM
SHWOO
BZZZZ

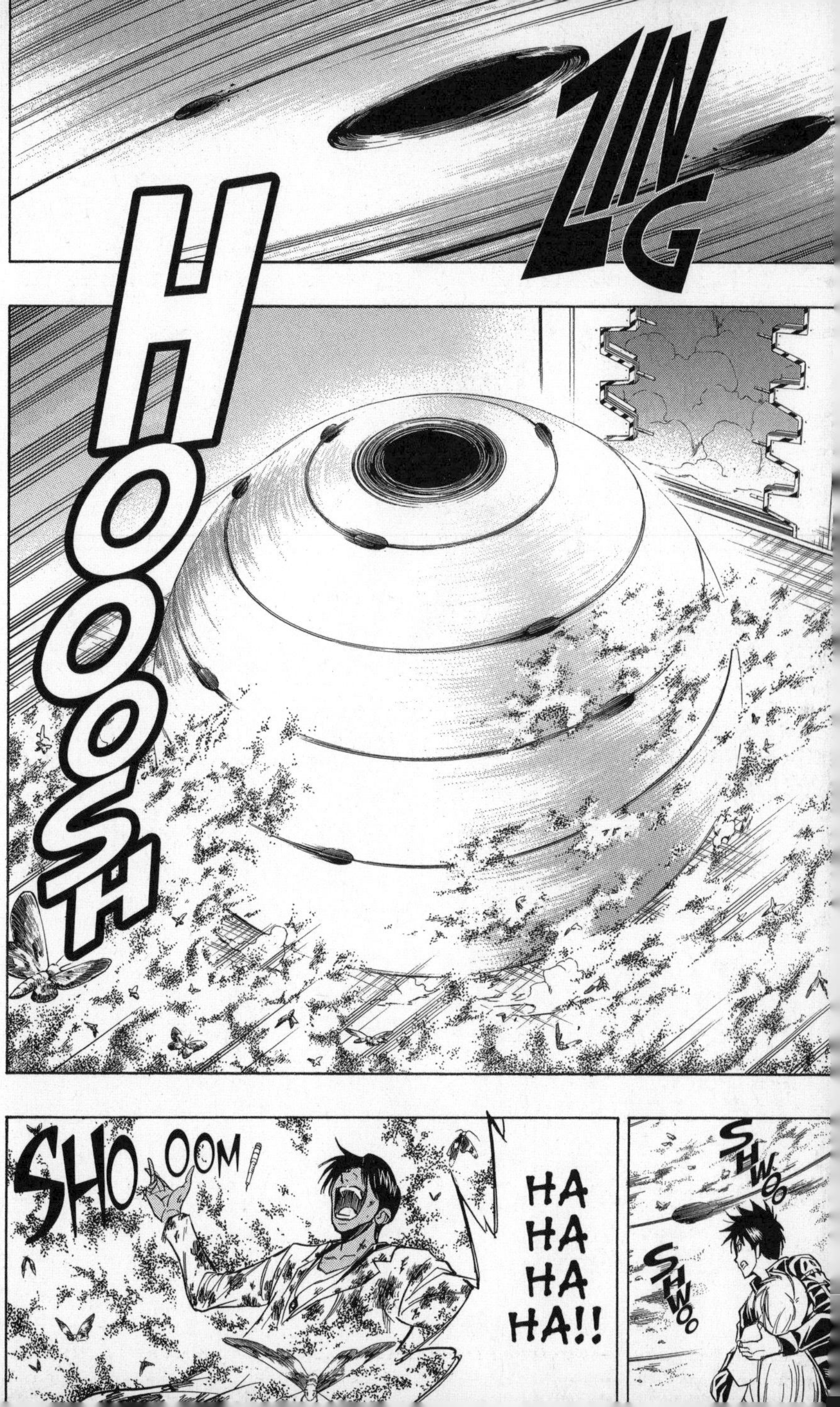
ZING
HOOOOSH
SHWOO
SHWOO
SHOOOM
HA HA HA HA!!

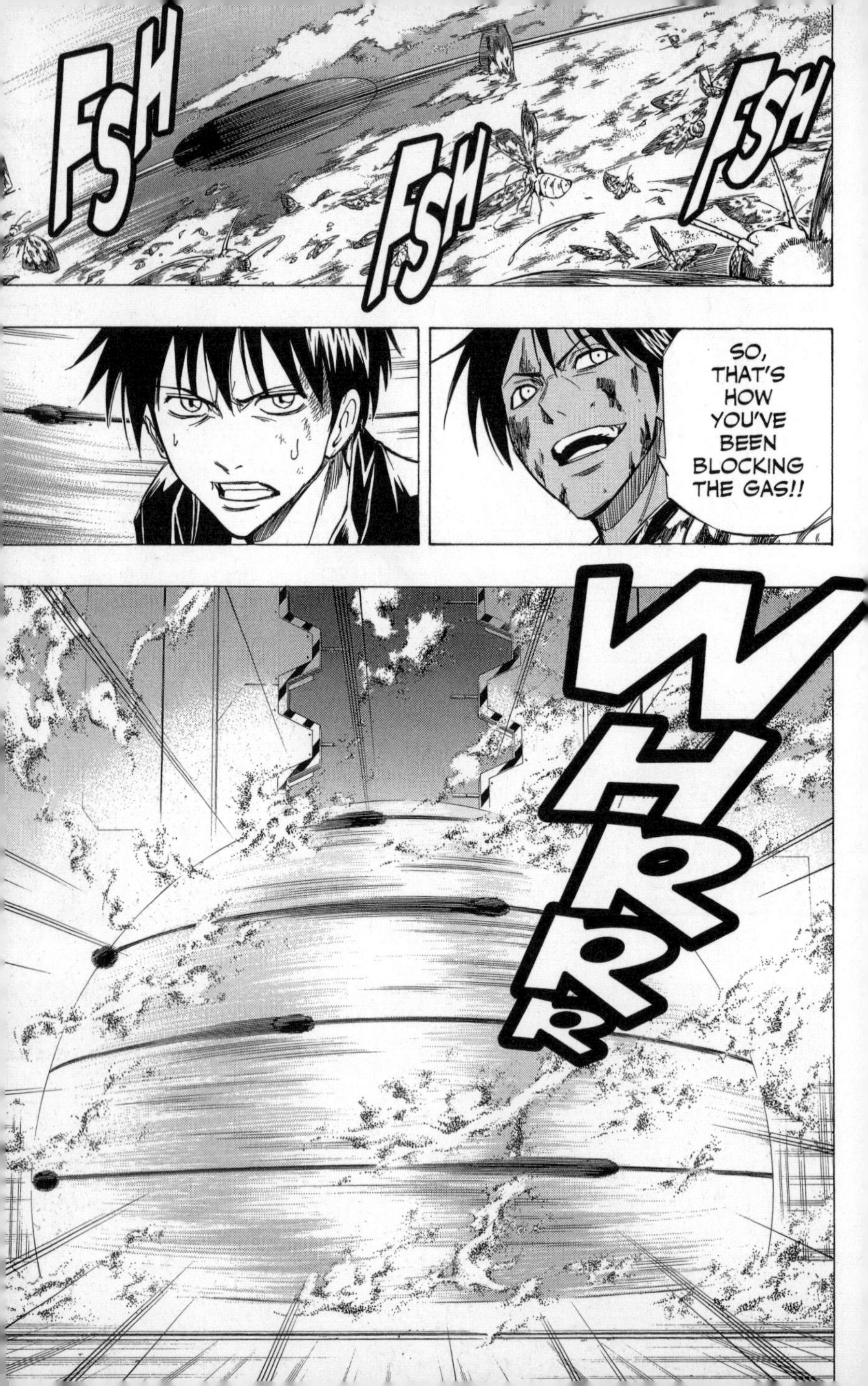
FSH
FSH
FSH
SO, THAT'S HOW YOU'VE BEEN BLOCKING THE GAS!!
WHRRR

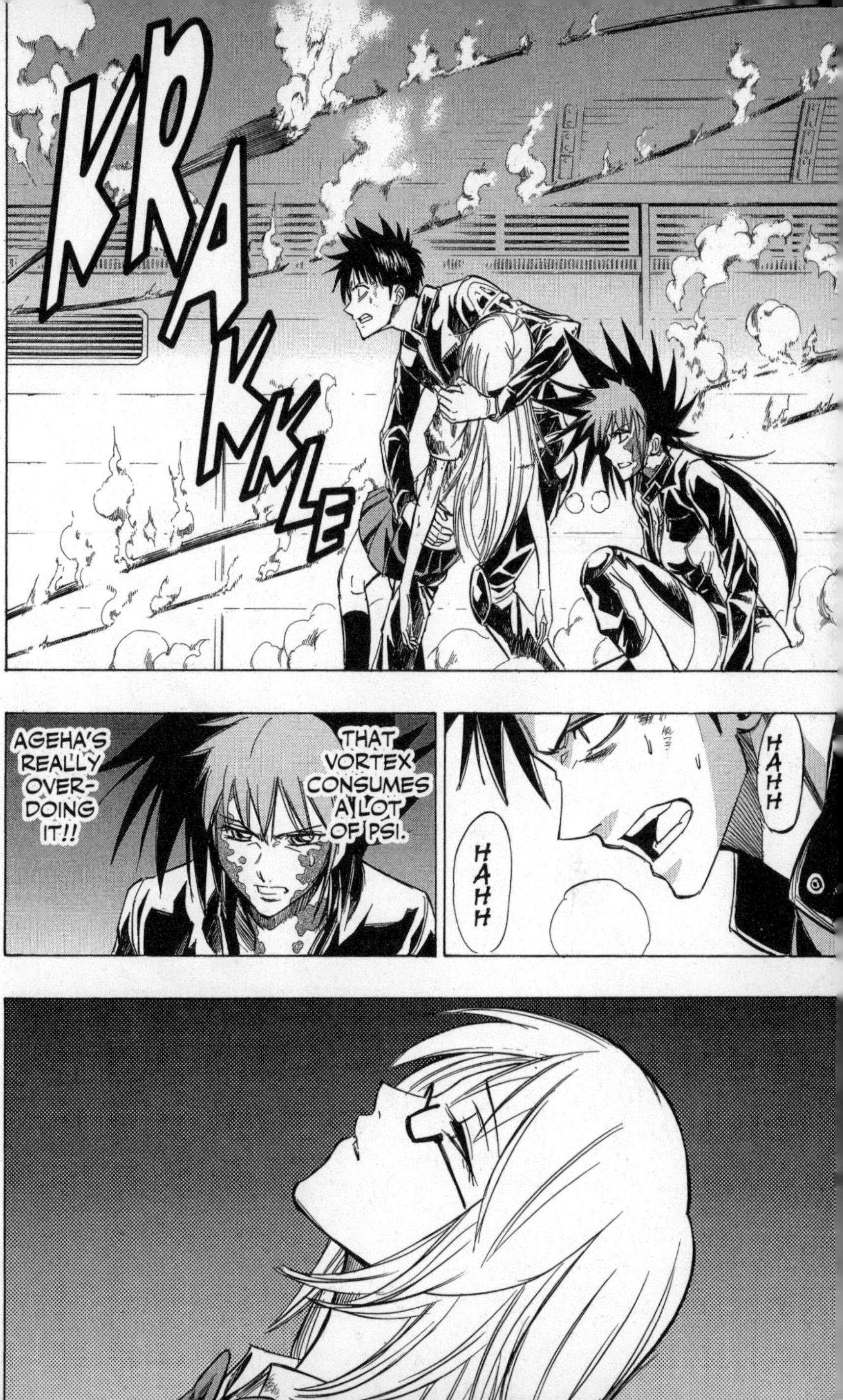
KRAKKLE
HAHH
HAHH
THAT VORTEX CONSUMES A LOT OF PSI.
AGEHA'S REALLY OVER-DOING IT!!

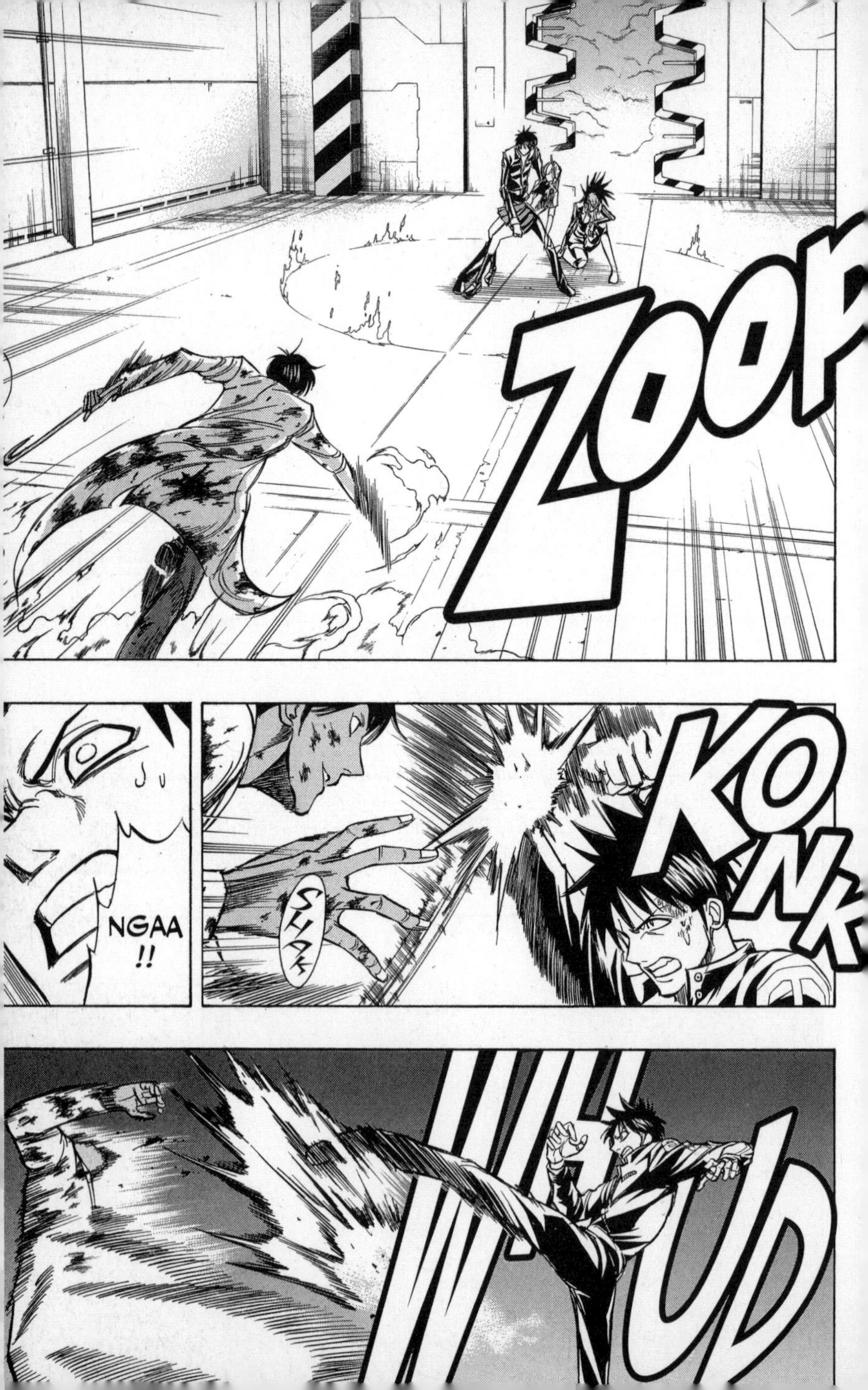
ZOOP
KONK
SHAK
NGAA !!
THUD

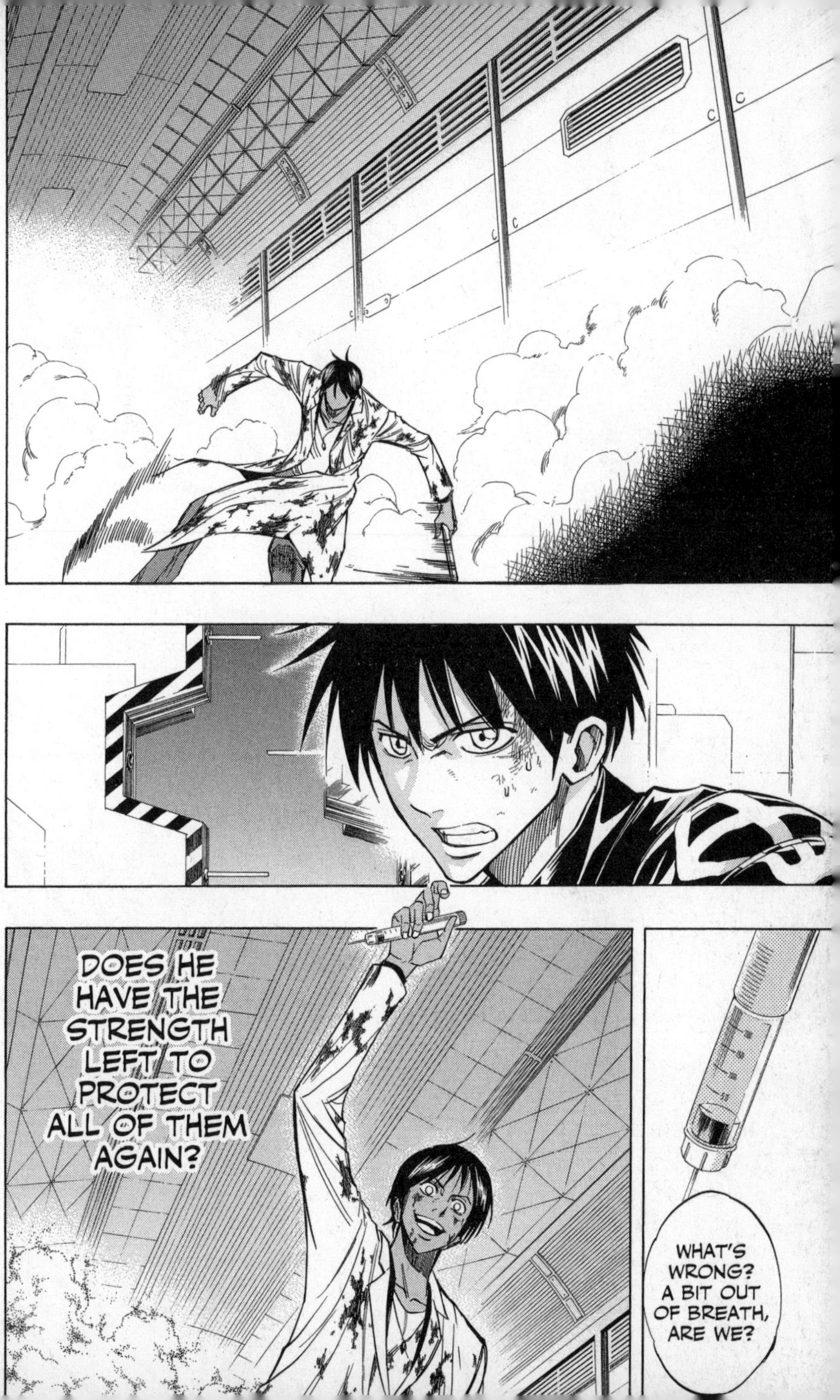
WHAT'S WRONG? A BIT OUT OF BREATH, ARE WE?
DOES HE HAVE THE STRENGTH LEFT TO PROTECT ALL OF THEM AGAIN?

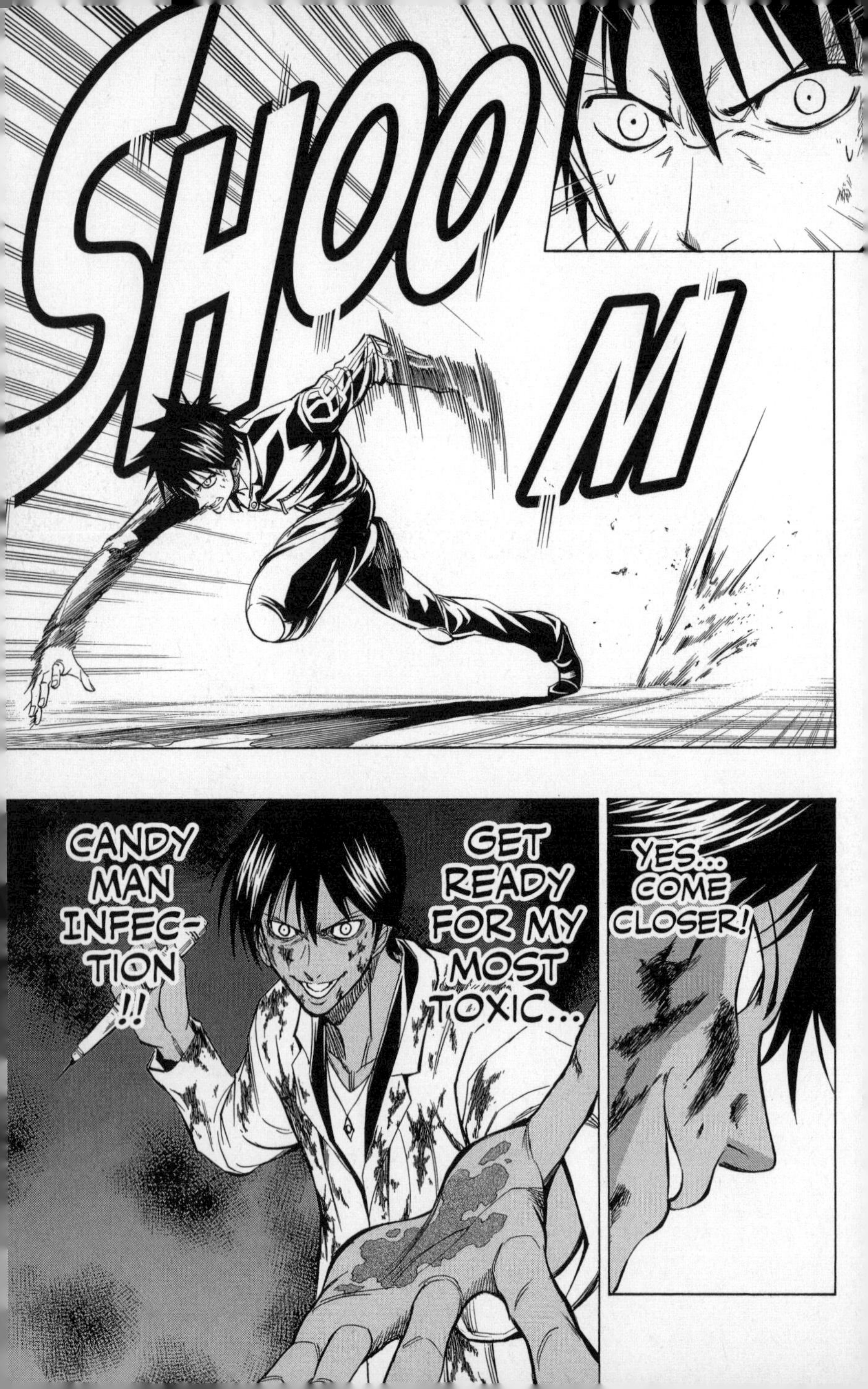
SHOOM
YES... COME CLOSER!
GET READY FOR MY MOST TOXIC...
CANDY MAN INFECTION!!

Mutters and mumblings...

I SIGNED POSTERS TO BE GIVEN AWAY
AS PRESENTS TO 100 FANS.
I DON'T GET TO DO STUFF LIKE THAT
EVERY DAY, SO I REALLY ENJOYED IT.
THANKS, EVERYONE.

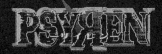

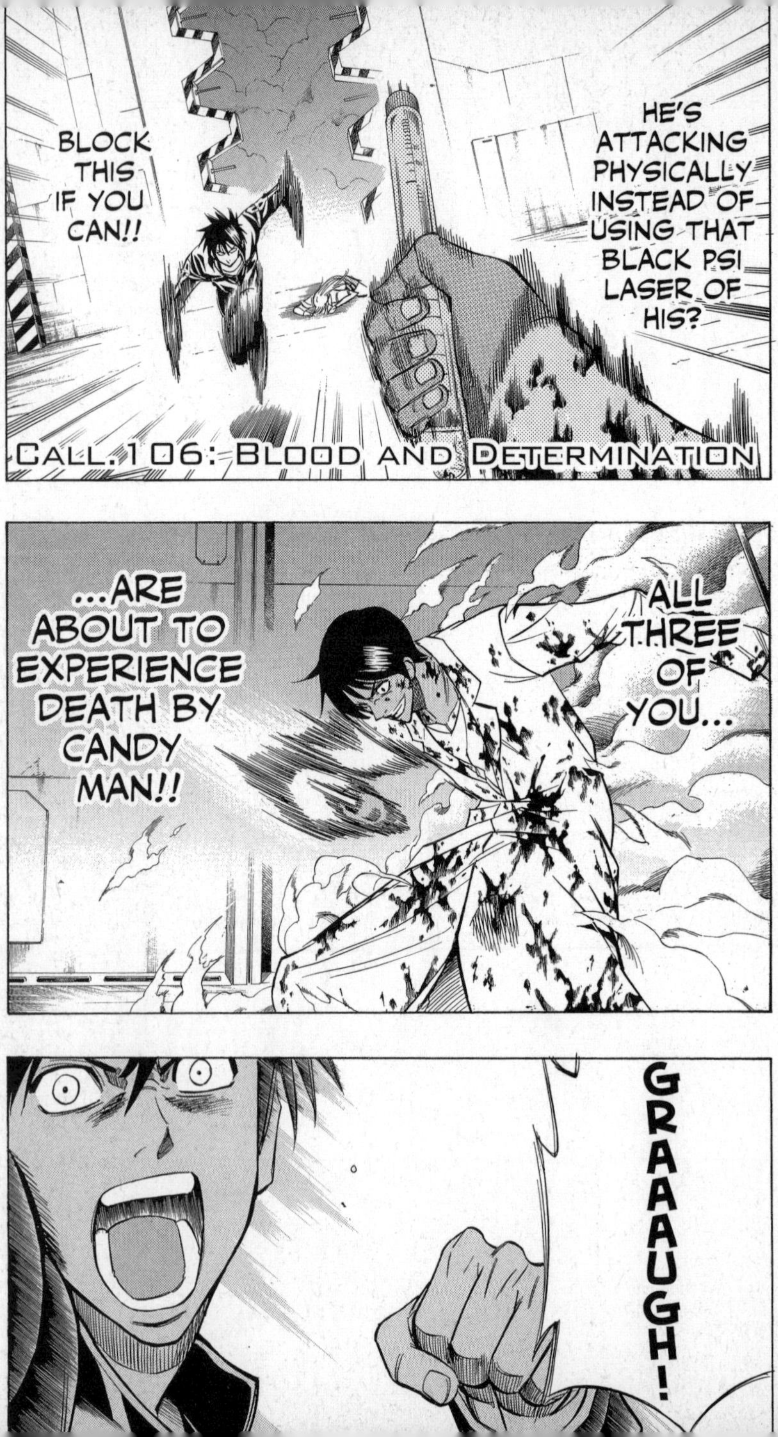
HE'S ATTACKING PHYSICALLY INSTEAD OF USING THAT BLACK PSI LASER OF HIS?
BLOCK THIS IF YOU CAN!!
CALL. 106: BLOOD AND DETERMINATION
ALL THREE OF YOU...
...ARE ABOUT TO EXPERIENCE DEATH BY CANDY MAN!!
GRAAAUGH!

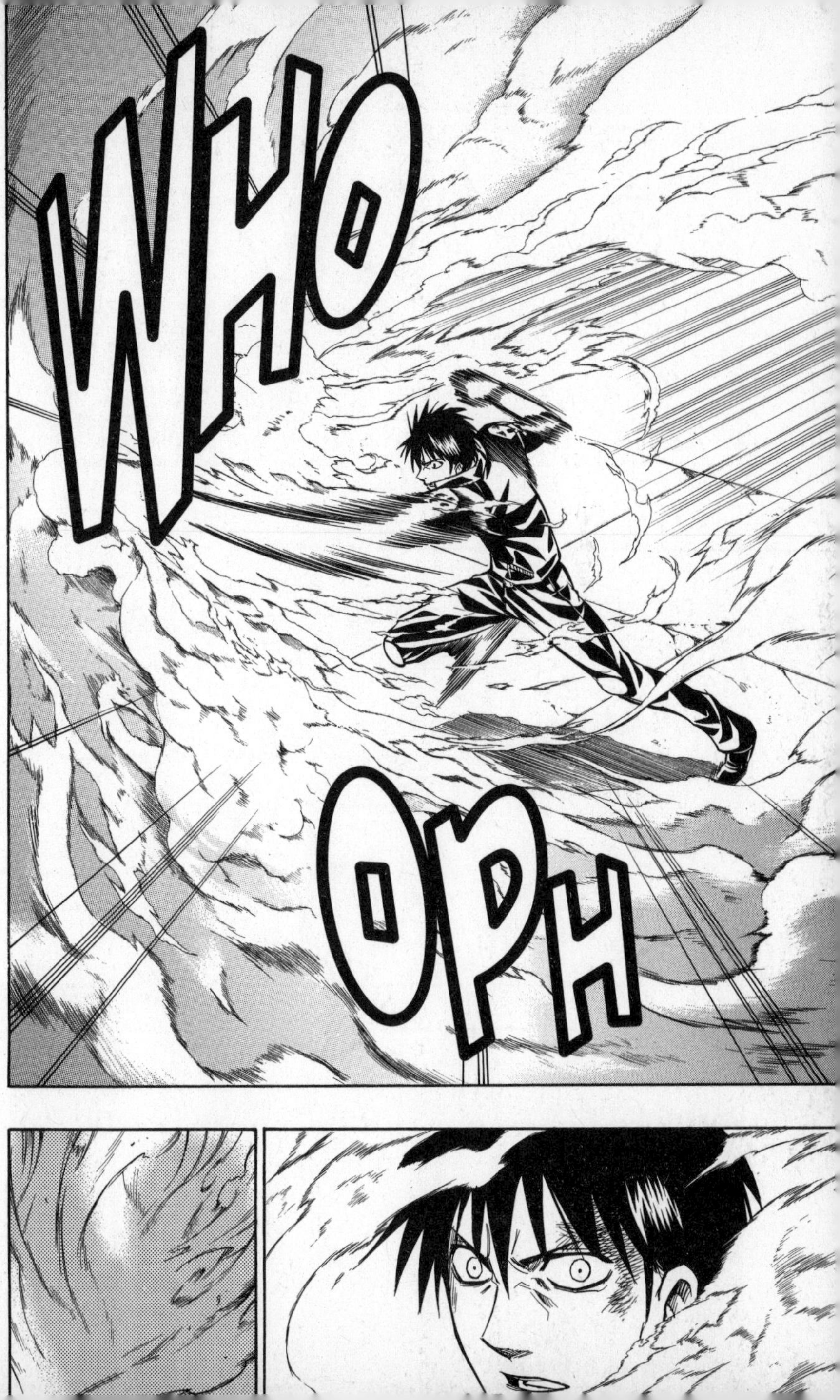
WHOOPH

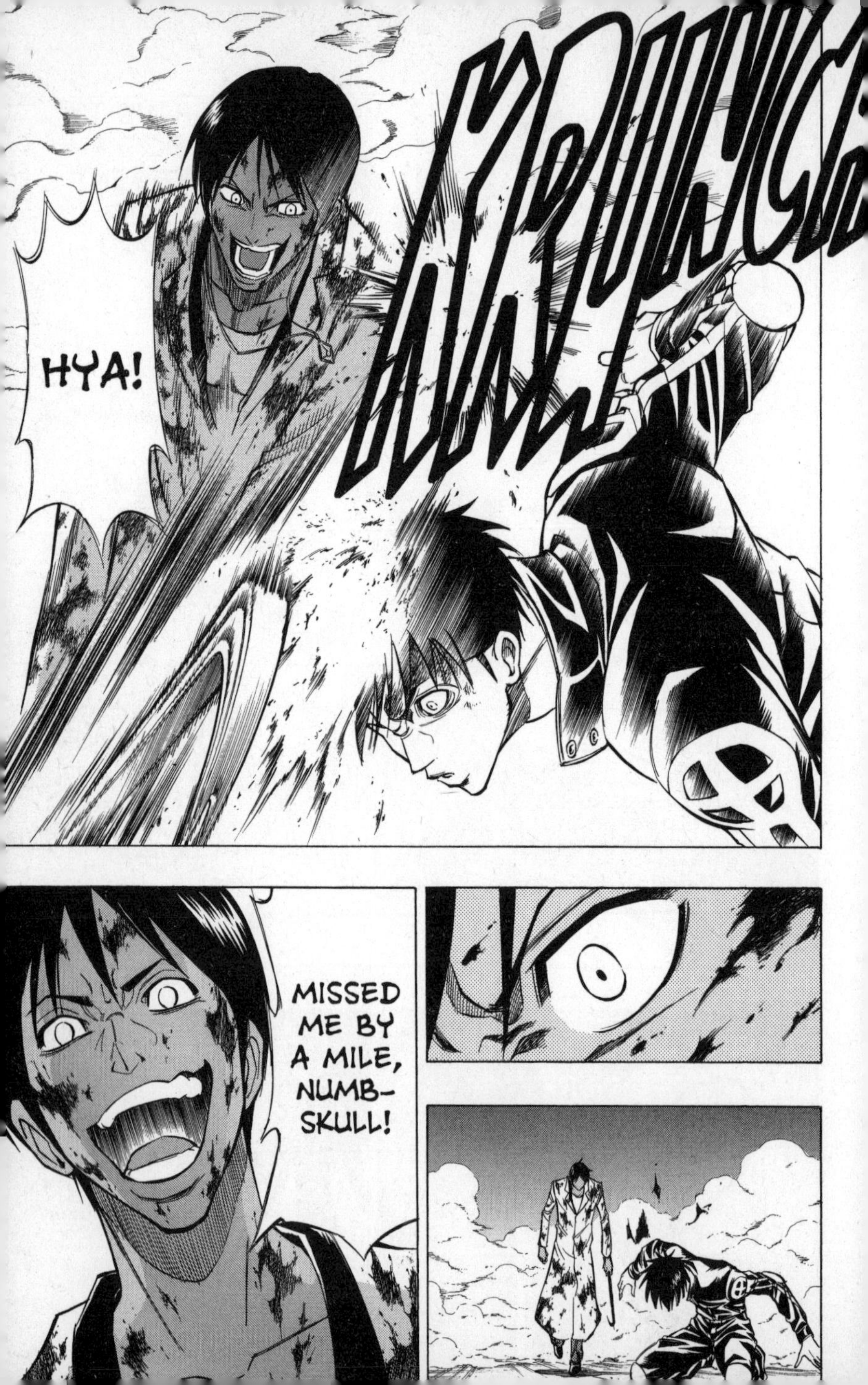
HYA!
MISSED ME BY A MILE, NUMB-SKULL!

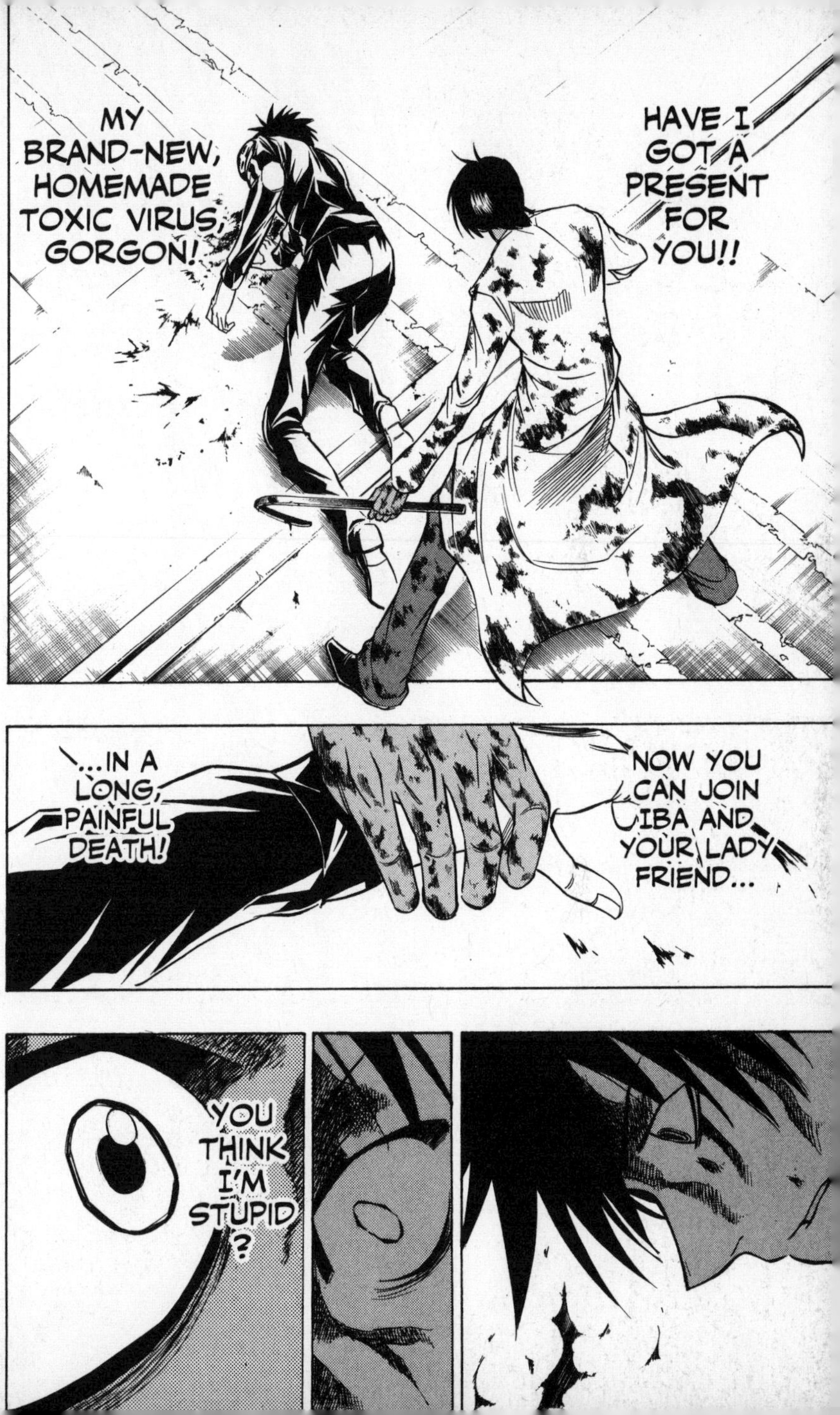
HAVE I GOT A PRESENT FOR YOU!!
MY BRAND-NEW, HOMEMADE TOXIC VIRUS, GORGON!
NOW YOU CAN JOIN IBA AND YOUR LADY FRIEND...
...IN A LONG, PAINFUL DEATH!
YOU THINK I'M STUPID?

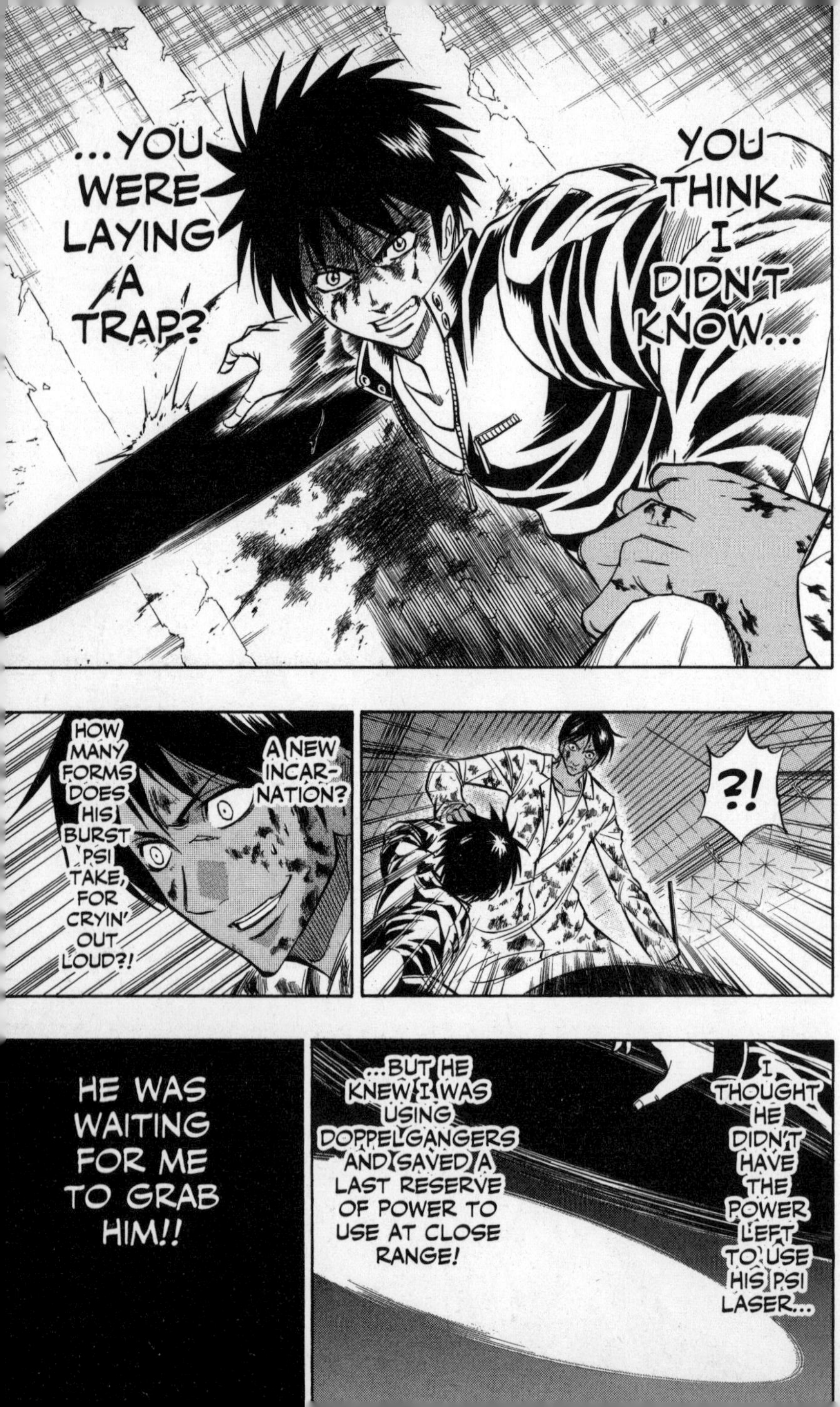
YOU THINK I DIDN'T KNOW...
...YOU WERE LAYING A TRAP?
?!
A NEW INCARNATION?
HOW MANY FORMS DOES HIS BURST PSI TAKE, FOR CRYIN' OUT LOUD?!
I THOUGHT HE DIDN'T HAVE THE POWER LEFT TO USE HIS PSI LASER...
...BUT HE KNEW I WAS USING DOPPELGANGERS AND SAVED A LAST RESERVE OF POWER TO USE AT CLOSE RANGE!
HE WAS WAITING FOR ME TO GRAB HIM!!

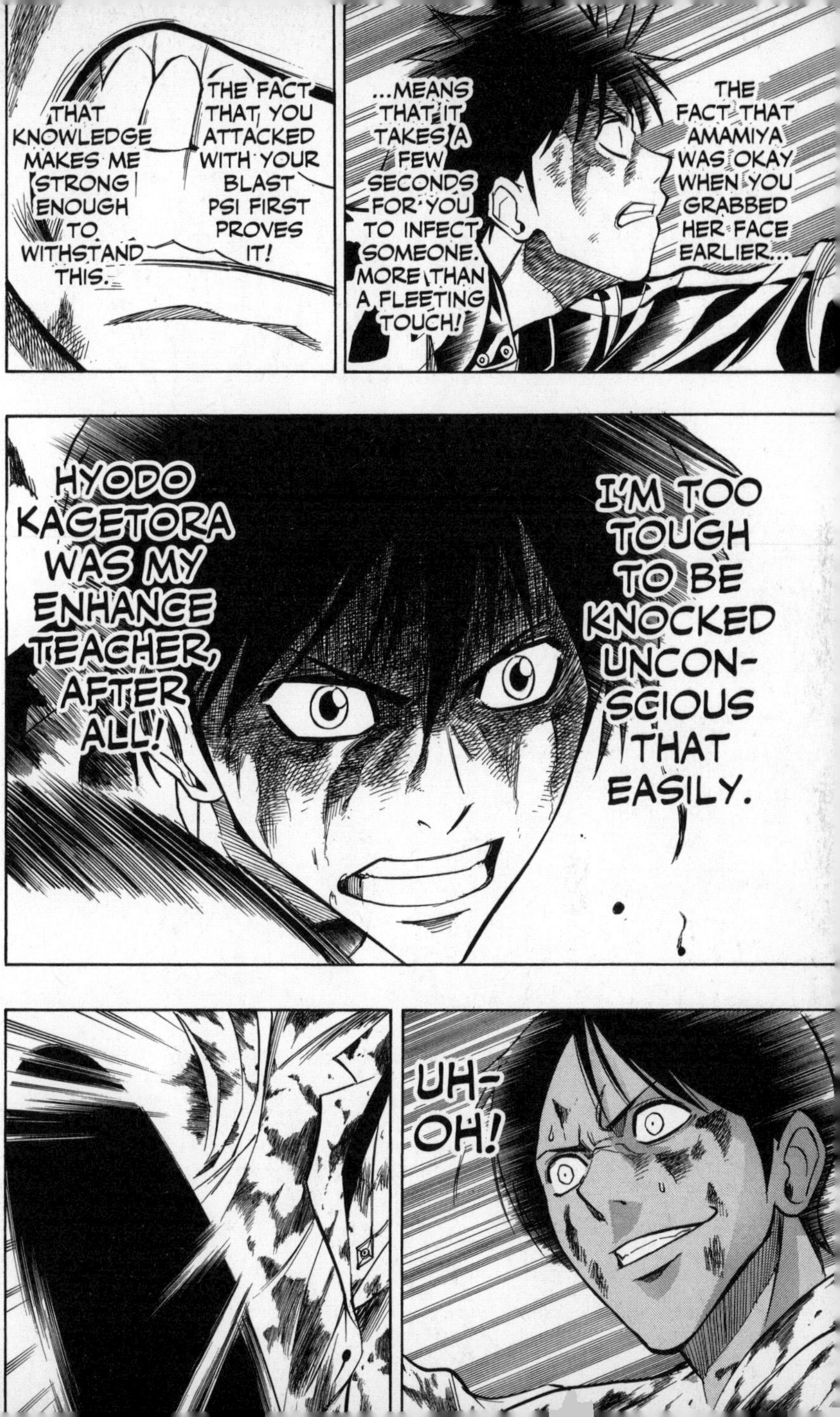
THE FACT THAT AMAMIYA WAS OKAY WHEN YOU GRABBED HER FACE EARLIER...
...MEANS THAT IT TAKES A FEW SECONDS FOR YOU TO INFECT SOMEONE. MORE THAN A FLEETING TOUCH!
THE FACT THAT YOU ATTACKED WITH YOUR BLAST PSI FIRST PROVES IT!
THAT KNOWLEDGE MAKES ME STRONG ENOUGH TO WITHSTAND THIS.
I'M TOO TOUGH TO BE KNOCKED UNCON-SCIOUS THAT EASILY.
HYODO KAGETORA WAS MY ENHANCE TEACHER, AFTER ALL!
UH-OH!

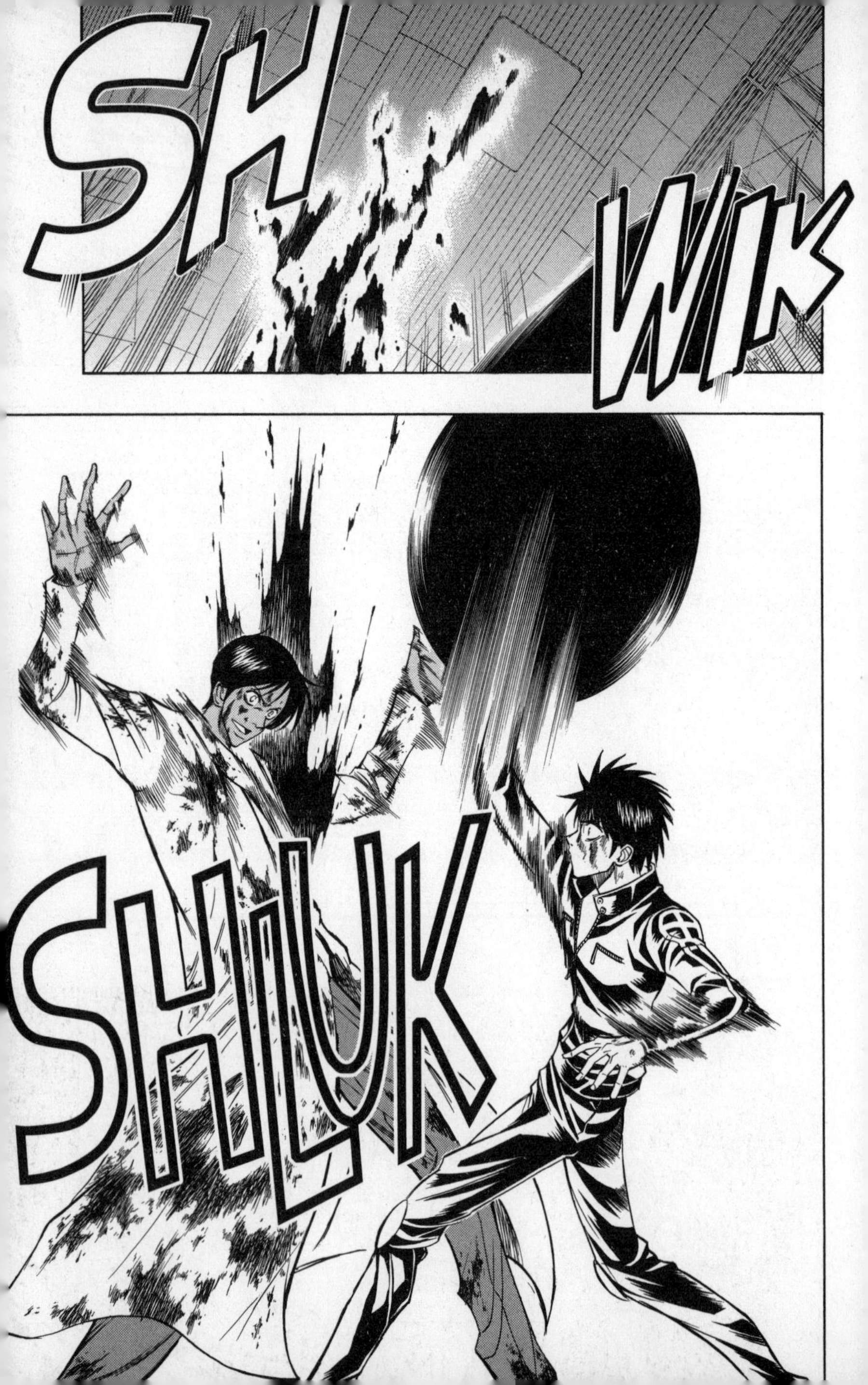
SH
WIK
SHLUK

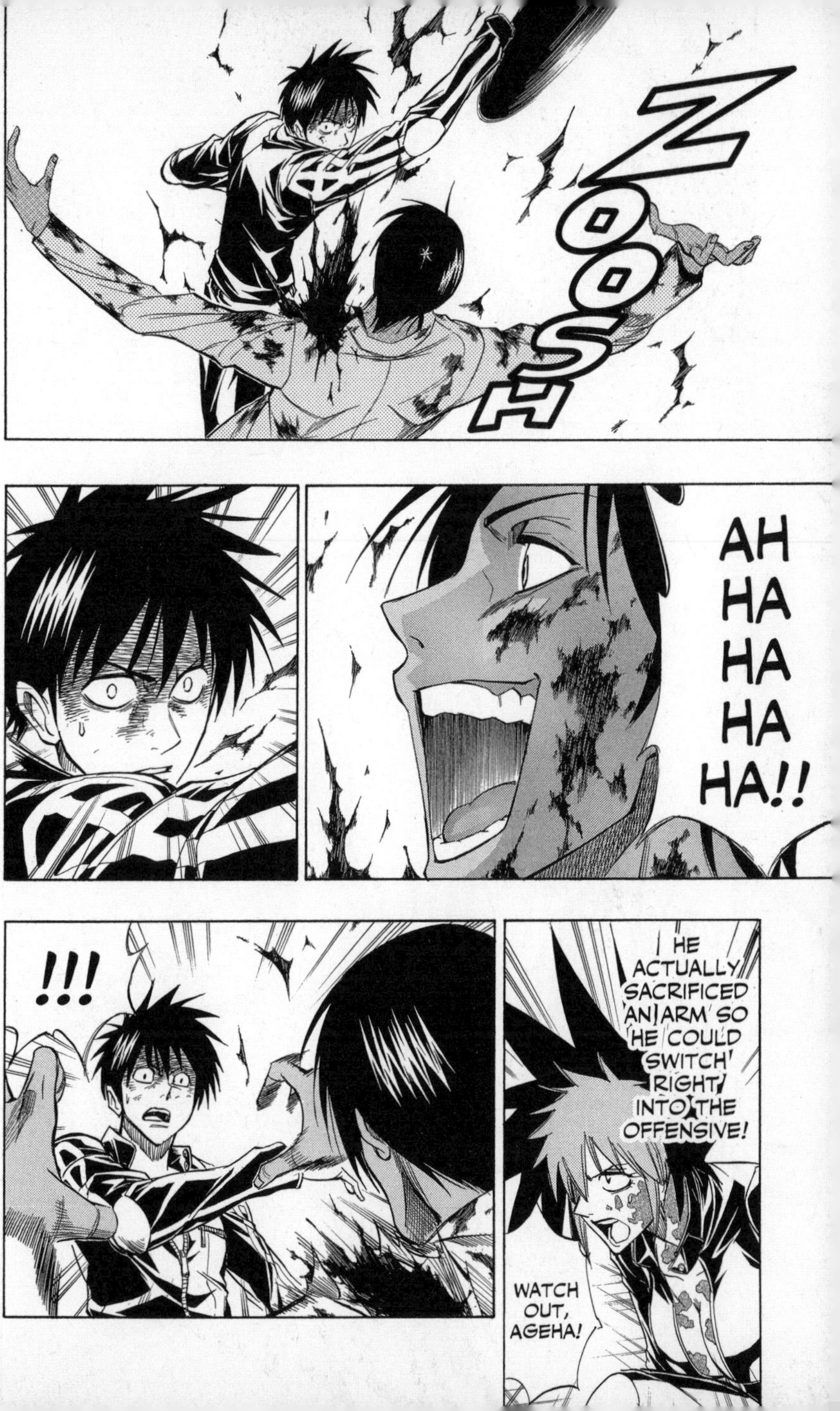
ZOOOSH
AH HA HA HA HA!!
HE ACTUALLY SACRIFICED AN ARM SO HE COULD SWITCH RIGHT INTO THE OFFENSIVE!
WATCH OUT, AGEHA!
!!!

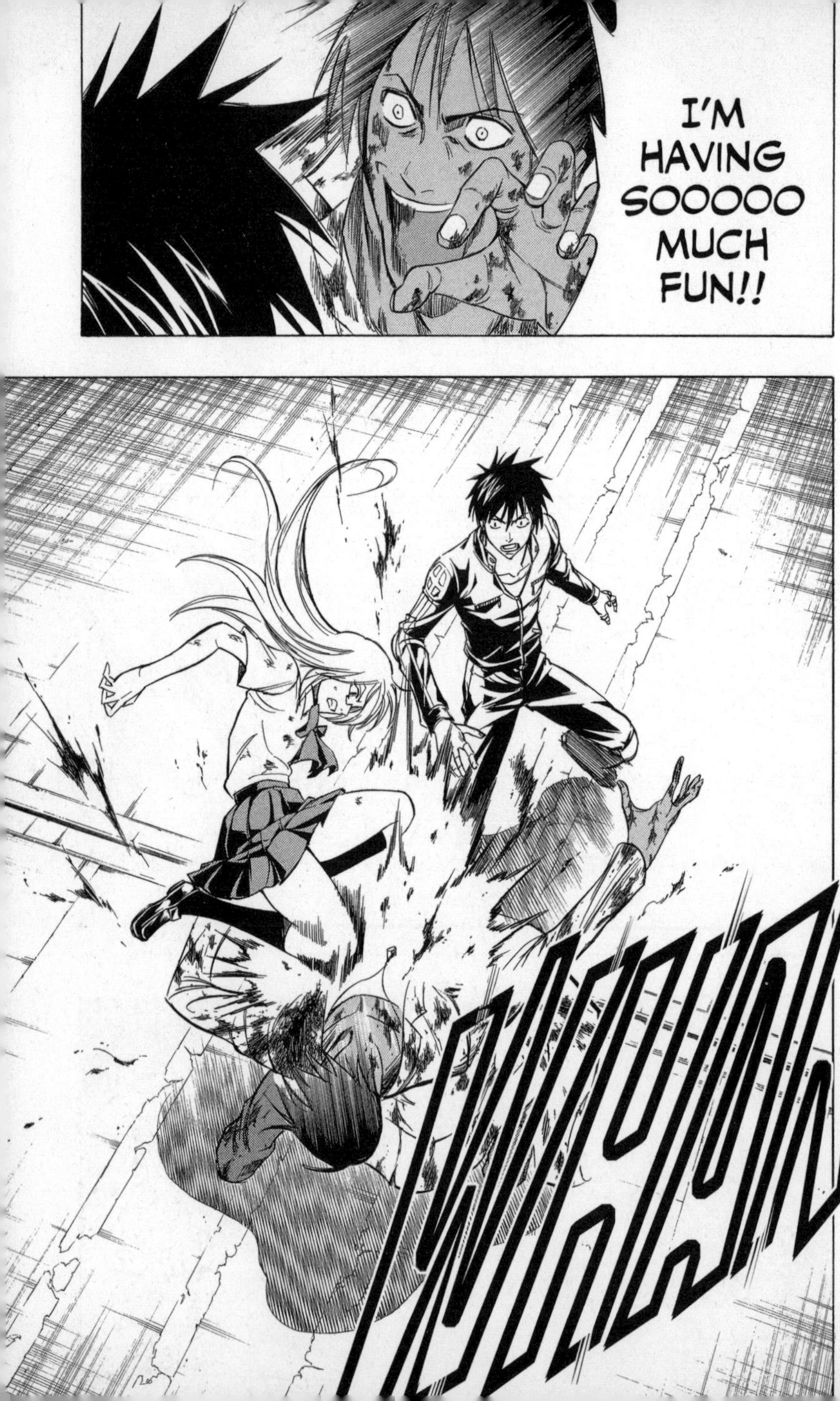
I'M HAVING SOOOOO MUCH FUN!!

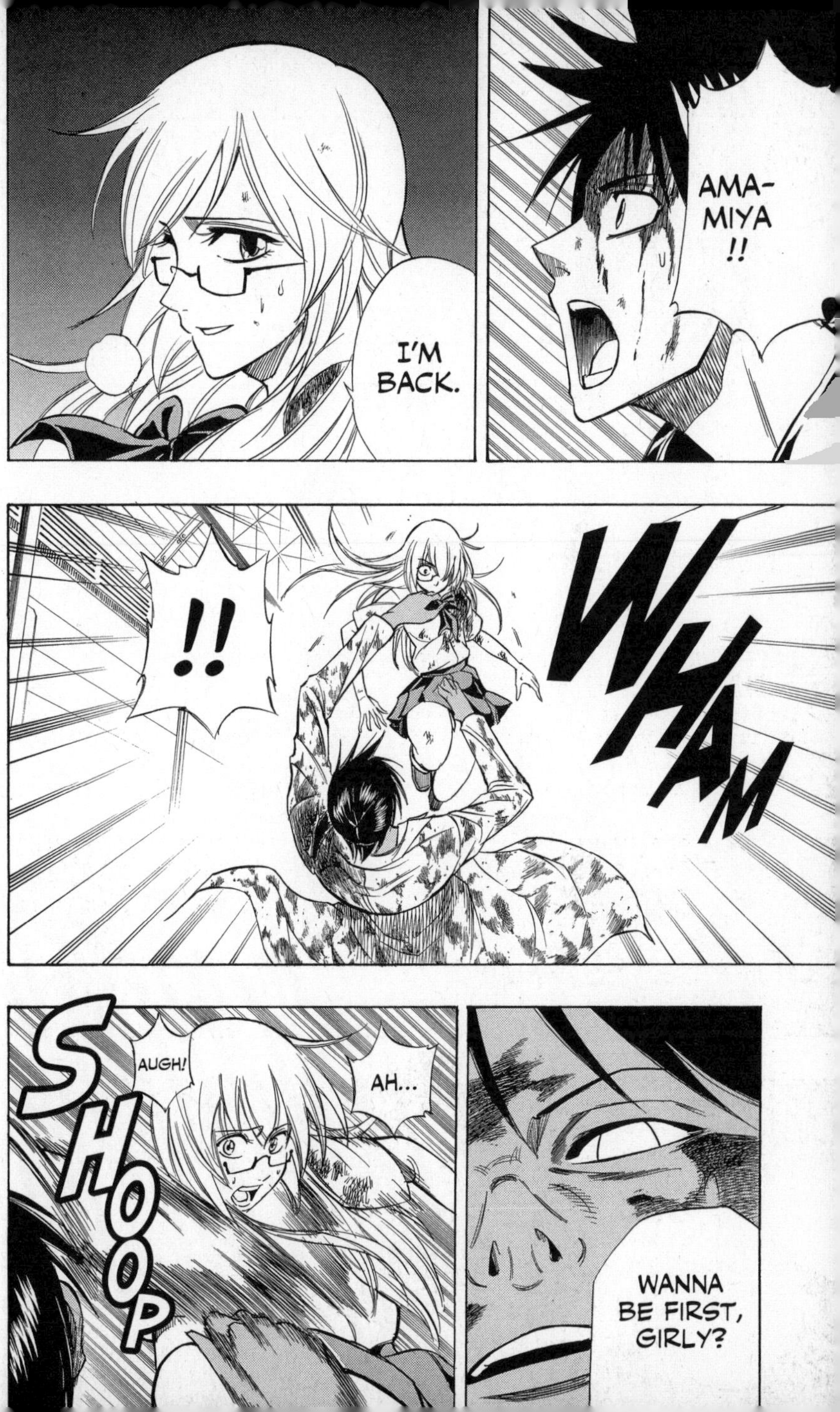
AMA-MIYA !!
I'M BACK.
WHAM
!!
WANNA BE FIRST, GIRLY?
AH...
AUGH!
SHOOP

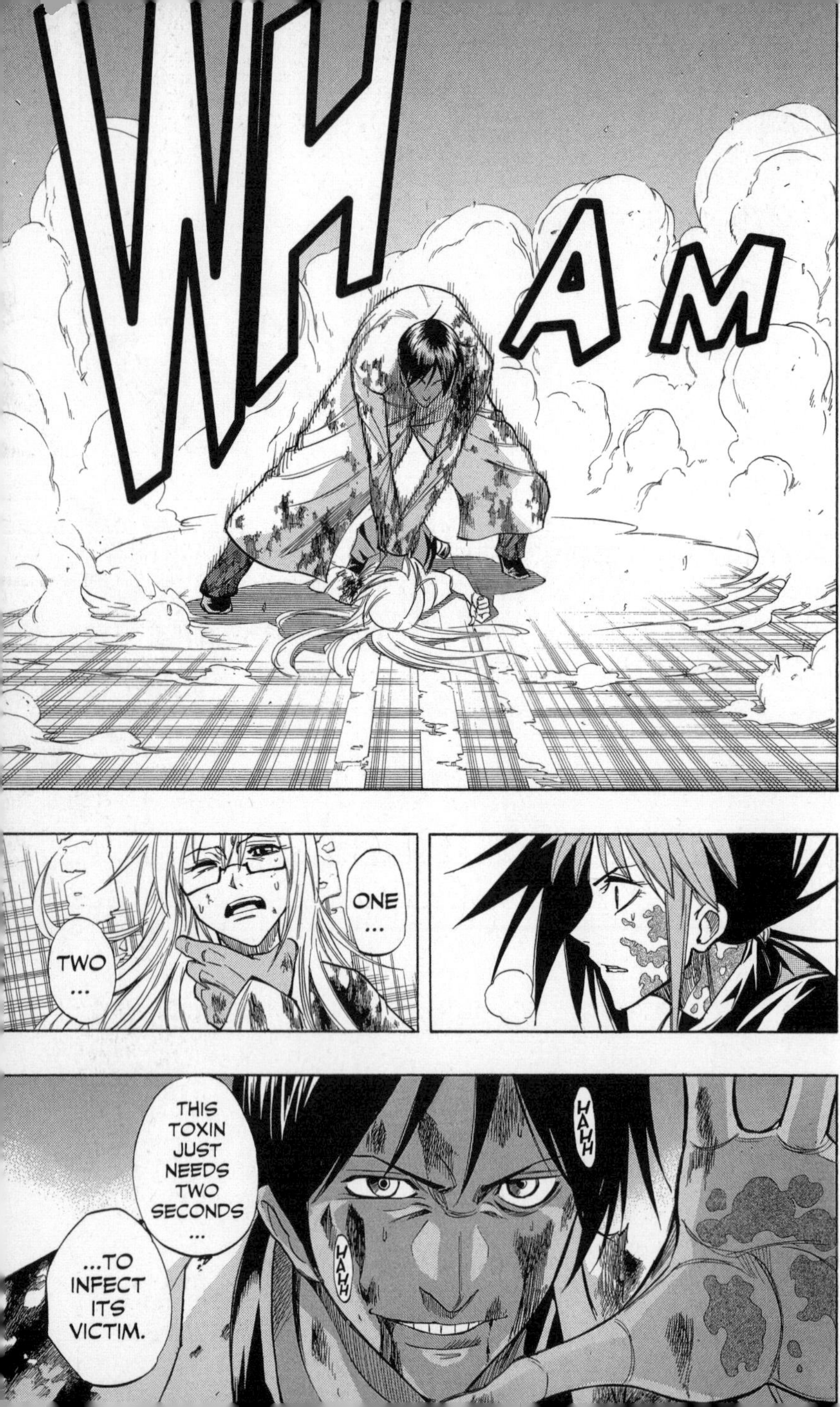
WHAM
ONE ...
TWO ...
HAHH
THIS TOXIN JUST NEEDS TWO SECONDS ...
HAHH
...TO INFECT ITS VICTIM.

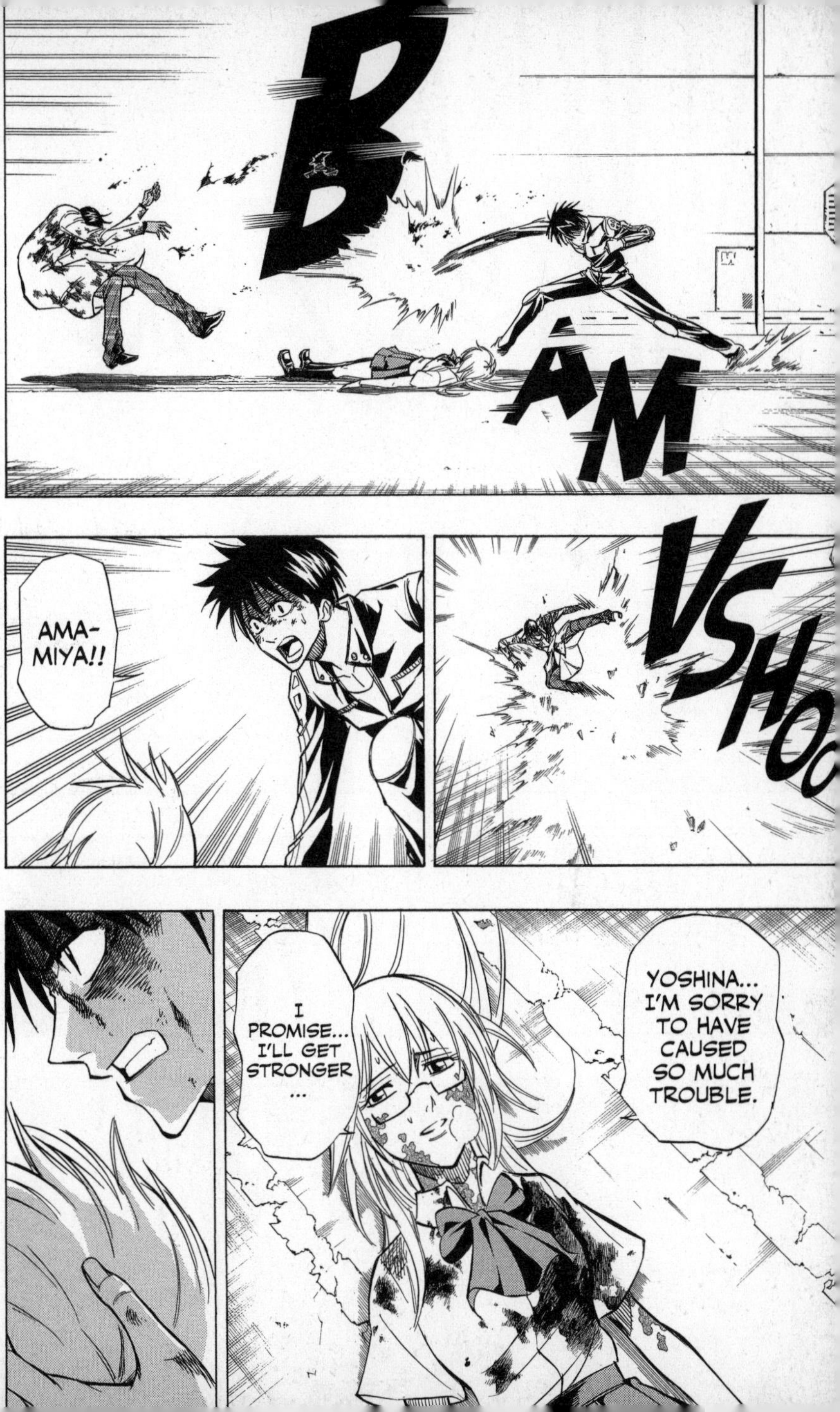
BAM
VSHOO
AMA-MIYA!!
YOSHINA... I'M SORRY TO HAVE CAUSED SO MUCH TROUBLE.
I PROMISE... I'LL GET STRONGER ...

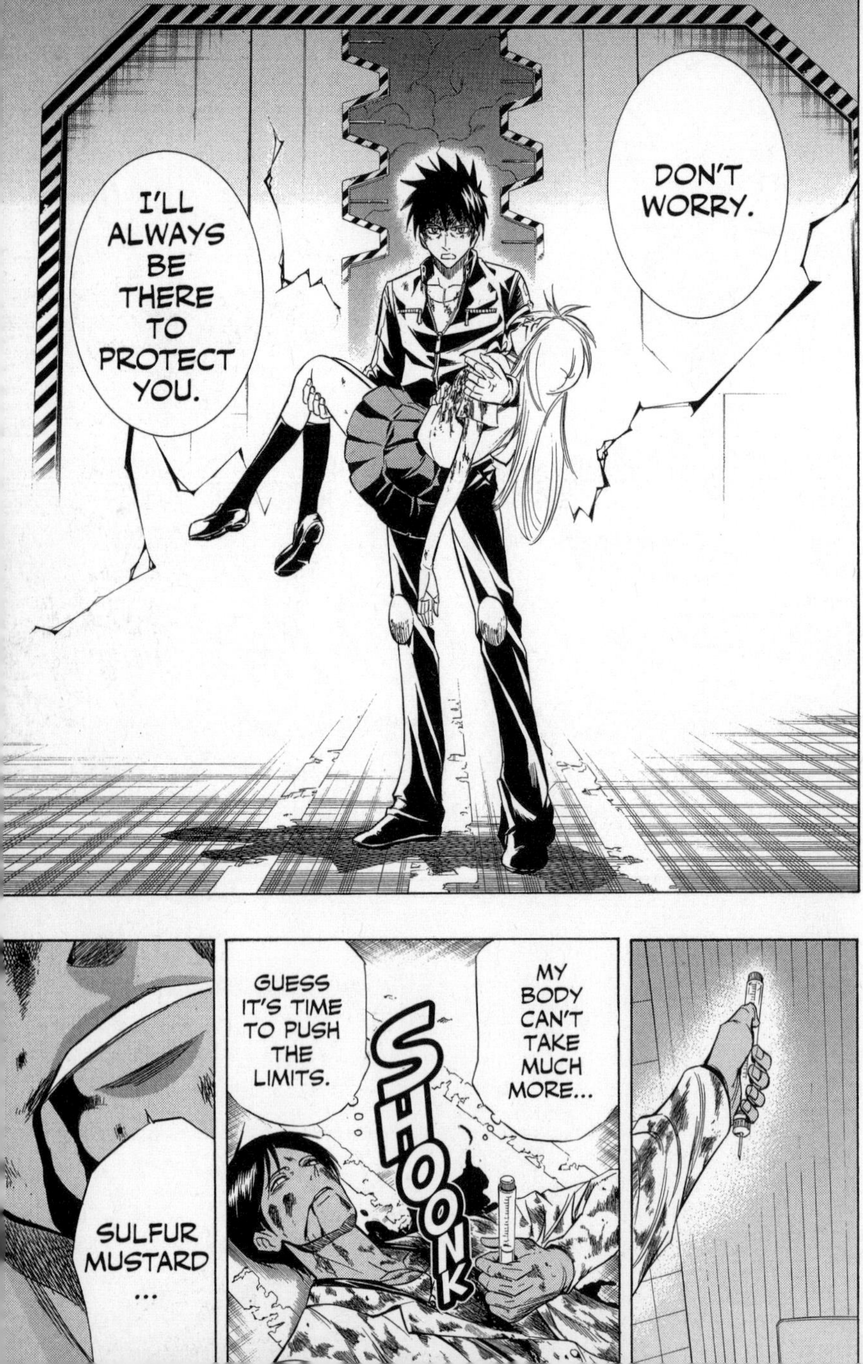
DON'T WORRY.
I'LL ALWAYS BE THERE TO PROTECT YOU.
MY BODY CAN'T TAKE MUCH MORE...
GUESS IT'S TIME TO PUSH THE LIMITS.
SHOONK
SULFUR MUSTARD ...

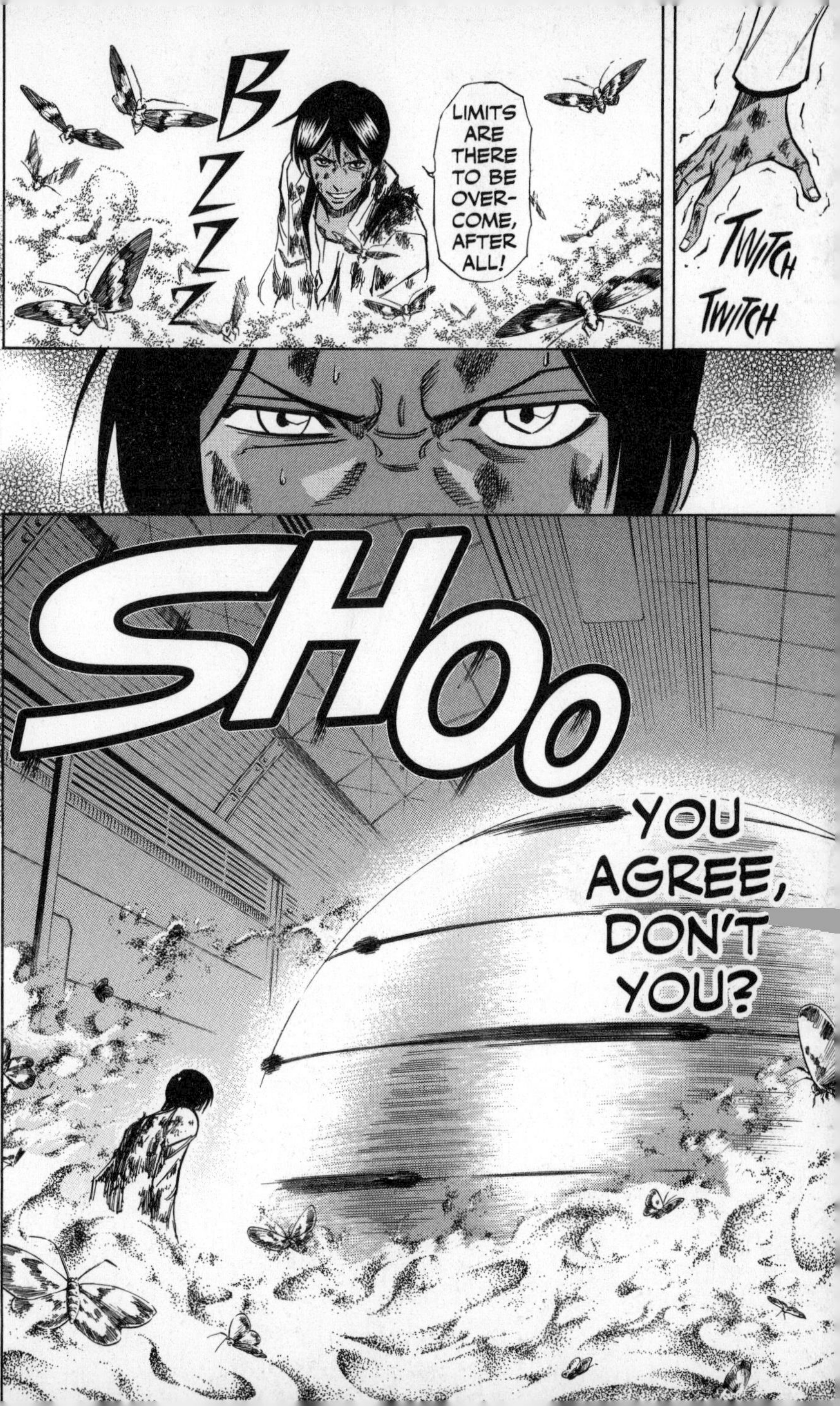
TWITCH
TWITCH
BZZZZ
LIMITS ARE THERE TO BE OVER-COME, AFTER ALL!
SHOO
YOU AGREE, DON'T YOU?

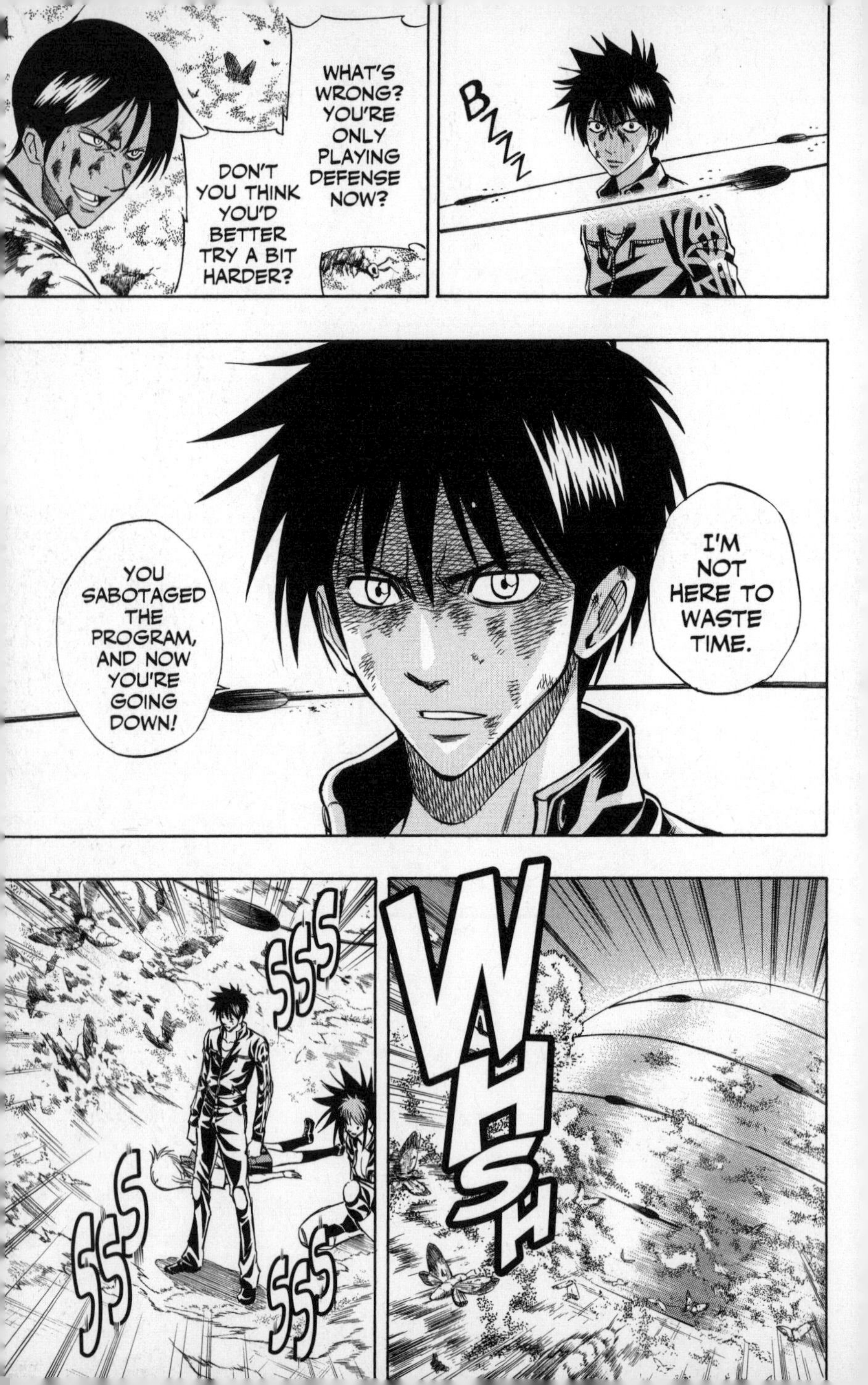
BZZZZ
WHAT'S WRONG? YOU'RE ONLY PLAYING DEFENSE NOW?
DON'T YOU THINK YOU'D BETTER TRY A BIT HARDER?
I'M NOT HERE TO WASTE TIME.
YOU SABOTAGED THE PROGRAM, AND NOW YOU'RE GOING DOWN!
WHSH
SSS
SSS
SSS

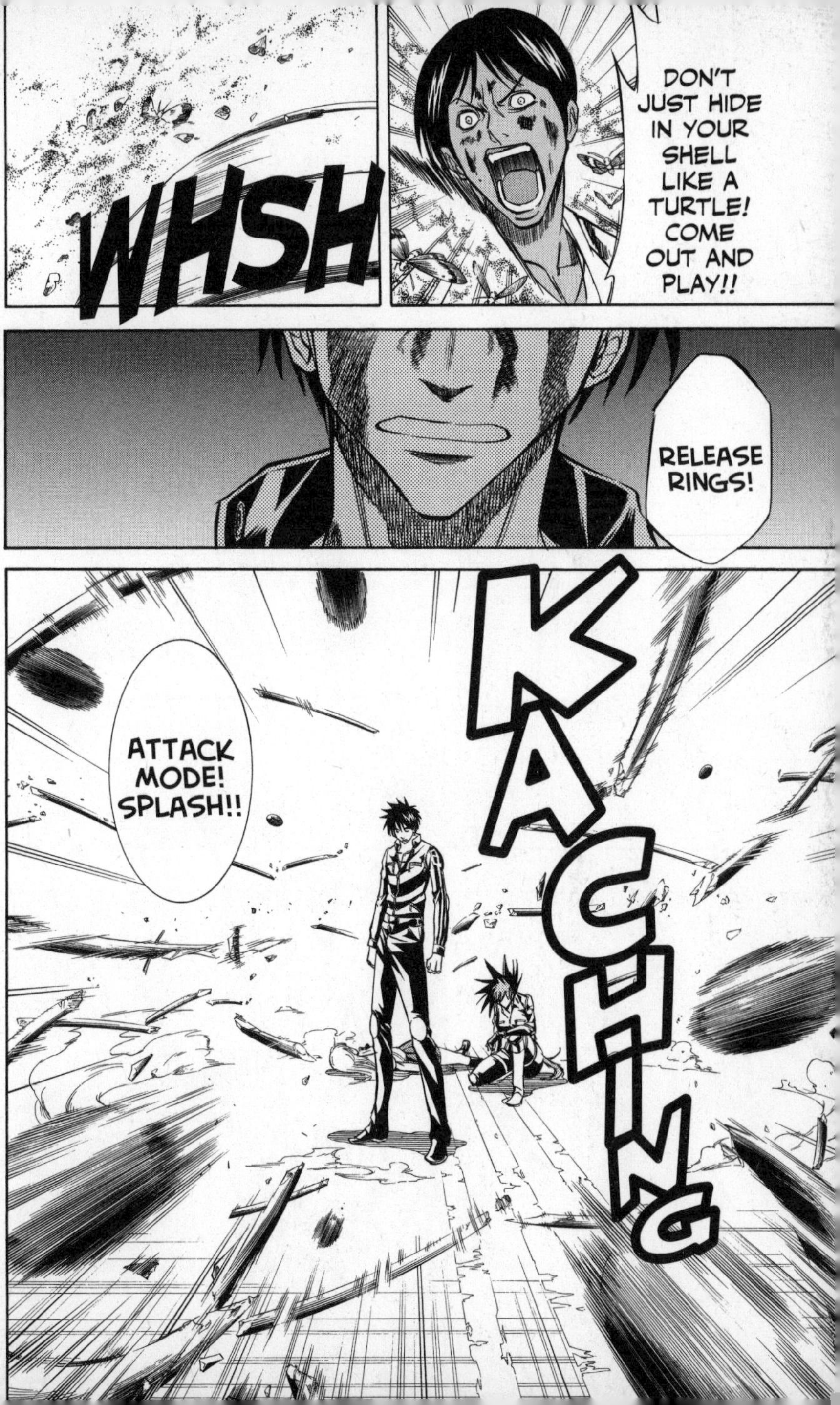
DON'T JUST HIDE IN YOUR SHELL LIKE A TURTLE! COME OUT AND PLAY!!
WHSH
RELEASE RINGS!
KACHING
ATTACK MODE! SPLASH!!

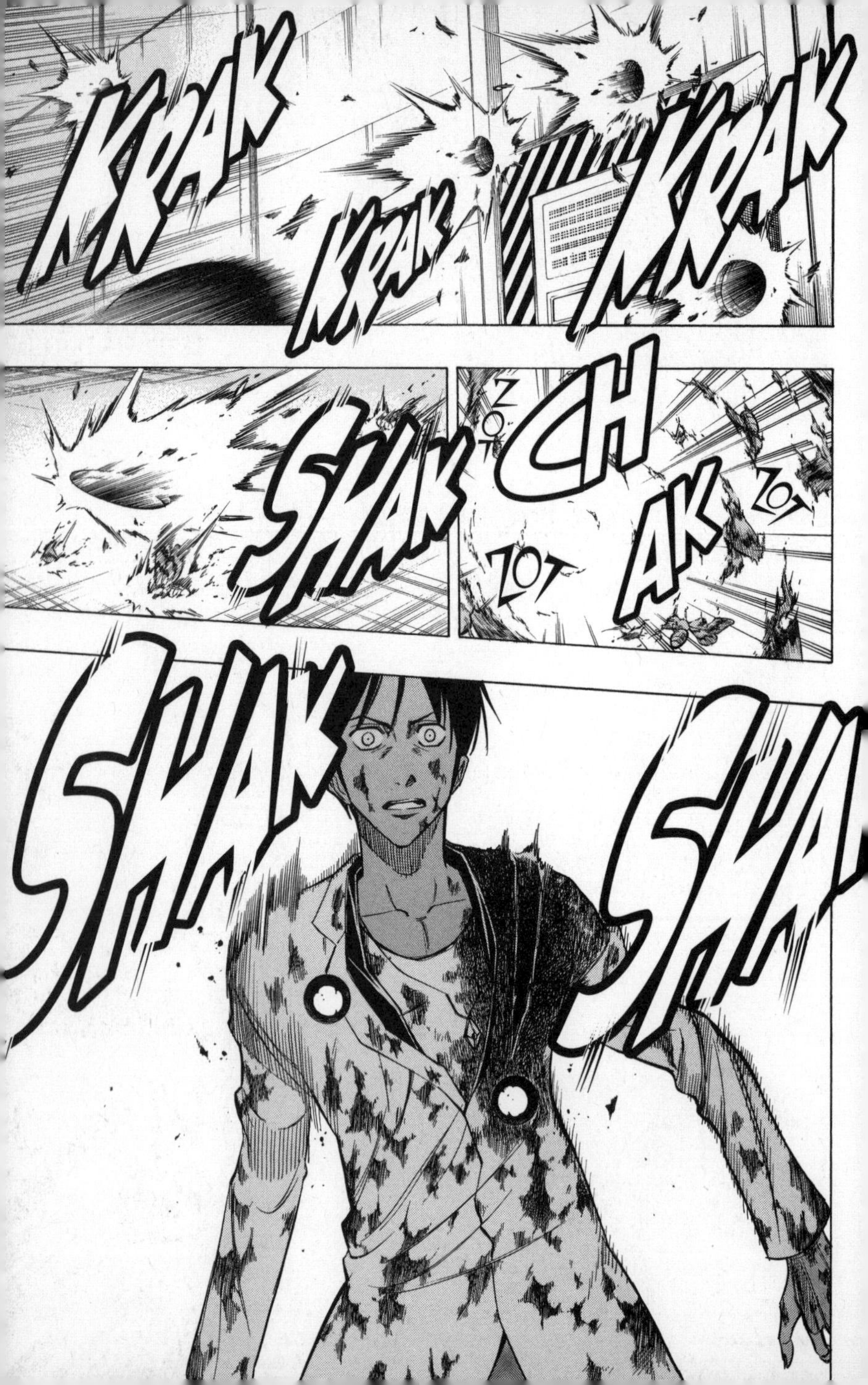
KRAK
KRAK
KRAK
ZOT
ZOT
CH
AK
ZOT
SHAK
SHA
SHAK

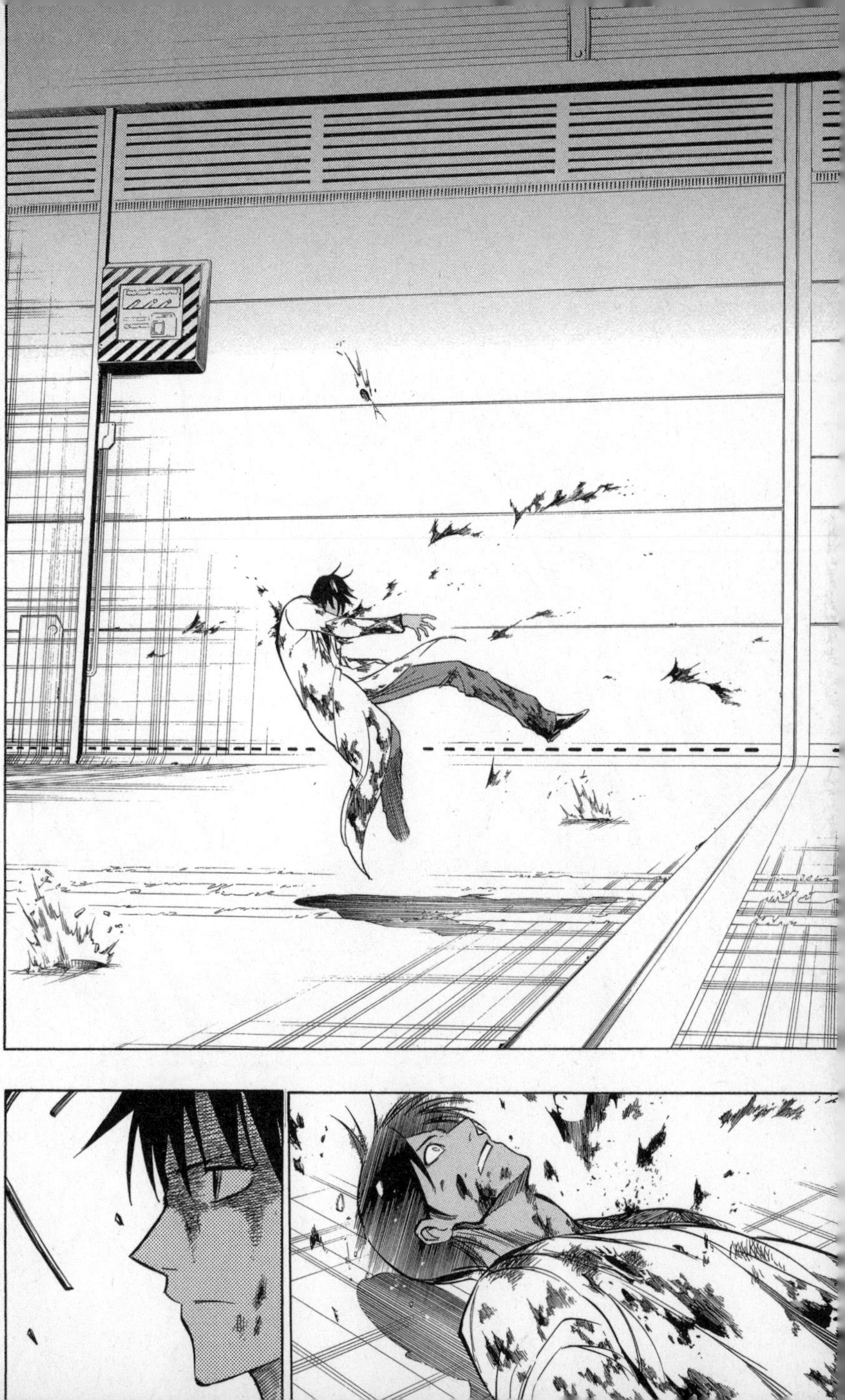

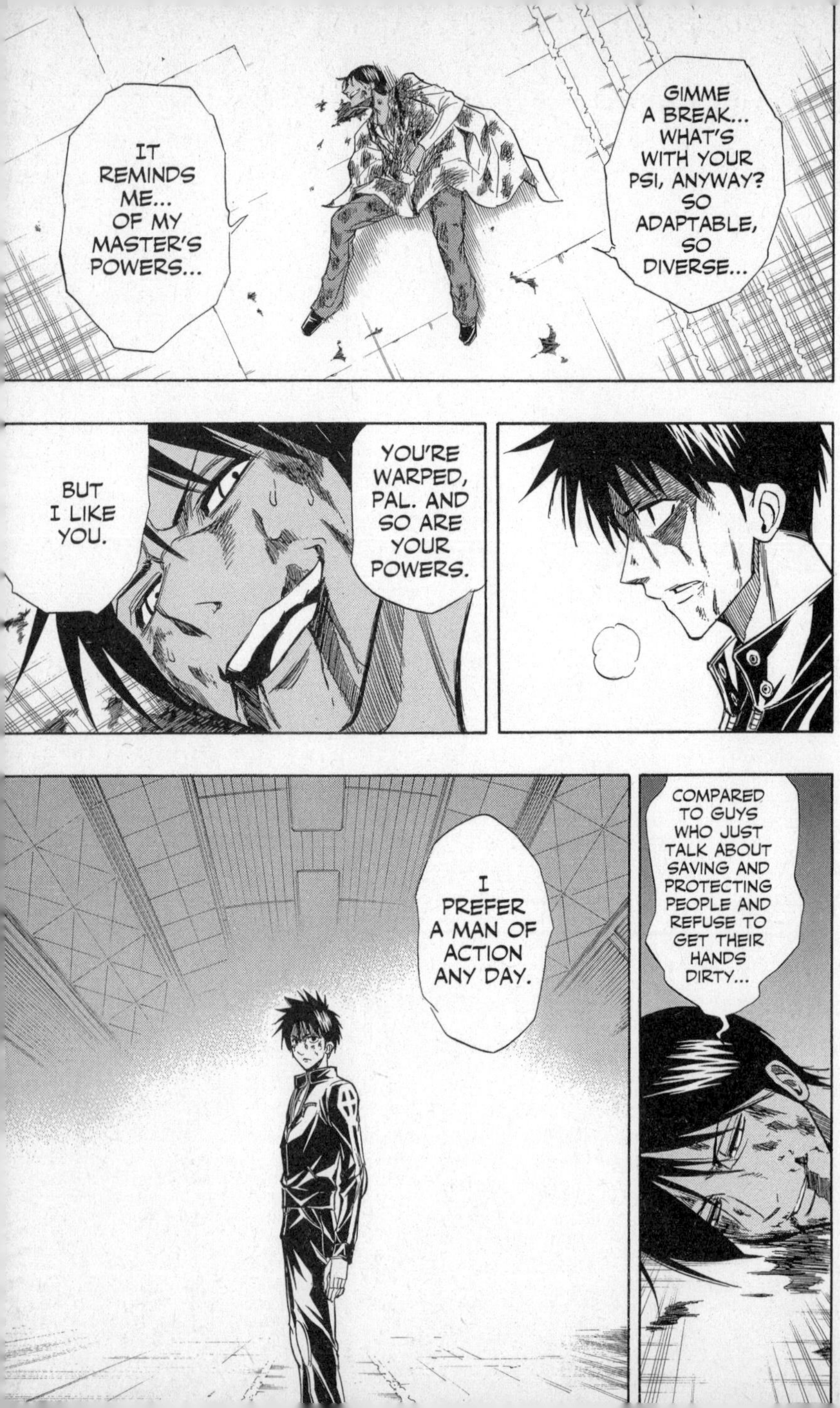
GIMME A BREAK... WHAT'S WITH YOUR PSI, ANYWAY? SO ADAPTABLE, SO DIVERSE...
IT REMINDS ME... OF MY MASTER'S POWERS...
YOU'RE WARPED, PAL. AND SO ARE YOUR POWERS.
BUT I LIKE YOU.
COMPARED TO GUYS WHO JUST TALK ABOUT SAVING AND PROTECTING PEOPLE AND REFUSE TO GET THEIR HANDS DIRTY...
I PREFER A MAN OF ACTION ANY DAY.

Mutters and mumblings...

I DECIDED NOT TO GIVE YUSAKA A PAINFUL,
SAD PAST TO EXPLAIN HIS MISDEEDS. I
HOPE READERS WILL PERCEIVE HIM AS
JUST BEING A TRULY HORRIBLE PERSON,
A DEVIL IN HUMAN CLOTHES.

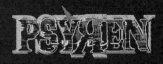

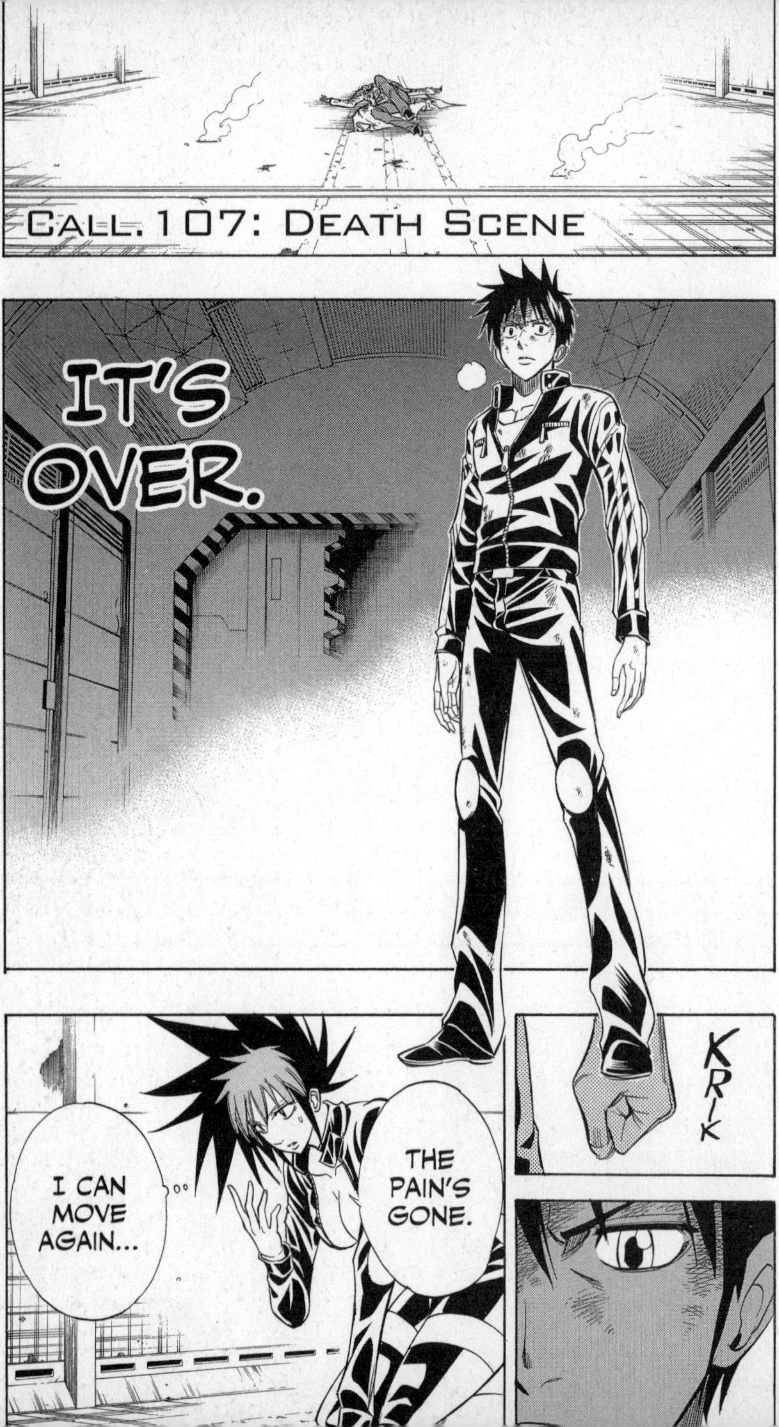
Call. 107: Death Scene
IT'S OVER.
KRIK
THE PAIN'S GONE.
I CAN MOVE AGAIN...

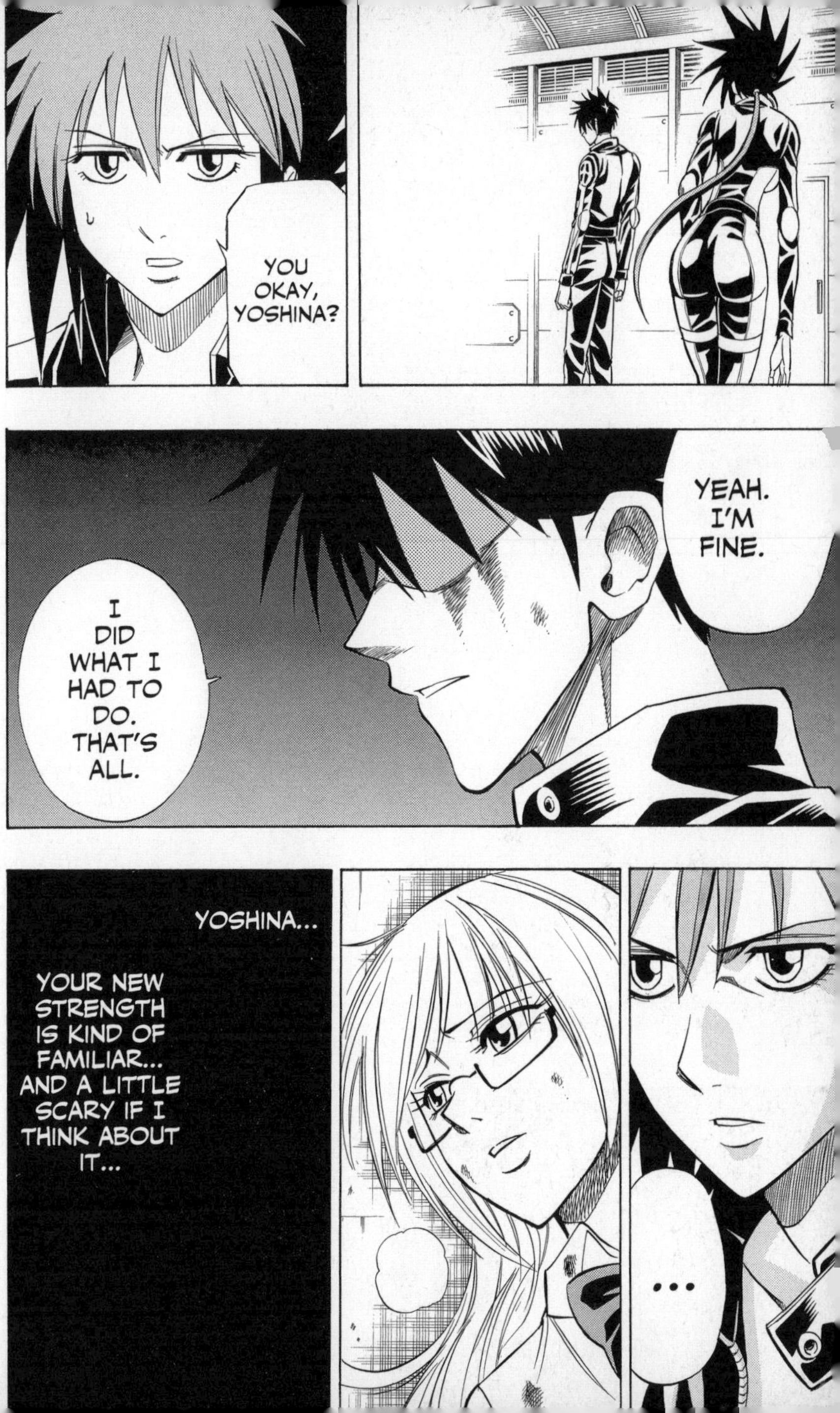
YOU OKAY, YOSHINA?
YEAH. I'M FINE.
I DID WHAT I HAD TO DO. THAT'S ALL.
...
YOSHINA...
YOUR NEW STRENGTH IS KIND OF FAMILIAR... AND A LITTLE SCARY IF I THINK ABOUT IT...

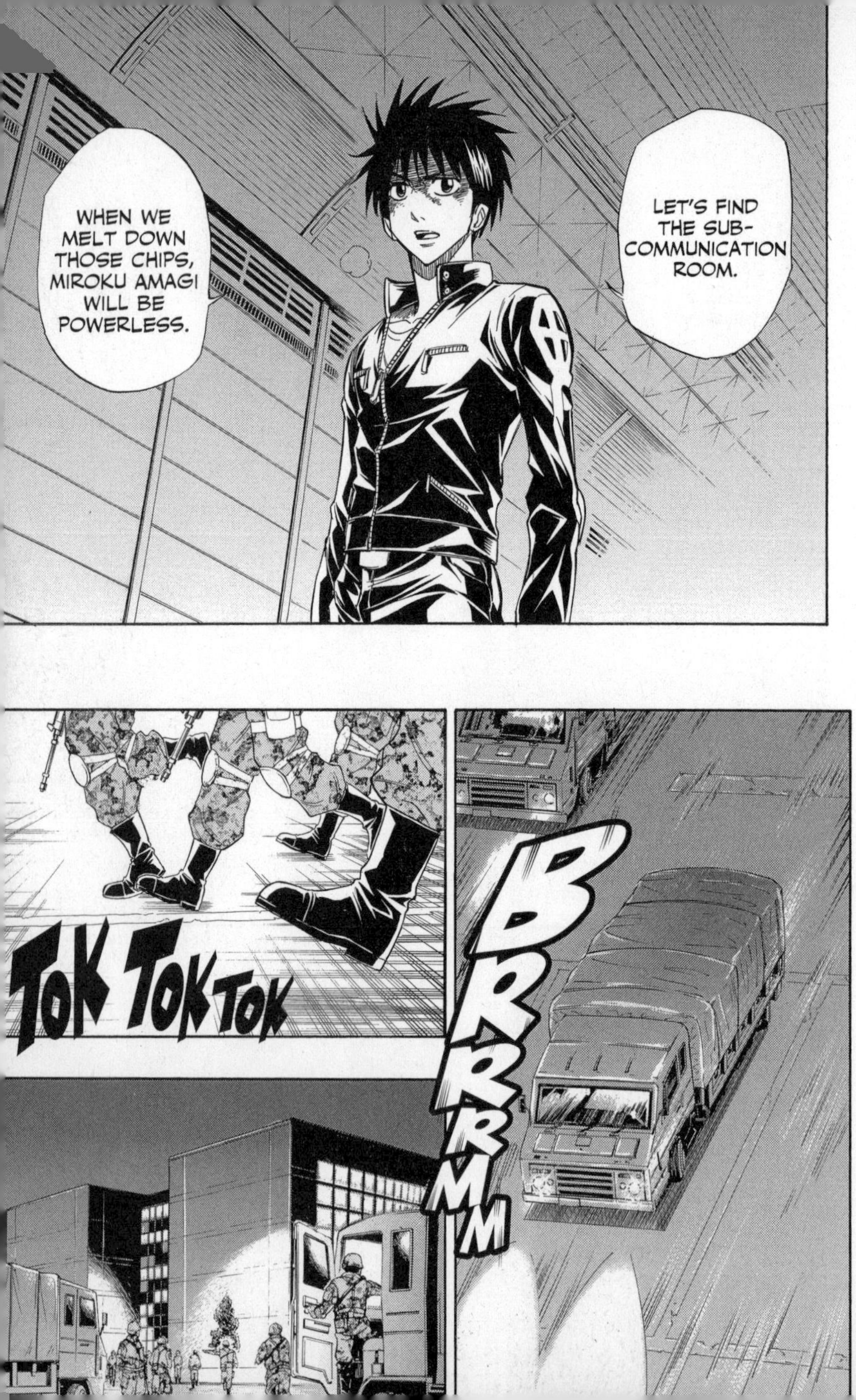
LET'S FIND THE SUB-COMMUNICATION ROOM.
WHEN WE MELT DOWN THOSE CHIPS, MIROKU AMAGI WILL BE POWERLESS.
BRRRRMM
TOK TOK TOK

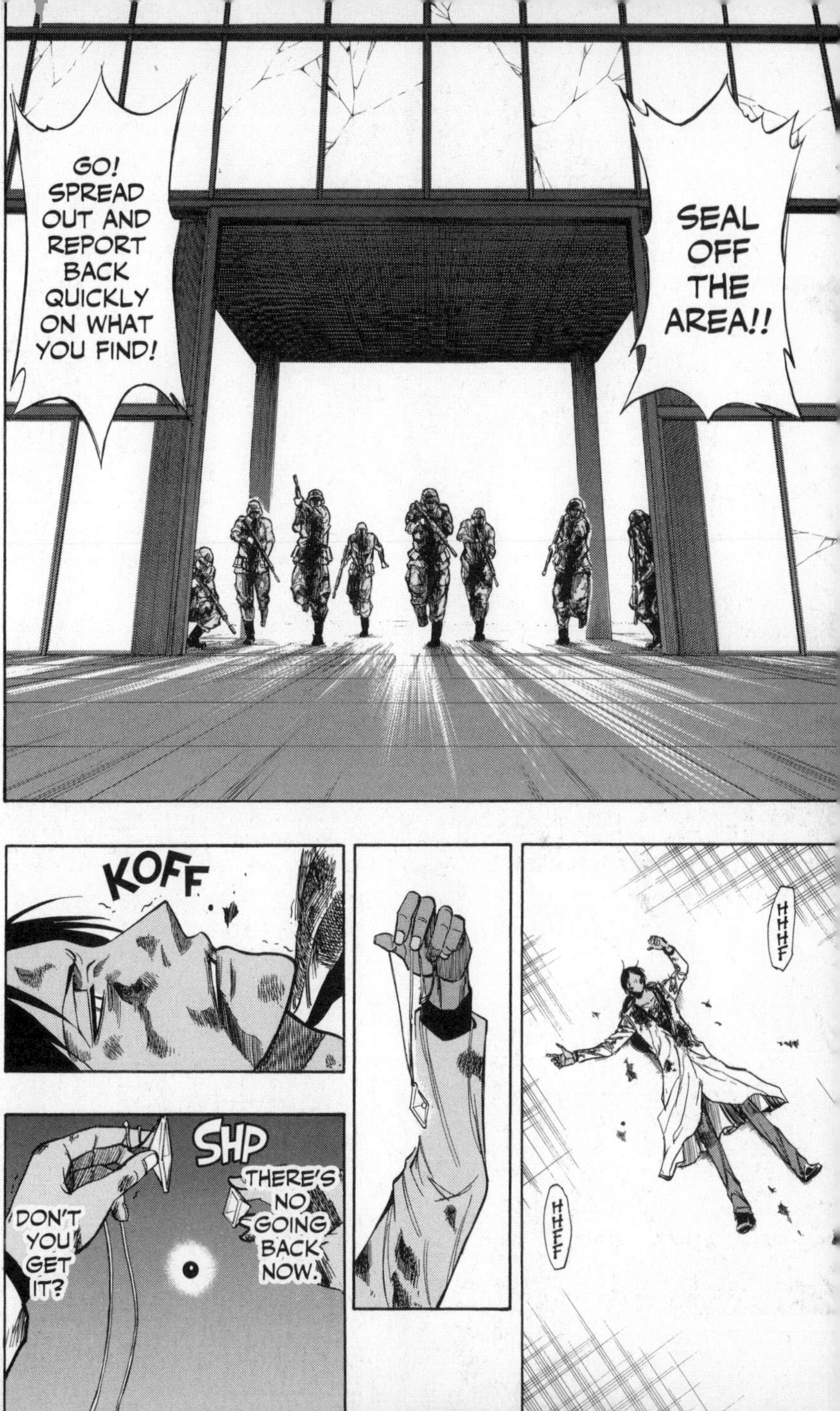
SEAL OFF THE AREA!!
GO! SPREAD OUT AND REPORT BACK QUICKLY ON WHAT YOU FIND!
HHHF
HHFF
KOFF
SHP
THERE'S NO GOING BACK NOW.
DON'T YOU GET IT?

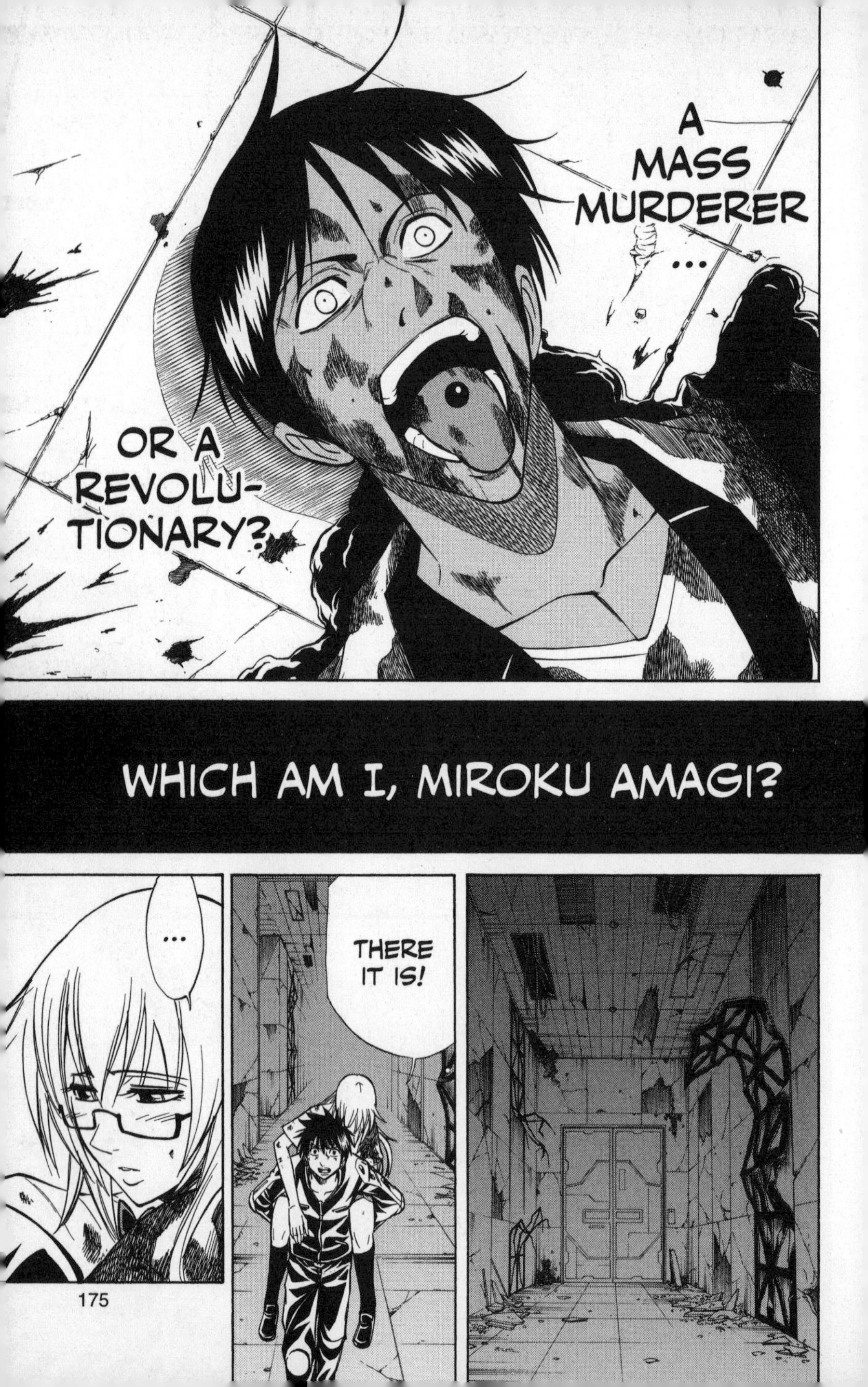
A MASS MURDERER ...
OR A REVOLUTIONARY?
WHICH AM I, MIROKU AMAGI?
THERE IT IS!
...

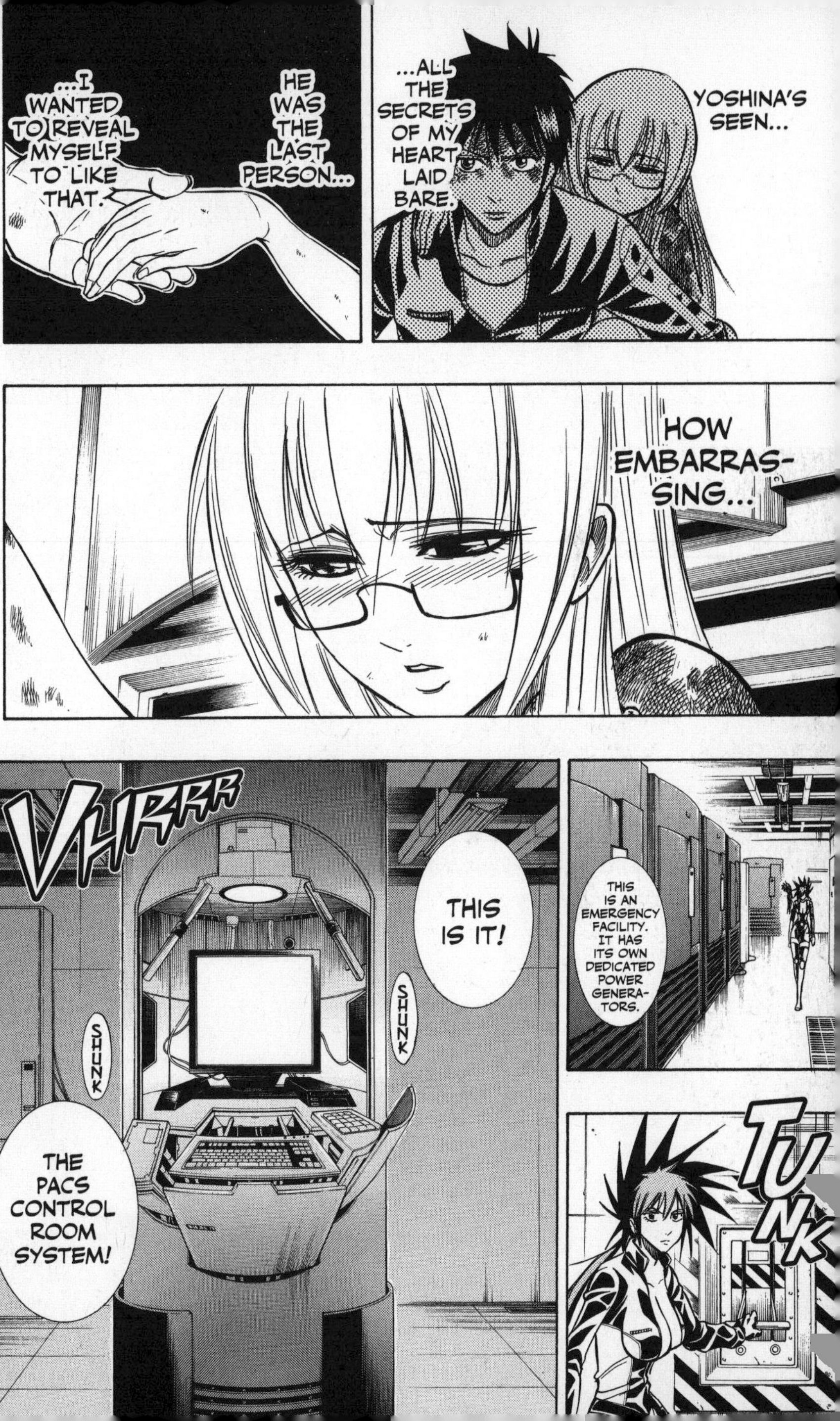
YOSHINA'S SEEN...
...ALL THE SECRETS OF MY HEART LAID BARE.
HE WAS THE LAST PERSON...
...I WANTED TO REVEAL MYSELF TO LIKE THAT.
HOW EMBARRAS-SING...
THIS IS AN EMERGENCY FACILITY. IT HAS ITS OWN DEDICATED POWER GENERA-TORS.
TUNK
VHRRRR
SHUNK
THIS IS IT!
SHUNK
THE PACS CONTROL ROOM SYSTEM!

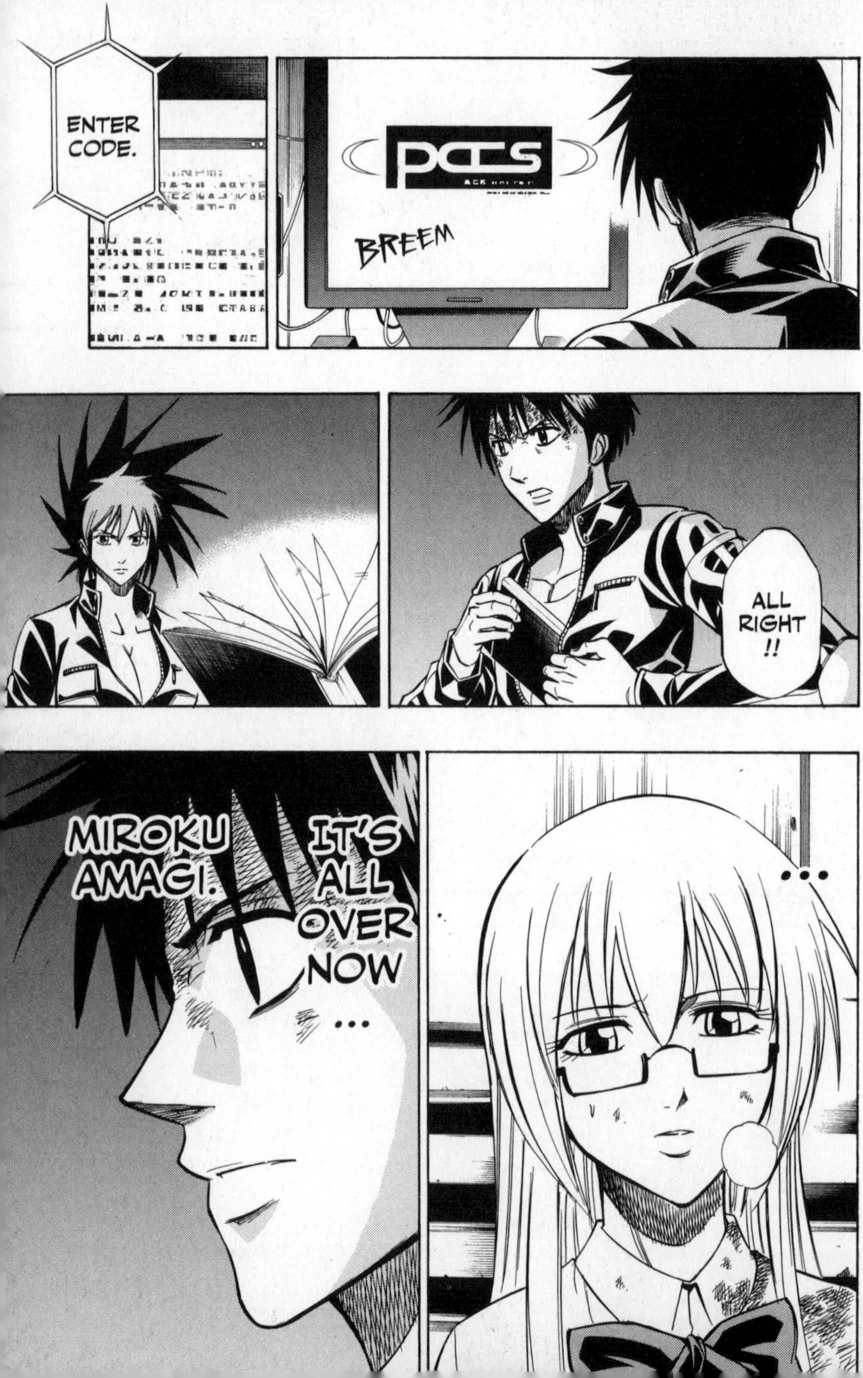
BREEM
ENTER CODE.
ALL RIGHT!!
...
IT'S ALL OVER NOW...
MIROKU AMAGI.

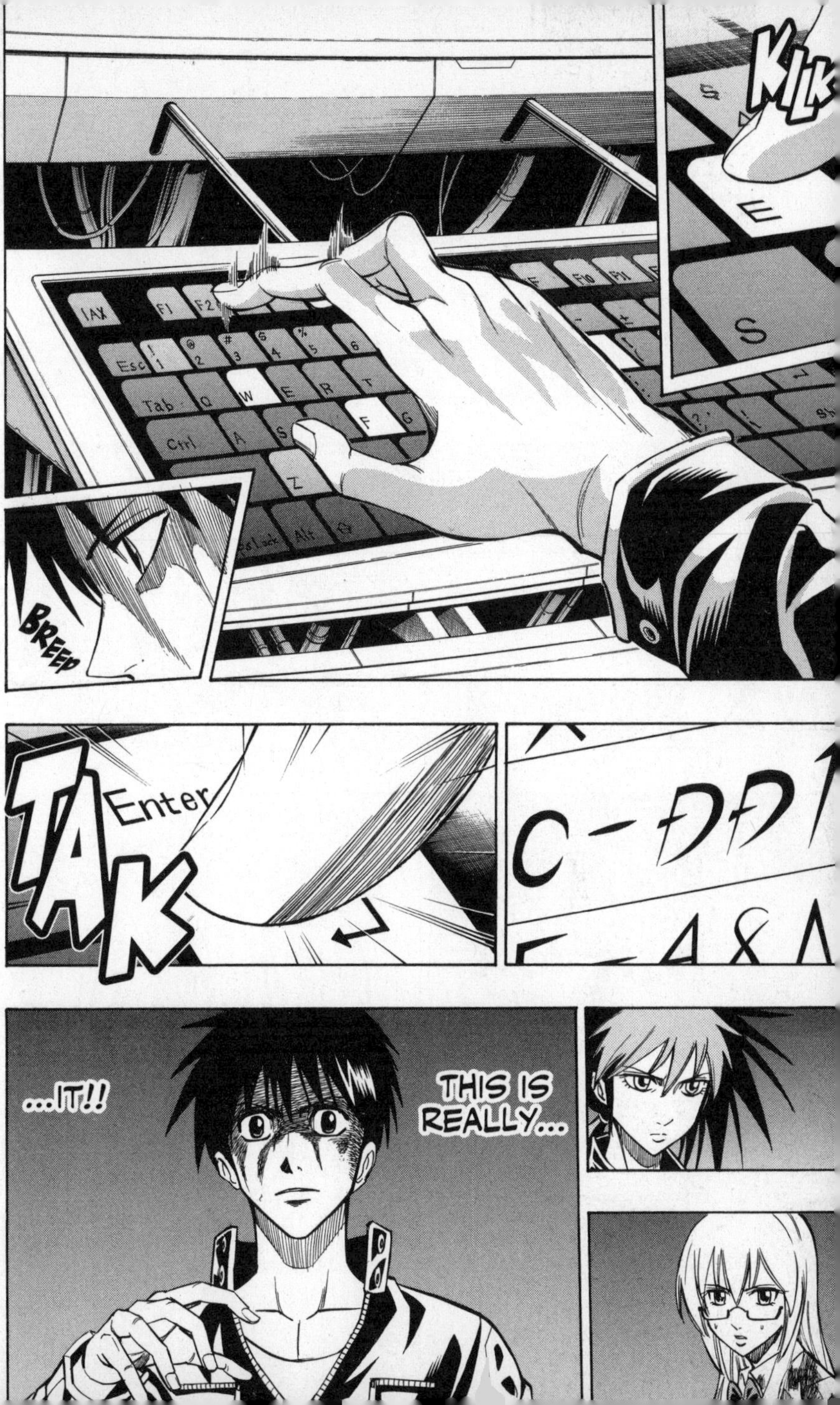
KLIK
BREEP
TAK
Enter
THIS IS REALLY...
...IT!!

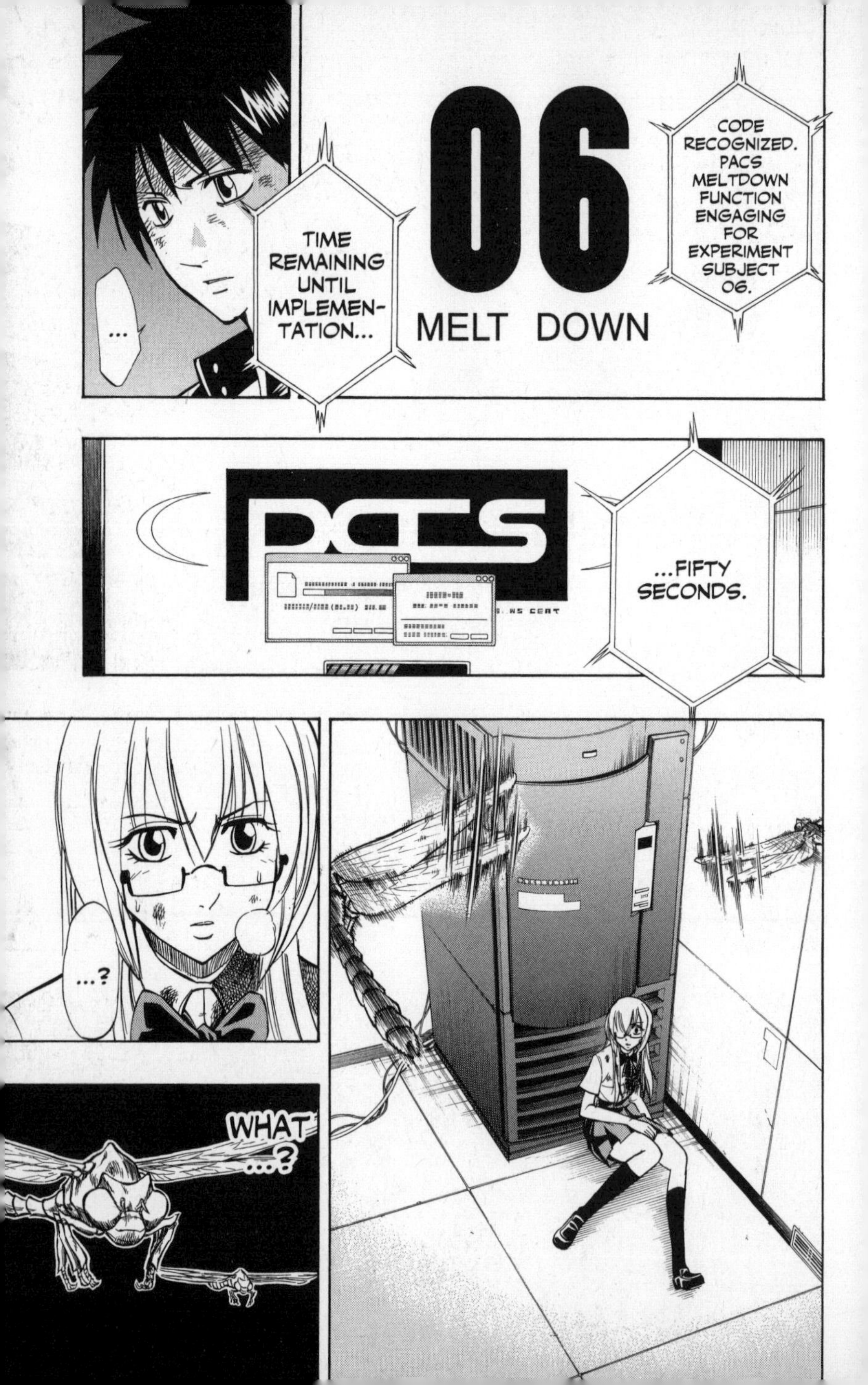
CODE RECOGNIZED. PACS MELTDOWN FUNCTION ENGAGING FOR EXPERIMENT SUBJECT 06.
06
MELT DOWN
TIME REMAINING UNTIL IMPLEMENTATION...
...
...FIFTY SECONDS.
...?
WHAT ...?

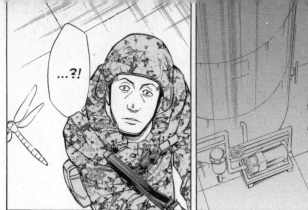
...?!

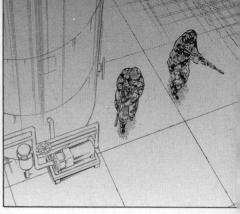

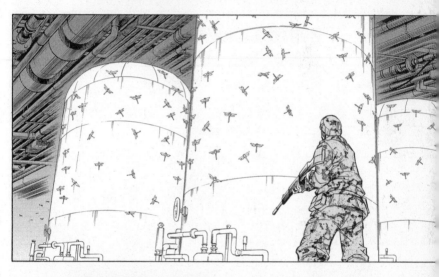

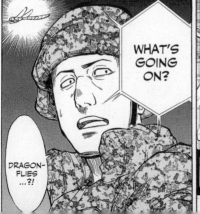
WHAT'S GOING ON?

DRAGON-FLIES...?!

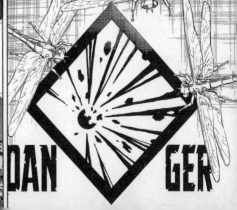
DAN GER

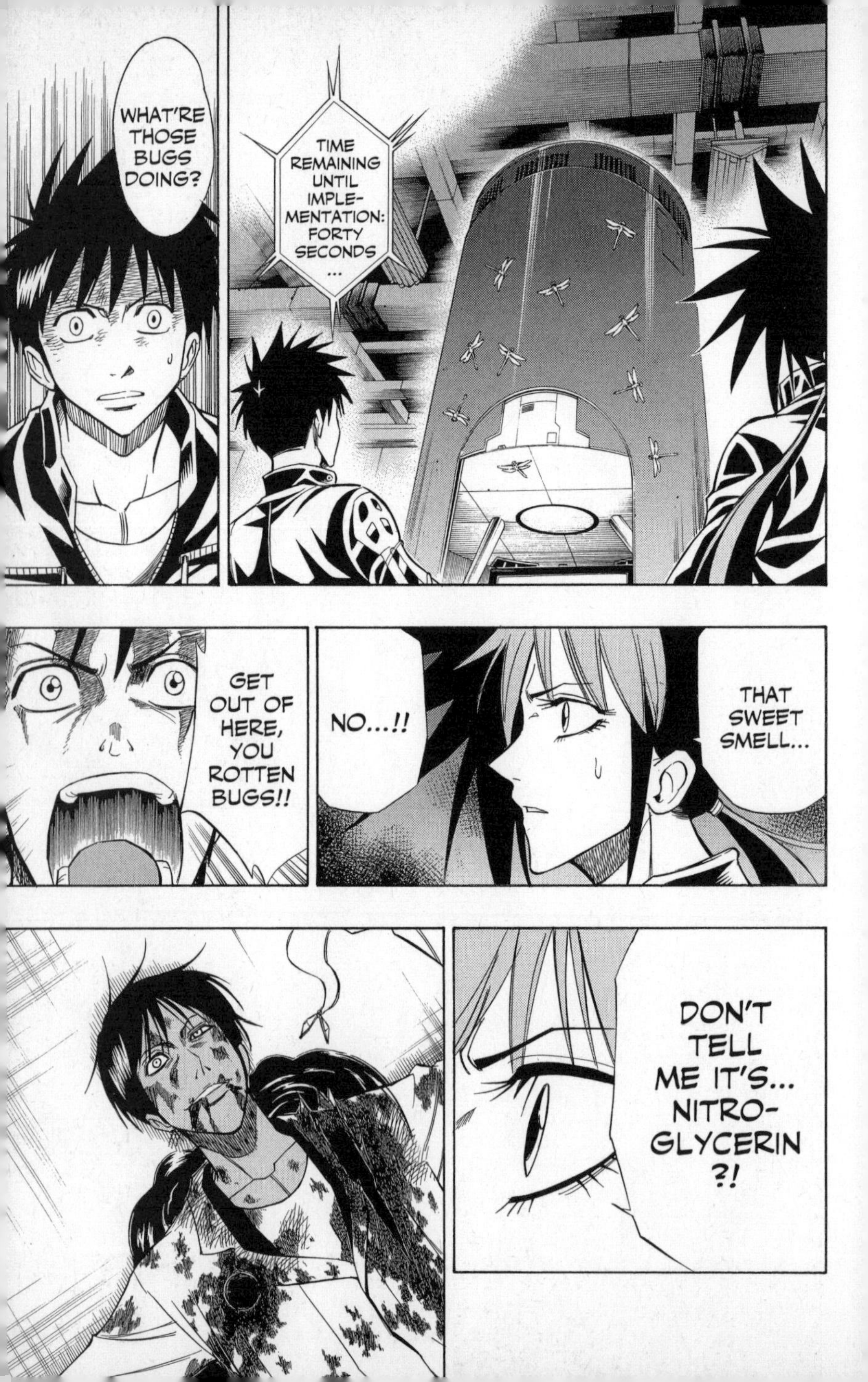
TIME REMAINING UNTIL IMPLEMENTATION: FORTY SECONDS ...
WHAT'RE THOSE BUGS DOING?
THAT SWEET SMELL...
NO...!!
GET OUT OF HERE, YOU ROTTEN BUGS!!
DON'T TELL ME IT'S... NITROGLYCERIN?!

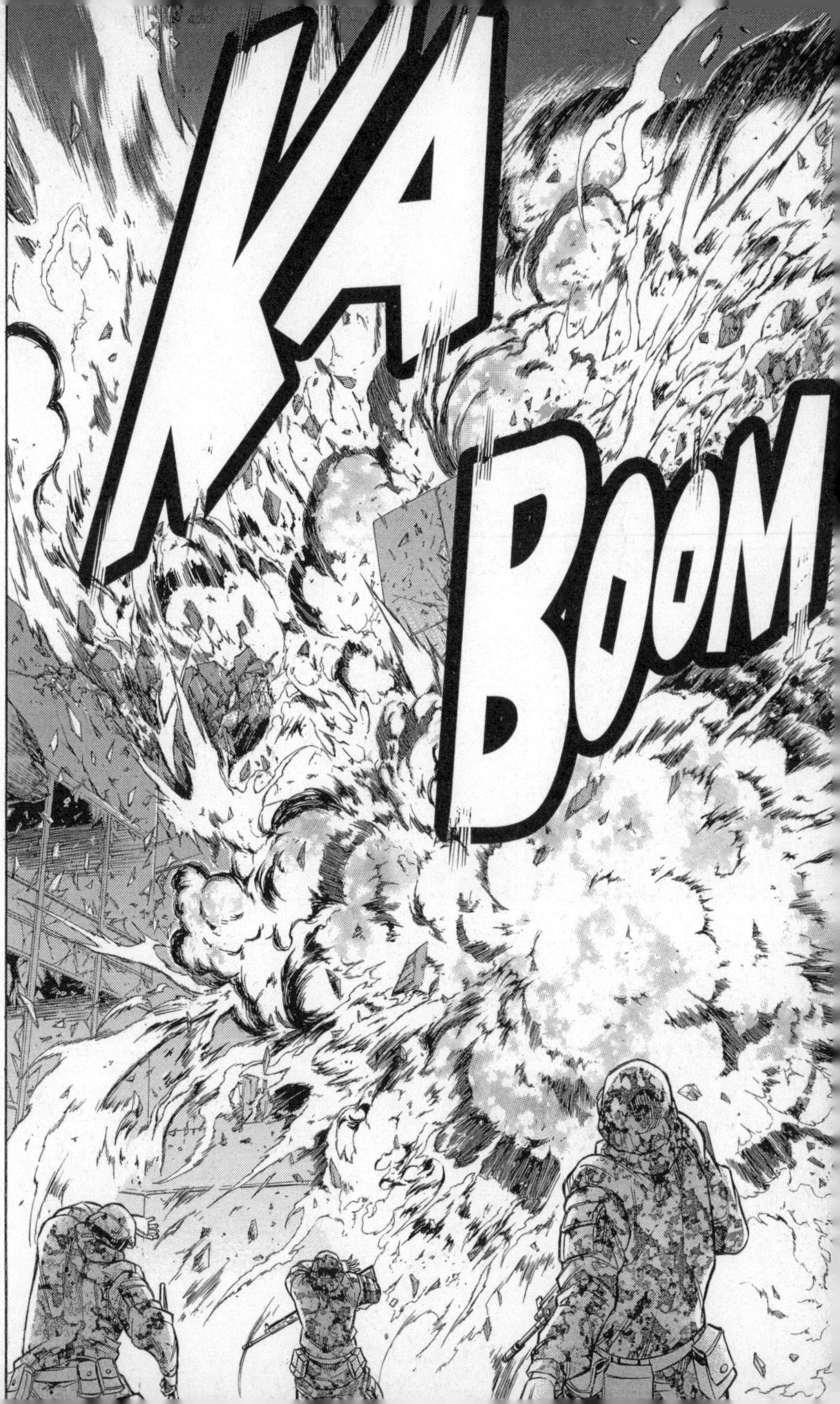
KA BOOM

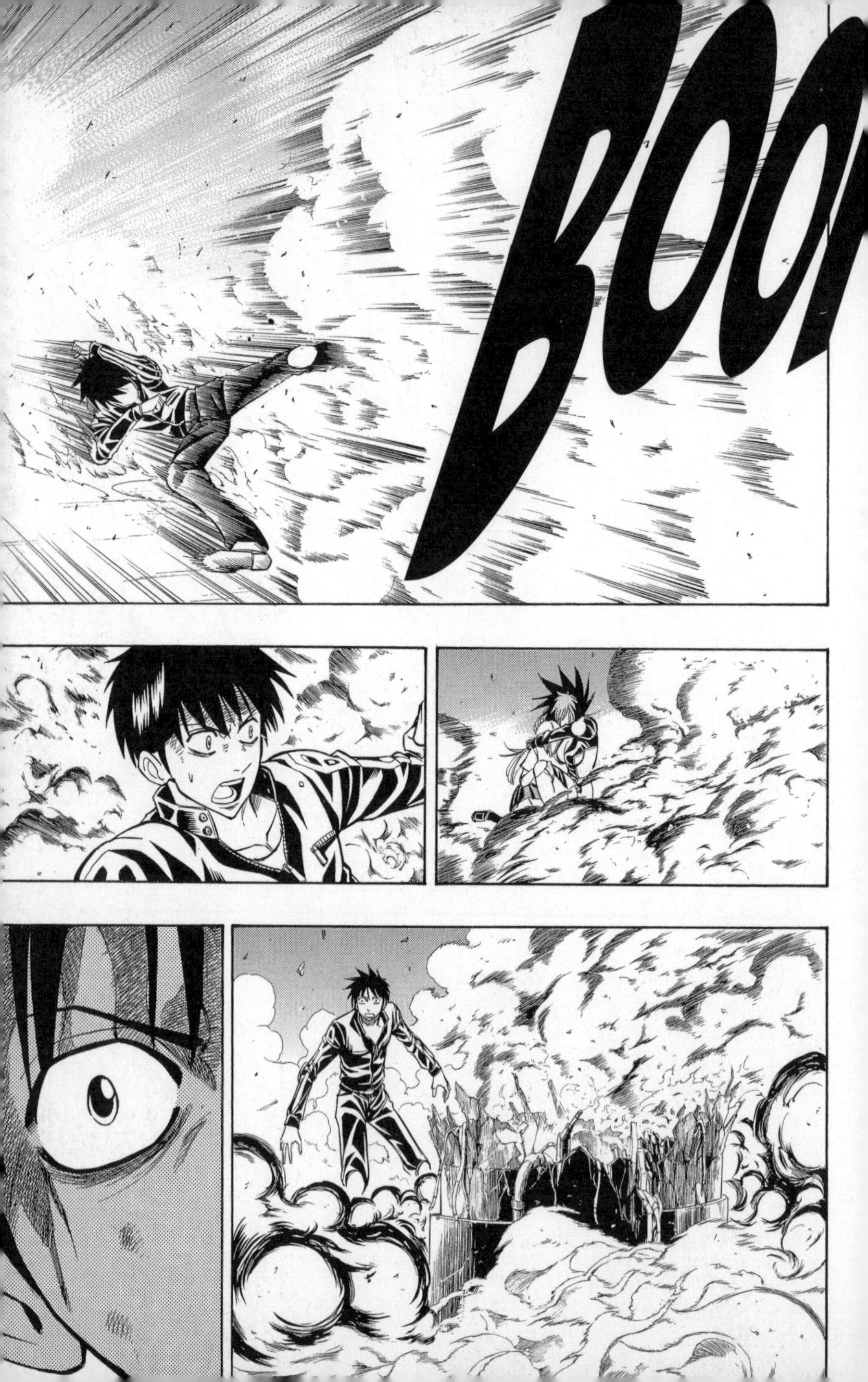
BOO

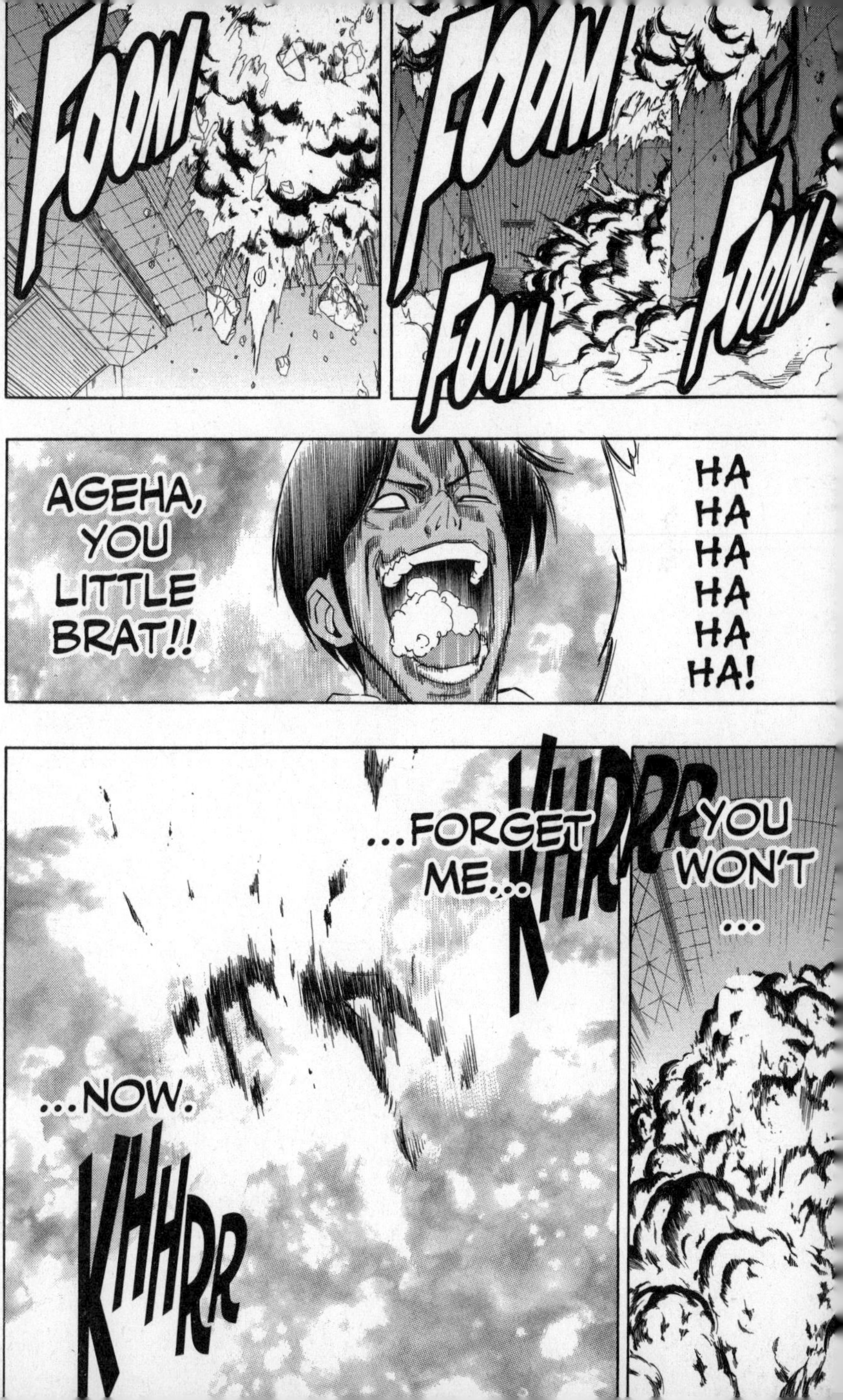

FOOM
FOOM
FOOM
FOOM
HA HA HA HA HA HA HA!
AGEHA, YOU LITTLE BRAT!!
YOU WON'T ...
KHHRR
...FORGET ME...
...NOW.
KHHRR

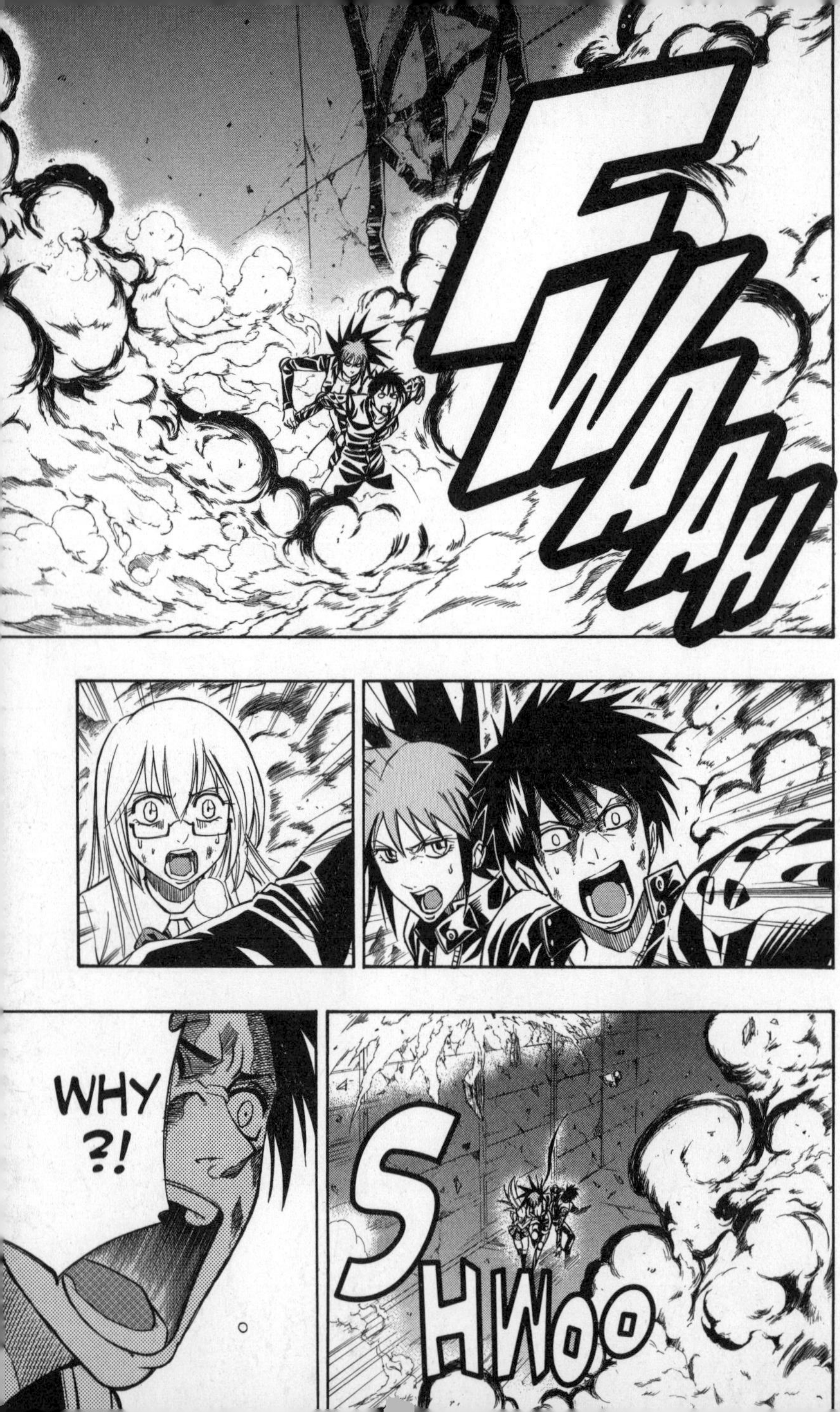
FWAAH
SHWOO
WHY ?!

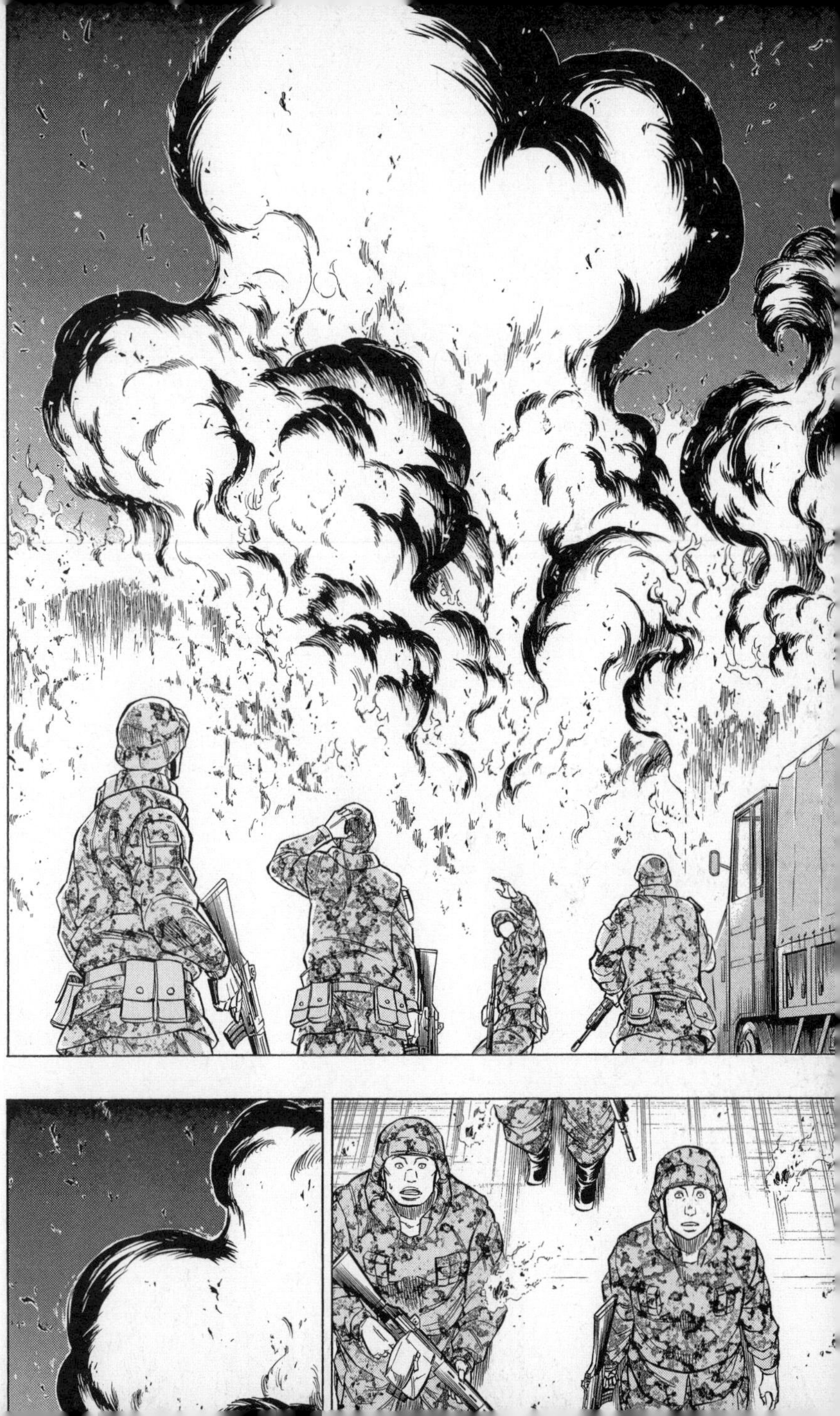

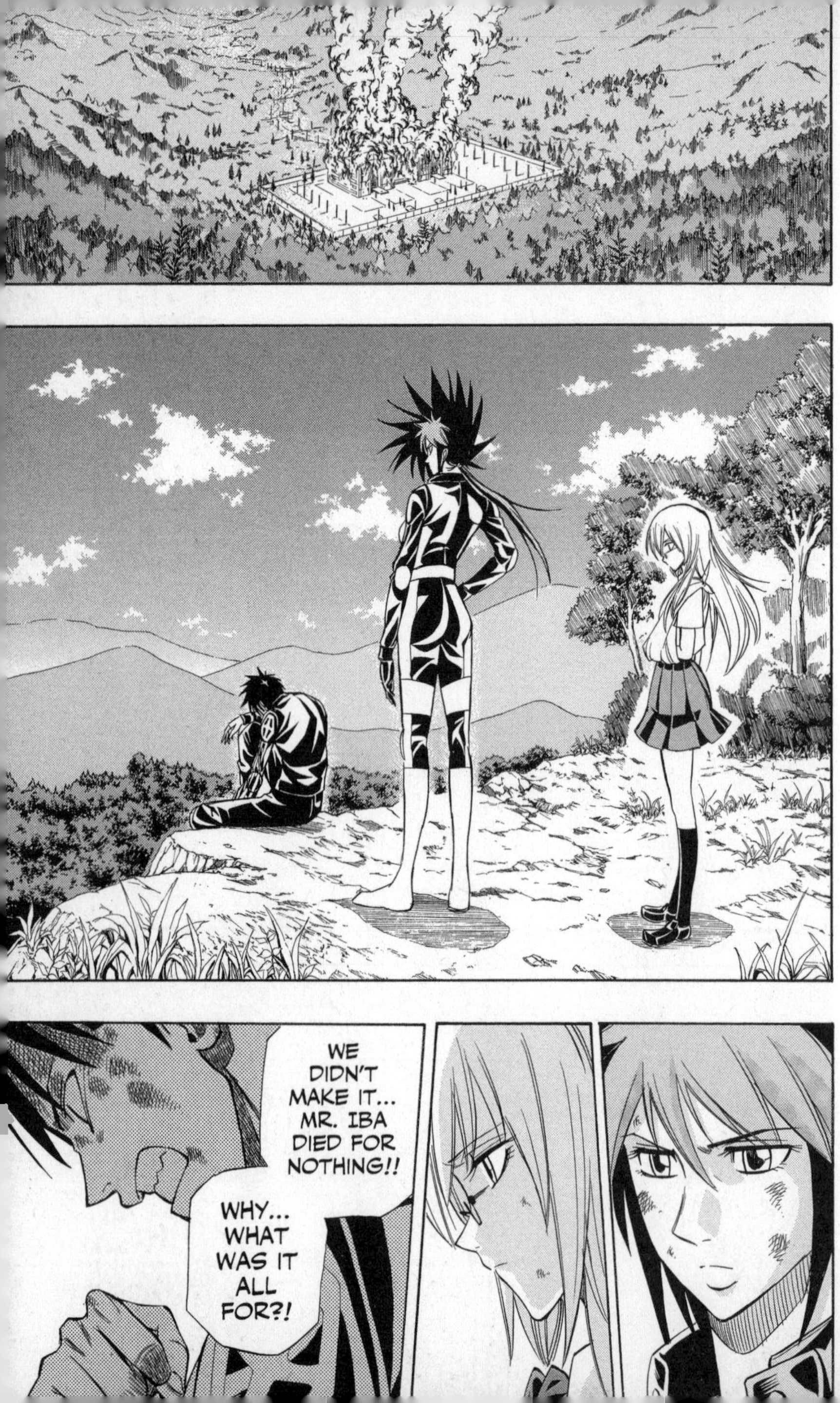
WE DIDN'T MAKE IT... MR. IBA DIED FOR NOTHING!!
WHY... WHAT WAS IT ALL FOR?!

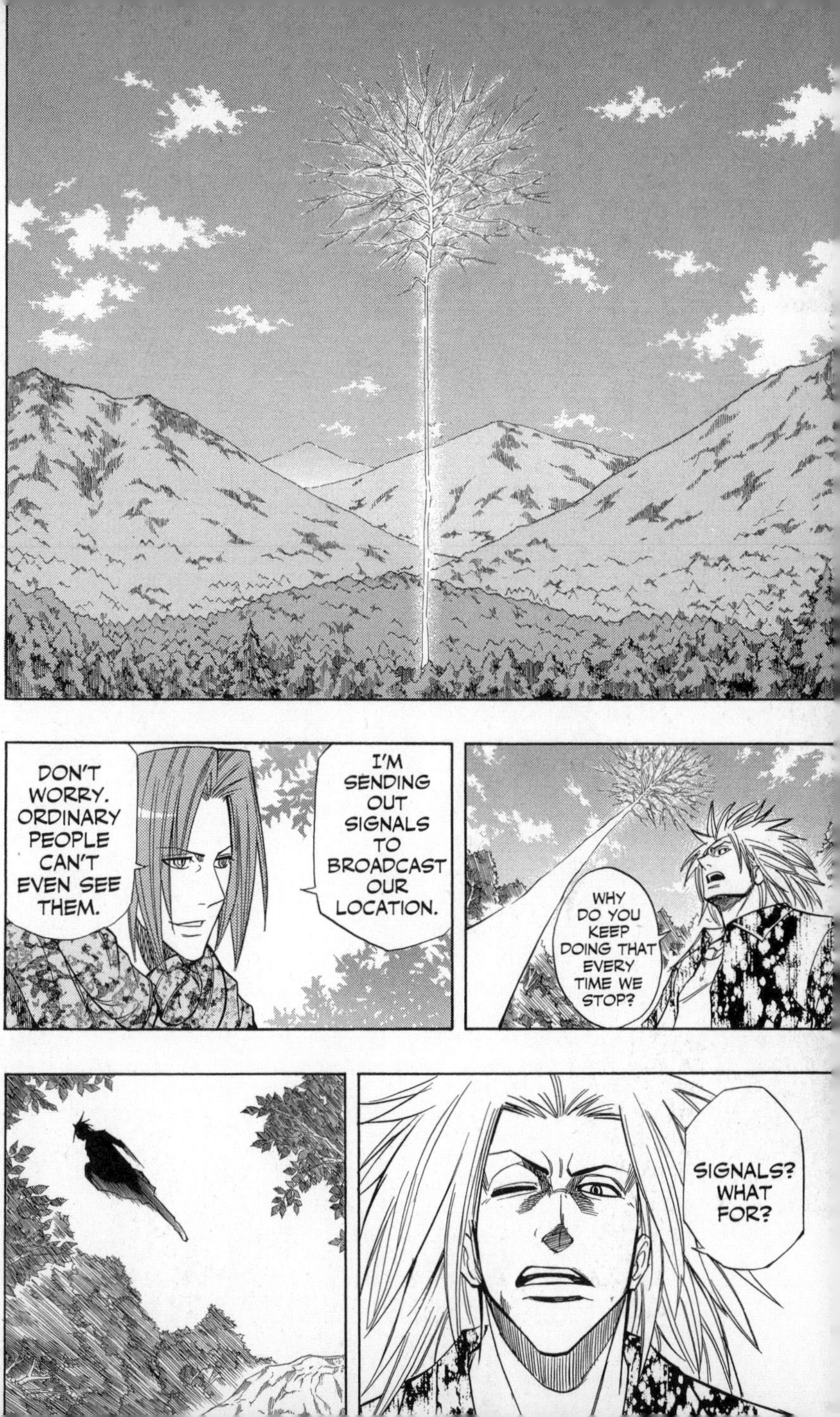
WHY DO YOU KEEP DOING THAT EVERY TIME WE STOP?
I'M SENDING OUT SIGNALS TO BROADCAST OUR LOCATION.
DON'T WORRY. ORDINARY PEOPLE CAN'T EVEN SEE THEM.
SIGNALS? WHAT FOR?

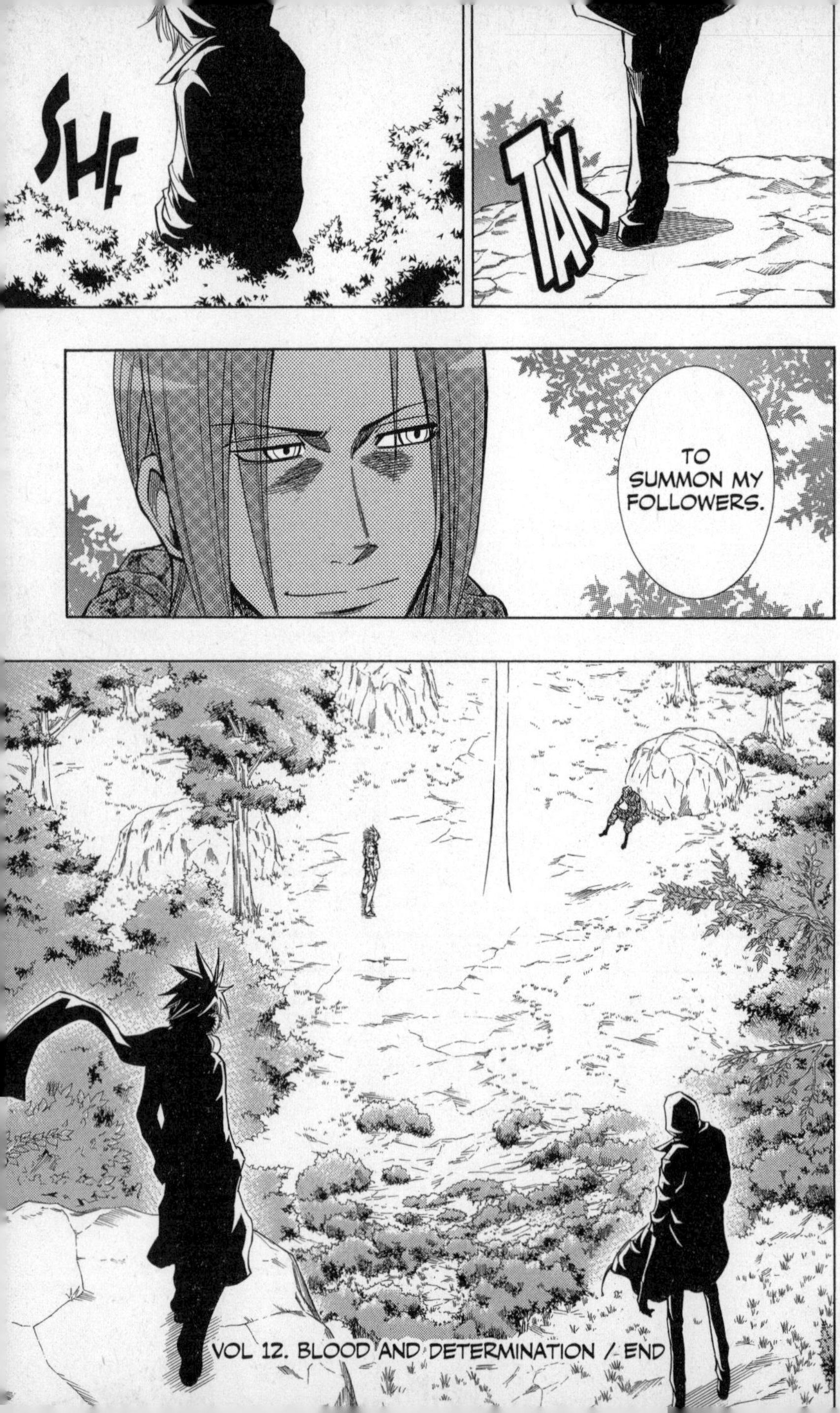
TAK
SHF
TO SUMMON MY FOLLOWERS.
VOL 12. BLOOD AND DETERMINATION / END

PSYREN

サイレン

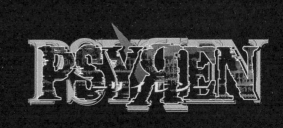

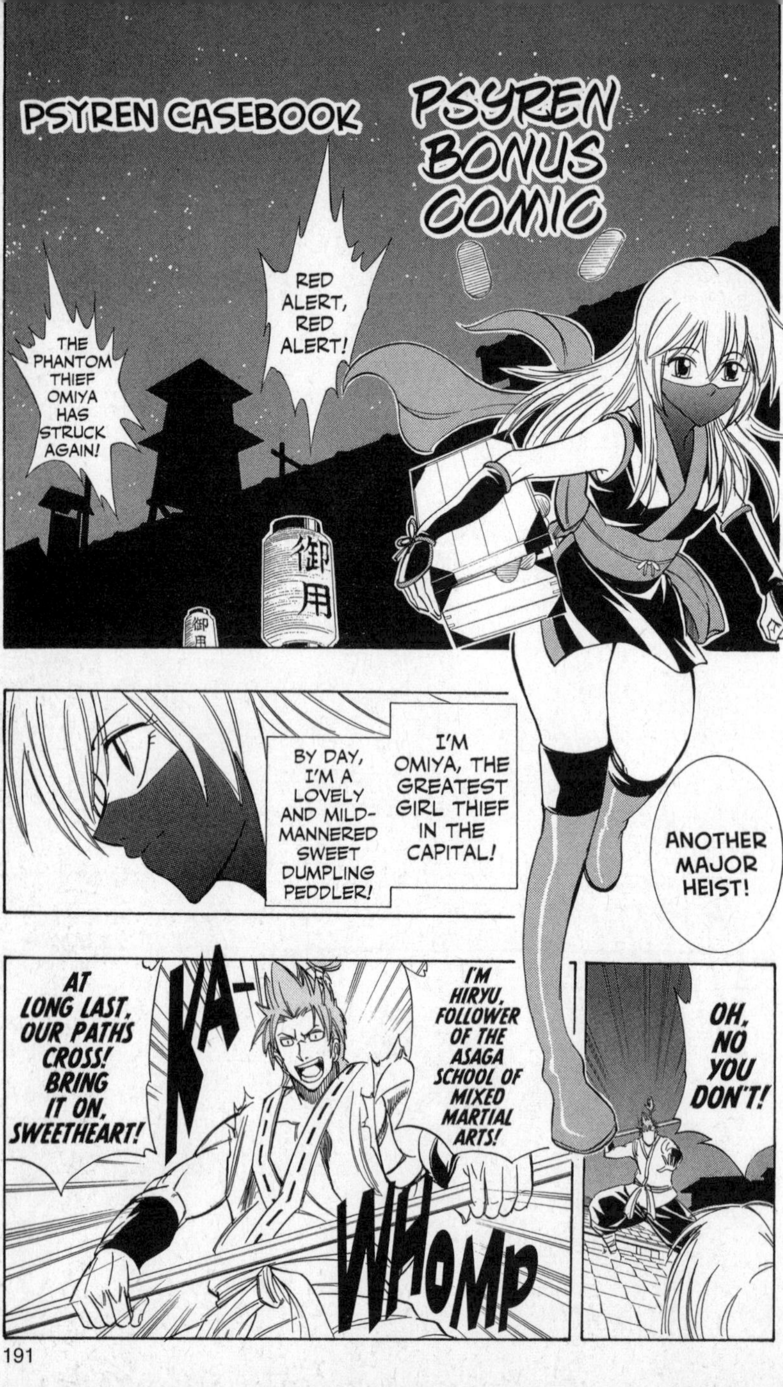
PSYREN BONUS COMIC
PSYREN CASEBOOK
RED ALERT, RED ALERT!
THE PHANTOM THIEF OMIYA HAS STRUCK AGAIN!
御用
御用
ANOTHER MAJOR HEIST!
I'M OMIYA, THE GREATEST GIRL THIEF IN THE CAPITAL!
BY DAY, I'M A LOVELY AND MILD-MANNERED SWEET DUMPLING PEDDLER!
OH, NO YOU DON'T!
I'M HIRYU, FOLLOWER OF THE ASAGA SCHOOL OF MIXED MARTIAL ARTS!
KA-
AT LONG LAST, OUR PATHS CROSS! BRING IT ON, SWEETHEART!
WHOMP

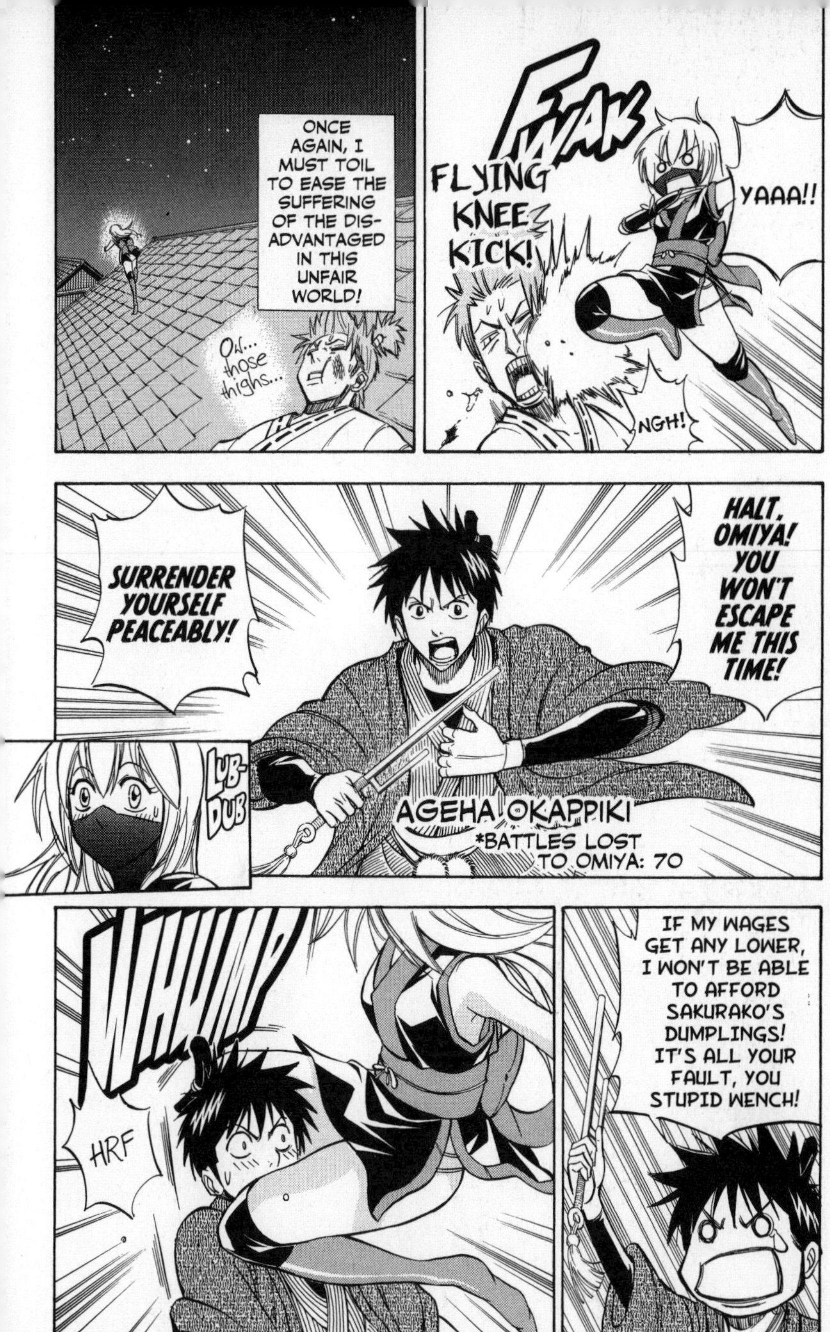
FWAK
FLYING KNEE KICK!
YAAA!!
NGH!
ONCE AGAIN, I MUST TOIL TO EASE THE SUFFERING OF THE DIS-ADVANTAGED IN THIS UNFAIR WORLD!
Ow... those thighs...
HALT, OMIYA! YOU WON'T ESCAPE ME THIS TIME!
SURRENDER YOURSELF PEACEABLY!
LUB-DUB
AGEHA OKAPPIKI
*BATTLES LOST TO OMIYA: 70
IF MY WAGES GET ANY LOWER, I WON'T BE ABLE TO AFFORD SAKURAKO'S DUMPLINGS! IT'S ALL YOUR FAULT, YOU STUPID WENCH!
HRF

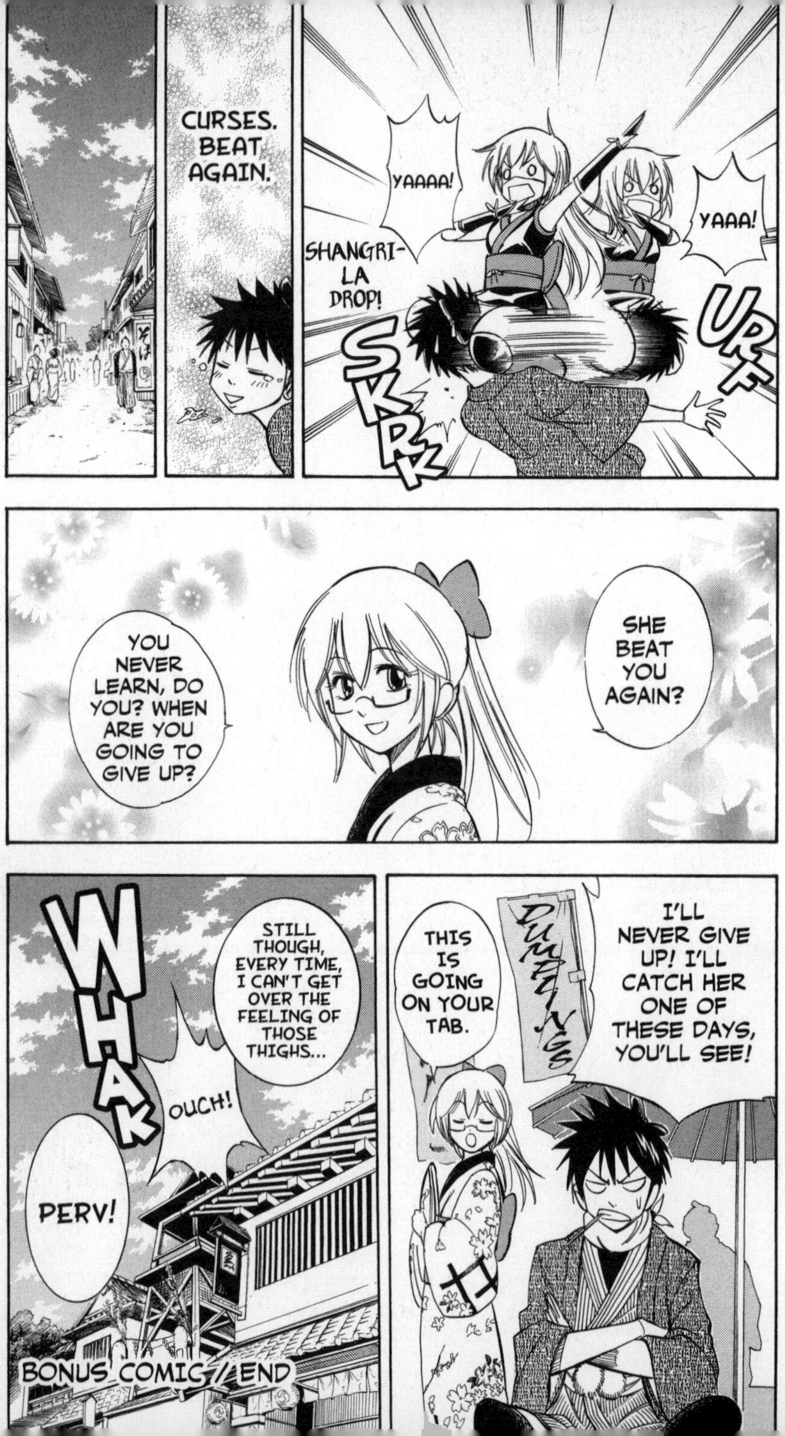
YAAA!
URF
YAAAA!
SHANGRI-LA DROP!
SKRK
CURSES. BEAT AGAIN.
SHE BEAT YOU AGAIN?
YOU NEVER LEARN, DO YOU? WHEN ARE YOU GOING TO GIVE UP?
I'LL NEVER GIVE UP! I'LL CATCH HER ONE OF THESE DAYS, YOU'LL SEE!
DUMPLINGS
THIS IS GOING ON YOUR TAB.
STILL THOUGH, EVERY TIME, I CAN'T GET OVER THE FEELING OF THOSE THIGHS...
WHAK
OUCH!
PERV!
BONUS COMIC // END

PSYREN

Afterword 12

THANK YOU VERY MUCH FOR BUYING VOLUME 12.

THIS VOLUME WAS FULL OF SERIOUS CONTENT THAT WAS REALLY CHALLENGING, WITH THE LAB, THE EXPERIMENT SUBJECTS' PAST, AGEHA'S BATTLES, AND SO ON.

ACTUALLY, I DON'T THINK I'VE DONE ANY EASY CONTENT IN A LONG TIME!

STILL, THOUGH, WITH ALL OF THESE SAIYAN-ESQUE BATTLES, I FEEL MYSELF IMPROVING AS AN ARTIST, WHICH MAKES ME HAPPY EVEN THOUGH I STILL HAVE A LONG WAY TO GO.

ON A TOTALLY DIFFERENT SUBJECT, THE FOREIGN TV DRAMA *CRIMINAL MINDS* IS SO GOOD, I CAN BARELY STAND IT.

IT SHOWS THE MEMBERS OF THE FBI'S BEHAVIORAL ANALYSIS UNIT SOLVING CRIMES BY PSYCHOTICS SO DEPRAVED THAT EVERY TIME, THEY PUSH THE BOUNDARIES OF ACCEPTABLE TV CONTENT.

THE SCENARIOS ARE SO HIGH QUALITY, IT REALLY MAKES ME WANT TO IMPROVE MY OWN SKILLS.

TILL NEXT TIME!

TOSHIAKI IWASHIRO, JUNE 2010

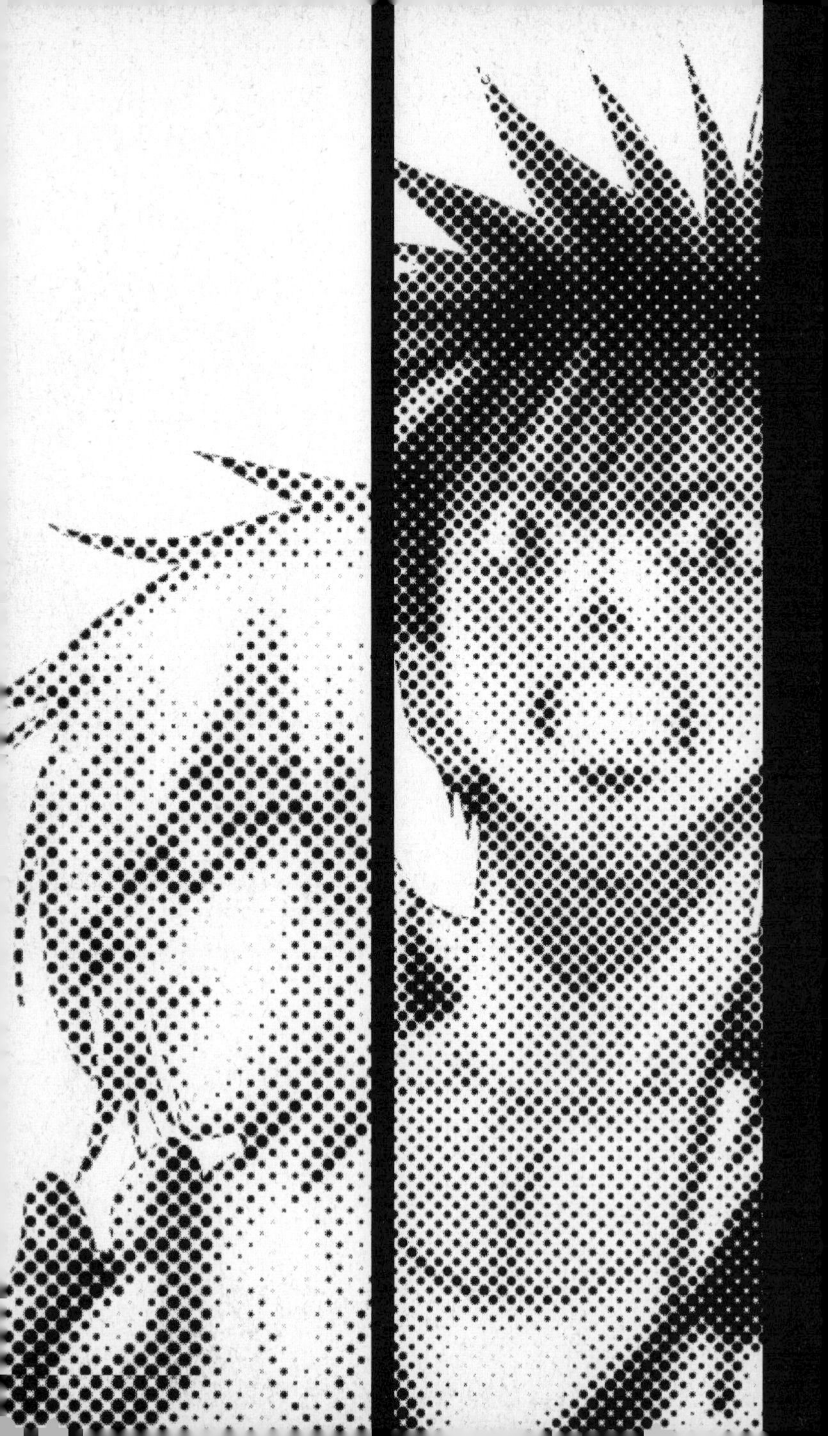

IN THE NEXT VOLUME...

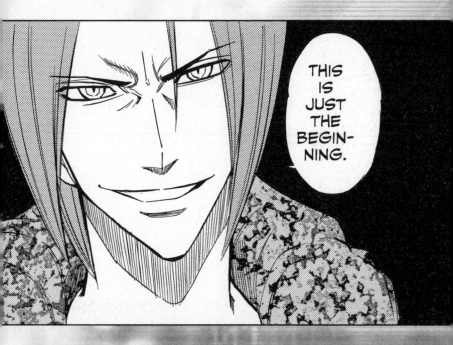

THIS IS JUST THE BEGINNING.

INFILTRATION

Under Miroku Amagi's leadership, W.I.S.E is growing steadily larger and more powerful, but Ageha and his fellow Psionists are unable to ascertain their whereabouts. In a desperate effort to prevent the giant meteor Ouroboros from striking the earth, Ageha hatches a dangerous plan...

Available NOVEMBER 2013!

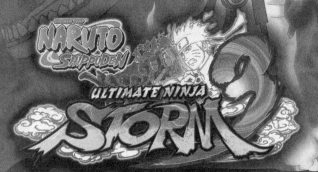

THE 4TH GREAT NINJA WAR AWAITS!

NARUTO SHIPPUDEN
ULTIMATE NINJA STORM

THE MOST EPIC NARUTO GAME EVER!
AVAILABLE NOW!

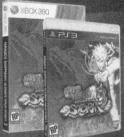

- LEAD THE NINJA ALLIANCE ULTIMATE CONFRONTATION AGAINST AKATSUKI'S DEVASTATING ARMY
- CONFRONT OVERPOWERING BOSSES IN MEMORABLE BATTLES DEFYING TIME & DEATH
- NARUTO STORM SERIES ENTIRELY REVISITED THROUGH TOTALLY REVAMPED STORY MODE & COMBAT SYSTEM
- 80+ PLAYABLE CHARACTERS – THE BIGGEST ROSTER EVER!

 XBOX 360   XBOX LIVE   PS3

DISCOVER ANIME
IN A WHOLE NEW WAY!

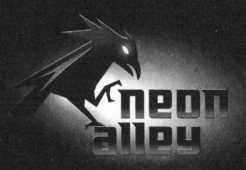

www.neonalley.com

What it is...

- Streaming anime delivered 24/7 straight to your TV via your connected video game console
- All English dubbed content
- Anime, martial arts movies, and more

Go to **neonalley.com** for news, updates and to see if Neon Alley is available in your area.

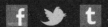

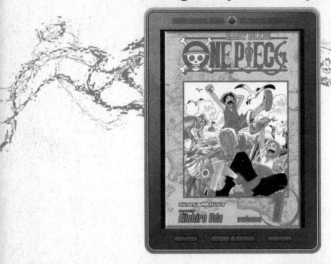
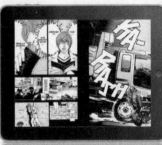
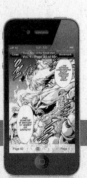

You're Reading in the Wrong Direction!!

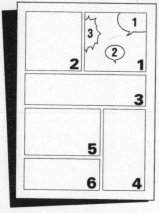

Whoops! Guess what? You're starting at the wrong end of the comic!

…It's true! In keeping with the original Japanese format, **Psyren** is meant to be read from right to left, starting in the upper-right corner.

Unlike English, which is read from left to right, Japanese is read from right to left, meaning that action, sound effects and word-balloon order are completely reversed—something which can make readers unfamiliar with Japanese feel pretty backwards themselves. For this reason, manga or Japanese comics published in the U.S. in English have sometimes been published "flopped"—that is, printed in exact reverse order, as though seen from the other side of a mirror.

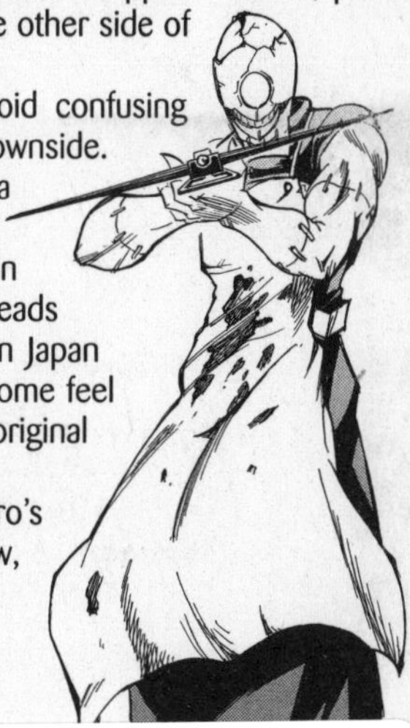

By flopping pages, U.S. publishers can avoid confusing readers, but the compromise is not without its downside. For one thing, a character in a flopped manga series who once wore in the original Japanese version a T-shirt emblazoned with "M A Y" (as in "the merry month of") now wears one which reads "Y A M"! Additionally, many manga creators in Japan are themselves unhappy with the process, as some feel the mirror-imaging of their art changes their original intentions.

We are proud to bring you Toshiaki Iwashiro's **Psyren** in the original unflopped format. For now, though, turn to the other side of the book and let the fun begin…!

—Editor